MW00387184

pursuit:365

A year of stories, perspective,
and inspiration from 365 individuals, 2022

SHELLY LYNN HUGHES

Copyright © 2022 by Shelly Lynn Hughes

ISBN 978-1-7776124-3-6

All rights reserved. This book or any portion thereof may not be reproduced or used in any manner whatsoever without the express written permission of the publisher except for the use of brief quotations in a book review.

Book Cover Design: Nicole O'Keefe

Typeset: Christina Moore

Copy Editing: Melissa Schilz, Nicola Arndt, Elizabeth Bennett

First Printing, June 2022

Published by Ho'ola Publishing

pursuit365.com

DISCLAIMER: Readers of this publication agree that neither Shelly Lynn Hughes nor Ho'ola Publishing will be responsible or liable for damages that may be alleged or resulting directly or indirectly from the use of this publication. Neither the publisher nor the authors can be held accountable for the information provided by, or actions resulting from assessing these resources.

FOREWORD
LORNA R. VANDERHAEGHE

Photo credit: Erich Saide

Inspiration, passion, determination and resilience are the key words to describe the people behind the stories in this book.

I was raised by a single mother who had not finished high school when my father left her with three children under the age of 5. In our catholic church community, we were known as the welfare family, the only family, with no man to take care of us... fatherless, husbandless, so shameful in that era. During those burdensome years she often fed us first before herself and she made our clothes from the second-hand clothes of others.

My mother was determined to take us out of poverty and to do that she got educated and became an accountant. Conversations around our dinner table were often about confidence and independence, especially financial independence. She never wanted her daughters to be left in the same vulnerable position she was.

Her passion for the rights of women and children to access healthy food, dental and medical care ran deep and as children we often sat on the steps of the parliament buildings in Victoria, B.C. while she took part in the low-income party demonstrations. Even as a catholic she was elated when Roe v. Wade became law in 1973 allowing women, of all socioeconomic status, control over their reproductive rights no matter where they lived. She knew from experience that bringing babies into poverty was a difficult path.

If she was alive today her passion and determination would be reignited, and she would again stand on the steps of parliament to voice how important it is for us to support all human rights. Her stories continue to inspire and motivated me to be the woman I am today – a woman with a strong commitment to family and social justice.

The 365 stories on the pages of this book describe the determination, passion and resilience of the people who had the courage to tell their stories. The courage to create a business, fulfill a dream, encourage others, make changes – whatever the story you will be inspired by the motivation, formidable determination and passion shared here.

Lorna R. Vanderhaeghe, M.Sc.
President & CEO of Headlines Promotions Inc.

Lorna R. Vanderhaeghe

Shelly Lynn Hughes is always on the go, finding new ways to elevate the people around her and showcase amazing stories.

PUBLISHER
SHELLY LYNN HUGHES

It's the stories we share that make up who we collectively become.

In many of our stories, we create heroes who are solely responsible for solving whatever problem society is facing. In reality, though, no one person can save the world—but together, we can. We need each other to find answers, get things done, and push society forward.

Creating the opportunity to elevate the voices of 365 individual stories in this second year of our pursuit:365 project has been such an adventure and such an honour. To launch on National Say Something Nice Day is so appropriate because that is the essence of this book. This large-scale endeavour serves to bring hope, excitement, and humanity to a national audience and beyond. There would have been no way to achieve this landmark accomplishment if I had not approached it as an entirely collaborative project.

When you go through this book, take note of the true value that these individuals have chosen to share with you. Take the opportunity to read and listen to the stories, and let yourself be inspired and invigorated by them. Let us take you on a journey to a kinder path and use this as a beacon to say something nice to someone today and every day. Say something nice about someone today and every day. This is your call to action!

I invite you not just to consume the voices of the select few phenomenal features throughout these pages, but also to share your own voice. Take to social media, call a friend, submit a story to a local publication, and share what you have to say. On behalf of all of us, I invite you to share your voice the way we are sharing ours here.

Shelly Lynn Hughes,
Publisher, pursuit:365

Dedicated to my father, Raymond, because he is likely the kindest, most loving person I know, always there to help another person and never expects anything in return.

Paul Henczel, BBA, is an Author, Podcaster, TEDx and International Speaker from Vancouver, BC, Canada. You can connect with Paul at www.inspiredinfluencers.com

PAUL
HENCZEL

My life was turned upside down when I was crushed by 12,000 pounds of wood in a traumatic near-death workplace accident. I could hear my body cracking, gurgling, and crunching; it felt like my head was going to explode, there was so much pressure. I thought: "if this doesn't stop, I'm going to die."

Then I blacked out. I was not breathing and went without oxygen for 12 minutes before regaining consciousness. The immense pain was overwhelming.

I was rushed to the hospital where there was a lot of confusion and panic. Something had to change. But then I was touched by an angel… IT WAS MY WIFE. I now had hope because I wasn't alone.

My accident has left me with numerous invisible injuries and physical impairments, including severe PTSD. I also have a permanent Brain Injury and Cognitive disorder; imagine having a concussion that never goes away. I had to learn a whole new way of living and my recovery has been long and challenging.

One of the most life-changing strategies I used in my recovery was telling my story. It was emotionally healing and helped me to move forward. Storytelling is one of the most powerful ways we have to communicate and motivate. Stories make the invisible, visible. I realized this wasn't the end, but the beginning, and when I changed my story, I changed my life!

I miraculously survived certain death to achieve what most would say was impossible.

"If you believe it will work out, you will see opportunities. If you believe it won't, you will see obstacles." –Wayne Dyer

I've gone from an injured millworker to an International Speaker by focusing on the possibilities.

Now, my passion is to inspire and empower others to find their voice. In my podcast, I interview today's top thought leaders, storytellers, and legacy builders. You're invited to join my community of inspired leaders.

So, I encourage you to share your story - the world needs to hear your message. The best part is that you decide your next chapter.

Paul Henczel

MICHAEL
ADRIAN LENSEN

In my 32 years of formula car racing I have found this statement to be so true, and I have found it equally applicable to life in general as well. At 73, I feel very fortunate to still be winning races. "We just want to beat the old guy," the younger drivers say.

Winning and happiness happen in the present. My thriving contracting business and 35 years of marriage to my beautiful wife speak to that.

In car racing, the ultimate goal, of course, is to win the race. If winning is not your ultimate goal, why spend the substantial amount of money, time and effort, just to stay home and read a book? It is also safer.

Like all success, before you get to the point of winning a race, there are many steps to take; let's call that building a level of experience. Experience which ultimately leads to winning.

Your physical and mental preparation, the preparation of your racecar to make it fast and safe, your concentration while on the track, all that and so much more are the ingredients which should lead to success. The same is true in thriving; you can't drop the ball in any important area of life without consequences.

And in life, as the years roll by, aren't you also building a level of experience? Of course you are.

Life's experiences. You can't buy them, you have to live them and learn from them.

And then you apply them in good times and bad.

So what do I mean by, "not focusing in your rear view mirror" when it concerns life?

Unfortunately, so many people live in the past, focusing on previous negative experiences that keep them a victim, blocking the path to happiness.

Every morning, you have the ability to decide to have a great day or a bad day. Choose the great day, nobody is going to choose it for you, it is up to you. Curve balls may be thrown your way but you are much better equipped to handle those if you decide to start on a positive note and commit to it.

Derek K. Miura, a personal injury and wrongful death lawyer of 30 years, on how to "FIGHT THE RIGHT FIGHT".

DEREK
K. MIURA

I have always had an innate sense and ability to stand my ground – a chip off the old block of my dad. I have also always had a childlike curiosity – my mom used to remind me that I would sometimes ask, "why?" for hours on end.

Growing up, I was always the smallest kid in my class as well as in most situations. Now, I stand between the "little" people and the "big guy," whether it be insurance companies, corporations or even governments. The vulnerable need advocates who can fight the fight for them, and this is where I come in as a lawyer.

Fighting for justice has been a cornerstone of my legal career for the past 30 years. It has been and continues to be an immensely fulfilling and rewarding vocation for me.

However, lawyers do not have a monopoly over fighting for justice. Whether in public, the workplace, the schoolyard or home, one can always stand up for what is right – both for others and oneself.

Here are a few things I have learned, and continue to learn, about how to "fight the right fight":

First, know your "truth". Know who you are and what you value. Knowing one's true values makes standing up for them that much easier.

Second, know your heart. One can find virtually unlimited strength and power when one fights from the heart.

Third, choose your battles. One cannot fight every single battle (as I am still learning).

And fourth, you cannot always be fighting. One needs balance in life, including things that bring enjoyment and peace. For me, when I go into nature or do my transcendental meditation practice, it makes a huge difference. It helps me recharge my batteries so that I can be the best that I can be for my family, my friends, my clients and others. Enjoy the little things and the small moments.

Finally, love. There is no doubt that love is the glue that binds all of us as well as the Universe itself. Love yourself, love others, and love all of life's miracles – both big and small.

May justice prevail in your life too.

Liliane Ulysse is a brave, ambitious, and powerful woman who always has this deep yearning to motivate others.

LILIANE MARIE
LAURENCE ULYSSE

I used to work for the Government in Canada from 8am to 4pm, Monday to Friday. I was dreaming of a life that allowed me to wake up when I wanted to, and starting my day in a peaceful way, rather than having to get up and drive to work in traffic every day.

Balancing work and life as a single mom weren't easy for me. The weekends I spend with my son never seem to be enough. I used to blame myself for not being present enough for him. I felt a little twinge in my heart thinking my son preferred his grandmother because she spent more time with him. I felt guilty every day. I worked a lot to have a good life for my son, but what discouraged me was the fact the money I received was never enough to meet our needs.

One day, I said to myself, "Life is never about doing the same thing every day. It's about exploring and learning different things which will eventually become a real-life lesson. I admit, it stands true to me and ultimately, it's about becoming your own boss."

That's how I got into real estate and simultaneously started my own beauty product company, Liliane & co. I found happiness when I decided to become my own boss, something I had to conceive, and was deeply passionate about. I went on to become an independent woman who always wanted to make my own money, trying to follow in my dad's footstep.

I have realized that becoming an entrepreneur is also about how much you learn. It isn't just about how to run a business, but about how much you can push yourself, endure and how to hustle. I also wanted to set an example for my son, instill good values in him and make him understand that money doesn't by happiness. I wanted him to know that the time he spends with his loved ones is worth gold.

There was no way I could have learned so much staying in a regular job (although my job was anything but regular). Being your own boss is more about becoming the "Queen" of the jungle.

Liliane Marie Laurence Ulysse

Sherrylyn is an Overcomer...
A Mama, a registered nurse, a community builder and an actor.

SHERRYLYN
VIVERO

Coming to Canada from the Philippines at 19, naïve and overwhelmed, the culture shock unfolded before me. A wave of challenges and rejections hit me as a newly licensed and internationally educated nurse. I remember having nightmares of dealing with patients, co-workers and using medical equipment. My self-limiting belief is on loop, telling me, "I'm not good enough."

I persevered until I became a charge nurse, mentoring graduating students in universities. I married my best friend and after a year, I edited our 12-hour wedding video into a 4-minute music video. I learned basic video editing; it was overwhelming at first but I enjoyed the process and the outcome. Me and my husband started a video company, capturing weddings and birthdays. It was enjoyable until we had kids and got burnt out!

We've been in and out of the children's hospital during winter as the weather is dry and cold. The boys developed winter induced bronchitis; as new parents, it was hard to see them go through this. So, we decided to move to a warmer province. Uprooting our family was very difficult; it almost cost our marriage.

While adjusting to a new city, I couldn't find any Filipino community groups, so I created one. I started a Facebook group and searched for volunteers to help newcomers. We registered the group as a non-profit organization and got recognized as a "Community Service Award" finalist in Canada. The group grew from 50 to 1700 members.

By then, our six year old son was hired to work in a TV series. He enjoyed the experience, got a talent agent and took acting courses. I couldn't find any groups to guide us so (again) I created one. The Filipino-Canadians in Hollywood (FCH) was born, a support group where we guide, nurture, advocate and celebrate Filipino-Canadian talents.

I'm a dream facilitator for our two child actors, and I was recently signed as an actor with a talent agent. I enjoy making projects about anti-racism and mental health, highlighting equality, kindness and empowerment while showcasing our rich Filipino culture. I've been a registered nurse for 19 years now, and I still enjoy it. I've learned to be grateful, choose my battles wisely, be physically fit and develop an abundance mindset.

Lesly Quiambao is finding her way through self-acceptance and learning what living with ADHD means for her life story.

LESLY
QUIAMBAO

For as long as I can remember, I have always been at war with myself. Always frustrated with the way that I am and the myriad of compulsive pursuits I would chase moment to moment. My outer, bubbly expressions with new and old friends would suggest otherwise, but no one would suspect the inner turmoil I was living through. From the ages of four to eight, I frequented the hospital to get stitches on my chin from a stubborn insistence of jumping from high tables trying to fly. I have held 15 different jobs throughout my 14 years of working and tried on various different identities during that process. The adoration I felt from new friends and the exciting experiences easily warranted regular life changes. Then the 2020 pandemic started, and the indistinguishable days endured, mercilessly stuck on repeat.

My home reeked of silence. There was nowhere to be but with my own thoughts. Life became so quiet that the silence made a habit of screaming at me, except only I could hear it. I would hear abhorrent cyclical thoughts like, "People don't even like you. No one cares about you. No one wants to be around you. You're not even good at anything. What can you even do?" As if my unspoken ideology incessantly reminded me that being useful to people was a prerequisite to being loved. For what felt like the longest span of time in 2020, I believed every word of those intrusive thoughts.

Then on March 17, 2021, I received my ADHD diagnosis. It marked the day that I finally decided to end the war with myself. That diagnosis explained so much about my past and I wanted to make peace with the cyclical thoughts of fearing that people would leave me, not being good enough, or being thought of as odd by others. Those thoughts made me too afraid of being myself. Self-acceptance might always be a work in progress for me and that bit of insecurity still occasionally visits as a humbling reminder to prioritize self-compassion. How might one live in tandem with an ingrained fear of yourself? Acceptance, I suppose, and taking it one day at a time.

Andrea Barone is the founder of Crystal Hills Organics and has been referred to as the Queen of Crystals.

ANDREA
BARONE

I have always been optimistic, looking for the bright side in any situation. It seemed like my life had quite an easy flow to it. However, things came to a screeching halt when my children were quite young and my husband, at the time, walked out. I was also just in the process of setting up my business.

I started to have panic attacks and was worried about the future; finances, how my kids were feeling, where we would live, and if I could still get my business going. I was consumed by fear and anxiety every minute of the day. In this lower state, it seemed like no matter how hard I tried to manifest goodness, it did not come to fruition. Although I could put on a happy face for my children and others, feeling positive was another story. I knew I had to work at achieving inner peace again so that I did not stay in a state of fear for years. I had two young boys who depended on me to give them love and show them how to have courage, peace, and happiness in their lives.

Through self-care rituals and inner work, a shift started to occur and I began to feel my positive spirit emerge again. I was able to re-evaluate everything that I wanted for my business, my children, and myself. I redesigned my business so the emphasis was on providing self-care rituals and crystal-infused beauty products to help women raise their vibration, set their intentions, and let their inner goddess shine forth. I wanted to help women feel empowered so they could manifest their dreams.

My business started to flourish, then I reconnected with a past love from twenty years prior. We now all live on a beautiful vineyard with lots of herbs and flowers. With my lab just across the walkway, life is just how I envisioned it. I share all of this to let others know that you can get through those difficult times. You can emerge from the darkest depths of despair and regain your confidence, happiness, and health, and let love flow back into your life.

Andrea Barone

Photo credit: Lee-Ann Richer

Mike Reno is the lead singer/song writer of the iconic 80's rock band, Loverboy.

MIKE
RENO

As you can imagine, I have collected many stories traveling the world in a rock band. Picking just one and keeping it rather short is turning out to be the hardest part.

Well, here it goes.

Early on in my career and shortly after completing the recording of my first album, myself and two of my band mates took a holiday with our girlfriends to the Mexican resort town of Puerto Vallarta. Now this, believe it or not, was a time before cell phones.

Just as we started to unwind a bit, a young man came running down the beach calling out my name. As it turns out, there was a call for me in the lobby. I ran back to the hotel and my manager Bruce Allen was on the line. What he said to me was a life changing conversation and got the ball rolling at a speed that seemed to never stop. He said, "grab the guys and head to the airport... Dick Clark wants you guys on his show American Bandstand on Saturday."

Saturday was two days away! With an opportunity like that in the music business, how could we fail? The group was/is Loverboy, and we haven't stopped since.

Loverboy has been going strong since 1979, and with shows all around the world there are many stories. However, this story stands out as it changed everything for us. We appeared on American Bandstand a few more times, and on one of the shows, we presented Dick Clark with a gold album which he went on to say was the first time he received one live on the air. It was very touching for all of us, and we went on to appear on the American Music Awards, which his company produces. One year, we presented Michael Jackson with the award for Album Of The Year! That was definitely another highlight for us. So many amazing stories...

Amada Jones is a certified life coach focusing on women, their self-worth and body acceptance.

AMADA
JONES

Not being enough. Contemplating this, I ran a list of all the big challenges that have impacted my life, starting from abuse, traumatic events, themes of rejection and people leaving me. Then it came to me, an encompassing theme that seemed to be a fit for all of these life challenges. The theme of 'not being enough'. I won't blame myself for things, especially for the abuse that I endured along the way, but I do realize I may never have been there if I had not thought I wasn't enough.

I view my experiences as lessons; those lessons played a huge part in shaping my life and bringing me to a place of "being enough," and now, being in a place where I help guide people. Being a life coach, I help individuals navigate through change and life transitions.

At age 13, I struggled with my body; I suffered from an eating disorder and major body dysmorphia. This challenge was and still is huge in my life. Although I have recovered, the idea of my body and body image has made me feel less than enough. It effected so many aspects of my life.

What I would tell my younger self, I also tell my clients: your body is not a reflection of your worth or who you are. In fact, it is a gift that should be seen as art. Embracing its uniqueness makes you even more beautiful.

Poor body image and self-worth can lead you into terrible situations. I know, because I lived it. I was three months pregnant, in an abusive and unsafe relationship. I had to leave quickly, and start fresh on my own as a new mother.

I want women to know their value. Their worth comes from a place so deep within. I feel that until we have taken that dive within to discover all the amazing possibilities, we are in fact really limiting ourselves.

Amada Jones

Frances Michaelson is the founder of Live the WOW (World of Wellness) in Hudson, Quebec. A former gym owner and body builder, Frances turned to Naturopathy to heal her gut and change her life. Now she aims to do the same for others through her practice.

FRANCES
MICHAELSON

Although I graduated university with a major in Sociology and a minor in criminology, after going to my first aerobics class, I found myself immersed in the Canadian fitness world. I co-owned a gym in the 80's and competed in body building competitions in the 90's. In 2001, I opened one of Montreal's first personal training studios while owning and operating an exercise product distribution company called Muscle Up Canada. This company started with just one small band and quickly grew to over 600 products! I had no idea what I was getting myself into – I was a young mom at the time, raising two boys and dragging them with me everywhere. I knew I was doing too much, but I felt compelled to keep going.

I began to question the true meaning of health after losing my mother suddenly in the late 90's. It was my first experience with hospital care and left much to be desired. Also, I was not feeling as well as I appeared to on the outside. I knew my hands were full, but I felt trapped with my business commitments.

As a personal trainer, I started to question why everyone reacted so differently to food. I created meal plans for my clients, but not all would experience positive results. I felt the nutrition world was missing something. In 2004, I went to a naturopath; this changed everything! I realized we are not what we eat – we are what we digest!

I switched gears; I went back to school to study naturopathy and this changed my life. I graduated in 2011, and by 2017 I published my first book: Let's Practice Health… Learn Why Your Gut is the CEO of Your Health. I was excited to tell the world about how incredible our bodies are and share stories of clients turning their health around with my guidance. I sold my businesses a few years ago and now have a naturopathy practice under the brand Live the WOW, with my own line of herbal products. My second book, Do you Have the Guts to be Healthy, was published in March 2020

My advice to all women is to follow your gut; it knows best. And remember that life is a gift, but health is a practice.

Sharad Kharé, Chief Storyteller at Human Biography, award-winning video content producer, biographer, legacy documentarian and speaker.

SHARAD
KHARÉ

In 1996, I learned that my lifework was to be a storyteller, and more importantly, a story listener. When I started my work in media, I hosted community TV. I loved it so much that I became a video blogger and did the same thing on the internet starting in 2008. I would take my camera everywhere and I would interview people. I learned to edit and make content; I was in control, I was creating. At times, it felt like it was enough. It wasn't a living, but it was a happy life.

Out of survival, my work had to aspire to be more focused and entrepreneurial. In 2009, my goal was to document and interview the most famed and accomplished, and they would be sitting across from me, and I would get paid to interview them. I went back to school in 2011 to do a master's in communications. My academic work looked at how people know their loved one vs. that same person's persona on the internet. Digital legacy vs. personal legacy.

Since graduating, I have had the honor of hosting and documenting the Dalai Lama, directing campaigns with Meryl Streep, interviewing media icons such as Arianna Huffington, creating content with Katy Perry, or asking Maye Musk what inspires her about Elon - the anecdotes go on and on.. In 2019, I was awarded the Disruptor Fellowship at the United Nations in New York, recognized by distinguished icons and visionaries globally for my innovative work in media.

My company Human Biography is globally recognized, and I am so proud of the work we do every day. I am focused on creating with communities and individuals that are changing the world. My work with Indigenous storytelling has also been a joy and gift. In 2021, I was fortunate to direct and co-produce an award-winning documentary called "The O Show," which follows an Afro-Indigenous and two-spirit leader, activist and humanitarian through her journey.

I believe everyone's story is iconic, and I encourage everyone to share theirs with the world. Our potential is never limited, our lives can be full of joy and fulfillment, and we, both as individuals and as a collective, can truly be happy.

Sharad Kharé

Marlyna Los is a Feng Shui master, astrologer, teacher, consultant and author. #TogetherWeAreMore #LivingWithPurpose #Love&LightAlways

MARLYNA
LOS

For the longest time in my life, I told myself I was fine. I truly thought I was okay and that everyone else was the problem. If only they would change, I could be happy.

My first inkling that I was part of the problem was in my early 20's watching Phil Donohue. I was sitting at home with my two young boys, watching a rebirthing ceremony. The therapist picked a male from the audience to sit inside a circle of chairs. Each chair was filled with audience members who took on the roles of significant people in this person's life. Each person was directed to go one by one, saying affirmative, loving statements to the person in the centre. The person in the centre was put into a light trance and told to imagine they were being born, and then one by one, each person in the circle spoke. "I'm so excited to meet you. I've waited so long to meet you. I'm so looking forward to getting to know you. I can't wait to hold you."

As I watched, a sound I had never heard before came out of me, this deep, forlorn howl emerged. What was that cry? I wept as I realized that when I was born, there was no one in the room saying those things. There was no one then who wanted me; I was being given up for adoption.

Watching that rebirthing ceremony was the beginning of change in my life. For the first time, I realized I was not okay and that I had work to do to heal. I saw how long ago, beliefs were formed that did not serve me. I started to take responsibility for what I could change and accept what I couldn't. I changed my story.

It is possible to reframe life; the past didn't have to define my future. I got help. I met my birth family. I learned that everything that happened was a choice made on a soul level and that I am not a victim. I learned to be the change.

Today I am curious and willing, I am strong and independent, I love and am loved deeply.

Life can be messy and juicy, and when things get hard, I remind myself I can do hard things.

Marlyna Los

Shayda John has been in advertising and marketing for different media groups for over 12 years. She recently launched a business, Badgirl Branding, with an amazing graphic artist and friend.

SHAYDA
JOHN

Photo credit: *Douglas Drouin Photography*

Well, I found this harder to write than I thought I would!

It's interesting that talking comes so naturally to me when communicating with others and giving advice, but when it comes to my story, talking about myself is difficult.

My life has been a roller coaster ride of experiences that have guided me into the woman I am today and continue to grow into.

I never knew what I wanted to be when I "grew up," I just went with the flow and did what I wanted to do at the time. I always loved being around people, and being the social butterfly. Always making an effort to see the best in things, and helping others to do the same. Learning the hard way, that not everyone is good for you. Not everyone you meet is meant to stay in your life, but meant to teach you a lesson that you will only understand with time.

Experiencing my fair share of toxic decisions and abusive relationships made me realize what I do not want. I believe I went through tough times to make me a stronger and better person for today.

I find happiness in bringing others up, helping them see that things will get better if you work hard and have a positive mindset. I have surrounded myself with an amazing circle of businesses, friends and family who are all supportive of my creative mind.

I love encouraging people to step out of the box and do whatever they set their mind to. Life is short. Everyone has a story and most are not simple, just never think you are alone as so many are wanting to help you do you.

Carol Sachowski is the founder of Storycoaching Inc., supporting clients as they craft and contribute authentic stories of active resilience and hope.

CAROL
SACHOWSKI

My Mother's teaching career started when she was 17 years old. Towards the end of it, she taught kindergarten in Toronto's west end, twice a day – 50 little ones in total, out of what had once been the school's library.

During this time, my Dad's health was significantly impaired; his personality altered and his spirit broken. Mom was somehow holding us all together. Holiday festivities were somewhat muted throughout this time, although during it, a wonderful tradition emerged.

After dinner on Christmas Eve became the time for Mom, my sisters and I to gather around the fireplace so Mom could open gifts her students (or their parents) had given her. While Mom said the night was for honouring the children, we were also honouring her. With each unwrapping came a story about that child, a particular trait or endearing moment, or better yet, a completely off the wall comment. Like the little girl who gave Mom's teacher's aide serious side eye, answering "no dice" when an attempt was made to coax her into her winter jacket! And we'd be sure to honour those additional little ones, also students, in the two classrooms, with Mom sharing a story of each as well, often with extra adoration. Laughter turned to tears then to laughter; Mom beamed through it all.

When I reflect on the work I do with individuals, teams and organizations alike, at the core, those client stories are not all that different. They include laughter and tears, triumphs and struggles, hugs and hurdles - honouring amazing people simply trying to do their best, be it alone or together.

In 55 years I've had countless moments of happiness and just as many of sadness; I don't think I'd want it any other way. Each experience – mine, yours, our loved ones, our communities, our clients – tells the tale of what it means to be magnificently human, lumps, bumps and all. How could we know joy if we hadn't experienced sorrow?

I'm excited by the future that awaits us. I'm equally anxious about it too. That's the polarity of humanity; of our collective responsibility to care for the earth and her inhabitants through it all.

Gloria Cuccione, executive director of the Michael Cuccione Foundation, philanthropist and loving mother living life to the fullest!

GLORIA
CUCCIONE

I met my soulmate on my nineteenth birthday, not looking for love but unable to deny it. We married in 1980 and had three beautiful children.

I can still remember our middle son Michael saying, "we have an almost perfect life!" Our precious child was diagnosed with Hodgkin's Lymphoma (cancer) at nine, three months later, which forever changed our lives. Michael became our constant inspiration. He accomplished more in his 16 years than most do in a lifetime. We lost our almost perfect son but learned to live life to the fullest through him. I feel blessed to have had his great light shine in our lives.

Despair came in waves at times, so I learned to steal moments to catch my breath and enjoy snippets of every day. I knew Michael would want us to be happy, not to have his illness tear apart our family. Hours before he took his last breath, he apologized to each of us. He lived an exemplary life, and I knew I would see him again!

Michael battled cancer twice and beat it, but later died of respiratory failure after six weeks on a ventilator. He established his foundation and raised $2.5 million to establish two lifetime endowments for young scientists to pursue their passions. After his passing, we carried on his legacy and raised over $25 million. We launched the Michael Cuccione Childhood Cancer Research Program at BC Children's Hospital. Every goal set in support of sick children has been surpassed.

Before Michael's diagnosis, fashion was my passion, and for ten years, I ran a flourishing business. My focus quickly evolved to helping our son and family through adversity. Our family now tries like Michael to live life to the fullest, pursuing their dreams. In my 60's, I have started a new business as the founder of a daily use unisex skincare mask, 1111 WISHFACE Cosmetics. My goal is to produce one of the healthiest, consistently performing skincare lines. My nurturing, caring spirit draws to me beautiful, like-minded people. Peace and love are my wishes for everyone. Our journey is short, so why not live it to the fullest!

LIAM
CHERNEN

I've had a lot of fun in my life, but like me, most people also experience not knowing what's next in their life at some point or another. My high school experience was busy and complicated, but I was amazing at finding time for everything. Despite expertly enjoying life's pleasures, I had a great deal of stress from needing to find direction. Having a greater sense of purpose and where I wanted to go next was becoming an aspiration for me. I used to get so worked up about the thought of losing time, needing to maximize my life. Although it might've taken a bit longer because I loved my life so much, I still had that question creeping up on me. What now? It was time for me to break through and plan for the future, a daunting but exciting venture. It was then that I found something to strive for, in cooking.

In 2016, I decided to do a trades program called ace-it professional cook level 1. I discovered that I love to cook. For me, cooking was this beautiful and calming experience. Food was something everyone, including me, loved. Turning raw, natural materials into delectable dishes that looked out of this world became my passion. Becoming a chef brought me to Vancouver Community College where I completed an intense cooking boot camp program to prepare for my ITA (Industry Training Authority) examination. After Graduating, I completed work experience at Vancouver's premier Gotham Steakhouse, later on to work at Nordstrom's Bistro Verde. Finally, I was hired at Cactus Club Coal Harbor, where I have worked for two and a half years now.

It astounds me that life can turn around so irrevocably; I was so unsure of where my life would go, not liking where it was, not understanding what it would become. Then, everything shifted, and step-by-step, I forged a new path for myself. I'm thankful for the joys of my past; it taught me that I have the ability to do anything. My vision of the future is clearer than ever before. Stepping up with determination and ingenuity, I launch myself farther than I ever deemed possible, into the future.

Jeffrey St. Germain, a musician since age two, is a performer at the Fremont Street Experience in Las Vegas.

JEFFREY
ST. GERMAIN

A two year old rock star!

I'm the first-born son of a young single mother. We didn't have much money, and we moved apartments every few months it seemed. The one thing that my mother had was her incomparable singing voice. She was the daughter of a very famous Canadian singer and was blessed with the ability to silence a room when she sang. To me, she was the biggest star in the world. I was only two years old when I decided I was going to be a 'famous' singer like the rest of my family. My mom, aunt and grandfather were the stars of a nationwide television variety show. They pre-recorded the music and vocals months before the actual on set filming. I would be at the studio watching them through the window that separated us from the isolation booth. I'd watch in awe, often mimicking and singing along, much to the chagrin of my grandfather. I wasn't even three years old yet when I decided I was going to be a rock star too! I started dressing in leather pants and t-shirts covered in clips, chains, and zippers. I'd perform for anyone who would listen. For the first few years of my life, I was convinced that all the big artists on the radio were performing my family's music and not the other way around. My tiny little bedroom became my rehearsal space and I'd spend every day listening, learning, and repeating every cassette or Betamax recording I could get my hands on. Occasionally, I'd have enough "D" size batteries to walk around the house with mom's oversized, early 80's boombox. If someone spoke to me, I'd usually respond with, "can't talk, I gotta 'hearse." Hearse being toddler language for rehearse; I was a two year old rock star. Forty years later, I'm living my childhood dream. With a little luck and a lot of help from a few close family allies, I did it. I am a "rock star." I have my dream gig in fabulous downtown Las Vegas at The Fremont Street Experience. I am everything I ever wanted to be as a kid. However, I can't talk right now, I gotta 'hearse.

17

Alex Delvecchio is a former Detroit Red Wing and eleven time captain of the team.

ALEX
DELVECCHIO

After spending the first half of my life in the demanding, fast-paced spotlight of professional sports, there came a time when I had to step out of it, as happens with every professional athlete. I had to shift gears, leave the demands and familiar routines behind me to find a different speed and a new normal. It wasn't as simple as it might seem. My "hockey" life was fast-paced, dictated by schedules, games, appearances, travel arrangements and a million other things that came with my career. So many decisions were made for me by others that making my own decisions was relegated to those parcels of time that existed between hockey demands. I'm not complaining, that's just the way it was and, in a way, although incredibly demanding, it had also become very comfortable, very familiar. You get used to things.

When I stepped outside of the hockey spotlight, all of a sudden I didn't have those demands and that fast-paced, familiar structure. Instead I had a leisurely, free slate and, seemingly, all the time in the world to do what I wanted, when I wanted. My life slowed to a different pace. I've never been one to look back, but I didn't quite know what to look forward to. It was all new to me and more than a little overwhelming. Shifting gears was necessary but what speed did I need to be at? I had no idea. So, as a first step, I decided to "cruise" by spending a lot more time just doing the things, big and small, that I already enjoyed. I played a lot more golf, took some ski trips in the winter to places I had always wanted to see, planted a larger garden, spent more time in the kitchen trying new recipes and perfecting old ones, and I spent more time with family and friends.

Soon I found that this new normal, although spent at a slower pace than before, was as rewarding as I could have hoped for. My life became and continues to be, very full; full of everything I choose to do, at the time and way I choose to do it. Life is good!

Marilyn A. Anderson's gift is communication - helping leaders and their teams answer 'yes' to 'are YOU feeling heard?'

MARILYN
ANDERSON

Today, I happily describe myself as a communicator, collaborator and confidante. I am fascinated by what drives people and take great pleasure in making appropriate introductions which can benefit both parties. The enjoyment of meeting new people and matching them to others with integrated needs and interests has established my reputation as a 'connector'; there is literally an endorphin explosion in my brain when I can make a 'great fit' connection, which helps others move ahead. I am also very careful to respect their privacy and the intel they share. What we call networking has long been an integrated part of my daily life.

Looking back, I suppose you could say I had a nomadic upbringing. We moved a lot when I was growing up, leaving the family farm when I was six years old and relocating again when I was eight, sixteen, and seventeen, before moving on to post-secondary education on my own.

In small towns, being the 'new kid' wasn't always fun, and I became adept at adapting to whatever I perceived to be the status quo. I recognized groups quickly and developed my own approach to 'social security' by connecting with people in several circles - not being a member of any one group. In time, I developed my collaborator role, connecting people from different groups where there was an overlap or shared interest. Bridging those gaps meant I had a pulse reading of social development, which helped me to help other people achieve positive outcomes of their own.

Today, all of those experiences have come together in my business practices, as I work with leaders and teams to achieve meaningful results. Many relationships in my life have been enhanced by those overlapping interactions, and have resulted in many successful business outcomes over time. My favourite motivating question is: "Are YOU feeling heard?" When everyone in a conversation/on a team/contributing to a project can answer "yes" to that, much can be accomplished in a very healthy environment.

My mom had a principle which I have incorporated into my voicemail to this day. "Make someone smile today. You'll be glad you did!" Wrong-number callers leave me messages because of it. Thanks, mom. Cheers!

19

Crystal is a living example of how far one can go, in distance and in life, by simply putting one foot in front of the other and refusing to give up.

CRYSTAL
FLAMAN

As a child, I was one of the most 'unlikely to succeed' in any athletic pursuit. Picked last for recreational sporting activities and rarely making the cut for any team, I grew up doubting my ability and value on the court or field and in my life.

Those hardships as a child taught me great strength, the power of the mind and resilience. I found a way to overcome seemingly insurmountable obstacles, including curing my Lyme Disease and bouncing back from a foot-crushing accident. As an athlete these experiences were both mentally and physically debilitating. However, I stumbled on a simple philosophy to accomplish just about anything I set my mind to. You can use this simple method to achieve your dreams, too.

My philosophy in life is simple: When the why becomes big enough, the how becomes easy. Make your why bigger, no matter what your goals are, and you're halfway there. Try it, and you'll see that it works.

With a greater sense of why and any goal in mind, whether it be Ironman triathlons or ultra-marathons, the next step to getting to the finish line and realizing our dreams is to surrender to the journey. Not surrender in the way that we often think – to give up or give in – but to become sure of the end. This is what surrender really means. If we can become sure of the end, and make our why big enough, we can and will realize any dream we have.

Along with creating a compelling reason why and surrendering to our dreams and goals, the final component of my method is to find a friend, be a friend, keep moving forward and do not get wet. I've endured great personal challenges, but this simple philosophy has helped me countless times. In business, in races and in life, when it feels like it's all up-hill, the wind is in your face and it's raining.

May we find ourselves in pursuit of what sets our soul on fire and use the simple ideas on this page and on every page of this inspiring book to help us bring all our dreams to life!

Jolene Laskey is the CEO & founder of Wabanaki Maple. She is proudly Wolastoqey, and a member of Neqotkuk (Tobique) First Nation, NB.

JOLENE
LASKEY

As I started this chapter of entrepreneurship at 50 years of age, one of the hardest parts was learning how to accept and adapt to the many changes I was now faced with. By this, I'm referring to mostly getting out of my comfort zone and gathering the courage to move forward with my business. It entailed a lot of hands-on learning on how to navigate through what I describe as "uncharted waters" and understanding this vast business ecosystem as an Indigenous woman. Within the first year of planning, I focused on finding opportunities that could help me build a stronger understanding of how it all works, and by the end of 2018, I'd successfully completed a Business Incubator Program, a Grow Export Program, launched our website and created new relationships with a solid network of mentors and advisors. Fast forward to now, it's been an amazing journey so far and with a few years of experience now under my belt, I'm much more equipped with many business resources, knowledge, and confidence to move the company to the next level.

It's really been a combination of driving forces for me, but what keeps me inspired on a daily basis is my family. One of my stronger characteristics is that I am a nurturer, so as a wife, a mother, and a grandmother, I am motivated and committed to creating a beautiful legacy that eventually can be passed down to our next generation. In addition, as a proud Indigenous woman my inspiration is often derived by the many aspects of my culture, community, and environment. At the end of the day, I simply strive to give back with a vision to help our communities thrive and to help support and preserve a healthy environment.

Mike Soloman is a Vancouver based visual artist and musician. When he's not in the studio he gardens and cooks.

MIKE
SOLOMAN

One of the major steps in choosing my life's path was to believe in myself enough to call myself an artist. Perhaps because I was self-taught, at first I felt as though I needed to earn the title, by having someone grant me permission to use it.

Once I began to regard myself in that manner, my awareness of possibilities expanded. I became a much keener observer of our natural world. We're surrounded every day by sources of divine inspiration: the remarkably intricate plant structures, the flow of water, the sacred geometry of a snowflake, and a fire's dancing flames.

The most amazing art exhibit is continually unfolding! It's designs are manifestations of the life force. The repetitive patterns reflect and echo the building blocks of Creation.

"If you want to find the secrets of the universe, think in terms of energy, frequency and vibration." – Nicola Tesla

Since I am a musician as well, the audible spectrum is as intriguing to me as the visible world. The unseen energy inhabiting everything is a field of resonance with no beginning or end, an energy that we are all connected to, and a direct link to our imaginations, unconstrained by time.

This makes me wonder whether we're merely aligning to the frequencies that yield such revelation and processing it into physical form, revealing what already is there. Often, it feels like a process of distillation.

Rather than conveying what was intended, the mediums themselves, such as musical instruments and paint, each add a dimension or direction of their own. This unintended, organic translation is where real magic happens. When a supposed mistake turns into an artwork's best aspect, was this element part of some core essence to begin with? The original vision generates all roads that lead to the final creation, so maybe...

Our lives are songs, and we are the conductors.

Justin Saint found their self-expression through art, drag, dance and working out. Living life beyond the binary perspective.

JUSTIN
SAINT

As a child, I had a clear idea of what I did and didn't like, but constantly found my interests being diverted away by disapproving adults. I was affectionate, theatrical, and hated anything involving running and rough sports.

Cast in a lead role in our kindergarten play, my mind conjured up fantastical landscapes as I read the script. Through them I fought villains, dodged obstacles, and willingly ran backstage to magically reappear in new spots moments later. I had to wear makeup for the show, and while other kids made fun of me, I didn't care. Even with lipstick on, I was the hero who rescued the queen and saved our kingdom.

As I got more opportunities to perform, I saw growing resistance, until I was blocked from acting completely. I tried to express myself through art, only to see my sketches burned. There was so much fear that I would become a sissy or deadbeat, that I would get beaten up or scolded for hours for doing anything remotely feminine or artistic. I became so afraid of speaking up that I started mumbling when I spoke. An awkward teen, stiff and unsure of myself.

Ending up homeless and being cut off financially was the beginning of my artistic liberation. I applied for scholarships and student loans, securing just enough money to study makeup artistry. I performed as a drag queen and found that feminine dance moves came quite naturally to me. Years of repression were replaced with womanly confidence. I loved seeing a queen staring back in the mirror. Straight and gay friends assumed I would get gender confirmation surgery, but that didn't feel right.

I started taking dance classes and yoga. Masculine spaces like gyms were terrifying, but as I went to more classes, I realized it was a meditative space. I eventually started lifting weights. I began to love my own reflection, even out of drag. Embracing my feminine side made me understand my masculine side.

Even without the words for it, I've known my gender since I was four. In a world that keeps saying 'no' to me, being non-binary means being able to say 'yes!' to my own gender expression.

Justin Saint

Brittany Hardy is an entrepreneur from Port Coquitlam B.C. who creates social media marketing plans for her clients around the world. She is a mother of four, is a true Gemini, and loves everything about personal development, lattes, and online shopping ;)

BRITTANY
HARDY

People are often fascinated with how I make my life 'work' with four children who have three different fathers, alongside the many ups and downs along the way. It comes down to a fierce will to care for my children; I have had to be resourceful to get to where I am today.

Earlier this year, I wrote a chapter for another book, which I titled 'Just Start'. If I have learned one thing, it's that the path is always blurry, until one day it isn't! You just take the first steps; eventually, you get to your destination.

I wrote about part of my journey – young motherhood, being alone, a failed marriage, a start-up business – wrapping it up with a newfound compassion for myself and all women; I felt an incredible amount of accomplishment.

I naively thought my tribute to my oldest daughter was going to make her feel proud and connected to her mother. Spoiler alert… teenagers don't work like this.

I've been told the teenage years between a mother and daughter are amongst the hardest – good Lord, I hope that's true, because I might not survive it otherwise!

I'm not the most patient person, nor am I good at letting go. Sometimes, I want to hold on, but in my daughter's eyes, I'm stifling her independence and creativity, smothering her when she wants space.

I made the heartbreaking decision of allowing my 15 year old daughter to live with her father, coming home every second weekend. It feels like part of my being has been ripped out.

I have to trust she will make her own mistakes, but will flourish and blossom into an amazing young woman.

So, here I am again, just starting! Navigating how to parent my other children in the absence of their big sister, discovering how I can be the best mom to my daughter.

I know the universe has my back. It's working in mysterious ways, but our path will reveal itself.

If you've ever had to 'let go' and surrender against your better judgement, I'm right there with you.

Oh… and send help for the next three teenagers I will soon have – I'm sure I'll need it ;)

Brittany Hardy

Meg loves the journey of becoming, which has resulted in many high-level successes. Married to her high school sweetheart and mama of two, she has earned the top Canadian PhD science scholarship, awarded top business accolades in her health company, as well as played in two Canadian masters' soccer championships representing Ontario...a sport she only began playing in her late 20's.

DR. MEG
HAGGITT

Do you believe in the rise? What traits or successes do you "wish" you had? Many believe you are born with certain abilities; you either have them or you don't, those "natural talents". However, studies of successful people fail to support that conclusion. You AREN'T born with a ceiling to what you can accomplish. YOU create your ceiling.

The question is not IF you have a certain skill or trait, but are you WILLING to put the time and effort in to attain it. Sometimes, the answer is yes, and you begin your rise. Sometimes, the answer is no, and you do nothing. In life, no one else can give you the "right" answer (though they may try), it is yours to own. But what would happen if you chose to rise?

My journey in life has been filled with "improbable" outcomes. From a university–bound farm kid to being chosen as one of the top 24 in Canadian graduate students, I rose. And have chosen to rise many times since then. It's never easy, it takes a willingness to do the work. And the key to rising is not to focus along the way on where others are in their journeys. Just focus on you and your efforts. I compete against the me of yesterday… am I better than her today? I take satisfaction in forward motion, even when the results aren't obvious. It is life changing to realize you have no ceiling.

You don't rise once and you're done. As a new inspiration will pop on your list, you will have another choice to make. Is it worth it? Are you going to choose to rise? Ah, the moments that determine our life aren't parade worthy at the start, it is just a quiet decision in our own mind. Yes, let's rise. Let it begin…

Dr. Meg Haggitt

DR. MARK
ROBSON

It's 1956, the Hungarian Revolution is on FIRE! And we're fleeing for our lives.

We've got one chance to escape tonight, so we're taking it. Border Patrols are shooting at us as we crawl across the corn field towards the Austrian border. We finally made it to freedom, but many didn't.

Seven months later I see my mother for the first time. I'm finally born, breast feeding and bonding with my birthmother. We're at the refugee camp in Abbotsford, BC, Canada.

After one week, I'm taken away for adoption. I wouldn't see her again, until 39 years later, when I finally found both birth parents just three weeks apart. That's a whole other story that filled in missing pages in the book of my life.

It's 1982, my chiropractic practice is booming in Victoria, and I'm on a crusade to save lives.

Ten years in practice, I've served thousands, made millions, created my dream life, traveled the world, went through two divorces, bought everything I wanted. Then, it happened.

Labelled a "maverick" by my profession, shot down, ridiculed, told to fit in and be like the rest of us. Fuck that shit!

I'm too different, practicing ahead of my time and way beyond the "status quo". But that's who I am! I'm either in the wrong profession, country or the wrong planet!

After 10 years in practice, I flatlined emotionally, spiritually and financially. Something's not right, and I can't figure it out here. I practiced for 13 more years before hitting a wall - HARD!

It's December 14, 2005, blowing cold, wet snow in Seattle as I board my flight.

I'm outta here, long grey winters, high fucking taxes, conservative mindsets and the frustration of being told to "just FIT IN!". Nope!

I sold my practice, gave everything away and headed to the other side of the planet for three months where nobody knows me, and I know no-one; I want to see who and what I become.

I never came back.

Natasha is a wife, mom, cop, actor, and co-author in "The MomBabes: A Motherhood Anthology." Natasha is the director of promotion and marketing for BC Women of Law Enforcement.

NATASHA
BRUCE

"Impossible" is not a word we say in our house. "I'm possible!" is the legacy I am seeking to create.

In 2017, I sustained yet another on duty concussion and my life changed catastrophically. My vision, hearing, speech, and cognitive capabilities were all severely affected.

As a police officer and mom of three, with the baby still nursing, the distress and sense of panic in seeing my world taken away from me was devastating. I poured my energy into doing the best I could and actively engaging in what I had hoped was healing therapy.

Finally, I felt strong enough to return to work. Right away, I began to experience panic attacks and sleepless nights, which revealed a PTSD diagnosis from years of trying to fight an on duty traumatic call I could no longer outrun. My brain was screaming at me to stop.

COVID-19 shut down one on one therapy; my healthcare team had to be creative in their approach to help me tackle PTSD and prescribed acting as therapy. This proved to be a natural fit as I am a born creative who had been silenced for years.

I said "yes" to embracing the fear of PTSD trauma brain voice. It became my job to unleash the trauma, constructively turning it into telling stories as an actor and writer. I said "yes" to joining other like minded individuals and their inviting communities. I said "no" to fear and "yes" to telling an important story about being a new mom and a police officer. A story I wish I had heard before I had three kids.

I realized that I could help others through my experiences, and the impossible became the possible. I designed my own website to continue my legacy, which helps other moms and is also a place to sell copies of my book.

Just because I live with PTSD and the after effects of a serious brain injury does not mean my life has to have limits. "I'm possible!"

Natasha Bruce

Justin "The Happy Mechanic" DaSilva is a fully certified diesel mechanic who loves making old iron live again.

JUSTIN
DASILVA

I have never been one for following the rules, or authority for that matter. Not in a rebel without a cause kind of way, practicality has always been a key touchstone for me. No, my perspective has always been that of being able to see the bigger picture, clearly seeing improved ways of doing things. I am a builder by nature, and that gift has always enabled me to look at things from multiple perspectives.

Ever since I can remember, I have had a deep curiosity around how things work. Add to that an intense fascination with trucks. As a child, I would take my toy trucks apart and put them back together so that I could understand what makes them move and why. Mechanical abilities always came naturally to me, so my path, quite honestly, couldn't have been clearer.

As I got older, my mechanical curiosity led me to old trucks. All the puzzle pieces finally came together, this was my calling: giving new life to old things and proving they still had a chance.

Entrepreneurship was undoubtedly my path in life, but not an easy one. Everyone thought I was nuts and kept asking why I couldn't just get a normal 9-5 job. I did try that, but the joy and fulfillment just wasn't there. So, I dove in and bought my first old truck – a perfect model that would enable me to use it as a service truck and help others. Everyone had given up on it, and most mechanics had written it off as unfixable. But not me.

I spent my first year working full time, fixing the truck at night and getting my business up and running in whatever hours were left. It was a lot of work, but seeing that truck revived to its full glory was worth it all. I had taken something that people had lost hope in and given it a second chance at life, and that is the essence of what I do now. I help others to keep their "old faithful" on the road, and their pride high. Everything deserves a second chance at life, even if it is an old truck. :)

Amanda Da Silva is an author, educator, entrepreneur, personal coach, and university mentor for students looking to pursue their dreams.

AMANDA
DA SILVA

All hell breaks loose at 40!

This is the title of the notes page documenting the symptoms I have been experiencing for over three years now. Aches and stiffness from head to toe upon waking up, constantly feeling ill, uncontrollable palpitations, violent migraines, extreme fatigue, eye pain, memory problems, difficulties with focus and attention, to name but a few.

When I hit 40 years old, I became a CEO, was driving a three-hour-long commute every day, running a household with three children, three dogs, and caring for elderly family members in need of assistance. Somewhere in between, I stopped looking after myself. This is when the physical and psychological stress took a toll on my health. I ended up in an emergency room on more than one occasion. After doctors ran a series of stress tests, heart rate evaluations, echocardiograms, and electrocardiograms etc., I received my diagnosis: Fibromyalgia.

As someone who's always been highly driven, energetic, and on the go, I had no idea where to start or how. The only thing I knew is that I had to reassess my priorities, starting with my job.

The doctor's input provided me with mortality motivation that I didn't know I needed. It taught me to appreciate the relationships I have, and it pushed me to pursue what I am truly passionate about. Because at the end of the day, it is your purpose and the people you surround yourself with that matter. Then comes the dream life and the financial wealth – in that particular order.

Coming out triumphant from such a taxing experience inspired me to create the "Discover Your Purpose" course. This was, in fact, what I did for myself to get to where I am today. While this was not an easy process, making the necessary changes one step at a time helped me regain control of my health and my life.

I now feel happier and more at peace than ever before. No day is without its challenges, but I find so much joy, meaning, and fulfillment in being surrounded by my loved ones, being able to generate my own opportunities, and take better care of myself and my family.

Amanda Da Silva

Shaun Peet is a Canada's first NASCAR Pit Crew Coach. In addition to his duties at the racetrack he is an author and a speaker. In his keynote speech, "One Good Shift," he asks us all one simple question, "If one good shift can change the course of something as simple as a hockey game, don't you think the same could be said for something as magnificent as your life?"

SHAUN
PEET

You are guilty. Your friends are guilty. Just about everyone you know is guilty. Heck, I'm guilty and I am the one writing this! I know you are guilty before I ever ask the question. Well then, what is the question you might ask? The question is: Have you ever tried to prove someone wrong? See, I told you. Guilty.

At some point in our lives, most all of us have tried to prove someone wrong. But have you ever stopped to consider when we get to do that? The only time we get to prove someone wrong is when accomplish a goal, get a promotion, win a championship, etc. It is at some hard-earned moment of brilliance. Yet, it is at these beautiful milestones in our lives that we think it best to remember the people who stabbed us in the back, lied about us, gave up on us, or worse, never believed in us? These people don't deserve to share this moment.

What if you made one simple shift? What if instead of proving people wrong, you prove people right? Think about it. We all have people in our lives that have poured their love and their time and their respect into us. Whether that's parents or grandparents. Coaches or teachers. Co-workers or friends. What if instead, you did it for them? The friend that always came through for you. The teacher that stayed after hours to deconstruct the complexity of an algebra problem. The father that woke up at 430am to take his son to hockey practice even though he knew his son was the worst player on the team. What if you did it for them?

When you shift from proving people wrong to proving people right, you unburden yourself from all the people who never deserved to be in your life in the first place. And you fill your championship moments with the people that do.

The life you have always wanted to live in right in front of you. And all that it takes to get there is, One Good Shift.

Kerri Anne Kedziora is a woman on a mission; empowering others despite their own perceived barriers, but because of them!

KERRI ANNE
KEDZIORA

UNLEASHING THE WOUND!

Having survived a traumatic and troubling childhood, and failing with government appointed counsellors, coming into adult life, I had no idea how to navigate the waters.

I spent my early twenties trying to figure out how to cope with trauma I had experienced at the hands of my extremely abusive stepfather and my own mother. I found the only way that I knew (or was taught) to cope, was to use alcohol.

As one might imagine, after suffering extreme trauma in my early years, continuing through most of my life (in reality, continuing until I finally got sober in my 40th year), family and friends became victims of my alcohol infused anger, despair and self-loathing. I was not what many refer to as, "a happy drunk." I spent my 20's and 30's wrapped up in emotions, anxiety and intense fear of making any move to better myself.

Years of brainwashing had convinced me I was unworthy of anything good… ANYTHING.

Having contemplated suicide many times, I wondered if life was really worth living; I was unable to commit to either dying OR living!

Fast forward to my 40th year, when I realized that the decision was quite simple. Either get sober or die. There was no in between. In fact, I realized if I didn't get sober, I would surely die, leaving nothing but the story of a sad and wasted life for my children to tell. If they bothered to speak of me at all!

That realization created big change. Summoning the courage to get sober, making sure to take the time immersing myself in programs that would help me heal, I have finally realized that life is worth much more than I ever understood!

I am thrilled that through my healing I'm able to help others. Spending my time empowering others to use their abilities to enrich their own lives. Employing people with different issues, I strive to help them learn to overcome every day barriers in order to succeed at work and in life!

I title this chapter of my life: "Unleashing The Wound," because I'm ripping off the band-aid, exposing the wound, encouraging it to heal.

Kerri Anne Kedziora

Vancouver-based creative director Robert Amado's constant curiosity and vast training is what makes him an award-winning hairstylist and entrepreneur.

ROBERT
AMADO

Born and raised in Vancouver I had a dream and a vision. It was over 20 years ago when I became a professional hair stylist.

Fast forward many years later, what better place to move than the big city of Toronto and plant my roots. It was the perfect recipe in becoming not only a professional hairstylist but also an entrepreneur, diving into creating the Amado brand.

I have so many amazing Canadians to be thankful for and you have all played a huge part in every aspect of my career.

Whether I've sculpted your hair, have been blessed to have you in my life or have had the honour to build a professional relationship in any way shape or form, each and every person that I have met along the way has contributed to what the Amado brand has become today.

God has paved the path for me to walk and has allowed me to become the stylist, entrepreneur and person I am today. Through hard work and so many wonderful relationships built along the way, I am truly grateful for every single day.

Life has many twists and turns and with all those amazing obstacles and opportunities it has led to not only developing my craft, but creating the silver lining into the Amado True Professional Hair Care brand.

If there is one thing that I have learned in the last few years, it is that if you take care of the people, then everything else takes care of itself. There are so many factors in creating a business and brand, but at the end of the day, it's the people that stand behind you that matters most.

Like the agile scissors of a polished stylist, my empathy towards everyone has shaped this cutting-edge brand into something of style and well-being. I've always concentrated on building relationships with so many wonderful Canadians to understand their needs and wants, to make them look and feel their best.

Life brings us as many joyful moments as it does downfalls, and although there are days we wish there was a manual to follow, it simply wouldn't be the same without the spontaneity. The journey of life may not become easier as we grow older, but we do seem to understand it better as our perspectives evolve.

At the end of it all, it's really quite simple; my focus and vision has always been about giving something more, and the best way to predict the future is to create it.

Robert Amado

Allison Lee Patton is a curious, passionate, energetic, and creative freedom seeker.

ALLISON LEE
PATTON

I always find that looking forward fuels my innovation and creativity. As I gather up the learnings and visions from 2021, I use these as the launching stage for what comes next.

Recently, I read the book Atlas of the Heart by Dr. Brené Brown. The book named and described 87 emotions and experiences that allow us to process our life experiences and build connection with each other. There were two profound things that happened as I read the book; one was emotional, the other practical. As for the emotional, I can only describe it as the ability to find closure to numerous pain points of previous life experiences that I did not even realize were hanging there in the background. The ability to define, understand, and connect to these emotions provided me comfort and peace.

As for the practical, the book described story stewardship as a way to deeply connect. This occurs when we listen to someone else's story and believe the story they tell us. The power of this simple concept is deeply motivating to me in my work, with my family, and in my community. I have a strong desire for my story to be heard and believed as well.

In 2022, as I continue to serve in public office and in my work at Ardour Wellness as a naturopathic physician, a focus on this natural and authentic connection is one that I am pursuing passionately.

The other definition I want to highlight from the book by Dr. Brené Brown is the definition used for humility.

"Humility is an openness to new learning combined with a balanced and accurate assessment of our contributions, including our strengths, imperfections, and opportunities for growth."

I really appreciate and connect with this definition and plan to approach my work in 2022 from a place of humility. I couldn't be more excited to fine tune the services that I am able to provide to my ever-awe-inspiring patients as I continue to help them work toward even better health and wellness in their lives.

As I cherish the precious nature of our lives, I aim to make every day count, and I feel immense gratitude for the opportunity.

Alyson Jones is a therapist, speaker, writer, educator, business owner and clinical director of Alyson Jones & Associates.

ALYSON JONES

"The opportunity you fear is the opportunity you need."
– Alyson Jones

I do not believe in living a fearless life. I believe in following fear even when we do not feel ready for where it leads us. Opportunities seldom come when we are ready. When I really look at each big change, turning point, or accomplishment in my life, they all scared me, and I was not ready for any one of them.

When I was in my 20's I had completed my psychology degree, and wanted to work in the mental health field, but was unable to get a counselling job in my community. My boyfriend (now husband of 30 years) and I packed our bags and moved to British Columbia without jobs. This was terrifying on many levels, but here I began my career as a child and family therapist.

When I was in my 30's I was increasingly curious about parenthood – but I was also afraid of all the responsibility that came with parenting. My curiosity outweighed my fear and soon we were parents of twins. I certainly wasn't ready for that, but thank goodness my curiosity won that day; parenting has been one of the most interesting experiences of my life.

When I was in my 40's I opened my counselling and consulting center Alyson Jones & Associates. I forged my way though those initial years and fears. I established myself as a business owner and operator of a mental health clinic with several associates serving many clients.

At 50 I faced more fears when I published my first book, MORE A New Philosophy for Exceptional Living, which was based on lessons learnt as I moved through fear to opportunity and growth.

Time keeps moving regardless of what we do. We will feel fear, but if we learn to follow our fear, we will have an exceptional adventure and many great stories to share. Not every opportunity has assured success, nor can we expect a great outcome from every choice, but each opportunity will bring growth and experience.

Maybe my fear has always been my wisdom speaking to me.

JENNIFER
UTLEY

I like to think of PR as the wind beneath your wings, and this other person's wings, and these newfangled wings over here. I get so excited about new ideas, working with innovative thinkers, inventors, and social causes. I'm the one in the back with the headset on, holding a clipboard and jumping out of the camera shot.

Becoming a publicist was never in the plans though. I was always passionate about the environment and politics, and figured law would be the most practical course of action for me. My other love for fashion and art would remain a hobby. Everything changed when I fell in love with an Englishman and moved to the UK. Armed with a political science degree to fall back on, I landed my dream fashion job in London and for a few solid years, I thought I had it all worked out.

However, after a bully of a boss and a bad break-up, I decided it was time to go home. I moved back in with my parents and started working as a temp, responding to calls like a cheese sampler at the mall. I went back to school and focused on PR. I interned a lot, wrote for an ill-contrived start-up magazine, styled some very embarrassing fashion shoots, and even wrote a book that never got published. It was my quarter-century life crisis.

Despite it all, I kept going, networking, and finally one day, met a dynamic woman who was co-producing a very large fashion, music, and art event, with guest host, Richard Dean Anderson - you know, MacGyver! After the event, she hired me and has basically been stuck with me ever since!

It was the beginning of a new career that has allowed me to do so much and give back so much too. As a small, boutique agency with women at the helm, having kids, making room for our passions, and leading with our hearts is not just allowed, but expected and encouraged.

From working on Vancouver's first Eco Film Festival, and supporting designers at New York Fashion Week, to representing clients at international cosmetic shows, and campaigning for mental health and environmental initiatives, life is never dull! It's a beautiful balancing act with my wonderful kids and husband and social causes close to my heart.

Dennis Wager, CEO and president of Apex Rock Pros LLC, is a leader and innovator in the rock breaking industry.

DENNIS
WAGER

Growing up, I learned that I was good at working with my hands. It was alongside my father in our garage where I began building projects with wood he brought home from the shipyards. I built lawn furniture and carved signs, saving up my money to buy aHarley Davidson motorcycle.

Back then, I didn't really care about much besides riding my bike and drinking beer with my friends. After high school I continued my carpentry projects. My dad was my best friend and biggest influence.

Although my dad had a regular job as a longshoreman, I somehow got my entrepreneurial spirit through him. Always busy, always building and creating. Over the years my building projects turned into substantial businesses.

Learning and expanding my skill sets have led me to places I sometimes couldn't even believe were possible. At one point, I was training blasters in the US Army on underwater blasting with low explosives and how to mitigate environmental damages to sea life by using deflagration versus detonation. I thought to myself, what do I know that these guys don't? But hey, they were paying me!

At times, I've underestimated myself. I often questioned what I was capable of, but I was never afraid of failure. I took leaps of faith and put myself out there; it was risky at times, but saying "yes" to things is what put me ahead. I eventually became a leader in my industry.

Everything changed for me in 2006. I was in a severe car accident that nearly took my life. Suffering from a head injury, the years following the accident were a blur. I couldn't keep my business running, some days I couldn't do much. After two years of struggling to stay afloat, I lost my business, my home, and other properties.

It was an awful time, but eventually, I bounced back. Losing everything was hard, but I'm so fortunate, and for that, I'm grateful every day.

I've since been able to rebuild; at 57, I love my life, my family and my two granddaughters. I am open to everything, and that includes failures – they are life's biggest lessons. Happiness is in creating a life you love.

Jillian Morris, writer, life-promoter, bridge-builder, mother, wife, is interested in the stories that shape us. She believes storytelling is a powerful means to finding connection.

JILLIAN
MORRIS

I am Kanien'keha:ka (Mohawk Nation), onkwehon:we (original person), from Six Nations of the Grand River Territory. I spent 13 years as a federal public servant. I was motivated by representation and the possibility of systemic change from within.

Reality finally sunk in. I am now a freelance writer, researcher, and collaborator.

I carry with me the blood of my ancestors, the heart of my community, and the spirit of generations to come. My knowledge, my gifts, and my blessings belong to them.

Reframing my actions through the lens of responsibility versus rights or entitlement has shifted my perspective and how I relate to the life around me. This does not mean I do not stand up for Indigenous and inherent rights.

I stand with my kin and demand action on broken treaties, land and water protection, reparations for all the harms and injustices placed upon us. I do this because I have a duty to do so. I do it for those who fought before me. I do it for those who will pick up the work when I'm gone.

As a Haudenosaunee woman I am guided by the philosophy of the Good Mind. It is not retribution that I chase. It is peace, balance, and friendship. The good life as a prospect for all.

A dozen years ago I lost my lifelong supporter, protector, friend, my brother. He loved me unconditionally. He was proud of me. He trusted me. He teased me incessantly. He made me laugh until I cried. He was the first person to make me feel like I was enough.

This world was too cruel, too unforgiving, too apathetic for his perceptive spirit. Society didn't see people like him, like me.

Countless Indigenous voices, like his, have been silenced. The shame of not using mine is greater than the fear of not being heard.

Trauma passed down, trauma lived, trauma experienced vicariously… trauma on trauma on trauma. This is not our story.

So now, I write.

I write to help redress the history that has been misrepresented. I write because truth must come before reconciliation. I write in hopes that you want to hear more.

I write so you can see us.

Dale is an artist, videographer, and outreach worker.

DALE
VILLAJUAN

One of my mantras is to create art and assist those in need. In order to support people, I needed my voice to be heard. I am the type of person whom people might think is arrogant or a snob; in truth, I have a quiet persona and keep to myself. It may take some time, but eventually, I can have a conversation and we can talk about the universe. I realized my personality was that of an introvert.

How did I overcome being an introvert? I stopped labeling myself with that trait; taking away the word was a start. There is nothing wrong with being an introvert and it is a unique trait.

One of the main ways was to step out of my comfort zone and go out to meet people and socialize. Be brave and start a conversation. My heart races 'til this day when I go out. It was difficult at first, but after overcoming the anxiety of being in a social environment and having that first conversation, I was at ease.

Alone time is great – I get to reflect, recharge, and especially, get creative. Balance is the key. Spending more time with people is an excellent way of overcoming being the lone wolf. The reclusive lifestyle almost leads me to not want to be around people at all. It is a dark and sullen place to be. Being out in the community leads to business opportunities, personal growth, improved mental health, and a healthier lifestyle.

Overall, I embrace the trait and take the leap to get out there, socialize, and evolve. It has helped me grow personally and at a professional level. It is an ongoing challenge, and with time and practice, it would be a natural flow to express oneself out in the world.

Today I use my voice to advocate, mentor, inspire, and share my art experience. To be bold and to get loud.

GINNI
MEHTA

My path was rocky at first, stunted by my immigrant status and ever slowed by my fears. I found strength in my own convictions; that hard work, compassion, and giving back would eventually pay off. Today, I am proud to say that my career stands for those exact same ideals while continuously empowering me to grow and help others do the same.

There is a fundamental shift in the spirit, a sudden realization of just how strong you can (and must) be when faced with the dread and loneliness that so often defines becoming an immigrant. To lift your roots from the earth—the very foundation of your formative self, history, and primordial sense of safety in this world—and move.

Photo credit: Kyoko Fierro from Fierro Photography

I was born and raised in New Delhi, India, and moved to Vancouver, Canada, in 2018. Equipped with my MBA, I was ready to pursue my passion in business operations, finance and marketing. Not only had I taken on the challenge of doing so as a recent immigrant, but I had moved into an industry that was entirely new for me.

I applied for a position at Okoko Cosmétiques that matched my skill set and my beliefs, from building cultural competencies and empowerment to ethical production while giving back to the community. Driven by female leadership by CEO Oyéta Kokoroko, the Okoko team made me feel instantly comfortable and welcomed after so much fear and isolation, challenging me with exciting opportunities to grow as both a professional and an individual.

If I could speak to my younger self, I would tell her to not give up because of fear. If you can grab your fear by the throat and hold it down as you trudge through each day, each challenge, and each task that seems to come so easily to everyone else around you, you will find something. Something that doesn't necessarily define you, but rather makes what was already there, shine. Your strength. Everything else falls into place so long as you keep going. Your sweat and determination will turn all those "cant's" into "cans."

My journey has taught me strength, and I will teach my daughter to find hers.

Mom, business owner, blogger, docu-series binger, fan of lazy day Sunday's, and obsessed with b&w films or antique cameras.

SHARLEY
NEILL

I am a former foster child.

At five years old I became the latest and youngest addition of four adopted kids in my newfound family. To the outside world we looked like a well-blended brood. To me, it felt the same as showing up to a party as someone's plus one that no-one else has met. It's awkward, everyone is staring, and at some point there's a good chance you'll end up with egg on your face. This was no exception.

Admittedly, there are some days I still feel that way (minus the egg). I have always struggled a little to find my role in the family. Being the last to arrive and youngest in the household, I never felt like I had much to contribute by comparison. Now in my mid 40's I can finally say, I'm coming into my own.

I am a survivor of both domestic abuse and addiction. I'm also one of many who live with bipolar disorder. Overcoming these obstacles has taught my inner foster child self-worth, esteem, and the quiet confidence that I somehow (through no fault of my adopted family) thought I was less than deserving of before.

I became my own boss in my 30's, I have just begun a second venture in my mid 40's, and now nearing an empty nest, I still wrestle with the idea of going back to college so I can work with addictions and mental health. It would be a full circle moment for me. We will see what the future holds.

Someone once said to me, "We each have our own Everest, but the path we take to get to the top is different for all of us." I have no doubt my path is similar to some of yours. Keep going...

I'll see you at the top!

Sharley Neill

Lesley Corte is an artist, writer, brilliant clairvoyant, intuitive guide and creator of lesleycorte.com

LESLEY
CORTE

We all want to know who we truly are. I certainly do. It is the journey I'm on in this life. Consciously, it began as I left home to go to university.

"You know, your mother wasn't ready for you to leave home," my dad said in the car after picking me up from the train station for Thanksgiving weekend of my first year. The statement turned my insides. I was eighteen. It was time to live as "me" and not be swayed by the family that imposed so many judgements and rules about how to exist in the world. I was in the grip of an identity crisis.

My art training helped me with expression of my inner self and I began to trust my intuition. This took me into an evolving career as a graphic artist, interior designer and finally towards event design, as well as endless renovations on my own home.

But my intuition blossomed when I began to meditate. It was the vehicle that led me to meet spirit guides, explore past lives and open to my soul's purpose. In my guidance practice I hope to help others to do so as well.

I have a deep inner wealth of talent and power experienced through past life recall, but to put it out in the world has been a challenge. In many periods of history I have fought against cultural and power structures and was persecuted for it. History has not always welcomed female power. But the world is now ready for women to step out, each to shine with their own individual talents and power.

I now allow myself to flow through my days with my inner guidance in charge. That's not to say I don't sometimes say, "no, I don't feel like doing that right now!" My rebellious self is still alive and well and is the jet propulsion I need to write a book about my past life lessons, which have brought me to the understanding that we are all truly magnificent souls.

My purpose is to guide others to experience their own true magnificence.

LAURA
TRAPLIN

Life is made up of choices. Some are free will, some are pre-destined.

I had a preconceived idea of how my life was going to play out. My soul had a different plan. My path was redefined when I was 35, after we adopted our four year old son. Within a short timeframe, all plans and normalcy were exchanged for daily behavioural crises.

Two years later, our son's seven month old birth sister joined our family. The odds of her being placed with us despite residing in another province was nothing short of remarkable.

Within weeks of her arrival, our son started having flashbacks to the severe abuse and trauma he'd suffered in his early life. This led to two years of intensive therapy, hospitalization, and severe behaviour that made daily living an unbearable challenge. At the same time, our daughter was diagnosed with a global delay. I felt an overwhelming, utter sense of despair as I tried to manage the needs of my children, all while grieving the normality of my old life and the one I had hoped for.

One night, emotionally exhausted, I prayed for help, questioning my path and the meaning of my life. The next morning my son said: "Mom, I had an amazing dream. You were asking an important question and I was told to give you this answer - you're the best mom I could ever have, please don't give up." This allowed me to believe in a benevolent force much bigger than myself. In my darkest hour I asked for help and received answers. I gained insight into past lives and soul contracts, and how relationships are beautifully yet sometimes painfully woven together from one lifetime to another, searching for healing. I felt the door to Spirit miraculously open. My mediumship and psychic abilities I had suppressed from my teen years were ignited.

Opportunities for the growth of our soul arrive when we least expect it. We can choose to embrace them or not. I chose to understand the meaning of my soul relationships. I chose to embrace my connection with Spirit. I chose love, compassion and understanding, for myself and others, and see life as a succession of gifts.

Lori Bagnérès is a mother, artist, curator and educator based in North Vancouver, BC. Through her mark-making and image manipulation, Lori has created a new niche of contemporary landscape painting. Lori's work is represented by private and public art galleries across BC and Ontario.

LORI
BAGNERES

When I was attending art school in Europe we frequently engaged in critique sessions with professors and professional artists participating in the school's residency programs. One of my one-on-one sessions was with an artist whose work had started gaining notoriety on the world circuit. I was within months of completing my MFA and five months pregnant at the time. The meeting was constructive all the way up to the last few moments, where she proceeded to offer me counsel rather than 'critique'. She commented on the fact that my impending motherhood would more than likely interfere with being able to manage a busy career as a professional artist, especially one that involved keeping up with the fast pace life of exhibiting, alongside the demands of gallery owners. I was stunned by her discouraging words and left feeling like my entire world had just been turned upside down. Unfortunately, I allowed her opinion to consume me for quite some time; I resolved to pursue a teaching career in art while raising my family.

It was years later, during a mixed media workshop given by a fellow artist/mentor, that I came to a realization about becoming a professional artist. Through her teaching wisdom and example, I felt less threatened by my previous art school feedback. I started to look at the bigger picture and the definition of what it is to be an "artist/bread-winner/mother". During this period of recognition I was able to focus on my passion and the need to dedicate my full attention on creating my own artwork.

I am grateful that I have learned a hard, yet valuable, lesson through this story. One that taught me that you shouldn't allow other people's insecurities, arrogance and negativity stand in the way of your own creativity. Once you discover this, it is wonderfully freeing to step back, accept feedback and put it into perspective.

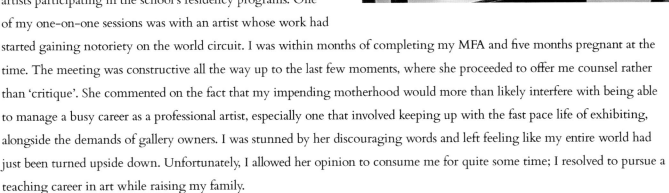

Maja Aro is a professional stunt coordinator/stunt performer, an indie film writer/director and a mother of 2 boys.

MAJA
ARO

The simple task of making lemonade.

Every day we are given obstacles in life. Most are small and do not alter the trajectory of our lives in any major direction, but every so often we have a day that is truly life changing. A day to learn from and evaluate which path you want to take next.

One of my big life changing days happened a few years ago. It was Mother's Day, the sun was very hot, my husband and I enjoyed a lovely brunch on our deck with some close family and friends. Everyone left, and we started some casual gardening. Oddly, not long into this mission, our fire alarms started blaring. My husband went to check, and I immediately heard his frantic yells. Our deck had caught on fire from underneath (what we would later be told was spontaneous combustion of a hay bale). The fire spread quickly, and as we fruitlessly tried to put it out, windows smashed before our eyes and the fire surged inside. It was so hot it took the fire department over seven hours to put it out.

Now I don't tell this story for its tragedy, as it really wasn't. It was a life changing day, and I had the choice of which path to take. I decided, while helplessly watching everything burn, to let go of everything. That way, anything that was recoverable would feel like a gift. We were surrounded by our community, taken in for the night by neighbours, given clothing by other neighbours and friends. It was one of the most beautiful and humbling things I have ever experienced, being on the receiving end of pure human kindness and generosity.

That kindness inspired us to call the path we decided to take "Project Lemonade," as it reminded us to always see the bright side of that life changing day. Making lemonade is about letting go and allowing the world to wrap its arms around you. It seems like such a simple task, but letting go can be quite hard.

I challenge you to let go, and simply make some lemonade next time you have a life changing day.

Jen Warrington is building a legacy for herself and her family, while helping others find, thrive and love their careers.

JEN WARRINGTON

From 2014–2017, I lived my life on autopilot and was 1000% in a fog. In a very short time span, I was 'this close' to losing my newborn daughter, my husband had two back-to-back brain surgeries and my mom passed away after an aggressively brief battle with pancreatic cancer.

I spent many nights walking the floor of my home making sure my daughter's heartbeat was stable, checking on my then seven year old son for good measure, while making sure my husband's head didn't explode while he slept. This was all while worrying and crying over my mom.

A few other unfortunate events and losses made it impossible to catch my breath and feel normal again. There was struggle, heartache and the inability to understand why all of this was happening literally back to back.

I functioned.

I managed.

I made it through each day.

I tried my best and really never let anyone, including those closest to me, see my rock bottom.

Fast forward to 2020, a global restructure impacted my job just two weeks before the country went into lockdown.

Honestly, it didn't scare me.

I (almost) immediately had a plan.

I was going to start my own business, and start my own business I did!

I'm a career strategist who helps professionals find careers they love with companies they're proud to represent, or we help them start their own! I take the overwhelm, frustration and worry away in figuring out what comes next or how to get to where they want to be. I give them the confidence and a plan to level up their career game and show them that 80% of what they need, they already have!

I've reflected on the chaos and pain and have coined the phrase, "from trauma and stress comes resilience and success!"

I am thriving!

Jenny Story is a best selling and award-winning author of the book series Dysnomia, a 2D and 3D animator, background actor, and the Self Advocate Award winner for AutismBC 2020.

JENNY
STORY

Being diagnosed Autistic at the age of three, I faced many challenges growing up. Though I knew that I could be smart, fun, creative and full of imagination, being shy, introverted, and Autistic, I've always struggled to communicate with others. So, when starting to go to school, I found it hard to bond with other kids my age. It was also difficult for me to learn in some of the classes that I did not care for, such as math.

Despite the bullying and being told there were certain things I would never be capable of because of my Autism, it didn't stop me from trying to achieve the impossible. When I wanted something, I would work hard to accomplish my goals and dreams.

With the love and support of family members like my mom and brother, friends I have made along the way, the kind hearted people in my life who believed in me and saw past my Autism, and never giving up, not only did I manage to graduate from elementary school and high school with good grades, I also got accepted into Vancouver Film School shortly afterwards and became a 2D and 3D animator. I have also written a best-selling award-winning fantasy YA book series, Dysnomia; I plan to turn this into animated movies or a TV series. I've also finished an animated short called Sparkles Loves Bacon during the pandemic, doing background work, and working on plenty of other projects that have yet to come.

I feel blessed to be able to follow my dreams when others doubted me and so many still keep on daydreaming. The doctor told my mom that my future was bleak and I wouldn't amount to much in life, yet I have been fortunate enough to achieve my goals and then some.

I am proud to be Autistic and wouldn't change a thing about myself; I would not be where I am today if I wasn't who I am. Always believe in yourself no matter what obstacles might come your way.

Jenny Story

Janet Walmsley is mother of two, retired dental assistant/hygienist, actor, talent scout, acting coach and teacher, best-selling/award winning author and advocate for Autism.

JANET
WALMSLEY

What is the definition of self esteem - confidence in one's own worth or abilities, self respect.

Something that I dealt with for many years, it took me into my fifties to truly embrace my self-worth and respect for myself. In hindsight, I'd have liked to have grasped this earlier, however, I learned to take the positive out of the negative.

I was ridiculed and teased about being flat chested in school. I was a cheerleader and once, when my top lifted up, a boy said, "hey Janet, you're so flat you don't need a bra," and, "your breasts are like fried eggs busted!" Those degrading remarks haunted me for years.

An ex-husband said, "you are fortunate to have me, as you're ugly being small chested." Many women have gotten breast implants, however, I remember my mother saying to me, "Janet, God gave you what he did, don't let anyone change you."

I never did until seven years ago, when I was diagnosed with breast cancer and had a double mastectomy and breast reconstruction. I remember my plastic surgeon opening up a drawer of sizes that I could choose from and I said," I don't want the Dolly Parton, let's go with the Jennifer Aniston model!"

In group therapy after two divorces, I saw nine other women who were mirror images of me; nice looking, professionals, successful, loving wives and mothers. We allowed men to take away our personas and hold us down. People would say, where is the Janet we know and love? We were given wooden flowers; written on mine was: loving, caring, giving and not a taker, which certain men take advantage of, use and abuse. They peg your low self-esteem, your desire to please. I was always blaming myself and thinking, "what did I do wrong?" I worked on myself, but those men wouldn't. I seemed to beeline for these types of men - I went from the frying pan into the fire from my first to second marriage.

The last 11 years, I have never looked back. I am no longer the shell of my former self. Yes, it took time to get here, but now I look in the mirror and love who I see!

Janet Walmsley

Priya Mehrotra empowers, elevates, and educates women, helping them navigate their career successfully without sacrificing their health and personal life.

PRIYA
MEHROTRA

I moved to NYC after graduating from university, wide-eyed and bushy-tailed, ready to start my career on Wall Street. Little did I know the challenges I would face in the big city - an intensely competitive and male-dominated financial services sector.

The corporate world is generally tough to navigate, and women face an additional set of challenges. Glass ceilings were nowhere on my radar when starting out! There were not many female role models in leadership positions and no rule book guiding women how to succeed. Consequently, I made mistakes early on in my career when I was learning by trial-and error, despite going through an expensive graduate school and earning an MBA in NYC.

That said, I've been fortunate to work alongside Fortune 100 male leaders for 15+ years, who took interest in my growth, helping me gain valuable experience along the way. Like they say, if you can make it in New York, you can make it anywhere! I now know firsthand just how true those words really are.

However, even as I was thriving in my profession and climbing the corporate ladder, I was also combating more stress with every new success, working crazy hours and juggling increasing responsibilities. Research shows that "Type A" personalities are especially at risk of burnout because of our exceptional drive and unusually high expectations of ourselves. I knew that if I did not change the way I functioned, I was headed for job burnout!

The sad reality is that so many women struggle trying to balance family life with professional endeavors. The pandemic has made this situation worse; according to McKinsey, 75% of female employees considered quitting their jobs due to burnout.

Thanks to my grandfather, who trained me in holistic health practices, including breathwork from an early age, I was able to restore much-needed balance in my life. Now, as a Work Stress Transformation and High Performance Coach, I am incredibly passionate about helping other ambitious women who want more out of life to overcome their personal struggles so that they can feel fulfilled in all areas of their life - without giving up their job or taking a step back in their career.

Dannii Freeman is an artist, designer and entrepreneur. She dreams of inspiring others around her with creativity, kindness and love.

DANNII
FREEMAN

In the blink of an eye my world turned upside down. I was in the darkest place I've ever been; the demons that lived there haunted my mind to the point that sleep was never part of my routine.

Everyone has a voice inside their head telling them one thing, then another. Making you feel one emotion, or nothing at all.

Life is hard, but being alive is beautiful. The man I fell in love with for four years took his life in the place we made our home. We believed in each other. He showed me that I shouldn't be afraid to be an artist, a dream I always chased but never quite felt confident about, until he came into my life. Art saved me, I just wish I could've saved him.

We're all a little broken, but I believe that's how the light shines through. I never thought I'd smile again, but I'm here, I'm thankful and I'm strong. I've learned to grow and move forward with love and kindness in my heart.

Memories live on forever. Life is meant to be lived and cherished with the people you care about most, while always believing in yourself.

When life knocks you down, remember that it's temporary. How you react is the true test. You'll pick yourself up when you feel like you have no energy to do so. People who make you feel whole and strong will come into your life at the right moment.

After losing him, I feared I had lost myself. Not only as an artist but as a human being. I slowly started to introduce myself to others and the energy came into focus – the universe was listening. It sent me the right people to keep me motivated. I've now started my own clothing brand, Danniifree. I'm keeping busy with orders for my small business, Barn Board Beauties, while managing to find time to enjoy the little things like chasing sunsets, making art and writing a book I hope to publish one day. I'm simply living the best life I can, and you will too. Remember to never give up. You are beautiful, you are strong and you are alive!

49

Brian is an award winning story teller, creative leader, director, writer, proud dad and adventure seeker.

BRIAN
MELLERSH

My dad once said: "If Brian fell down a sewer, he would probably find a gold watch."

When I first heard this, I thought he was saying that I am simply lucky, and I am in a lot of ways. I have everything I need and am grateful for that, but what he meant is that I would try to make the best of things, explore my surroundings, and get my hands dirty.

I have always been adventurous and willing to dig through the mud searching for something shiny. For me, experience is the gold, not material things.

Over the years I have had many twists and turns in my career. I spent years playing in a band, and when I eventually ended up working in television, I knew I had found my home. I was surrounded by fun, creative souls, with a deep passion for sharing stories. It was the perfect fit for me, and I even met my future wife on one of my first gigs.

I worked my way along from a sound assistant, to a camera operator, and then on to directing and producing. I've had the privilege of travelling the world, meeting incredible people, enjoying once-in-a-lifetime experiences, and bringing awareness to important issues. I even co-produced a show with my 11 year old daughter! What an incredible experience as we laughed, learned, and had some amazing outdoor adventures together. It was art imitating life.

I have found "gold watches" all around the globe, and even won some awards while doing it. I am grateful to everyone who helped guide me along the way.

One of those guides was my dad, who passed away six years ago. He never got to see a lot of my successes, but I know he has been along for the ride in spirit.

My goal in life is to have fun, never stop learning and to lend a hand to those still digging around in the sewers. You may get dirty, but that's all part of the adventure.

Caroline Blanchard is a single mom of three, #1 best-selling Author, podcast show host and serial entrepreneur who focuses on women's empowerment, media, network marketing, recovery, and coaches people to optimize their life and business.

CAROLINE
BLANCHARD

This picture means so much to me! It was my 45th birthday; I had separated from my husband a year before and was alone with my three kids, running my business from home, feeling scared, lonely, and like a failure. At my age, single mom, second divorce, and in recovery for only six years, I felt pretty low and hopeless to ever be loved again.

There are moments when, even if you have achieved incredible heights professionally and accomplished outstanding projects, you still feel worthless because someone or something broke your spirit. On the outside, I had it all together, staying strong, sober, and productive. On the inside, I was in pieces and hated myself.

My BFF, Elizabeth, surprised me and brought me to a photo shoot in a studio on my birthday. She brought clothes, jewelry, a hairstylist, and a make-up artist. It felt wrong and weird at first, but the women there were amazing and helped me feel so special for a few hours. It turned out to be so fun, and I couldn't believe Liz planned this, that I could be worth all these efforts and money to someone.

When I saw the pictures, I felt so empowered and actually thought I was beautiful for the first time. I always struggled with my self-esteem, image, and self-worth. I saw the girl I used to be in business: fearless and strong. I remembered all of my strengths and how much I had to bring to the world. I began to fall in love with myself and hope again.

I revisited my dreams, life plan and dove into my business with more confidence and determination. I even dared to start a media company and coaching business to help other women. It gave me back my fire.

The point of this story is that I wish all of us could see ourselves through the lens of a professional photographer. Yes, there is lighting and make-up involved, but what they genuinely capture in the end is the person we really are when we feel beautiful, and our worries and inside negative voices are shut down.

Thank you for being in my life, Liz! Love you.

Steph Purdy is an entrepreneur & eternal optimist who does her best to look on the bright side of things & shine a little brightness into peoples' lives

STEPH
PURDY

I remember it as if it was yesterday. I was sitting across the table from my husband of just over a year, buried in shame and telling him that I would kill him if he breathed a word of this to anyone. Especially to his parents.

I had just left the doctor's office with a stress note telling me to take two weeks off work. I was sick. I was burnt out. I was ashamed. Burnout and stress, for me, meant weakness, and weak was the last adjective I would ever want to be associated with me. The moment of diagnosis confirmed my belief of weakness. Today I know that this is a fallacy; burnout is far more prevalent than I ever realized, but I suffered in silence because I kept myself shrouded in shame. Shame is a silent killer; it does us no good.

Shame typically comes when you look inward with a critical eye and evaluate yourself harshly. This negative self-evaluation usually has roots in messages you've received from others, especially during childhood. My messaging ran deep.

Entrepreneurial parents raised me. My dad was my hero, I idolized him. I watched him work from before sunrise until long after sunset. I watched my mom battle cancer, survive painful surgeries, and be right back at her desk mere days later. No pain, no gain. The bar was set incredibly high.

Reflecting on this moment in life no longer brings me shame. I use this to remind me that I am resilient and capable. I overcame. Grinding and hustling are no longer words that serve me. Today I speak up and most importantly, I ask for help. I've learned that it's okay to say "no" and that "no" is a complete sentence.

Today I am the proud owner of two businesses, I still work incredibly hard and always will, but the "why" that drives me is entirely different today than it was back then. My "why" for my newest business, Red & Ko, was different from any previous reason. My "why" is because it lights me up. I love to connect with people over food and because I get to tap into my creative side.

Steph Purdy

Amy Sussex is the owner of Revive As Wellness, a wellness centre that offers holistic services and products to help with your mental, physical and emotional needs.

AMY
SUSSEX

Being a people pleaser, I often tried to shrink myself to fit into whatever the circumstances were. The last thing I ever wanted to do was hurt or disappoint someone. It took a long time to realize I was always putting myself last, never paying attention to what I wanted. I was so concerned with what others thought of me, with other people's happiness; I rarely shared my true voice.

In 2015, my circumstances began to take a toll on my mental and emotional health. After years of hard work, which led me towards a supervisor role in my corporate job, I started noticing things; I was not feeling right. I had become almost obsessed with perfectionism in my role, trying to please everyone. I wasn't feeling fulfilled in my job, I felt like I was meant to do more. It was around this time that I started having panic attacks; I didn't realize what was happening and thought I was having a stroke. I made a doctor's appointment and he indicated it was a generalized anxiety panic that I was experiencing. I looked at him and said, "um, nope, that's not me, there is something seriously wrong."

It took some time for me to realize that, oh yeah, there is something seriously wrong; it was my mental and emotional state which was now affecting me physically. I was so embarrassed and ashamed because I was having panic attacks during team meetings I was leading. I had lost my voice and didn't know how to use it anymore. In hindsight, I was finally discovering my true voice that had been locked away for who knows how long.

I started making some life changes; who I surrounded myself with, what I watched and listened to. I started exercising more and using holistic therapy. I added more movement into my life, started reflecting, journaling, practicing gratitude, meditating and figuring out what the heck I really wanted to do.

This led me to leaving my corporate job of 13+ years and starting my own business. What started off as a need to help myself physically, mentally and emotionally has now transformed into this amazing ability to help others as well.

Melissa Mancini Burbridge is the founder and CEO of Alisei Creative Solutions, a successful digital media firm.

MELISSA MANCINI BURBRIDGE

Right now, I am the CEO of my own company. I help women push past their fear and rediscover who they are so that they can chase their dreams and start living for today instead of waiting on tomorrow.

But this wasn't always. the case. In 2019 I was a stressed out, overworked nurse who was dreaming of a better tomorrow.

I always wanted to make an impact on the world and help people. Originally, the plan was to become a lawyer, but somewhere along the path it didn't feel right. I took some time off to raise my children and figure out my next steps. I took a quiz that said I would make a great nurse or police officer and I chose to become a nurse. Nursing was great in the beginning, but it started to take a toll, then after a move from one province to another, the politics and stress made it difficult.

Then trauma forced me to make a decision: keep living as a burnt out and tired nurse, or forge a new path. While driving home from a trip with my kids, I made the decision to walk away from nursing.

With no idea what I was going to do next, I began working as a business development manager while doing social media management on the side. That hobby became my passion and I started my own digital media firm.

During a coaching session, I realized what I was truly meant to do – help women avoid the pain, frustration and heartache that I had experienced, facilitating them to rediscover who they are by offering them coaching, support and guidance.

I am a mother of two plus a fur baby, who loves living away from the hustle and bustle of the city in a peaceful country setting. Travelling, coffee and the ocean are my favorite things.

"Carpe diem," or "seize the day" has been a quote I live by ever since seeing the movie Dead Poets Society.

Make sure to look at the possibilities and opportunities; don't let them slip by, because that opportunity might be the one that changes your life forever. Live for today instead of after retirement.

Melissa Mancini Burbridge

Sonya is a weight loss life coach helping clients lose the unwanted weight of debt, stress and pounds.

SONYA
JANISSE

The power of positivity: a cape of courage.

When any year comes to a close, we're filled with a level of excitement that only seems to crop up at this time of year. Anticipation of a brand new chapter, a clean slate. But before we jump into 2022, let's reflect on 2021.

Everyone had hardships, struggles and hurdles throughout the year (I call mine hiccups). It's all too easy to become a victim of circumstances, getting stuck in a negative headspace. My insatiable curiosity and my relentless optimism lead me to believe there's a solution to every problem. I found 2021 to be a chance to shift, and that's exactly what this small-town girl with big dreams did!

This past year has been full of "hiccups." It started with falling through the ice of Lake Erie, when my dog couldn't resist the birds' taunting anymore, then having to rescue her AND myself. If you know Lake Erie in March, then you know how cold those waters get! It's still as vivid today as it was in that moment!

Between escaping an icy end, rescuing my dog, deaths in the family, a stolen truck, loved ones in car accidents and the loss of my job; I could have ended up in a pretty dark place.

But guess what? I bounced back even stronger! You can too! Ask yourself:

Do I want to be the victim or the hero? (Grab your cape!)
How can I flip the script? Develop memories rather than self-pity?
Can I help others with the lessons I've learned.
Move forward and grow? (Find your super power!)

One of my biggest takeaways was my surprising tenacity. I absorbed more than I thought possible. I let go of the trauma. I found ways to stay positive. I allowed myself to be guided to the other side. Now I have the time to do what I love most: helping people discover their best self and live their best life. Life works out the way it's supposed to, even if we can't always see it right away. Stay positive, keep moving forward, and inspire others along the way. Be the hero in your story, not the victim!

Clarissa Gibson, an Allied Health Professional and Bowen Therapist from Burnaby, B.C., is an entrepreneur, who assists clients on their healing journey.

CLARISSA
GIBSON

As a lifelong learner, I have learned how experience in the work environment and learning from courses, books, and intuition happens simultaneously. My magic place is listening, observing, communicating, and honoring the journey of others and myself. Facilitated by an active daily habit of exploring inner and outer curiosity, my time is spent in this place of curiosity, holding presence and allowing a space for self-healing. My hope is this will enrich the lives of those who come across my path.

After receiving my Master of Science (MS) from Simon Fraser University, I found myself on an adventure in Cardiac Rehab and Bowen Therapy. Applying scientific knowledge combined with life illustrations made from everyday ordinary things we do and enjoy, enables me to create an environment where others can learn and connect to their own perspectives and bodies.

Giving clients the lead in their own healing journey from the first intake session is a power move I use in my business every day. "What would you like to accomplish through our time together? It has been surprising to see the response of clients when asked this question: Many times, the answer is simple: "to be able to play with my grandkids," "to decrease the amount of discomfort my body feels," or "to move with greater ease." Learning what their goals, ambitions, and medical literacy levels are through our dialogue provides me with the framework to communicate effectively and easily with clients. This personal approach enriches my life experience while learning and growing with clients over the time we have together.

My time spent with friends and family helps create balance in my life, as does gardening and spending time in nature. I enjoy finding beauty in the world. So far in my life, I have lived in 3 countries, which has provided me with the understanding that all people have the same needs, wants and desires, although expressed and celebrated in various ways. Sending light, balance, and a zest for life to all!

Lily Ahonen is proud to be Ms. Calgary 2021. She loves to travel and has been to over 40 countries.

LILY
AHONEN

When I look back, I remember all the hard times. Growing up in severe poverty in a dangerous neighborhood. Multiple attempted kidnappings. Attacked by neighborhood kids and wild dogs. No activities other than growing up at the racetrack and pawnshops. Broken windows, stabbings, sirens. Moving out at age 15, spending the first few months alone in Europe. High school dropout.

Fighting to finish high school, doing two years' worth of courses in Grade 12. Working two to three jobs to support myself. Finishing a diploma in mechanical engineering technology but having to stop multiple times to help others with their problems. Suddenly moving overseas, for no real purpose other than to escape, to have my own life without putting everyone else's needs first. Moving to other countries with no money and not knowing a single soul. Somehow surviving, even thriving, and collecting many incredible stories for my old age. Making a best friend in Helsinki, my soul mate. Two years later he committed suicide, completely crushing my world.

Returning to Canada and wanting to work in the engineering field, but being told by people close to me that it's "not suitable for women". Giving in and going back to school to become a nurse. At age 25, craving stability and love, I got married; a decade-long marriage that ended in divorce. Starting over at age 35 with no money and zero self-esteem.

Fighting to get my life back, working seven days a week. Buying two houses on my own, travelling and living an amazing lifestyle, supporting my little family. Too good to be true. And then, a sudden back injury, which left me partially paralyzed and hospitalized for close to a month. I lost my boyfriend, my house and my job. I had to start over once again. During this time, my house flooded. Over time, things got better. I had surgery and was no longer paralyzed. I became a published author, an IMDb credited actor, a pageant titleholder, a living organ donor, a business owner and winner of multiple awards for community service. I found strength though all of my challenges, and with proof of what I had overcome, I knew I could do anything.

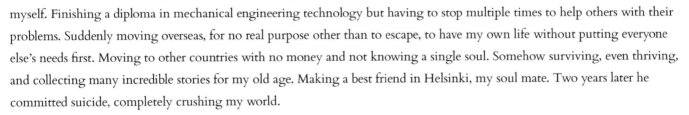

Kelly Baker-Pabla is a social entrepreneur who works with nonprofits and corporations to leave this world better than we found it. Mother of 2 and sister to 7 other siblings she knows that collaboration over competition is the key to creating impactful change.

KELLY
BAKER-PABLA

It is amazing what happens when your soul knows what's best for you and propels you forward without hesitation or permission.

For quite some time, unhappy in my corporate life, the voice in my head screamed, "Get out! This is not the place for you!" but I kept burying it, too afraid to leave because I had worked so hard to get where I was. I had the respect of my peers and an office with a water view. How could I leave the career I had spent almost a decade building with my family to provide for? Responsibility dictated I just carry on as usual, miserable, or not.

After another humdrum meeting where the old boys club had the only voice, I could not stand it another minute. There had to be a better place for me.

As if possessed by outside forces, with no backup plan, I felt strangely calm when I picked up the phone and called my boss to give my resignation. The words "I quit" came out of my mouth, and I did not feel sad or panicked; a peace washed over me.

After the amazement of what I had done set in, I took time to understand what made me tick. I uncovered a truth that had been long staring me in the face, but I was too scared to see it.

The eldest of eight children, I am a nurturer by nature. Motivation and happiness come from helping others. Affecting positive change that helps build businesses and leaves this world a little better makes me feel accomplished. The day I uncovered this certainty was the day my baby T.H.I.N.K. Funding was born.

I founded my company on being TRUE, HONEST, IMPACTFUL, NECESSARY AND KNOWLEDGEABLE. I aim to do business differently, growing both corporations and non-profits by fostering lasting, trusting relationships that put people first.

In the years T.H.I.N.K. has been in business, the application of this people-centric connection has achieved business success quickly, building profitable companies that are making a difference in our world. I am so proud of the legacy T.H.I.N.K. Funding is creating where my purpose meets my passion.

My advice to anyone too afraid to change is to be courageous! I promise you can shift that negative narrative! You never know what is waiting for you on the other side of fear.

58

Gillian Mott is a violinist/educator/foster carer. A "Gill of all trades" from White Rock BC, now in London UK.

GILLIAN
MOTT

I'm an eternal optimist, even after discovering I've been depressed most of my life. My diagnosis came at age 39, after a huge meltdown that had me contemplating walking in front of a bus.

There is still such a stigma attached to depression. How can I be depressed? I have the most amazing parents who gave my brother and I a happy home and are continuously supportive. I was very shy; even being on sports teams and in musical ensembles, I had low self-worth.

Self-sabotage ruled my life into my late 30s. I grew up thinking that putting myself first was selfish. My first two boyfriends gaslit me to the point where I had zero self-confidence; that has carried over into friendships and other relationships.

But, no matter how bad things would get, my violin Siobhan kept me going. Siobhan came into my life when I was 13; we have had amazing moments of happiness and sadness in our travels. Performing and teaching allows me to share my experiences with others, with the hope that they find a connection to help them get through a happy or hard moment in their own life.

It took three weeks to take that first SSRI. I was so nervous, but that cloud gradually dissipated. I can now manage the stress of living in almost Central London as a single woman. I stopped caring what people thought. I realized the roadblocks I'd faced were put there by me, but they started to clear. I now know it's OK to have a bad day.

Outside of my teaching and performing schedule, I started doing things I had wanted to do for a long time; I filled in an application to become a foster care provider and was approved. In April 2021, I welcomed my first teenager. She's now moved on and I have welcomed another teenager who is strong, with confidence that I wish I had at her age. I adopted my kittens, Bubble & Squeak, who saved my mental health in lockdown. And I recently learned I qualify to buy a three bed shared ownership flat, so I'm going for it. Why? Because I'm worth it.

Originally from B.C., Andrea Szopa is an IT consultant, co-founder of Silver Stratus Global, international photographer and a global citizen.

ANDREA LEE
SZOPA

It was never my goal to visit fifty countries and live in seven of them before my 50th birthday. How did I end up an expat world traveler? It all started with moving to the next town, then the next province, and suddenly, a new country didn't seem so hard. It wasn't easy; it involved hard work and stress, yet the payoff enriched my life in so many ways. I have spent the last 20 years learning new ways of thinking and new ways of living while making new friends all over the world. I am not a big risk taker; planning and research has been a big part of my achievements and I can tell you that no matter how much you plan, you must always take a first step.

When almost everything is foreign and new, you learn quickly what is important to you. You discover that you can live without a lot of things and most influences are only regional, cultural, or social. I met my Polish/American husband while living in London, UK and we continued journeying around the world together. We lived in Spain, Kuwait, Panama and the Philippines. I am now that person that has a story for every situation in life and have done things I never could have imagined growing up in a small town in BC.

I welcomed the new age of digital photography, capturing all these delightful experiences and places for my future self and to share with my family and friends. Photography or any art gives you new perspectives and insight by focusing on the big picture and all the little details at once. It is very easy to hyper focus on one thing and miss what is right in front of you. Enjoying the location and the moment while still getting the shot takes balance and resolve.

Make and embrace new experiences for yourself. I am now living in the United States and have launched Silver Stratus Global, an international information technology services company. You don't have to rush out and move countries, just say yes to something new, notice a new detail, expand your horizons and see where it takes you!

Michele Thomson believes that leadership starts with an understanding of how to hold space for others to create thriving workplaces.

MICHELE
THOMSON

I was born an only child to a single mother who created a world of opportunity for me. Loss came early for my mother when she lost her father at sixteen. The youngest of three girls, she gave up education for work to help pay the bills. My grandmother never remarried but approached life with a child-like curiosity and created a life full of love and laughter, all the same qualities that I see in my mother. I am incredibly humbled by the sacrifices my mother made so she could create a life of abundance for me despite challenges that did not make it easy for her. She always stressed the importance of family and education, surrounding me with strong and independent women.

I knew very early that I wanted to be a nurse. I was strongly influenced by my mother, who was a lab technician. My grandmother would take me to the hospital and I would finish my homework while waiting for mom's shift to end so she would take me to go see the nurses care for tiny, frail babies in the neo-natal unit. Nurturing others has been deeply rooted in my sense of purpose.

At 22, I became a Registered Nurse, specializing in Gerontology Nursing. I have worked in long-term care for over 16 years. In 2018, I created Curis Consulting because I was feeling burnt out and disillusioned with Canada's healthcare system and ready to challenge the status quo. My vision is to guide leaders who value human connections over bottom lines to create thriving workplaces, so they can be the boss that everyone wants.

The day I wrote this is my mother's birthday. I want to honour and thank her for showing me the value of my worth and shaping my core values. The greatest compliment I have received is, "you are just like your mother."

The 5 Things I live By
1.   Get involved in things that you are passionate and curious about
2.   Fear is the only thing between the life that I have and the life that I want
3.   Be kind and humble – especially when nobody is looking
4.   Surrender – the universe has a plan
5.   Every day is a new beginning

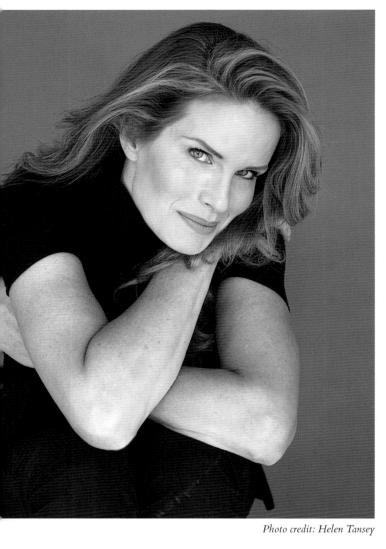

Photo credit: Helen Tansey

MONIKA
SCHNARRE

Hey there! My name is Monika...

My passion for the past decade has been inspiring women to build and renovate their own homes. I have my own tools and simply love the process of building, renovating and sometimes creating new furniture. Often, I am met with hostility when dealing with men in the building trades. So, I understand why women are hesitant to get started, but I want to inspire them to pick up the tools and defy expectations. And really – who cares what people think?

When I lived in Toronto, I saw a woman almost every day in the elevator at my condo, looking obviously distraught as she went to work, which weighted heavily on my heart. We only have so many 365 day trips around the sun and we have the ability to change our situation on a daily basis. Yes, it takes risk and motivation, but trudging to work each day and hating your life is no way to live.

People say to me, "but you're so lucky!" "You made money modelling!" "You had it easy!" While it's true that I made money when I was younger, that was 35 years ago, and that money is loooong gone! Everything I have accomplished has been outside of modelling and with hard work. I bought my first house at 23 and have flipped 14 properties. This is simply to say that nothing comes easily in life. What I lack for in talent, I make up for in tenacity.

Right now, I'm on my sixth career. I've been a model, actor, television host, writer and have flipped homes. Currently, I'm getting my real estate license and starting a side hustle which will have a charitable component. As I enter my 50th year, there are still so many things that I want to accomplish. I want to leave this earth feeling like I've done some good. My mission is to help as many single mothers get back on their feet as I can. It's selfish, of course, because it makes me feel good. When my son goes off and starts his own adventures in life, I will move to Italy. It's where my heart is happy. It's important to set goals. So, here's to Tuscany 2032!

Monika Schnarre

Having learned so much from living with Multiple Sclerosis, she can't imagine what her life would be like without it.

SHAUNA
ZINGG

I was 22 when I was diagnosed, more than half my life ago. I was very sick, but once out of the hospital, I resumed training for a marathon. MS replied by giving me another relapse. So it was – when I pushed my body too hard, I had a relapse. Over the years I learned that if I supported my body, through things like nutrition, rest, exercise, and meditation, I felt better.

I took the drugs doctors recommended, but after adverse reactions to them all, my doctor said they had no other drugs for me. I realized that doctors could only help so much. I had to take responsibility for my own health.

I struggled with my grief – over the person I wanted to be and the person I might become if the disease progressed. I heard the term, "external validation" and I wondered: what do I do for the approval of others? What's most important to me?

My health.

Dealing with a diagnosis for a chronic disease means it doesn't go away. Every day I make choices with this in mind. I make small adjustments and am consistent with what works. Little steps make a path. I do what I can today to support my feeling as good as possible tomorrow.

During the pandemic, I committed to daily meditation. It helps me detach from my emotions so I can choose how to respond instead of just reacting. This means I can be a better listener and participate more authentically. I am now better at sharing the love and support my wonderful friends and family have shown me, which is so heart filling!

What has worked for me may not work for everybody. Luck, friends and family have buoyed me and MS has taught me. I have slowly learned how to support my body, to maintain the equilibrium it needs. I also assess my priorities often because MS holds me accountable. As Victor Frankl said, 'it's not what happens to us but how we react to it that matters." Most days I go for a walk or hike, but sometimes I go for a run when my body feels like it.

Shauna Zingg

Tinuke Adebowale is a mom of two and the culinary creator behind Tempting Delights.

TINUKE
ADEBOWALE

There's no such thing as perfect. In business and in life it's easy to get caught up in the desire and pursuit of perfection. I consider myself a self-starter and a "doer," so I tend to leap and then figure out how to fly along the way and sometimes I do bump my head – ouch. As a single parent and with my business, I believe in leading by example and creating a space for fun and growth. We learn from our mistakes.

Raising my amazing kids, and now as an entrepreneur, I really dove into the deep end, headfirst, no water wings – and I learned quickly not to be afraid of failure.

"Failure" is a difficult thing to define, especially when we eventually move past those perceived failures and onto new endeavours. My most difficult hurdles or moments of "micro-failure" always include that overwhelming paralysis that comes when comparison takes over. I've fallen subject to the common mental roadblock of comparison many times. It's that feeling you get when you see someone doing what you want to do, and you start second-guessing your own value and ability. It creeps in and tries to settle in your mind, attempting to stop you from moving forward. When that paralysis hits, it makes it difficult for me to stay motivated. The key is pushing past the negative voices in your mind. I know… easier said than done.

It's a challenge to overcome mental blocks, and I'm still reminding myself daily to just push through and go for it. It helps to have an intimate network of family and friends that are supportive and encouraging. When I show up for myself and "just go for it," I find the responses so positive, and that reinforcement has helped me over time to adjust my thinking and learn from these moments of micro-failure.

Don't be afraid to modify the plan as you go along. Be ready to pivot, but success lies in sticking with it. Perseverance is key.

Perfection is never the goal and that's just perfect for me!

Tinuke Adebowale

As a 26-year spa industry veteran, Gordon Tareta has opened hundreds of spas and learned a lot along the way.

GORDON
TARETA

I feel fortunate to have opened 140 luxury spas on every continent, in some of the most stunning destinations in the world. I credit this to a lot of luck and being surrounded by good people. It all started after being hired as the health club manager for the world-famous Banff Springs Hotel. This landmark hotel needed some TLC and I was tearing apart the locker room and rebuilding it when my boss, Ted Kissane, asked me if I'd like to build a spa. That night I had a vivid dream that I will never forget. I was climbing a never-ending sand dune and the sand kept filling in with every step I took. I thought, "I'll never make it to the top." When I awoke, having no clue how to begin, I just knew I had to start with the first step.

After researching the globe and some of the most beautiful spas in the world, I had created a design and business plan from scratch. I was 21 years old, asking for $11.8 million and I was excited when my plan was approved. After completion, Conde Nast named the Banff Springs Hotel Spa number two in the world; the company loved it so much, we dreamed up and built six more. After this, I set my sights onto a more global perspective. I joined Hyatt in Chicago as it's first global vice president and I was privileged to oversee 110 spas all over the world.

My best work and problem solving happens when I sleep. Recharging one's body is very important, but sleep for me isn't idle. Processing issues happens for me at night, and I often receive downloads at 3:00 am. Keeping a notepad and pencil under my pillow has served me well. I realized that the thousands of grains of sand in my sand dune represented new knowledge and experience. Regardless of the task or challenge, it's important to not worry about where to start. You just have start. It may take 10,000 steps or even more. Knowledge will flow to you and with perseverance, you will make it to the top of your mountain.

Gordon Tareta

Alex Kazentsev is an entrepreneur and musician who believes in the pursuit of excellence and the importance of surrounding yourself with the right people.

ALEX
KAZANTSEV

Music and entrepreneurship are similar they both require technical abilities, a significant time commitment, and spark from within. Being a musician can be an endeavour that is taken on solo or with a group or team. To be truly successful, we require the presence of others – whether a network, a team, a mentor, or an audience.

I recently lost my father. Losing a loved one has a way of immediately delivering us into the present moment. Time has so much more meaning and the time I have suddenly became so much more significant. I looked around and discovered the ways I was keeping myself stagnant in my own status quo by listening to the voices around me telling me that I "couldn't accomplish" or that I "wasn't enough." The voices that I gave credence to were the ones I was allowing in, and I capped my own success and happiness by immersing myself in the narrative that kept me there.

They say we are a sum of the five people we spend the most time with. I believe that if we are purposeful about who those people are, and surround ourselves with good, kind, and ambitious people, we can collectively improve our pursuits and lives. The voices I choose to let in today are supportive and empowering, and I reciprocate those voices by building up the people around me.

I grew and learned the importance of cultivating community and network of people who support me. The people I choose to surround myself with are integral to achieving success in music, in business, and in life.

66

Sonja Picard is an artist, jewelry designer, adornment alchemist, entrepreneur and teacher.

SONJA
PICARD

"I believe it is our true nature to be surrounded with beauty, it elevates our soul and our physical well-being."

I never thought as a jewelry designer I could have such profound impact on peoples lives. I have utilized my expertise in jewelry design and the inherited knowledge passed down to me in mantras, symbology, gem therapy, ancient rituals of adornment and word construction for powerful affirmations to create Recycle Your Love™.

Recycle your Love is a service of creating, prescribing and making jewelry specifically for my clients as their 'medicinal jeweled elixir" to promote physical and emotional well being, career or relationship enhancement and connection to your future self. It was inspired 15 years ago from listening to stories about heirloom jewelry that was hidden away, unworn, that evoked deep sadness of a loved one long gone or old wedding rings attached with broken hearts and unfulfilled dreams. Jewelry is always given in love; we then become the custodians of these gems that witness the journey and hold the energy of the wearer. I knew this was an opportunity to create something magical rather than making something 'pretty' from 'old jewelry'. The result: one of the most powerful pieces of jewelry your can wear, your life story, a jewel that becomes your own secret signal to the universe, celebrating and manifesting your omnipotent future self.

My inspiration comes from the limitless resiliency and strength of the human spirit. My clients show me that when they choose to rise up, let go and celebrate, they transform and bloom. We are all searching for that elevated path to heal our wounds, stay close and true to our voice, our dreams and aspirations for the future. Therefore, jewelry is not mundane with this sentiment and reflection – it becomes a touchstone of our inner affirmations and strength, a beautiful daily witness to wear that carries our life story, inspiring us to choose and create an extraordinary life through our own destiny, free will and beauty. Find your daily ritual and hold it close!

"Jewelry is more than decoration, it is an extension of ourselves, our personal evolution and cosmology."

Jeff Hardy is the founder and chief executive officer of Lifeguard Digital Health.

JEFF
HARDY

That's the Idea, an App to Save Yourself from Yourself

It's funny how facing the unthinkable led me to finding my true life's purpose. For a long time, I held together a fragile shell of success. I balanced a wonderful wife and kids, a beautiful house, and a thriving company, all while nurturing a deep addiction to alcohol. A few years ago, my alcoholism finally won out. My life eroded until I lost everything.

I tried various treatment centres, but it took many failed attempts before I genuinely wanted to change. At my last treatment centre, I met a young, vibrant man named Evan. Despite our age difference, we became good friends and helped each other. While I was still in recovery, I was devastated to lose Evan to fentanyl poisoning.

Evan's tragic death infused me with a new purpose in life. I was inspired to find a way to keep people safe and help prevent unintentional deaths from drug toxicity. Driven by the shocking number of lives needlessly and accidentally lost to the opioid crisis, I called on friends and family to help me.

I connected with programmers and IT specialists to develop ground-breaking technology that brought my idea to life. I named the patent-pending platform after Evan, and called my new company Lifeguard Digital Health: a digital health solutions company powered by Evan.

The first App that we created is not only a life-saving overdose prevention tool, but it connects individuals directly to mental health and addiction services in their area. The App works by having an activated timer that connects the user to emergency medical services when an overdose or drug poisoning occurs.

In partnership with the BC Provincial Health Authority, the App launched in 2020. It has now saved over 40 lives in BC and been successfully activated over 60,000 times. Lifeguard recently launched in Northwestern Ontario and created a customized App for the Métis Nation BC and the construction industry. As we look out for ways to improve people's lives, our next application under development is for seniors in residential and care homes.

Today, I am happy to have reconciled with my wife and kids, having funneled my addiction into an active and healthy lifestyle, like my passion for tennis!

Holly is hard working and passionate about her family, community, real estate, music, animal rights and life.

HOLLY
CALDERWOOD

I work with buyers and sellers of real estate in Vancouver, specializing in luxury view and waterfront homes. I have been selling real estate for 16 years and I currently work for Sotheby's International Realty Canada. With offices in British Columbia, Canada, and around the world, I can help you buy or sell in any of the top global luxury market destinations including Paris, New York, Beverly Hills, London, Milano, Seattle, Hawaii, Cabo and more.

I am a 25-year West Vancouver resident and proud to call British Columbia home. I was born in Winnipeg, Manitoba and was raised with hard working prairie ethics, but nothing could have prepared me for the tragic and sudden loss of my 18 year old daughter, Amora, in October 2017.

Life and family are the most precious gifts of all, especially our children. Once you lose a child you are never the same. You are an empty shell of the person you once were. On March 10th, at 7 am at St. Paul's hospital, when my beautiful, once in a lifetime daughter was born, I never could have imagined as I held her in my arms and looked her into her beautiful eyes, that she would be gone 18 years later.

If you would have told me before she was born that I could have a beautiful daughter, Amora, but only for 18 years, I would do it all over again. I now live with a heavy and grateful heart, taking time to smell the flowers and to enjoy the simple things in life. I enjoy time with my mom, son, and my daughter's dog, Ceely. A daily routine of walking the seawall and up the mountaintops of West Vancouver keeps me mentally strong, zen and balanced.

Since the passing of my precious daughter, I have spent the last four years writing and making music and I have my own Soundcloud page.

I plan to write a book about the heroic rescue of my daughter's stolen dog, Ceely. I spent most of 2018 searching for her in the streets of Los Angeles; we found her September 11, 2018.

Every day is a chance to start over, to make a difference.

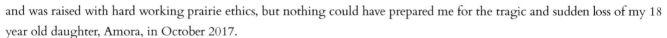

Martin Prchal is a multimedia artist creating primarily through still and moving images.

MARTIN
PRCHAL

The Washing Machine's Grief Cycle: Cold, Slow, Cleansing

Physically, I've never been much of a runner, but man can my mind go the distance. Strange that it's the negative thoughts, running on a diet of fear and anxiety, that never seem to tire. After my mother unexpectedly passed at the very onset of the pandemic, my mind ran its longest race.

She choked on a pierogi which, before being removed from her windpipe, had caused brain damage so severe there was no chance of recovery from life support. It happened in the four day window after I'd finished quarantining at my girlfriend's house, but before returning home. This wasn't the plan. I was supposed to be spending the next six months travelling the world, establishing independence and drinking in freedom, not coming back to my old room and old life.

I sunk into my grief like a stone dropped in the ocean, slower than expected but with the same result: rock bottom. On the journey down, hypotheticals escaped into my consciousness one after another:

What if I had come home right after quarantine.
What if I had taken her out to dinner that night instead of her eating in.
What if I had never gone away.
What if I had been a better son.

When I eventually stopped sinking, I found that I'd finally run out of new "what ifs" to torture myself with, and in mulling over the old ones, I found perspective in my misery. None of this was ever in my control.

I can't change that my mom will never know that I dropped out of university to pursue art, and though it would've caused her a great deal of distress, I know she would be infinitely happier to see where and who I am today: a happy person in pursuit of something I love. I can honour her memory, make beauty where once there was sorrow and live the life she sacrificed so much for me to have.

I was the perpetrator and the victor of the war inside my head. In the peacetime that has followed, I'm starting to understand that my journey is just beginning, and with it, the soul of my mother's journey forges ahead.

70

Paul Becker is the co-founder and chief curator of Art Rapture.

PAUL
BECKER

As a young boy, I was shy.

Large groups or being put in the spotlight crippled my insides. I was quite content to sit alone, solving math problems or immersing myself in music. My parents bring this up on occasion. I guess they are as intrigued as I am with the way humans can adapt and change.

My emotional state transformed once I began working in the restaurant industry at 16 years old. The restaurant industry didn't just teach me the merits of work ethic, it also gave me a boost in confidence due to the innate camaraderie associated in the back of house. Soon after sharpening knives, washing dishes and cooking guest meals, I moved to the front of house where there was no option other than being a "people person." I loved it.

Fast forward to today; I'm 40 years old, and if you spoke to any of my family or friends, I'm quite positive that "shy" would definitely not be a word associated with their description of Paul Becker.

I have an insatiable love for art. That love transformed me into the chief curator, founder and auctioneer of a boutique art company called Art Rapture. Art Rapture curates group shows, solo exhibitions, auctions and publishes fine art prints & NFTs for leading Canadian artists such as Ola Volo, William D. Higginson, and urban legend, iHeart. We strive to bend the boundaries of the traditional Canadian landscape to achieve rapture through visual art. Our curator talks and seminars instill passion, enthusiasm and respect for art. My soul fills with joy when I'm able to vocally share my profound and deeply ingrained intimacy on the subject of art. Art is relevant to all our lives as human beings. Whether you understand it or not. My role is to guide you through the journey.

As an auctioneer I have conducted hundreds of live art auctions in front of crowds ranging from dozens of people to over one thousand patrons.

Hand me a microphone and I'm "on."

As a father of two young girls, it's important that I remind myself that change is inevitable. What is today, may not be tomorrow. The world turns, the seasons follow.

Heather Nightingale is an internationally acclaimed makeup artist with over 20 years in the beauty industry. She is known now as the "Nurse of Beauty"!

HEATHER
NIGHTINGALE

I believe education is the key to happiness, love, and success. You must seek to learn before you can teach. Understanding yourself permits you to see others clearly and care for them with compassion.

My mantra is a theme that has wound continuously throughout my life: The power of education can't be reversed. Create with passion, energy, love, and health. Your imagination is your only limitation.

Educated at Mount Royal University in Calgary, I began my first career working with our youngest citizens using my Early Childhood Education degree. I was drawn to this field because my own childhood journey had its ups and downs. At 10, I moved from Trinidad to Montreal with my mom. My initial introduction to school in Canada included bullying and discrimination, from fellow students. I knew then that I wanted to provide young children with a safe environment where they and their parents could learn about appropriate developmental stages, the importance of self-understanding, self-respect, self-confidence, and the necessity for creating appropriate boundaries. These skills grounded in love, gratitude, and hard work would enable children to navigate most future circumstances.

I carried these beliefs into my second career as a makeup educator and brand executive with MAKE UP FOR EVER. Flying worldwide with work, I sometimes listened without always hearing. One day during the flight, the attendant's safety preamble caught my attention, "When the oxygen mask drops down, please place the mask over your mouth and nose FIRST before proceeding to help your children or other passengers!! " It reinforced the idea that we can only help others if we have helped ourselves first. It was one of life's little reminders. I am the best educator ever when I charged my batteries first. My education and my careers underscored the need to develop personally and then reach outward to share wisdom, learnings, and knowledge with gratitude. Surrounded by vibrant, positive people who believe in me, I have learned it starts with me! To love someone else, I must love myself first!

Heather Nightingale

Elisha Bonnis is a teacher with a Masters in Math. In addition to being a JUMP Math Mentor and trainer, she is also an artist with a jewelry company, Naked Silver Designs.

ELISHA
BONNIS

"We like to weed out the losers here."

Those were the words spoken by my principal as I was expelled from the second high school by the age of 12. School had always been a nightmare for me.

My family was fractured and living in poverty. I had chronic health conditions as a small child and was often in the hospital or too sick to go to school. When I was at school, I was lost. My teachers seemed angry with me; I was always losing things, never meeting deadlines, daydreaming and distracted. I was either ignored or teased by my classmates. I was often told I was not trying hard enough, that I was stupid, lazy and irresponsible. I believed I could not learn (particularly math, which was my greatest struggle), that I could not take care of valuable things, that I was not worthy of having friends.

How did that girl end up evolving into a woman who pursued a career as a teacher, obtaining a Masters in Math Education, becoming a portrait artist, a sculptor, a stand-up comedian, a math mentor and a jewelry designer? There were transformational events that led me there.

My parents found an alternative high school where I felt seen and understood for the first time. I became the first person in my family to graduate and to complete university, with the encouragement and support of my family and my then-husband. I discovered John Mighton's book, The Myth of Ability, which awoke me to the knowledge that I could learn math, and that with practice and belief in myself, I could pursue my dreams.

After a lifetime of feeling scattered and disordered, I was diagnosed with ADHD. I had been a child with ADHD. I am now an adult with ADHD. I can see the profound negative impact this neurological condition had on my life, but I also see the gifts it has brought me: my ability to connect with and support my students, and my ability to nurture multiple creative passions. I finally see myself clearly…as a powerful, talented woman who has overcome many challenges, survived many traumas, and fulfilled many dreams.

MICHAEL
HEFFERON

"It's the passion for creating that blazes the trail for business"

Looking back, it was a pretty big thing to set up my own animation studio right after graduating from Sheridan College, but I was following my passion for storytelling. They say that if you love what you do, you will never work a day in your life. Well, that still rings true for me after 30 years in the animation industry!

My first studio, Phoenix Animation in Toronto (later became a part of Britt Allcroft/Gullane/HIT Entertainment), best known for the iconic children's series, *Thomas the Tank Engine*, opened the doors for me working at studios in Europe, Australia and Canada. I found my niche was turning studios around. My success pivoted on two steps – looking at a studio's raison d'etre, asking "what story are we trying to tell?" and secondly, achieving buy-in from both creative and business stakeholders. Without buy-in, a leader's vision is useless.

My biggest, most satisfying challenge is Mainframe. Formerly Rainmaker Entertainment, when I came on board the studio's feature film business model had proven unsuccessful. I eliminated everything that wasn't working, returning the studio to its creative roots. I shifted the business model to produce episodic television and movie specials for broadcast/streaming services, all while restoring Mainframe's focus on the art of storytelling

At this time, my son Austin also began to inspire my direction through his interests. For example, one of his favourite movies was *Spy Kids*, which sparked the idea to turn it into a series, *Spy Kids: Mission Critical*. This, along with my next project *Reboot: The Guardian Code*, which went on to receive nominations for creative and technical merits, including Daytime Emmy nods.

Austin continues to inspire the projects I am working on. My latest upcoming original series was sparked by my teenage son's current interest in Fortnite and gaming. As I watch his interests develop into talents, I am constantly reminded how at our heart, all humans are creative thinkers. My life is not split into isolated silos of work and family life; they inspire each other, and that passion helps foster a work environment where creativity can thrive.

74

Deborah is a certified BCCDA Career Development Practitioner, coaching actors, writers and directors to find fulfillment in their career.

DEBORAH
GILLAM

I heard this saying at a very young age: "it's not what you know, it's who you know." That never really made sense to me; I can know a lot of people, but how would that do anything for my career? So, I decided to change this saying to: "it's not who you know, it's who knows you," and who likes you! This saying has proven true to my blessed career as a career coach, producer and talent agent for the past 30+ years.

I have been an entrepreneur since the age of nine; I knew I would be in a career that involves helping people. I am a firm believer in networking- yes, this works in getting people to know who you are! I would have friends come talk to me to help them find a solution to their problems, it's always been that way for me. It's this mindset that has allowed me to build a successful business as a career coach.

Don't forget to take the time to volunteer - it really helps build your network of people who know you, and is so very rewarding. It all starts with who knows you and likes you!

I have a challenge for all of you. If you really want to see change in your life, step out of your comfort zone and face your fears head on; try it, you'll like it. This is truly a way to see yourself grow, it can open up the doors of opportunity. And of course, you need to keep an open mind and heart to be able to recognize the doors of opportunity when they open. It is unfortunate that a lot of us miss these opportunities when we go down a path that leads to roadblocks. When you hit a roadblock in your life or career, this is telling you to change the direction you're taking.

Never forget: the quality of your thinking determines the quality of your life. If you are seeking a more healthy and balanced approach to this often-challenging industry, don't hesitate to reach out.

75

Deborah Gillam-Harris

ALEXIS GAIL
ELLIS

I have had more adventures since the last book and I would like to tell you more.

So, 2020 wasn't amazing since COVID hit our world and a lot of normal stuff got delayed or cancelled. I didn't do a live pageant, but I wanted to keep doing pageants, so I did a few virtual. One was in the UK, called Regal World. It's an amazing pageant since you can meet others from around the world and now I know some pageant queens and ladies.

I had bad news and good news in 2021. My bad news was my mom was diagnosed with pancreatic cancer, stage four. There was no cure, but we tried our hardest to keep her and have the best time possible while also doing treatments. She passed away in September, 2021. I support the cancer society and will keep doing so in her memory.

The good news came in November – I won my first nationals pageant. It was amazing and I know my mom was there in spirit. I have a keepsake necklace with her and I spoke to her on my knees on stage. I told her it's all for her. My title is new, and I believe I was the first transgender woman to win a Canadian national pageant. I was excited and proud.

In 2022 I walked as a model at New York Fashion Week. I am also going to Florida to enter for the first time in an international pageant. I don't know if I'll win, but I feel that I always win in my heart. I hope in taking part I can empower and inspire others. This is my fourth chapter and I would love to see more LGBTQ and people living with disabilities telling their stories. The inclusion allows everyone to learn what it's like to be in our shoes.

I am so grateful for my life and that I've had the opportunity to inspire others to never give up and follow their dreams. I believe one day we will all be equal; it doesn't matter who you are, we are all humans.

Alexis Gail Ellis

Cindy Van Arnam is a possibilitarian and COO of MindSHIFT LLC.

CINDY
VAN ARNAM

In August of 2020, I was living a life full of adventure, freedom, and play. I was full of life and making an impact in my world; things were good. But I was broke. I was living PayPal to PayPal, borrowing money from the Bank of Mom, and wondering how I was ever going to get my rent paid. Somehow, at the end of each month, I managed to find what I needed to survive.

Deep down, I wanted more. I didn't want to simply survive, I wanted to thrive! All around me, people I knew were doing well, making lots of money, and fully thriving, despite the economic circumstances. Knowing that everything we see outside of ourselves is a direct reflection of what's happening in our own inner experience, I saw that wealth was available to me. I just hadn't chosen it to be included.

So, I made a decision. I decided to include wealth in my experience. In that decision, I had to rewrite a story about money that I had carried for over 20 years. It wasn't easy, but it was definitely worth it. It resulted in making some big changes in how I was operating my business and taking a massive leap of faith.

Three months later, I experienced my first $20,000 month in my business. Three months after that, my first $40,000 month, and three months following that, I became the COO of an eight-figure impact business. I had tapped into the power of three and the law of divine timing to create an experience that was well beyond my wildest dreams.

There are a set of rules we need to follow to lead a life fully lived. They are not man-made, but rather universal. By tapping into these laws, I moved from surviving, to thriving, and am now living my best life while showing others how to do the same. What I know to be true is that if I can shift this quickly, so can every single human on the planet. All it takes is a willingness to choose.

Cindy Van Arnam

Nicole McCurdy, certified intuitive coach and horse guided healer.

NICOLE LEE
McCURDY

I was born with a deep connection to animals, mother earth and an extreme sensitivity to the energy in the world around me. Life was not always easy because I could feel the heartbreak, the sorrow and all the highs and lows of everyone else's emotions.

My relief came in the moments where I could find my sense of calm in the presence of animals and nature. Little did I know, my path would offer moments that would take me to my knees in defeat, mixed with moments that would make me feel like I could fly with a profound sense of freedom.

I conquered many different challenges in my life, but there was always something within that kept me going, even in my darkest moments. It was a driving force and intuitive knowing that there was something greater directing my life. I was consistently called to nature and animals to support my healing, and my intuitive gifts began to blossom and grow.

Although I didn't fully understand my abilities, I was full of wonderment and curiosity. My parents said, "you never pick the easy path, but you always beat to your own drum". Their words were confirming and resonated on a very deep level. There was a rhythm I was following to guide me toward the life I was meant to live. It took courage to walk my unique path, especially when others didn't approve or understand why I made the choices I did.

In my twenties I embarked on a spiritual journey of self discovery which lead me to embrace my gifts as an intuitive healer. The more I began to really listen deeply, not only with my ears, but with my heart and soul, the more miracles I witnessed. I could feel my commitment to follow my inner knowing strengthening, as it became non-negotiable.

Today, I proudly live my life to the beat of my own drum. I offer sessions combining the healing power of sound, nature and horses to support others to heal trauma and find a sense of peace within. I found the answers to my deepest heart's calling and I am finally free to be me.

Sandy Rutherford is an elite success mindset coach and founder of both RF Success Academy and The Unstoppable Success System.

SANDY
RUTHERFORD

From massive success to mediocrity!

That was part of my story.

I was one of those people who seemed to attract success easily.

I was a highly sought after physiotherapist, went back for an MBA to switch into corporate, and enjoyed wonderful success in leadership roles in multi-national companies.

Because success came so easily to me, I never had to look at myself and learn to course correct – it seemed I was already on the right course. But I was what's called an unconscious competent. I was successful, but didn't know how and why.

So, when I switched from corporate to an entrepreneurial environment, I was expecting the same ease of success; when it didn't happen, I didn't know how or what to course correct. I got frustrated and discouraged. I had never had to work at success before, and the longer I struggled, the more I began to doubt myself.

To go from high level success with a strong self-image and confidence, where everything came easily, to struggling for success and increasing self-doubt, was humbling to say the least!

I was proud of my accomplishments, so to admit that I was struggling was painful. Admitting I didn't have the answers and needed help was not easy for me, yet this admission was the best thing that could have happened to me!

I set out on a journey to become a conscious competent, immersing myself in the teachings, being mentored by the legendary Bob Proctor, and giving up "my way" for a better way, a proven way.

I learned that not having the answers did NOT diminish who I was, that my self-image was strong in many areas but NOT where entrepreneurial success was concerned. And here's the big one – I learned that it wasn't enough to intellectually understand how success works – I had to learn how to internalize. Only then did I begin to think and operate on a whole new level.

I am now one of Bob's top tier coaches with a thriving global coaching practice, mentoring people hungry for the same breakthroughs, showing them how to #StoptheStruggle and go from mediocrity to meteoric!

What a journey! And it's only just begun!

Sandy Rutherford

Katayoon is one of the most successful Vancouver real estate agent with 16 years of award winning service and an impeccable reputation among her clients and her peers.

KATAYOON
WEBB

If you ask me to explain in one word how I got where I am now, I would say that word is certainly resilience!

By the time I was four years old Iran had a revolution, our lives changed overnight forever for the worst.

Memories of my elementary school days are dark. They consist of power blackouts, sirens, bombs, being misplaced from our home, many lost lives, and fear. Severe paralyzing fear. Fear of being killed in a bombing, fear of being imprisoned by the revolutionary guards for nothing other than being a girl or showing a few strands of hair from under the hijab. Everyone knew girls that went to that prison never came out the same. I survived a war.

Memories of my teenage years are being extremely oppressed by the regime and also by my brothers as they feared for my life as a young woman in that environment. I survived oppression.

Memories of an 18 year old refugee in Montreal, alone, severe culture shock without speaking a word of either languages trying to survive. I worked for five dollars per hour sewing and altering clothes, while putting myself through learning the languages and then university. Working full time and studying full time while having all the other responsibilities like paying for rent and food without any help. I survived poverty.

I moved to Vancouver when I was 26, worked two jobs to pay for life and an apartment in New Westminster that had fleas. Saved up a five percent down payment and bought my first condo in Vancouver when I was 28 almost 10 years to the day after I had moved to Canada at 18 with nothing but a suitcase of clothes. I was thriving.

That condo and the circumstances under which I had to sell it three years later, inspired me to become a real estate agent and give the absolute best client service one could train for. As once being a stateless refugee person myself, finding a place for people to call home became my passion. Making the process as memorable as I can and as stress free as possible is what I am very good at. The success that has ensued is just the by product of really loving what I do. I wake up everyday with heart full of gratitude for being where I am, given where I have been and where I came from and I know I owe it all to resilience.

Today, I run a successful real estate and home staging business. Combining art and real estate has been a really rewarding and fulfilling life and career for me.

Daughter, Wife, Mother of 2, Coach, Singer, Networking Sales Boss, Customer Service guru but mostly a Lover of Life. Using my life experiences to Empower, Coach and Stimulate women and men to confidently walk in their purpose. Living a heart centered, very blessed life.

STEPHANIE
DON WICKS

I became deaf in my right ear when I was under a year old. I have always been louder than everyone, that has always drawn attention. Living with this impairment has taught me a great deal. I have learned it's part of my purpose.

I was born in London, raised in Camlachie, where my childhood home is still my parent's home. My parents celebrated 53 years of marriage, this past year. My folks have always been my favourite cheerleaders. I am the youngest of 4, 2 from my dad's first marriage and another brother, with my mom. My father passed on April 22, 2021.   He was my drummer in my band, which he named, Stephanie & the Aikin Hearts. I will always sing, I love how music makes me feel, I want to give people that feeling back. Music has always been a staple in our family. I have 2 beautiful children they are my lifesavers. We have all moved into better life adventures.

On my mother's side, my Grandmother was a war bride from England. She passed a day before my first birthday. My grandfather was a Sargent Major when he served in the Army. On my father's side, my Grandmother was one of the first schoolteachers in Lambton County for both boards and was a principle as well. My Grandfather was searched out, to work at Imperial Oil, as a Pipefitter, to play football for The Sarnia Imperials. He played in the Grey Cup. I'd say I have some serious bragging rights.

I have had many jobs throughout my 50 plus years. Each one has taught me everything I needed through that season in my life.   I've taken bits from each and paid it forward. I started my company Sales Plus with Steph in November 2020. I was tired of working "for" someone instead of working for people. I am using my life experiences to empower, coach and stimulate women and men to confidently walk in their purpose.

Stay heart-centred and life will bring an abundance of blessings.

Jaala Wanless is a Canadian multidisciplinary artist at large. Jaala's disciplines include being a published writer, screen writer, sculptor, painter, filmmaker, illustrator, photographer, musician, and retired dj.

JAALA LEIS
WANLESS

The story of my life as an artist and human being could never be simply summarized nor condensed into 365 words. And, even if I did write the story of my life and the obstacles I've faced to get where I am in life, the giant tome I would create would read like a unbelievable fiction novel set in a universe full of adventure, adversity, serendipity and struggle.

What I will share here, however, are some of the lessons I have learned from my creative processes in terms of overcoming obstacles and adversity.

The perception one has of obstacles directly affects how one is able to achieve their goals. In other words, how you perceive a problem, whether you see an obstacle as an impasse, or, as a stepping stone to greater learning, will affect the outcome that you want to achieve.

Most of the time, when I change how I see something, I can usually see a new way forward or see something I never considered, and then approach my subject with an entirely new way forward.

Being able to see new perspectives and keep your thinking loose and flexible allows for innovation and invention. Change is always necessary! There are many paths forward in life, just like art, should you choose to see them.

Some obstacles aren't meant to be solved or removed…and these are situations where one has to learn acceptance of things they cannot change, trust that the obstacle/problem had appeared for a reason and surrender to new possibilities and directions.

An artistic masterpiece can be made with anything in any medium at any time!

Don't waste your previous time with those who say something can't be done. Just say thanks and then go do it anyways. If you have the will, you will find a way. No matter the timeframe, if you want to achieve or overcome an obstacle, keep trying, take every closed door or opportunity as a blessing, and change your perspective. The way will appear should you choose to look.

82

T.J. Corman is the author of the best-selling romance novel To You, From Me – A Story of Seduction, Love and Lust (available worldwide - FriesenPress).

T.J. CORMAN

My mom died of breast cancer when I was fourteen. Her death is the primary event that shaped the course of my life. In those days, we didn't talk about cancer. Cancer was a death sentence; it was as though if you talked about it, you might get it. There was no such thing as grief counselling - people dealt with loss and fear by not acknowledging it and carrying on.

Her passing devastated my family and crippled us. The economy had taken a downturn, and my dad lost his job. With that, he lost his ability to support me, financially and emotionally. As an only child, I went to live with my aunt and her family while my dad got his life together. Even though I was enveloped in the arms of a loving family, I was alone and devastated. I had lost both of my parents in a matter of months. When I was seventeen, my dad was diagnosed with colon cancer, and I became an orphan at nineteen.

Before she died, my mom's advice was to be sure I finished school. She told me that no one could take away my education, and if I had my schooling, I would always be self-reliant. A few days before he died, my dad sat me down on his knee and made me promise that I would complete university. It was the most important promise I ever made.

Even though I stumbled and floundered in my early twenties, I persevered and continued with university. My life was hard. I didn't have enough money, and I didn't have enough adult guidance. I eventually graduated from my five-year program, but it took me twelve years of living at the poverty line, juggling three part-time jobs, and forging onward to reach my goal.

Life has thrown me many nasty twists and turns, but I've learned to trust myself and overcome adversity. My mom was wise to give her little girl the advice she did. And I was smart to listen. No one can take your education away, whether it comes in the form of a university degree or life's hard knocks. Once you've got it, it's yours forever.

Erin Vogt is a wellness coach who focused on shame resilience, specifically around mental wellness and motherhood.

ERIN
VOGT

In pursuit of freedom around self-acceptance and fulfilled living, the road can be filled with potholes and quicksand. Overcoming years of struggle in my own mental health, I am passionate about living an open, vulnerable life on purpose and in service for others.

My silent battles started as a teen with unknown ADHD and anxiety. I continually tripped on my own feet, was stuck in a dark swamp while denying I was trapped in mental anguish. I couldn't accept myself and truly did not feel "enough" in the world. I recognized this as a universal issue with lasting consequences, if not confronted with love and patience.

No matter how hard I fought to escape that swamp, I seemed to sink further into the sludge. I would dream and journal about turquoise waters shimmering in the sunshine, as I swam among darkness in my head. I saw fun, energized people around me in this pond of possibility – my freedom pond. I knew one day I would find my way over there and swim, regardless of the mystery around how to get there.

When we don't know the "how," the why will find a way.

Entering motherhood was an ultimate test of resiliency and strength. My dangerous first childbirth lasted over 100 hours and resulted in an emergency cesarean that nearly took my life. Inevitably, this feat would become my Mount Everest climb. It propelled me forward into possibility, faith and accepting me as myself, unapologetic, a decade later. Today I see this was my destined path to prepare me as a mother, social worker and wellness coach.

Having overcome multiple depressive episodes, today I reside in turquoise waters (even while landlocked in southern Alberta). I now stand for women and men who are stuck in their own swamps. Choosing to live outside of stress and overwhelm is possible when connected to your purpose and allowing others to hold your vision high. I believe every person deserves to find the freedom they seek around accepting themselves and finding fulfillment in the magnificence they bring to the world.

Paula is a musician who experienced healing through music. She is an inspiring public speaker with a message of hope.

PAULA
DeWIT

One horrible night in June 1984 my life changed forever. My ambitious joy for life was taken away from me. As I walked away from the sexual assault, the shame began; I felt tarnished and undesirable. Emotionally, I was stunted. I knew I had to keep the assault a secret if I was to pursue my dream of becoming the first female conductor in the Canadian Armed Forces Music Branch.

Shame latched on like a leach, it sucked out my self-worth. Two days later, I travelled across the country. I was excited, not because I was going to start my music career, but because I was putting distance between me and my assault. My life was never the same. I found myself in situations that exacerbated more shame. I looked for love and acceptance in all the wrong places; I was moving further into the hole.

In 1986 I noticed I was having trouble getting out of bed, especially on the weekends when I didn't have work to distract me. I was consumed by negative thoughts; I was depressed and felt alone. I also faced workplace bullying and felt ostracized.

By the time I was released in the 90's, I had developed agoraphobia and was afraid every time I left my house. I thought I was going insane! I happened upon a late infomercial about panic attacks – I was not alone. Later, I Googled rape in the CAF and came across a Maclean's Magazine article. I finally received real help in 2016. I am now on a better path. My life goal is to help others who are experiencing shame and share a message of hope.

It took a lot of hard work and cognitive therapy to start to love myself again.

If you have experienced a sexual assault I would like to encourage you to reach out to someone you trust. Don't keep it a secret like I did. It won't serve you or make you stronger; it will steal your life from you. A person can heal by telling their story. The antidote to shame is empathy. Have patience with yourself. Be consistent and persistent with meaningful action. Healing will happen.

Paula DeWit

Mark Acheson is a Canadian voice, film and television actor

MARK
ACHESON

Photo credit: Gordan Dumka

"I've got to get out of the flow."

Ad lib words from Elf, a part that was supposed to be a one liner, but Favreau and Ferrell wanted to play. Now it will be on my tombstone.

At six years old, I wore a red cape and all the kids threw rocks yelling "kryptonite!"

At 12, I turned a Lloyds cassette deck into a Walkman by connecting Koss headphones with tape, and walked outside in 1969, 10 years before Sony, as people pointed and laughed.

At 16, I enrolled in theatre, before film and TV, and played hidden souls in Anne Frank and simple souls in Of Mice and Men. My father shook his head, doubtful of my future.

After 10 years of stage, the camera found me and I played again. Hitmen, homeless men, victims and victimizers, monsters… stunned that anyone would notice or care or pay me to play. Then cartoons that I had feverishly watched as a child captured me and my voices, and I played again.

During my play, I married three times, I failed three times, I hurt and was hurt three times. But all along the way, I stayed out of the flow and I played. So many roles, so many voices, so many faces, but always the same eyes; watching as my makeup, first created, then simply filled in the lines that were already there.

In many ways, truly a life well lived. Luck from above, support from those that once loved me, and the unending desire to stay out of the flow and just play. More mistakes than successes. But it's the takes that are kept that mark a career. And what is left on the editor's floor is not counted. Life also allows for bad takes, but you're a fool if you fail to learn, and learning never stops.

At 64, I start again. Learning again to play and to stay out of the flow, for this is living and the key to a life well lived. Don't allow the rocks stop you from being Superman. Don't let the laughing faces discourage your love of music. And don't let the shaking heads make you doubt your childish desire to play. And always stay out of the flow, for fortune favour the foolish, and God loves those that play and make his people smile.

Angela is a mother, author, creator and founder of Pups On The Pier.

ANGELA
ABBATE

Pups On The Pier, a multi-media brand that focuses on delivering creative solutions for tackling mental health issues among children and their parents told in the perspective of the most adorable pups, Chloe, Lulu, and Sparky has been my journal, my art, and my vision board throughout my healing process following an unexpected divorce. This creative journey began when I became a new mommy to "My Very First Pup", Chloe, in April of 2020. My daughter had finally convinced me to get a pup after she expressed the therapeutic benefits pups had on anxiety, something I have struggled with for years. I also thought a new pup would be a great companion on my parenting days off, "Mom's Weekend" a time of relaxation, self-care, sunshine, nature, and of you guessed it, Pups On The Pier, my baby, my passion, my joy.

While watching sunsets on the pier with Chloe and our new friends, I was fascinated by all the neighborhood pups on the pier. I started taking pictures of the pups, making videos for Instagram, and found this was bringing me immense joy while bringing many smiles and laughs to my growing followers. The name Pups On The Pier came to me one day on the pier, followed by a detailed dream I had of the exact logo I trademarked. The setting of the pier itself, therapeutic, the ocean waves, the picturesque city skyline, the salty breeze, I began to feel a sense of peace and belonging I had never known before. I wanted to combine my passion for writing and mental health advocacy and simply knew that Pups On The Pier was the medium and Chloe, my very first pup, the muse. I have published books, music, comics, and an animated feature film.

While finding my passion, I started losing my fears and gaining back my light. My vision for Pups was clear and my ambition, unstoppable. Have faith in yourself, when you think you can't cope, your dreams, manifestations, are your destiny and hope. Don't give up when others say you can't do…your truth and your purpose, you've got to pursue!

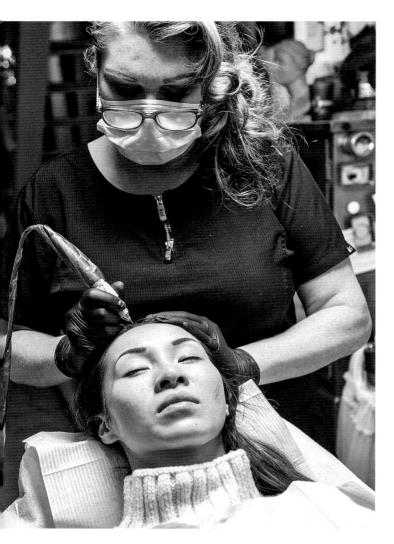

Shauna Magrath CPCP, a pioneer, innovator and thought leader in the cosmetic tattoo industry, attributes her success by overcoming FEAR!

SHAUNA
MAGRATH

Fear is (normalized) when you live in a constant state of fight or flight. Unknowingly, it will become an emotional addiction. Your perspective is EVERYTHING! If you truly want to find happiness, you must face your fears head on. I was fortunate to learn this in my 20's.

Growing up around violence, I was naturally conditioned to not know the difference. Having dyslexia, I was brutally bullied in school, which ended with me in the hospital at age eight. Every day was a struggle fighting fear and anxiety, not knowing what was to come. Teachers' ridicule only made things worse. Living in constant pain conditioned me to feel worthless and led me into the darkness.

At 22, I was a dancer working in the underworld, living in hell. After being assaulted, I had enough. I walked off stage that day and fell to my knees sobbing, praying to God for relief in that moment. I felt a warm hand on my shoulder, and a voice saying: "Follow your heart, you'll never go wrong. It's not until you jump off the cliff will you learn how to fly, and I will guide you along the way." I knew GOD had touched me and I felt fearless beginning my new lease on life.

In the last two decades my soul has been tested over and over. Life brought me to my knees again. I found myself with a new business, homeless due to a fire, dealing with seven family deaths and a breakup. I was alone, hanging on by a thread, standing vulnerable with my fear. I immersed myself into my business, BEAUTYINK® Permanent Cosmetics, helping my clients overcome their biggest insecurities. Their healing journeys empowered me to forge ahead, knowing that I was put on this planet to help others flourish.

After 52 years, I realize that making friends with fear is empowering. With this skill, everything you can imagine is achievable. Through sobriety, meditation, positive affirmations and self-love, I've developed the strength and trust in myself to conquer any fear. Building courage, confidence with faith made me the tenacious woman I am today.

Empowering others' lives is now my greatest achievement!

Shauna Magrath

From LeiLani's pro bono work, she created potent, plant powered complexion products infused with skincare that treat and benefit the skin.

LEILANI
KOPP

My story is simple. "Lead with an open heart and positive intent."

Every time I see someone creating change and making life better for others, I am inspired.

Inspiration is something that makes someone want to do something, or gives someone an idea to create something. I think and believe that there is so much more to this word.

Inspiration is something that motivates you to be better and do better.

Inspiration came to me through my pro bono work. Since beginning philanthropy in my own life, that look on someone's face, when they are smiling after crying, is contagious and gives you perspective; it shows you what truly matters in life.

My pro bono work is a specialized area with corrective makeup working with cancer/trauma/burn surgeons. People ask me if I was burned or had cancer, and no, thank god I have not, but I am humbled every day working with these people that climbed up from tragedy and rebuilt their lives. These patients inspired me to create Sweet LeiLani Cosmetics with no idea how or where to start, but they impacted my life, so much so that I had to find a way. Not only did it inspire me to build a thriving business, it helped me grow as a person.

It makes you a better parent and truly sets an example for your children to help others. It connects you with others who want to help change the world, which re-energizes you. Volunteering your time to support a cause you are passionate about is something you will never regret. It will enrich your life, and connects you to people and ideas that will positively impact your life. Helping your community is an opportunity for you to grow as a person, to better understand how you fit into the world around you.

After a certain point, money doesn't increase well-being, but giving to others does. I contribute to causes that will change one life somewhere, so we can change lives everywhere. Philanthropy should be embedded in the purpose of every business. It keeps me going even when I don't feel like continuing after having a bad day.

This is what truly inspires me.

Suzanne Durnan is the Principal and CEO of Simplified Financial Inc. since taking over and reinventing the business in 2008. Their focus is on life insurance solutions, investment strategies, and Employee Benefit Plans.

SUZANNE
DURNAN

I have been life licensed as an advisor for 30 years, have my CHS Designation, and licensed in British Columbia and Alberta. An active Board member of Advocis for the past number of years, I am the current Vice-President/Incoming President of the Vancouver Chapter. I love to promote the benefits of being a part of a professional membership and connecting with other advisors, business owners, and colleagues from across the country in sharing their stories and best practices.

My amazing team of 5 works out of my combined, yet separate home and office. I have trained my dynamic team to focus on exceptional customer service, effectively take care of administrative details, promote the business through various marketing strategies, and offer credible, creative, affordable financial and insurance-based solutions to existing and prospective clients.

Throughout an ever-changing industry, numerous challenges, and some difficult times, I have consistently proven that with determination, heart, and compassion, I always find a way through.

I have proven that this traditionally pressure-laden sales business can be done in a kind, caring, compassionate way. Helping clients to make informed decisions about ways to protect their families, businesses, savings, and livelihood…these are the goals that take precedence.

It is through building relationships, connecting with people at different levels, and continuing to grow professionally and personally, that creates a successful business model and sets you apart from others.

My main message is to get to work. Show your clients and your team that you appreciate them. Surround yourself with exceptional, trustworthy, reliable, loyal, supportive, caring, and driven individuals that can help you and your business grow and thrive beyond your wildest dreams. Have it all and share it with the ones you care most about…then do even more!

When I am not in the office or with clients, I am enjoying my beautiful home with my loving husband of 5 years and our two energetic cats. You can find me outside in my backyard relaxing, working out at the gym, spending time with my dynamic daughters and their supportive spouses, or in my art studio painting my newest vibrant creation.

Fynn Mansbridge-Fafard is a Canadian national team epee fencer, with an Olympic dream. He also coaches young aspiring athletes.

FYNN
MANSBRIDGE
-FAFARD

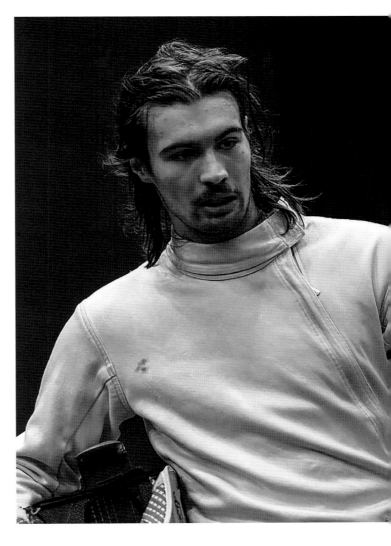

I started fencing a few weeks before my 13th birthday. It was the first sport I was ever truly passionate about, despite growing up surrounded by athletics.

For most of my life I've felt like I was different. Not necessarily in a good or bad way, just different. Especially as a kid. I was extremely shy and reserved, and didn't make a lot of friends. I didn't really know where I fit in. The friends I did make, however, were very important to me. In most of my early memories I am playing pretend with my best friend and cousin, William. We spent hours in our own imaginary world. That's where I felt most comfortable.

Fencing came at the right time in my life and I poured my heart and soul into it from the beginning. I still remember putting my mask on for the first time and feeling the same as everyone else in the room. It gave me something to be proud of, and I was pretty good at it.

I experienced success quickly, medalling at my first local competition, and winning the next. It gave me a feeling of accomplishment I had never experienced before. At 15, I made national team for the first time. Around this time I started making fencing my identity. I began measuring myself by my results and performances. Which made me feel on top of the world after a win, but completely crushed after a loss. This unhealthy mindset led to overtraining and exhausted me after a few years.

By the time I was 18 I was completely burnt out. I took time away from fencing and made a lot of important distinctions about the impact the sport had on my life. The first being that my competition results and performances have nothing to do with how much I am worth as a person, or my passion for the sport. The second being that fencing is what I do and not who I am.

I'm 21 now, and no longer confuse my success with self worth. I am currently ranked first in Canada, but more importantly, I am comfortable with who I am outside of the sport.

Fynn Mansbridge-Fafard

Saireen Neilsen helps women prepare and manage their menopausal symptoms in a natural way. Saireen hosts The Loving Menopausitivity Show.

SAIREEN
NEILSEN

Menopause was a nightmare for me. I struggled with symptoms such as weight gain, mood swings, brain fog, hot flashes, and insomnia. These are just a few of the many symptoms that women experience as they go through perimenopause and menopause.

I spent five years in each of the perimenopausal and menopausal stages. I spent a lot of time, energy, and money searching for relief and quick fixes. I was seeing a doctor, a functional medicine specialist, a gynecologist, and a naturopath – all at the same time! They gave me medication, supplements, and remedies, but I was experiencing side effects instead of the relief I was seeking. I said to myself, enough is enough.

I researched, read every book, took courses, and interviewed women who were going through it or had gone through it. I found that there are some safe, natural, and effective strategies that can be applied to reduce some of these symptoms. If I only knew then what I know now. I wish there was someone there to help me when I was going through it. I realized that I could help other women going through this.

I designed a program called Loving Menopausitivity to help women prepare for and manage their perimenopausal and menopausal symptoms in a graceful and natural way. I help women transition from struggling and surviving, to healthy and thriving during their menopausal journey and achieve "Menopausitivity" which is about being strong, healthy, sexy, and thriving during menopause and loving yourself, and living your best life.

What keeps me motivated is knowing that I am creating a Loving Menopausitivity movement that will provide a forum where women can be seen and heard, address the stigma of menopause, change how women view themselves and shift the way women are perceived at home and at work. I want to serve women and equip them with strategies that they can apply every day and throughout their busy lives.

I would like to impact as many lives as possible through my program. So far my story has been shared with 1.1 million people. You never know if you or someone else will share your story to impact other people's lives.

RACHEL
FRUSTACI

Life is short… live the life you imagined…

As young girl, I watched my grandmother welcome people into her home with open arms. She loved to visit and talk and feed people. She got pure joy out of it. She literally would invite anyone in off the street. I get it now, it made her feel good to make others feel welcomed and she showed love through feeding and entertaining people.

I was raised by my maternal grandparents and my mother. My mother had to work hard to provide for the two of us. My father wasn't present in my life, too busy chasing his musical dreams and women. And then he passed away before I turned 12 years old. I had to grow up fast.

I started working young, both at school and where I could make money. I put myself through college, interior design school, culinary school and then started my own family. I wanted to be a good mom and partner to my husband, so I shaped my career and myself around them.

I wasn't living the life I imagined though; I felt it and my family knew it. I was unhappy, and I got sick, really sick. That was a wake-up call; if I didn't change my life, it not only would kill my soul, but me physically. My 'aha' moment came when I got to plan an event. I realized how much I loved it. I was doing it personally in my life with over-the-top birthdays, baby showers, etc. I loved creating beautiful moments for people.

I decided to go back to school and combine my skills and knowledge over the years, and most importantly, I decided to take a chance on myself. I left my job and focused on myself, my family and my career. I opened a travel business and now my own wedding and event management company. I have decided that I want to work hard and invest in myself while making it work for me and my family.

I want to leave that legacy to my kids. Work hard towards your dreams, but don't forget what is most important. We sometimes forget to include ourselves.

KENDRA
VYSE

In many ways my entrepreneurial journey started like so many others; I wanted the freedom to spend time with my family and friends and be able to help when needed. But in many ways my journey was not typical because I grew up in a family of entrepreneurs. I grew up knowing that understanding your numbers and having a plan was key to success when it came to business.

When it came time to start my business, I was not going to have the standard, give me your records, I'll enter them, and here's your numbers accounting business. That was not why I was starting my business. My purpose was to help people have clarity and understanding with their accounting and bookkeeping. And I've been told I'm good at it.

And for years this is exactly what I did.

After some ups and downs, I had an established clientele and was looking at other ways to help entrepreneurs. But then Covid hit. Like so many others, I had to make an adjustment and my business was forever changed. I was already mostly remote with my clients, but I changed to a fully virtual practice.

However, this also allowed me the opportunity to take my business on the road with my fiancé. As a semi driver he drove across Canada, and I missed him. Armed with a cell phone, 50GB of data, and my laptop, I went to work in the cab of a semi, loving being with my fiancé and seeing the country with him.

But I wanted to do more than just help business owners with their accounting, I wanted to help them develop their business plans and implement them. So, when we decided that it was finally time to make the move back to Nova Scotia, my second business was born – Clear Direction Advisors.

I still help business owners with their accounting and bookkeeping, but there is a renewed focus on educating Canadian entrepreneurs. Accounting, bookkeeping, business plans and strategy, these are all topics that I know every entrepreneur needs to understand. My renewed mission is to bring this knowledge to everyone, and make it easy to understand.

Sally Omeme is a knitwear artist who specializes in hand-knits. Creating her one of a kind pieces by using repurposed garments, and interesting textiles.

SALLY
OMEME

From the moment I stepped off the plane, I knew I was in love with Vancouver. Small town girl hoping to make it in the big city, I definitely knew I was no longer in Kansas, or Sylvan Lake, Alberta, the place I grew up amongst the safety and shelter of friends and family.

From a young age I dreamt of working in fashion, often browsing through fashion magazines after school. I watched shows like Fashion Television or Fashion File to find inspiration. As I watched the models glide down the runway, the hair, the make-up, and the beat of the music kept in time with my heartbeat, making me feel ALIVE.

Living in Central Alberta, the world of fashion seemed worlds away. I felt as though I had been put into a glass jar that had been labelled with expectations of what others thought I should be. It wasn't until I discovered a fashion school program in the heart of downtown Vancouver that I was ready to break through the glass barriers that could be looked through, but not easily seen.

Determined to make it, no matter what anyone said, I hopped on a plane and headed into the great unknown Vancouver, with one night stay in a hotel. I had less than 24 hours to find a place to live, otherwise I would be living in my friend's van. Within hours of landing in Vancouver, I headed to JCI Institute. One of the staff found out I didn't have a place to live yet, and together we came up with a compilation of places to see. I was fortunate that the first place I checked out was to be my new home. I was so excited to be living with two Vancouver actors above a Starbucks.

The year brought many challenges, including my school funding falling through, near homelessness, and even having to walk two hours to get to class because I couldn't afford public transit.

The biggest lesson I learned was: "Obstacles are what you see when you take your eye off the goal." Looking back, attending JCI was one of the scariest, but best decisions I've ever made.

Sally Omeme

Andrea Menard is an accomplished Métis singer/songwriter, actor, speaker, wellness trainer and the founder of the Sacred Feminine Learning Lodge.

ANDREA MENARD

Fear has stalked me in my pursuit of fulfilment. Not just because of the hazards of being a Métis woman in this country, but because I have continually stepped outside my comfort zone to pursue spiritual fulfilment in both my personal and professional life. If you were to look at my resume, my journey as an actor and singer has seemed charmed. In many ways it was. But scratch the surface a little, and you will find a lot of tears, anxiety, and gut-wrenching fear. Stepping out of my comfort zone does not come easy for me. Even though I continue to do it again and again.

As a Métis woman, I was groomed to live small and dream even smaller. Not that anyone suggested that I do. It's more like the colonial system itself trained me to occupy the bottom rung of society because there is not a lot of room at the top for Indigenous women. I was groomed to fulfill the exact role my parents fulfilled. And their parents fulfilled. And play it with obedience and submission. But in the pursuit of fulfillment, this role just doesn't cut it.

I admit that, although I have fiery Métis ancestors who fought to be heard in the development of this country, I have been trained well. It shames me to say it. But my first instinct is to hide away and not be seen or heard. To not stand out in any way. Hence, the fear. But I was born to be a performer. I am a performer. My name is Fire Woman, for goddess' sake. I am here to set hearts and minds on fire with possibility. And love. And transformation. I am here to be seen. So as much as that colonial training wants to claim my courage time and again. It cannot win. For I am here to buck the system. I am here to pursue happiness. And expansion. And decolonization. And unity. And love. In my pursuit of fulfilment, I have made friends with fear. It's not the presence of fear that hinders your fulfilment, it is the giving in to the colonial training that keeps you small. And unfulfilled.

Huriye Sefayi is an international certified life coach and image consultant, founder of HS Vancouver brand and lifestyle blogger.

HURIYE
SEFAYI

I'll be honest, my youth was spent living a pretty ordinary life. I spent my days travelling between my family and obligations. Through bland days I had trust that every single ordinary task was important in leading me to my dreams.

My mission is to become a respected person by family, friends, and my chosen communities. I am here to make a positive difference despite being imperfect. I aim to have no regrets about the things that have happened in my life that have led me to who I am today. So, I decided to take experiences as lessons and move on.

I have learned that the most painful struggles can grant us our most necessary growth. I like to travel a lot, and after falling in love with Canada, I decided to take a leap and make a change in my life. Change is a part of everyone's life; while some people don't like change, I've accepted it as a necessary part of growth.

Canada was a big change for me, having to start from square one. Years of past work experience meant little in Canada. I had to begin at ground zero with only a belief in myself and my abilities. I had trust that I would figure it out along the way. I have had to work very hard to achieve my current life, which only became possible once I believed in myself and my potential.

I reached peaks in my life and I reached those peaks with my activities in cooking, judging, teaching, coaching and fashion. Along the way I successfully ran a vegetarian restaurant, I held a conference called "Attitude Behaviour Communication" at Henan and Xi'an University in China, I grew as a lifestyle blogger, I became a national artistic swimming judge. I also realized my passion in being a life skills coach, where I get to help others find success in their personal and professional lives. I challenged myself by modeling for brands, and I was the public relations coordinator at Vancouver Fashion Gala. All of these achievements have something in common; I had to first believe in myself to turn my ordinary life into my dream one.

Amy is a naturally gifted holistic health practitioner who helps people of all ages live the life they love.

AMY
McVEITY

There I was, in what seemed like the darkest abyss, having given in, awaiting my fate. I didn't know my outcome, but in that moment, it no longer seemed to matter.

2020 was a life changing year for many; for me, it was for a different reason. That year I was joyfully anticipating completing my family. However, instead of joy, I was met with great sadness, as I wound up burying two babies at separate times. At the time, my daily practices of prayer, meditation, affirmations, personal development and exercise helped me meet those losses with an optimistic perspective. I was proud of myself, considering losing a child has been one of my greatest fears.

Almost two years later, grief struck me in unbearable ways, I found myself struggling. My daily practices, including counselling, were no longer helping. The fight to resist began to consume me. My three beautiful children who needed a healthy, happy, loving mom, were experiencing a tired, angry and frustrated mom, which broke my heart. The fight was long and hard, until one day, I let grief take the lead.

Recently I rediscovered a beautiful painting that my best friend made for me in high school. It's a picture of a hippo dancing with an alligator. The caption reads, "Sometimes you just have to let loose and forget you're dancing with an alligator." Truly metaphorical of my experience with grief.

In this so-called dance of life, the alligator's invitation to dance was annoying, impractical and illogical. Once I realized the alligator wasn't giving up, I decided to submit and began to dance. I felt the brilliant footwork and movement of the dance, and that indeed, the alligator is an inspired teacher.

Letting go has shown me such empowering lessons. There is always light despite darkness. Faith alleviates fear. Joy stomps out sadness and anger. Unclear paths become clear. Brokenness always heals. Lastly, I am never alone, for with God, all things are possible.

This experience has brought me more life and understanding to what matters most. And this dance with the alligator is exhilarating, beautiful and healing and will leave you discovering who you truly are and how magical life really is!

ANGELA K.
MARKUSIC

I was a naïve, insecure child who was transformed by life's experiences into the strong woman I am today. An only child born to older European, Catholic parents, I grew up in a strict, sheltered environment. I would have never imagined my world would have gone the way it did … Divorced. Single Mom, Business Woman.

In my youth, my mother, father, and uncle were the most important people in my life. While I had them, I felt that someone always had my back. Losing them changed my life immensely. Now, it was just me.

While at McMaster U working on an economics degree, my mother had a "brilliant" idea. "Why don't you get your real estate license?" During the summers, I studied and obtained my real estate license. Upon graduation, I worked for the Federal Government. I wasn't meant to be a government employee. After six years, I quit. I had my children, and when they were quite small, I began my real estate career. It gave me the ability to earn as much or as little as I wanted and still have the time to raise my children.

At 26, my beloved father passed away. An absolute shock. I was left to deal with his sudden, unexpected death while caring for my grieving mother who continued to run their business to the age of 84.

Soon after, my uncle was diagnosed with cancer. In the last three month's of his life, I took care of him while parenting two small children and dealing with a marriage that was slowly failing.

In 2010, while still running her business, my mother suffered "mini strokes" which lead to dementia. I closed my parents' business and moved my mother into my home with my children and I. I lost my "mojo" and struggled to get through life emotionally and financially.

In July 2020, I lost my mother. She was the most influential person in my life. I felt that I lost a part of me that I will never get back. She was a woman "ahead of her time."

My work is not solely about business. It is about relationships and emotional connections, and my clients can become like an extension of family.

Though I didn't realize it at the time, what I went through in life made me stronger. Not only do I get stronger as I age, with my mother's death, the torch has been passed to me to usher forth the next generations and preserve our family legacy. My family's legacy is made up of survivors who are incredibly resilient, and who most importantly have a strong belief in FAMILY.

SUE
NOBLE

Dreams are the connecting threads that have travelled through life with me; some dropped but many achieved in part or whole and some in disguise.

Dreams chart our course forward if we dare to act upon them. They do not always look the way we imagine, and they don't always arrive when we expect them, but if you look closely, you discover they do come, sometimes cloaked.

In my twenties, I dreamt of becoming a journalist for National Geographic. I loved the stories and glossy photos of foreign places and different cultures. Although I did not become a journalist, I did have the opportunity to visit several other countries and immerse myself in their cultures. I also went to British Guyana in South America to build a school with a not-for-profit organization during my thirties. While there, I blazed trails into the jungle, wary of the snakes and panthers. I observed that heritage, customs, and traditions influenced how individuals moved through the world. My interest in sociology was solidified.

After graduating with a BA in Sociology, I worked in Human Resources and recruitment. I observed that background influenced one's understanding of the social contract and hidden hiring agendas. I wanted to help our most vulnerable populations achieve their dreams as well. Thus, my interest shifted from a social focus to an individual one; my dream of a master's degree was born.

After working in Human Resources, I moved to individual counselling. I spent 10 years in Employment Counsellor followed by 17 years in the addictions field as a Clinical Counsellor. However, if I wanted my own private practice, I would have to follow my lifelong dream of obtaining a master's degree in Counselling Psychology to become Registered as a Clinical Counsellor. So, in 2016, at the age of 55, I began my master's degree while working full time. Now, at the age of 60, I have completed my degree and enjoy working in a collective with other clinicians.

I used to ponder the pressure people put themselves under because of missed opportunities. There isn't just one opportunity; there are many. Recognize them and know they connect the threads of our dreams.

Dori holds braves space for people to be seen, heard and understood. She invites you to a path inward to a truer you.

DORI
HOWARD

Under the Vesuvius Sun

"Mom, why are you taking a course on compassion? You're one of the most compassionate people I know," claims my daughter. I prided myself on being a compassionate and empathic person. As a pediatric oncology nurse, mom, sibling of five, daughter and executive coach, compassion was my work and way of being. When therapist #3 established that I was 'practicing' idiot compassion, the next 59 minutes were a blur. As I sat stunned in my car, googling idiot compassion, words including enabler, delusional, loose or no boundaries, not saying no, no self-compassion, lacking in loving kindness to self-appeared.

Was this me? My intellectual self did not want to be an idiot and believed I was a few counseling sessions away from wise compassion. However, this would be the first of many wake-up calls to summon my courage and discover the path inward to my truest self. A journey that would bring me an open heart, a softened presence and being 'enough'.

My downward spiral was insidious and unconscious. Pretending, avoiding, indulging in bad habits and caring for others at the expense of myself helped me cope in an unhealthy marriage and toxic workplace. A series of unfortunate, life-altering events brought me to a place of choice. I chose to dig in and do the deep work that would liberate me to a state of ease, joy and peace. My rising up focused on radical self-care. Once a nurse, always a nurse – I developed my own self-care care plan. My renewed resilience focused on four pillars: nutritional harmony, mindset elevation, heart and soul alignment, and synergy with nature; adopting practices that plunged me deeply inward, surfaced wounds, mobilized emotions, and soothed my soul.

My resiliency care plan included creating peace with food, daily meditation, kundalini yoga, therapist #4, forest bathing and renovating a tranquil oceanfront property soaking up Vesuvius sunsets. The renovations mirrored my own healing and caring journey. Together, with my late brother, we envisioned a place where people would gather, learn, heal, recharge, celebrate, relax and share stories. This West Coast meets Zen Buddhism inspired design is enso, the Japanese symbol for enlightenment. It is where people share their stories and healing begins.

Dori Howard

Barb Pearson is passionate about environmental protection, wildlife and choosing whatever path is best for your own healing journey.

BARB
PEARSON

Each morning I wake up grateful for the turn my life has taken. This has only been the case in the last few years. Several years ago, I had to shut down my practice as a successful litigation lawyer due to the ravaging effects of multiple autoimmune diseases. I went on disability and floundered about dealing with anxiety, pain, frustration and boredom. I began to paint in earnest, hoping to fill a void however my symptoms continued to flare. I knew I needed to change something; I started to examine what I needed in order to heal.

First and foremost, I needed to forgive myself for not living up to the ideals of our culture. Second, I knew I needed to become grounded and be in nature doing something that felt real. Not having a clue what we were doing, our family moved to a 20-acre piece of land where we now raise dairy goats and free range poultry, in addition to growing much of our own food.

We turned a barren landscape into a sea of flowers and grasses, creating visual beauty. Most importantly, we set out to heal the earth by using sustainable farming practices; rather than using harsh chemicals to make our job easier, we think first about creating a thriving ecosystem that is a haven for wildlife, birds and pollinators. It was, and is, very hard work, but it is incredibly meaningful.

I now host classes and events where people come and learn about what we are doing, giving me the opportunity to share values that are important to me. It is the joy and enthusiasm of our class participants that was the impetus for creating a centre on our farm. This is a gathering place for people where they can spend a few days escaping from their fast paced lives. Here they can participate in workshops, give themselves permission to be creative, and most importantly, connect with nature.

I am delighted to share that what could have been a tragedy turned out instead to be a blessing, allowing me to once again use my skills as an advocate, however, my role now is to represent the environment.

Barb Pearson

Lauren Morris was born in Cape Town, South Africa and moved to Vancouver in 2000. She studied at the Cape Technikon as a Graphic Designer before moving on to pursue the Fine Arts.

LAUREN
MORRIS

As a young child I remember feeling happy and loved. Little did I know that as I waved good-bye to my five year old sister from the top of the jungle gym, that I would never see her again.

She went to get her tonsils removed and died during the night at the hospital. Our family dynamics were changed forever. I became the eldest with two siblings to follow. When I was 10 years old, my mother was diagnosed with breast cancer and died at the age of 35. We all turned inwards, dealing with our pain in silence. It was a time when no-one spoke and feelings were suppressed.

My memories of my mother, though scarce, are of her bright smile, loving kindness and creativity. For years the barriers of pain stifled my ability to be present. At the age of 21, after finishing my studies in graphic design, I decided to travel the world for a year. I was fiercely independent, traveled and worked in numerous countries, but returned back to South Africa with the same demons I had left with.

After immigrating to Canada, I started to paint, using my kitchen floor as a studio. Painting allowed me to tap into my vulnerability, to introspect and realize that it's not about how hard we fall but about how we bring ourselves up from diversity.

Through painting I have learnt to gain confidence, to love who I am and to be present for all those around me. I've also learnt that by sharing experiences, it enables us to understand and support each other.

When looking back, I am grateful for all I have experienced in my life; it's the foundation of who I am and how I see the world. I find joy in simple things like a good cup of coffee and believe that humour is the best medicine. Painting has been a healing factor in my life and I look forward to continuing the journey.

Elizabeth Douglas is a journalist, writer and fencer who is passionate about breaking the stigma around mental health through writing.

ELIZABETH
LOUISE
DOUGLAS

I don't remember a day in my life when I wasn't aware of my body. When I was seventeen, mere weeks away from graduating high school, my mother called and said we had to go to the hospital. Four women sat concerned and uncomfortable on plastic chairs, clipboards perched on their lap and pens at the ready. I sat and listened through foggy thoughts as they listed numbers, procedures, and possibilities. Slipping seamlessly through it all were two words I never thought I would hear: Anorexia Nervosa.

At the age of eight, I started fencing at a local gym in my hometown. I qualified for the Canadian National Team when I was sixteen and competed at my first World Championships that Spring. Everything spiralled after that competition; my focus turned from the love of my sport to scrutiny over my own body. A figure constantly under construction – never quite skinny enough, muscular enough, athletic enough. I received my diagnosis at 90 pounds and a heart rate of 32.

The past five years has been a long and winding road. But to this day, asking for help and choosing recovery has been the best decision I have ever made. To me, recovery means I get to live, write, and use my artform to elevate issues that are important to me. I started studying journalism and creative writing in university, and that's where I learned that I could use the challenging experiences in my life to fuel change. I am currently working on publishing a poetry collection titled From Roots and Remedies, which has become a meditative practice of working through trauma, self-acceptance, and love. For me, writing, whether fiction, non-fiction or poetry has allowed me to express myself in ways that I wouldn't have otherwise been able to. Through my journalistic practices, I have focused on stories surrounding mental health and perseverance through hardship. I have had the honour in speaking with inspiring people who are using their adversity to make a difference in the world.

I'm still aware of my body, that hasn't changed. But now I can appreciate what it does for me, and how it allows me to move through this world authentically.

Elizabeth Louise Douglas

VERONICA
PLEWMAN

WOLF

One day when I was six, I climbed to the top of a small hill near our home. Looking down, I saw a crowd gathered around a pick-up truck parked on the road below. Someone had rigged a wooden tripod in the bed of the truck, and from it was hanging the body of a large dead wolf. The scene remains vivid in my memory: the grey of the fur, the limp and fluffy tail curving downward from the chokehold of the rope tethering it to the tripod, the murmur of the crowd, my feelings of sadness. I think that was when I had the first inklings that something was not right with the world I lived in.

THE IMPORTANCE OF ART-MAKING

After the turbulence of my twenties and early thirties, I began to understand what I could do with my life. A year of back-packing around Europe in the mid 1970s helped me to see that I really could do the artwork that I'd been dreaming about for a long time. I started, and first showed my work in 1979. I have discovered since that making art covers all the bases: the physical, emotional, mental, intellectual, and spiritual elements of being fully engaged in the world. I believe that to be so not only for me but also for the community I am part of. For us, making art is a necessity. Making art is making an authentic connection with a material creation. Ideally, a viewer of the work also connects with that creation, sparking a non-verbal conversation across time and space.

CHANGE

Common wisdom holds that change is the only constant. The world's climate has been changing for a while, most dramatically so in the last twenty years. Climate change arguably is now the biggest existential threat facing us. I ask myself how I can adapt and still find meaning in what I am doing. It probably means starting small, on the inside, changing the way that I think (no easy task) to find the hope in myself and in the actions of others, and above all, to always remember how I felt when I saw that wolf.

Veronica Plewman

TATIANA
GREGORYANZ

I grew up in the Soviet Union. In my family, success was directly related to survival. Each accomplishment was preparation toward the next task for advancement. Advancement was more important than living. It was living and it left little time for joyful pursuits. My focus was on the upward climb.

Life changed when my son was born with cerebral palsy; the world stopped turning on its axis. I began motherhood, like all things, as a task to be completed, a job. However, my son was not a job, but a gift. One day his tiny all-knowing stare seemed to say, "don't worry, because it will be okay." I realized to be a good parent, I would have to sublimate my learned behaviours and desires to my son's needs. We needed to create a new path together. When I began to see him as a person, rather than a puzzle to be solved, or a job, I was able to give up who I thought I was supposed to be and carve out a new existence for us both. We came to Canada.

Like all parents, I struggled with knowing when to push him forward and when to accept his reservations. I learned compassion from watching how hard he worked at things that others took for granted. He taught me to accept the things we could not change and be patient because all good things take time. My son showed me the path to contentment. Our hard-won lessons shaped the way I move through the world today. My son helped me see that a by-product of helping others is happiness. If our gaze is constantly focused inward, we miss the beauty in the world around us. Selflessness creates wonder, and wonder creates amazement and joy.

I know that love is a practice we must commit to every day, and that the acquisition of skills governs harmony and human purpose. Feelings of anger or frustration indicate missing abilities required to navigate certain situations. With practice, patience, and time, we acquire the needed skills. A life that includes compassion, patience and acceptance is a happy life, well-lived.

Carrie McEachran is a wife, mother, CEO, founder, writer and advocate.

CARRIE
McEACHRAN

When I hear someone being described as "powerful" or "having ultimate power", I automatically think of someone who sits at the end of the table and has the authority to make significant decisions. Someone like the sunshine list CEO who would never know my name or consider me someone in their power league. NEVER in a million years would I have ever thought about putting myself into that same league. I can't even recount the number of times I found myself falling into the hole of self-pity hitting rock bottom, feeling worthless and unworthy and questioning myself. I always managed to climb back out and brush myself off, but it was never without the thought that it would be so much easier to give up and live the status quo life.

I just never wanted to live in the status quo world, so rather than hiding from the narrative, I have spent my entire adult life trying to prove it doesn't work for me (my parents will tell you that I have been trying to prove this narrative doesn't work for me since the day I was born).

Through my mentorship business, I continually hear from emerging leaders that they have had similar feelings to me on the subject. They are rarely putting themselves in the "power" category for many reasons, but mostly because they have allowed the world to determine their value and place them in challenging boxes to get out of.

Perhaps it's the experience from years of smashing my head against the glass ceiling and fighting to claim my seat at the table, or maybe it's because I've hit that magical age that all women talk about when they leave all self-doubt behind, but I am ready. After hitting numerous potholes, I am gassed up with the power to keep me moving forward to the next beautiful destination. I have made it my life's mission to pick up as many friends as I can along the way and help each one of them find the incredible power, they have within to live the life they have only dreamed of.

Carrie McEachran

Photo credit: Oshy Parasol

Laura Mennell is a Canadian performer who recently starred in Robert Zemeckis' PROJECT BLUE BOOK, as well The Farrelly Brothers' LOUDERMILK.

LAURA
MENNELL

I'm fortunate to have a weirdly wonderful job where I play make-believe as an adult. I am an actor.

It's a creatively fulfilling career that also includes uncontrollable factors. The job's instability can easily make any of us anxiety ridden; it can leave us questioning whether we're good enough, or wondering if it's wise to commit to such an unpredictable path. These feelings were definitely a driving force in my younger years and, at times, debilitating.

When I became a working actor, it often felt like no one truly understood what I was doing for a living. A well-intentioned family member once insinuated that my creative work was simply "a delightful hobby" and she hoped it would soon be overshadowed by "more serious endeavours."

Another reality of an actor's life is that you rarely know what the next year, month or even day will bring. As an actor, auditions for new roles pop up out of nowhere and looming deadlines often squash plans you've made with friends.

I work on series lead roles, creating shows with people who feel like family. When these jobs ultimately end, I must start over. We are up and down, yo-yoing all over the place. It's the nature of the job.

Despite job uncertainties, this enigmatic creative life frees you to be your authentic self—there's magic in the unknown. Forget the what-ifs, the have-tos, the I'm-not-good-enoughs, and just do what you're driven to do. Become more present in the moment and find a sense of calm. You don't need to know the outcome.

To all the creative souls out there grasping for certainty—there is none, but that's okay.

It's an exciting gift to live a life that doesn't follow the norm and is full of unknown possibilities. Give yourself permission to not know all of the answers. Ditch perfection for the quest of constant learning and allow life to surprise you.

If you're passionate about following a career in the arts, embrace all it has to offer, including the unknown. It'll show itself soon enough.

Jennifer Mercer lives in St. Thomas, ON and has just opened her own HR consulting business. Her biggest goal is to help recent grads secure jobs in their field.

JENNIFER **MERCER**

Life's ups and downs, love, and blessings.

One of my favorite aspects of getting older is acquiring wisdom and looking back on my life. In my early years, it was just my mom and I. She faced sacrifices but did not waver in her dedication to caring for me. She met my step dad and married him when I was five; he became my dad. Years later, I was blessed with an amazing little sister. They were there for me, provided security, and opened the door for new opportunities.

Even with their love, I struggled with abandonment throughout my life due to my biological father's departure. It is amazing how his leaving impacted my life for years to come, even though I have no recollection of him.

Abandonment happens in so many ways, perhaps as a child, through divorce, loss of a loved one, a dear pet or a job. I believe it impacts a lot of people. It is something we do not talk about, and I am guessing many do not realize the underlying impact it has on their lives. It set me back a few times and took a lot of years for me to be able to talk about it. For some reason, it was a secret. I kept it buried. Once I decided to tackle this demon, life changed for me. Focusing on the people that did not abandon me and realizing my father's decision to leave was not mine to own.

In 2008, I found my soulmate. When we met, he had two amazing daughters who I am so proud to call my own. I am thankful every day that they brought me into their life and that we became a family.

I like to focus on the blessings I have experienced throughout my life, specifically the amazing people who have been there for me, supported me and cheered me on. From my humble beginning with my mom, to my life now with many friends, family and mentors. They have taught me about unconditional love, dedication and are my biggest cheerleaders. They deserve my attention, focus and most sincerely, debt of gratitude. Thank you! When you focus on the good, the good gets better!

Taisha Teal is an artist, art therapist and event planner.

TAISHA TEAL
WAYRYNEN

As women, we often struggle to feel safe. Safe in our bodies, our minds and out in the world.

In high school, my parents warned me to keep my drink safe at parties. I had hopes of playing professional volleyball at the University of Santa Barbara. I also enjoyed being with friends on the weekends. Everything changed when I was taken advantage of. A few weeks later, I found out I was pregnant.

It became difficult to play volleyball as my body rapidly changed. My athletic dreams disappeared, but the hardest part was having an abortion and trying to finish high school without telling anyone. Knowing that women often aren't believed about being assaulted, plus the guilt I felt over the abortion caused me to keep this a secret for five years. I fell into a deep depression, filled with multiple attempts of suicide, PTSD, and daily anxiety.

When I found out I may have breast cancer, I saw several doctors. While the medication had some negative effects, it had some positive ones as well. It numbed my pain and anxiety enough that I was finally able to talk about what happened. I finally got the help and support I needed to overcome this trauma. I've found it liberating to help others overcome their own traumas through art therapy. Suffering in silence makes us feel disconnected from ourselves and others. The goal of my work is to help women and youth who are suffering to connect through art.

In 2019, my older sister Allexanne died of mysterious causes. With her connection to some powerful people, no one will share what happened to her for fear of their own safety. Unable to get justice or closure, I feel I've been silenced once again. Creating art has become an outlet for my grief. As painful as it's been, I'm grateful for the lessons that have come from this. I feel motivated to make the most of every opportunity whether I feel ready for them or not, embracing what comes from pain and darkness and turning it into something else. I choose to create uplifting, positive art that inspires self-love and happiness. We are all here to create!

Taisha Teal Wayrynen

Heather Mason is a survivor and advocate for traumatized incarcerated women.

HEATHER
MASON

Survival…hallowed be thy name! If my name wasn't Heather, it would be Survival. No memory exists that is not informed by drug or alcohol addiction. Addiction led me to federal prison.

Until 2018, my life path had been rocky and rife with dangerous pitfalls, like stumbling up a mountain in the dark, never sensing the edge before my foot slipped off it, stalked by hungry bears and cougars, no guide, my destination unknown.

With the grace of God, help from an excellent addiction recovery home and the Elizabeth Fry Society of Toronto, I have done much inner work. I have begun to understand why some of us are left to navigate life without a guiding light. The generational trauma of my caregivers led to trauma in our family unit, which then transformed into personal trauma from those within the family circle. This led to self-harm, medication use and extensive institutional trauma perpetrated by a government system designed to punish rather than rehabilitate.

My unique experience is enveloped within the broader familiar story of women. In one degree or another, the routine, covert, accepted life trauma happens to many of us so often that it becomes unrecognizable as a systemic problem. Instead, it is normalized as a hazard of being born female.

Now, I stand for women.

My daily life revolves around speaking up for women held behind bars who will face the life consequences of injustices inflicted upon them. Five other resilient women and I have resurrected an organization, Strength in SISterhood Society, designed to advocate for incarcerated women and ultimately abolish women's prisons. Working towards that end has led me back to school to train as a paralegal, allowing further insight into the justice system from the flip side. Alongside that organization, I am aligned with national and international women's rights groups. I tell my story and use my voice to educate and empower all women to speak up and work towards change.

My name is Heather; I have survived trauma, addiction, and prison. I am an advocate and truth-teller. My path lights the way for others to thrive.

Heather Mason

SURAYA
SOPHIA

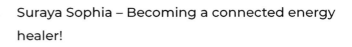

Born in war-torn Kabul, Afghanistan, at a young age, following numerous relocations, my family and I finally found refuge in Canada. Inspired by the sacrifices made by my parents, a desire to help them and others was forever instilled in me. I was driven to make a difference in other people's lives from an early age and knew I could help in some way.

Before I had any conscious awareness about energy healing, I experienced many personal challenges. Somehow, every day was a struggle for me; I felt uncomfortable in my own skin, and for a long time battled depression, anorexia, and a need to cut myself to release pressure. I then remember this beautiful, sunny August day, driving to work and looking up to the sky, when I suddenly became so overwhelmed that it led me to weep unstoppably. Pulling over to the side of the road, I looked up and asked, "Divine Spirit, I need your help"! Somehow, I knew a force was around me, willing to help and protect as I kept asking for guidance. Suddenly, I felt warmth and the sensation of someone hugging me. It was the most incredible feeling, and my sense of loss and deep sadness turned to tears of joy!

During that surreal moment I totally surrendered to a more divine power, which pulled me, quite literally, out of a dark place. Blessed to be a in a country that cherishes freedom and is plentiful with so many opportunities, my life was about to be become different. Suddenly, I started meeting some of the most amazing souls on earth, people who would guide me in the path of healing; something that I was unknowingly already intuitively practicing. I began understanding sentiments I had never known or appreciated before, learning new senses, and effortlessly receiving reiki harmony. I started becoming a pillar of light for which I understood was meant to define me.

With my new enlightenment, I was able to heal myself and began exploring how my healing work could help others. My purpose has finally been made very clear to me in this life; to be a conduit of love, strength, compassion, and healing!

Guinness World Record holder, 4x international best-selling author, founder of The Magic Within Coaching and Consulting Co.

ALAN
WADE

Never Ever Give UP

My story. At ten years old, my life would take a very drastic turn. I went into a church to look around. While in there, I was playing with some of the candles when I was grabbed from behind by someone. The man yelled at me, asking what I was doing. I did not even have time to answer him before he shouted that I was bad and deserved to be punished. I remember being shaken, and suddenly, there was a sharp pain and a ringing in my head. I remember feeling dizzy and unsure of what had happened. I remember being dragged and sort of walking, struggling to keep my balance within the room.

That man pulled my pants down, and the pain was excruciating. I remember the words, I deserved to be punished. When it was over, he dragged me to the church stairs and pushed me off them, saying I would be punished again if I told anyone. The pain was terrible, but I ran home; I'm unsure how, but I did. I cried the whole way and lied to my mom when she asked what was wrong.

The following five years were so bad and full of fear that I took a friend's father's gun at sixteen, went out into the bush, and pulled the trigger. I had been living in total fear, with night terrors whenever I slept. After the failed suicide attempt, my sadness and fright turned to anger and violence for 12 years, give or take, before starting the process of acceptance and forgiveness. The forgiveness was for me. I had blamed myself for all of those years. I would not tell anyone this story until I was nearly fifty years old, and it came out accidentally as I was giving a lecture on abuse.

That experience, and all of the other experiences in my life, have made me who I am today. I am grateful for everything that happened in my life. Today I have a coaching company that helps people overcome limiting beliefs and trauma quickly and effortlessly, without having to relive the experience. Love and light!

SABRINA
QUEIROGA

I was born in Brazil and grew up in a lovely family. As a kid, I was a quiet and attentive observer. I borrowed my parents' dreams as my own. I wanted to study and work in economics, become a successful executive, marry, travel around the world... but most importantly, be financially independent! I followed that plan. Life was good, filled with great moments and loads of hard work.

Inside my head, I had these nagging questions, asking what life is about? Why do we suffer so much when everything is so fleeting? I kept moving ahead, grateful for my life, but these questions lingered in the background. Suddenly, things started to change; I had a moment of enlightenment. I call it a click; I bet you know what I'm talking about. It's that moment when all the answers to your questions begin to pop into your mind.

This "click" is a sparkle, a brief moment that leads to a sequence of events, directing you toward your true path. Your body, mind, and spirit become aligned, and everything around you becomes more fulfilling: the time spent with your kids, your work achievements, time with friends, and life enjoyment overall.

I founded Click-y Health Coach because I believe that all you need in order to change your life is this "click" that wakes you up, inspires and guides you towards your purpose. My initial click happened in my first yoga practice more than 20 years ago. After that very first class, my life started to transform. Yoga gave me the space and the ability to look deeper within myself, helping me to understand that I'm responsible for my reality. It empowered me to change what wasn't serving me anymore.

I'm not saying that now you must run to try a yoga class... I believe that we are all unique. So will be our "clicks". But if you haven't had your sparkle yet, don't give up, follow your intuition. It's inside of you, just waiting for the perfect moment to show up.

Laura Lynn Ross has found her way to living a happy, healthy life.

LAURA LYNN
ROSS

Why do anything if it doesn't sustain you, enrich you, and make you feel happy and fulfilled in some way?

Life isn't always easy, nor has it been enjoyable every step of the way, but it has been one heck of a journey! Through ups and downs, I have come to learn that living doesn't require people to remain enmeshed in daily struggles just to survive. This is the message I strive to share with others.

At one time, struggling was all I knew, and even though most of my physical needs were met, I was extremely unhappy. I moved through life under the weight of responsibility, experiencing little to no time for fun and play. This perspective and mindset created my reality, but I didn't like the darkness. I tend to process fine details and abstract concepts with focus and concentration because I find a lot of meaning in creation, production, usefulness, and practical application, yet … my soul also yearns for whimsy, lyric, music, and movement.

In my early 30s, I recognized that other people seemed to have greater wholeness in their lives and a sense of balance, placement, and purpose that I had not yet found. Purposeful soul-searching, exploration, discovery, and heightened awareness have brought new understanding to my existence and life purpose.

I am happiest when I feel free to be who I am when I can choose what to do and how and when to do it. When I am myself - without restraint, constraint, or limitation- I feel a buoyancy that imbues all aspects of my life, maintaining positivity through adversity.

The most important lessons I have learned in life are reframing my thoughts and recognizing how strongly my thoughts drive my actions. I can choose to respond with grace to what life presents me with rather than react to it.

Actually, we all can!

Ever in motion, I seek to establish and maintain balance in all I do. In this, I am a work in progress. My days include curriculum development and training, Health, and Wellness coaching, writing, and publishing children's books, furthering education, and being a loving wife, mother, and kitty mamma.

Nira is a radio host and professional speaker who believes that one's true voice is the most powerful of all.

NIRA
ARORA

When I finally found MY voice, I found a true level of happiness.

Many people find this statement ironic coming from me since I have talked for a living for 20+ years. But there is a significant difference between being a professional communicator and connecting to your authentic self.

I'm still navigating how to use MY voice to represent my truth. But one thing is for certain; there is a level of happiness that has been triggered since I found MY voice.

MY voice now gives me the confidence to represent:
My beliefs
My passion
My vulnerabilities
My truths
My strengths
My weaknesses

I didn't realize this until later in life, but I was somehow stuck in a realm of knowing what to say and how to say it in order to appease those around me. To somehow make life less complicated for those in my circles and make others feel more comfortable around me. Not necessarily realizing that I was making more work for myself by adding all this pressure while simultaneously not being me. I was actually making MYSELF uncomfortable in the process.

As I reflect, it's not that people asked this of me, but somehow it became an unspoken expectation. Did they create this? Did I? Where did it come from?

Whether it was a cultural expectation, family expectation, social expectation, or professional, the basic idea was to not come across as 'difficult.' Whatever that means??

This is especially a common denominator for women and even more so, for women of color.

However, one day I realized the nonsense of 'difficult' and thanks to MY voice I have the confidence to say standing up for yourself does not make you 'difficult'! It makes you a resilient force to be reckoned with! A shining star! A beam of light!

And that perhaps may be why people try to suppress you with labels such as 'difficult.'

Find YOUR voice – your authentic voice.

It's usually sending you whispers from deep inside. Allow those whispers to become louder, allow them to shout at you to make those changes. Allow yourself to find and follow the path of your true happiness.

Nira Arora

Christina Wyatt is a Certified Financial Planner® based in Nova Scotia with a passion for lifelong learning.

CHRISTINA **WYATT**

"Experience is the hardest kind of teacher. It gives you the test first and the lesson afterward." – Oscar Wilde.

I believe my experiences have shaped the person I am now. At the age of 20, I became a mother, and by 22, I was a single mother with maxed out credit cards, loans with interest rates at 27%, a house I owed more on than it's worth, no savings, and seemingly no way out. There were days the furnace ran out of oil, weeks with few groceries and months without a cell phone – I knew I had to fix this for me and my son.

I started my financial journey and career at 22 – I became client #1. I spent years studying and taking courses while being a full-time single mom. There were long days in the office, learning from other advisors who became mentors and late nights studying, but never missing a baseball game, concert or important event.

I learned the strategies and planning that have enabled me to become debt free, sell my old home, save for my beautiful new home and accumulate savings and investments, all while building a life for my son and I that I had never imagined.

Now, 10 years later, I am a Certified Financial Planner,® a Chartered Life Underwriter and a Certified Cash Flow Specialist. I believe in lifelong learning and may never stop my midnight study sessions. I am a financial planner who shares my experiences with others so they can take my life lessons and learn from them.

My son is 12 years old now. We had a wonderful man join our lives when he was 6, who has become his father. He is an entrepreneur as well. With his dad owning and operating a construction company and me running a financial planning practice, it is almost inevitable that our son Ryland will also become an entrepreneur. For now, we enjoy watching him grow, never missing a game and providing a life where anything is possible.

It is amazing what you can do when you are truly determined – learn and grow from those experiences and create a life you are truly proud of!

Christina Wyatt

Trevor is based in Nanaimo, BC. He's inspired by pop culture and influenced by artists like Warhol, Lichtenstein and Basquiat.

TREVOR
AMON
PHILLIPS

In August 2013, I went to the Commodore Ballroom in Vancouver with some friends to see a band called The Breeders play. This would be a night that would forever change my life. On my way home I got off the bus at Main and 12th to walk as it was a nice night. I was waiting on the corner for the light to change, texting my buddy about plans to go fishing, when all of a sudden I heard a loud crash. I looked up to see an accident happening in the intersection, worse yet, I was driven into the building behind me, then, darkness.

I was in a drug induced coma for several days when I awoke in a room surrounded by curtains. I couldn't move and I was in a lot of pain. After what seemed like forever, a nurse popped into the room. I asked her, "where am I?" She told me I was in Vancouver General Hospital and that I had been in a terrible accident. Over the next five years, I worked extremely hard during my recovery to get back to where I was before the accident.

The accident made me think about my priorities in life and the need to follow my heart with my painting. Once I was able to stand on my own again and had the strength to move, I began to paint. I found a new life in my paintings as therapy and the absolute satisfaction in completing a project. I contacted a friend who ran Kimoto Gallery and asked if he would consider showing my art. He liked my work; from there my journey began.

I sold a handful of paintings through the gallery and was inspired to produce as people were interested. My wife and I moved to Nanaimo, BC to start fresh. We ended up separating two years after the move because of irreconcilable differences. Suddenly, things started turning around. I got into a boutique called Guava Apparel in downtown Nanaimo and a gallery called Le HangArt in Vancouver and Montreal. I've had to make tough decisions, but I'm getting recognition for my hard work.

Trevor Amon Phillips

Justin Madder is a former RMT turned real estate agent based in Kelowna, BC.

JUSTIN
MADDER

At 46 years old, I'm still continuously evolving and learning. After years of putting my all into my career as a registered massage therapist, teacher, and school director, the immense amount of stress combined with the inability to take time off led to burnout. I knew in my gut I was on the wrong path, but I felt like I had to forge on. I realized that I was so focused on achieving success, that it was becoming detrimental to the people around me, including my newborn son.

Emotionally, at this time I was becoming completely exposed; a realization came to me. The image I projected to the world didn't match what I felt inside. I was angry and frustrated; I felt confused as to why I was feeling this way. I had unresolved issues from my past that I had attempted to bury in work and other distractions. That's when I realized I needed significant change, and that change began with switching careers.

Moving into real estate was something I had casually dreamt of doing, but it took years to make the leap. Even when I did take that step, I struggled with letting everyone know, especially my previous students and colleagues. I felt as though it was a betrayal to my work in health and wellness.

The pandemic hit just as I became officially licensed as a realtor. The pandemic was hard on many people; I'm lucky to say that for me, it was an opportunity to seek growth and change in both my personal and professional life. It changed my emotional direction and gave me the most precious gift of all: time with my wife and son.

I once thought a career change was my biggest transition, but I've since learned that being vulnerable is not akin to being weak. The truth is, change is happening around us all the time, and we must embrace life as it's happening. Building a business in real estate has shown me firsthand that we need to consider our vulnerabilities when at an impasse with change. I appreciate the trust my clients have in me, it has allowed me to find my true purpose and embrace the fact that it's never too late to change.

Justin Madder

Petra Hermes is founder and owner of Fly & Sea Dive Adventures, a boutique style travel agency specializing in scuba diving travel.

PETRA HERMES

Scuba Diving's Lessons of Faith

1. BREATHE

A critical aspect of diving is proper breathing. Consistent breaths allow divers to be efficient with their air supply and enjoy longer dives. The same can be said for above water, throughout life. When I'm anxious or stressed, I don't breathe properly and I lose the ability to function well. Slowing down to take a deep breath can be calming, while reminding me to trust God.

2. EQUIPMENT

Diving equipment must be maintained and checked regularly. If it malfunctions, I may be in danger. This also applies to my connection with God; it must be kept "up-to-date." It's important for me to read the Bible regularly and be involved with my church. Checking "my equipment" is vital to keeping my faith real.

3. FRIENDS

The first rule of scuba diving is to dive with a "buddy" - a diver's buddy is their lifeline, not to mention someone to share the incredible experience with! Life can be difficult. In these circumstances, I need people to come alongside me. My faith in God ensures I am never alone. He provides friends to encourage me along the way.

4. TRUST

Panicking underwater makes me prone to forget what I've learned about diving safely. Panic is the biggest culprit leading to a diver's death. In the midst of life's challenges: illness, strained relationships, I'm tempted to panic. Psalm 56:3 "When I am afraid, I put my trust in You." Trusting in God's plan allows me to pause and pray, and remind myself He's in control.

5. HANDLING PRESSURE TO ENJOY THE RIDE

An important piece of gear is a "regulator". It takes the high pressure air in the tank and regulates it to the correct pressure. Life brings high-pressure times. God is like a "regulator"; He controls how much pressure comes into my life and provides me with the strength to handle it. He calls me to breathe and stay close to Him. My tendency could be to give up, pass, or head to the surface. In these moments, I choose to trust all I've learned and receive His peace. Psalm 46:10 "Be still and know that I am God."

CINDY
STIBBARD

I was raised to be fiercely independent. My mother may have described me as assertive, stubborn, and driven, which are the key traits that helped me become who I am today. My journey took me from a university student to a broke restaurant server to wine shop manager to elementary school teacher, to a married stay at home mom for 11 years, to today a single mom of two teens, a Radio Talk Show host, entrepreneur, and founder of two successful businesses.

Always being a go-getter, I never anticipated how my life and sense of myself would change when I got married. The truth of who we are is so essential that its absence takes a heavy toll, typically causing us to lose our sense of self.

During my marriage, I tried to be someone I wasn't. We had a lifestyle of abundance which unfortunately came with entitlement and control. At first, I accepted it because of the sense of calm security it brought. As I slowly fell into the background of my own life, lost financial independence, and adopted a martyr identity, resentment started to build. Who I was, and who I wanted to become was lost.

Accommodating the needs of others often leads us to reveal only the expected, dissociating us from our true selves, leading to emptiness and feeling alienated. Regulating for others in my marriage no longer worked for ME, leading to the hardest decision I have ever made.

Since my divorce, I have been exploring the layers of my self-limiting beliefs. I didn't become a "different" person, as many people assume might be the reason for divorce, just a stronger, braver, more confident, and authentic me emerged. My decision to leave resulted in a reawakening of a ReDefined me; a leader, starting my own business, running my own company, and making a difference in the lives of others.

My very public divorce drew others to me. I received countless texts and messages from other women struggling in soulless marriages. I knew I had to help. Today as a Certified Divorce Coach, Divorce Specialist, and qualified Discernment Coach, I am changing the experience of divorce for others.

Cindy Stibbard

Danielle Anderson is a freelance editor who loves helping authors improve their writing while maintaining their unique voice.

DANIELLE
ANDERSON

When I was in Grade 12, I sat down with a list of degrees offered by my preferred university and tried to decide what my career path would be. My top mark was in English, but I didn't want some desk job. I wanted to help people; to me, that meant working in healthcare.

Over the years that followed, my career took a winding path. I pursued a degree in kinesiology and health sciences, my intended profession changing every year. After graduating, I found work making and fitting custom orthotics, then switched to teaching exercise and fall prevention classes for seniors. Neither felt like the right fit. Throughout this time, I did editing on the side—a blog post here, a magazine article there—but never took it seriously. After all, editing seemed like the definition of a desk job, and while I wasn't sure what I did want, I knew it wasn't that.

Then, just as I started to think about returning to school, an opportunity presented itself: the chance to edit a book, start to finish. I normally wouldn't have considered a project like this as I was too busy. However, I was off work at the time due to a knee surgery, so I thought, why not? And as I worked on that book, everything clicked. I have always loved reading, and I found helping shape a book into its final form to be unbelievably satisfying. When everything wrapped up, I received a message from the head of the project: "This is your vocation in life, I hope you embrace it!"

As I switched gears and started pursuing a career as a freelance editor, I felt conflicted about giving up on my desire to help people. But as I worked with more and more authors, I started to see that I was still following that passion: I wasn't helping them with their physical health, but I WAS helping them find their voice.

In the end, I have learned that sometimes, finding your passion is not the end of the story. You also have to find the way you want to express it—and for me, editing is that expression.

David Burrows is the host of The Show with David Burrows. It promotes Music, Events & Community in Sarnia-Lambton. "The Show" is also a part of "The Video Show Network".

DAVID
BURROWS

When you think you're on top of the world, everything can come crashing down. One night I went to bed happy & doing what I loved & woke up losing it all. It was a distraught time in my life. It turned out to be the best thing that could've happened. What happened doesn't matter as much as what it taught me & how I overcame the obstacles. At times our advantages can be our disadvantages, and our disadvantages can become an advantage.

With support from family & friends, especially one friend who said to me, "get up and do something." I discovered that I had let myself become consumed in the fall so much that I forgot to look upwards. His words, although blunt, hit me. But what was I going to do? What skills did I have? I didn't know exactly. I just knew I had to start.

I had been a DJ & Karaoke host for 25+ years. So I took those skills to help carry me to my next journey. But, everything didn't come easy.

"I believe in you" is one of the most powerful statements another person can say to you. As a family man & friend, I love being involved in my community & supporting others. This is why I created my online talk show, "The Show with David Burrows" This would lead to my live-streaming business, The Video Show Network. This would then lead to me being the first in Canada to teach live-streaming & marketing at a college & then continue on to become an Amazon live influencer, which has taken my business to an international level.

It was up to me to get to where I wanted to be. It was essential to learn new philosophies that would help me grow. Changing how I think would be critical to my success.

The questions I had were, 'Can I do this, 'am I good enough, 'will this work,' and the answer is yes. Yes, I can!

I think everyone wants success; the problem is most people aren't willing to do what it takes to be successful, so don't be like most people.

David Burrows

Tyler Hatch, Founder & CEO of DFI Forensics, resides in suburban Vancouver, B.C. and started his company in July, 2018.

TYLER
HATCH

What is digital forensics and how did I get into it? I get asked this question a lot.

Well, I grew up in a world without the technology that many people couldn't live without in their daily lives now. I don't think I've ever taken technology for granted, but it's an incredible tool to learn, access information and make life incredibly efficient. I've always been fascinated by technology, but I never thought it was going to form the basis of my career and business.

It's not really surprising though. My father was an RCMP Officer and I practiced law as a litigation lawyer years ago. You might say that it was almost inevitable that I would find myself in a career with some form of investigation skills and a search for the truth at its core.

That's why I love digital forensics. We get to examine computers and cell phones to pick up clues and investigate a crime or legal event. That is what my business, DFI Forensics, does. It's a very specialized field that many people haven't heard of.

Imagine an employee stealing your company's proprietary data and intellectual property to take to a competing business? You'd be upset and probably contact a lawyer pretty quickly to take action against the former employee. But lawyers need proof to take to court and the crime scene is the employee's computer. It takes special skills, training and tools to examine that computer and gather all of the evidence to present to court in order for you to have justice against the thief. This is incredibly common and much of what we do at DFI Forensics.

Being an entrepreneur wasn't the direction I expected my life to take. I simply grew frustrated with not having the decision making abilities to run a business with integrity and a focus on the best possible work product provided to the clients.

Being an entrepreneur is the best thing that has ever happened to me in my professional life. I'm fulfilled, passionate about what I do and proud to build a small company with incredible future potential that is being realized more and more every day.

Lise Parton is a storyteller, expressive writer, author, poet, reader and artist who grew up on the west side of Vancouver.

LISE
PARTON

The Gift of Expressive Writing

I can gratefully write my way through anything! I've discovered my gift is the way I can capture words from inside my mind, my heart, my soul, or floating by in the Universe where I can capture them to create my pieces. I feel eternally blessed that my written words are my friends, my allies, my warriors, my cheerleaders, and my pocket therapist. I have learned that I am a 'playful' poet, a storyteller, an artist, and an 'expressive' writer. The ability to express myself through writing is a very powerful tool, in the toolbox of life. Journaling, or keeping a diary, are good examples.

I feel that my life, beginning in my childhood, was a bit different; I am quite sure it is because of the blueprints set down by my family, especially my father. Born the daughter of a baronet, my childhood was somewhat regimented. Set down was the proper and sequenced way I should act, what I was allowed to say and do, and how I should present myself to the world. All of this affected my belief system and how I saw myself. I also found myself not having the ability to freely speak or be authentically heard, resulting in me often being rather shy and lacking confidence. Being able to express myself through written words is the way I found my voice and bloomed.

I wrote myself through teenage angst, my first love, and parental divorce in my teens. I wrote myself a romance novel during a time in my life I think I needed more of it. I wrote stories to teach my children about the world around them in a wild forest on the edge of a beautiful lake. I wrote through a severe injury, my divorce and a life-altering move. Today I also write poetry for friends and celebrations, and by request. My life nugget for you is sharing that I write my own affirmations in times of trouble, record them to music, and then listen to them back as my own pocket therapist; that is so powerful. I also find my voice through song, laughter, dance, reiki, and decorating, but writing truly is my bliss.

JANINE
JONES

When people ask, "What do you do?" Do you talk about your career, or do you delve excitedly into your passion?

I used to think the correct answer involved one's career direction and recent accolades, maybe a house purchase, having children, tons of monetary gain, notoriety — all the things I was programmed to equate with success. I don't own a home, never have, I don't have tons of money, but I've lived and travelled. *I think it's the gypsy in me that never settled.*

In all truth, if you have health and happiness and a place to rest your head, you have everything. Peace, for me, is about appreciating what I have, not striving for something I don't.

I'm an artist by trade. It's my passion. I love to paint and draw, and I will always pursue it. I fall in love with the solitude of concentration every time I pick up the brush. But this story isn't about that part of me.

I moved back to Ontario from B.C. last year with the hope of a better work-life and closer proximity to family. The result has been reconnection with many I hadn't seen in 14 years living in Vancouver.

In November, I started working with The United Way Oxford and Women's Employment Resource Center as the new Program Coordinator for Food Forward Oxford. I now help Food Producers get food into the hands of Food Access Providers. My work in this area has deepened my gratitude and opened my eyes to what is truly important in life.

During the pandemic, many families saw lost wages, and the Home Insecure had it even harder, with insurmountable barriers limiting their access to safe, nutritious food. Each community needs to evaluate its food waste and concentrate on distribution to help the food insecure. Education is essential to understanding the difference between Best Before and Expired. The issue of Food Security is more important now than it's ever been. Not only does food chain efficiency help people, but it keeps more items out of landfills, also helping our environment. Has your meal planning ever required you to choose between paying bills or feeding your little ones?

Isah faced hardship for being gay in Uganda. Now in Canada, he strives every day to be his authentic self.

ISAH
NSUBUGA

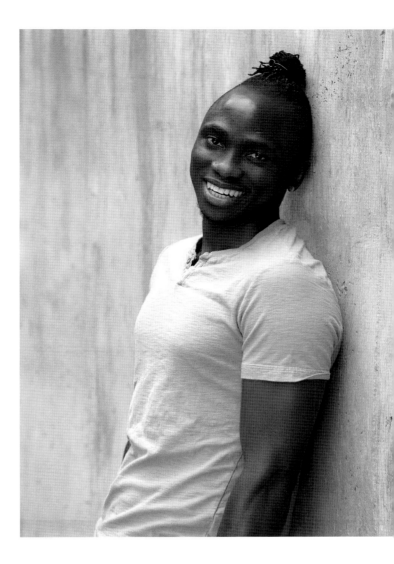

I was born in Uganda, but people who knew me would say that I didn't belong there, that I looked different. We have a lot of cultures and tribes; none allow homosexuality. The religions all say it's an abomination. They think it's a bad habit, something you choose.

I prayed that I wouldn't be gay. Fasted and cried. But nothing changed. The more I fought it, the more I felt an attraction towards men. I had to be very discreet, but people still noticed that I was gay.

I thought the end of my life had come when I was beaten up so badly that I couldn't walk. I managed to call my brother. He found me on the floor of my apartment and had to rush me to a clinic. I went into a coma for a week. When I woke up, I couldn't eat for three days.

Someone can face charges or be imprisoned for gay bashing, but they eventually get out. The law is on their side because being gay is illegal. You either go to prison for life for being gay, or you'd be beaten to death. I had to move away.

It wasn't easy applying to be a refugee. Some people wait for years. The offices were not always open. I stood there for hours for a piece of paper that got me into the system. They took refugees to a camp in the desert. The drinking water was salty, you got one meal a day. I had to talk about the times I had been beaten up for being gay, and they had to check with the hospital if my story was true.

When they told me that Canada had accepted me, I couldn't sleep for three days. I was worried that if I closed my eyes, I would miss something.

Even though people say that I'm safe in Canada, I still don't feel it sometimes. There is still fear in the back of my mind that someone may come to beat me. But I've seen myself changing. I've been doing projects that I didn't realize I could do. I'm grateful that I survived. I'm proud of myself now.

Isah Nsubuga

Nila Mushlovin-Cook. Dedicated Corporate Manager for one of 500 fortune companies and creator of an all-natural skincare line.

NILA
MUSHLOVIN-COOK

Two is the number of balance and the number of conflict and opposition. Without the number two, the positive and negative could not exist. Two is a number that has been intricately woven into my life. I am of two cultures, Ukrainian and Russian, and I have lived in two countries, Ukraine and Canada. I moved in the year 2000, dividing my life into the life before Canada and the life after Canada.

Growing up in Ukraine, I saw political unrest in the surrounding environment. After marrying and having a daughter, I wanted to reside in a peaceful place—my extensive research led me to Canada. It is the most tolerant and welcoming country, accepting immigrants as equals. Looking at Ukraine's current situation, my heart goes out to its people while validating the choice I made 22 years ago.

Arriving with a master's degree in Food Sciences, I started over as a lab technician and slowly climbed the corporate ladder. As difficult as this was, I was grateful to work and support my family in one of the most peaceful countries.

I currently enjoy employment in two different occupations, which correlate to various aspects of my personality. I am the national manager of forty facilities for Coca-Cola, committed to their ideals and upholding their brand, engaging my personality's structured, precise, problem-solving elements.

Secondly, I have created an all-natural skincare line, Neo Naturelle, which captivates the creative side of my personality. Dare to go bare! Neo Naturelle premise is that beauty has no expiration date, and we want to empower women and showcase their skin. A woman's journey is imprinted on her face, which is beautiful because her skin reflects the echoes of her soul. The skincare line embodies the beliefs and goals I have created for myself.

Advice for those embarking on a journey in a new country, come with an open heart and face your circumstances with love and kindness. Consider new possibilities to be opportunities; don't close your mind! I have never doubted my decision and am grateful to a country that accepted me as its own.

Nicole is a therapist, author and speaker. She is passionate about helping women live in the knowledge of their worth.

NICOLE
LANGMAN

What if we decided the rejections in life are actually divine repositionings?

And what if we could see them as pivot points leading us away from things not meant for us, towards a life more in line with our calling?

I never wanted to be a rejection researcher, but there I was, face down in the darkest valley of my life. When my husband of 20 years walked away from our family, I was catapulted into a new identity and a painfully up-close relationship with rejection.

Rejection is a soul wound. It shakes us at our core, sabotages belonging and connection and seeks to confirm everything we fear is true of us – that we are not enough.

I wrestled hard in those early days in that valley of rejection. The grief was thick, and the heartbreak, real. Very real. Little did I know I was actually on the cusp of true happiness. In a divine plot twist, rejection launched me directly into my true identity and a new found purpose.

My frontline research on rejection taught me three life changing truths: First, no human opinion gets the final say on our value. One person walking away does not represent the position of the masses. Second, rejection offers a training ground for building resilience. What we overcome no longer holds power. And finally, in my heartbroken struggle with identity, I was reminded that the only opinion that truly matters is the one held by my Heavenly Father.

He calls us chosen. And He pursues us with passion fueled by unconditional love. Understanding this truth offered the greatest healing.

As a therapist I work with brave and beautiful women who have experienced betrayal or rejection – leaving them wrestling with their worth. If you've been there, please know this - you are not what has been done or said to you. Your value does not hinge on the acceptance of others. You are made for greatness, you are highly valued. No human experience changes that truth.

If you have faced rejection or need to be reminded of your worth, pick up my new book, 'You Are Wanted - Reclaiming the Truth of Who You Are'.

Susi Vasseur is a youth life coach, mentor and math tutor energized by helping young people thrive and grow.

SUSI
VASSEUR

Free to be me.

I see myself living life as a treasure hunter, filling my map with wild and wonderful experiences, leading me to my life purpose. I love trying new things, being active and having fun. Fortunately, I grew up in a supportive environment that allowed this evolution.

My go for it attitude has been my strength to overcome life challenges, the first happening at birth. Unnoticed until my cute toddling was more of a limp, I was diagnosed with a dislocated hip that required surgery and a body cast for nine months, stifling my treasure seeking. Thankfully, surgery was successful and I was off and running again! In my early twenties, I injured the same hip playing soccer. Misdiagnosed for 10 years, my treasure search was embroiled with overwhelming highs and lows of emotion and pain.

I tried just about everything to gain back pain-free movement. In the meantime, I found a pot of gold. I got married to a wonderful man and had two beautiful children to love. I stopped looking at conventional medicine and instead worked with mind-body practitioners and energy healers.

The limitations in physical activity I experienced offered me time to focus my energy on learning all about human behavior; the power of the mind in healing, learning challenges, parent-child relationships and so much more. Books and courses in these diverse areas fueled me in my search for the magic wand to heal and grow.

My right hip became my constant teacher. Ironically, pain was one of the gems through which I learned lessons in patience, stillness, gratitude, perseverance and, most importantly, hope. These life lesson jewels are now my constant guide as I work with youth who need compassion and help in their learning journeys. Whether I am coaching, mentoring, or teaching, I realize that I really have a treasure trove of wisdom and experience to offer. If I can help youth in any way to find their purpose and strengths, I feel joy.

There truly is treasure to find when you decide to let challenges send you off to explore possibilities with an open heart and mind!

130

Laura's a children's author, podcast host, inventor, and mindset, sales & marketing coach who believes that everything starts with a dream.

LAURA
FOX

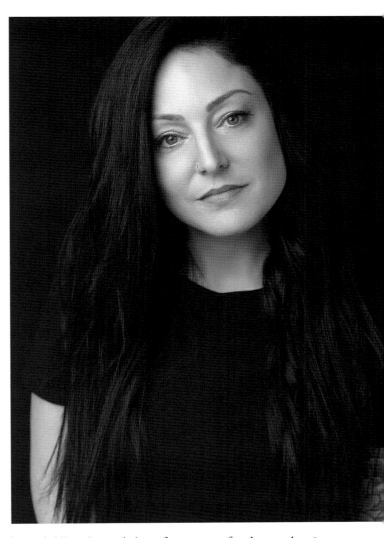

Life's Little Secret

A child's mind is fragile, literal and complex…

Lifting my desk, a scrunched up scribbled note rolled open…

"Meet me in the basketball courts at recess… don't tell anyone" - Scott

The most popular boy in school…was this for real? I had no idea this note would open my eyes to life's little secret.

At the courts… no Scott.

"THERE SHE IS!" belched out a young voice.

There stood the entire school- laughing, pointing … at me.

"She thought the note was real!"… someone chuckled.

My heart sank. I'd been tricked… ridiculed on purpose.

Tears streamed down my face as I dragged my feet home.

I went from feeling invisible to feeling like I was nothing, worthless. I wanted to die.

As an introverted child, often alone, battling other mindset ailments from childhood sexual abuse from a non-family member, I felt out of place and unseen.

"What's wrong?" my mom asked. "Nothing…" I replied, eyes down. She kept on…

"I can never show my face again…" I said, swallowing.

"Do you trust me?" "Do - you - trust - me?…" raising her voice.

"Yes," lifting my eyes for the first time that afternoon.

"Then trust me when I say; when you go back to school tomorrow, not one person will laugh, not one person will point and not one person will even talk about it. The only person who wanted to hurt you was the one who wrote that note, and 'who cares' about that person! Everyone else was just a follower and they didn't want to hurt you. I promise."

Holding her promise tight, I went to bed with a heavy heart.

I braved my bullies that next day…And you know what?

Not one person laughed. Not one person pointed. Not even one single person brought it up.

It was like it - never - happened - at - all.

Choosing death that day still shakes me to my core. If it weren't for my mom being present when needed, I may not be here today.

Life's little secret: Build a "who cares" mentality; the only part of life that matters is you.

A child's mind is fragile, literal and complex… it is also strong, confident and resilient.

MINDY ZARA
SMALL

I CAN HAVE IT ALL! A popular adage that doesn't ring true for me. I don't think it ever has. It comes from targeted messaging that focuses on the belief that a woman can efficiently juggle the four pillars of her life: family, health, employment, and personal interest. Life is busy as wife to one, mother to two, mother-in-law to two and grandmother to one with a full-time career. My active life is like a four-legged table, and when one leg of the table gets too short, it starts to wobble. Weekly visits with my grandson, Elias, bring my priorities into sharp focus. Keeping the table steady is about setting priorities and finding balance while maintaining a positive outlook. It comes from an awareness that we can not always have it all, but we can have what we need and want.

Now fifty-five years old, I remember growing up in Windsor housing with my mom and five siblings, sharing a single bathroom with a tub and no shower. Those were challenging times. When I was ten, we moved to London, which afforded me better opportunities. I rushed to meet them. Sometimes, when all the stars align and move us in a specific direction, we think that to be fate, but perhaps we can recognise it as an opportunity and say yes.

As a successful mortgage broker, I have spent the last 20 plus years building trusting relationships and using outside the box thinking to help families understand their options and achieve their goals. My client relationships are sacred, and I hope the knowledge I impart is lasting. Do I use the same method as my colleagues? No, but I have created a system that reflects my priorities and the needs of my clients. Do I have it all in the quintessential sense? Perhaps not, but I have everything I need. I have formed lasting friendships with many clients using my sense of humour.

Laughing with the people I work with spreads joy and creates positive outcomes. My supportive attitude, willingness to share knowledge and desire to pay it forward has changed my trajectory and the paths of others too.

James Eddington, chef / restaurateur of Eddington's of Exeter, host of Chef Table Tours and a farm to table ambassador.

JAMES
EDDINGTON

It is hard to imagine that one could fall in love with something by the feeling of the simple sounds of it.

I was a 13-year old mid pubescent gangly boy who visited a friend at their family's restaurant. Abruptly, I was told by a screaming chef with a Gordon Ramsey persona to "wait in the basement." Patiently, I sat quietly on an old card table littered with over flowing ashtrays and remnants of a half-witted coffee break that abutted an old overworked washing machine heaped high with colourful linens and soiled kitchen rags. I could feel the energy above me, and the sounds. Oh the sounds! The grind of the kitchen dazzled me with every heavy footstep, chop, sear and sizzle balanced between the sound of joy, laughter, cocktails being shaken and cutlery being piled high on a server's platter. I was enamored, I was curious, I was instantly captivated.

The next morning, I woke up early to hand write my very first resume. I put on my Sunday best, with all the intention to march back into their doors and apply for a job in the restaurant industry. Now, at age 44, it has been the best decision of my life.

Starting as a bus boy or full-time plate scraper, I worked my way and years through the industry ranks while earning enough to subsidize my restaurant management/chef post-secondary diploma.

Now in my 25th year of business as an independent restaurateur and internationally toured chef, I still take that moment to head downstairs to the basement and listen to that soft magical sound. The sounds of delight, laughter, enjoyment, hard work, dedication, commitment and balance is what represents WHY I work in an industry that I am so passionate about.

This industry has further extended my passion towards nature, farming and the appreciation of local, sustainable living and ethical practices, personally and within my business.

My lesson from all of this is to take those special moments to listen. Open your senses and follow your instincts, whatever they may be.

Cheers, "We truly hope you enjoyed your experience."
Chef James Eddington

Terrance Richmond is a creative visionary, activational speaker, and cultural pioneer focused on transformative relationships rooted in love.

TERRANCE
RICHMOND

I believe that everyone has a path to purpose, but how we get there is what makes each of us unique. Purpose never changes, yet the quest to fulfill that purpose is ever-changing.

Born in Oakland, CA and raised by a single mother alongside my grandmother and aunties, they committed to keeping me focused and sought to raise me right. This was anchored by their commitment to the Lord and their church family. As a child, I had a deep respect and reverence for the spiritual leaders in my life. From my childhood pastor to Dr. Martin Luther King Jr., I saw how they changed the communities around them, which in turn enabled them to affect a bigger global change – all fuelled by unconditional love. As I matured, that deep-seated purpose kept calling to me. Sports was a lifeline; I eventually played professional baseball straight out of high school and NCAA Division I Basketball, but the purpose to lead with love remained.

It wasn't until June 2007 when I truly committed to my purpose and made a decision to never look back. It called me out of destructive lifestyle choices that were not only affecting me but affecting my new wife and young daughter. I put down the alcohol, drugs and destructive language, fully committing to pursuing my purpose to lead. I now pastor and creatively develop people into global-minded leaders that remain rooted in unconditional love. I can confidently rest knowing that I'm wholly fulfilling my purpose as my wife and I lead an active and dynamic church community called Love Quest International Church. We are leaving a legacy of love and hope for our three children.

When you look at my circumstances, my path to purpose could have been one that kept me trapped in generational cycles of brokenness, and for a while, it did. From drugs and alcohol to crime and a lack of self-love, my path was filled with the same obstacles that many around me also fell into. Yet even in the midst of my brokenness, PURPOSE remained.

Tommy Chong is a multi-award-winning actor, director, writer, musician, comedian, cannabis rights activist, and one half of the comedy duo "Cheech & Chong."

TOMMY **CHONG**

The great thing about being a comedian Is that you're always searching for truth. And when you find it, truth will make you laugh.

That's why people have a hard time at solemn occasions, you'll have this uncontrollable urge to laugh; because that's the natural outlet for emotion. You can go angry, or you can go funny. You've got a choice. A lot of people go angry. They start ranting and raving. But the best way to handle it for your body Is to find the humour in everything – and there's humour in everything.

That's why when I was a kid, I always had a friend like a Cheech. He was like me, just bullied because I was small and couldn't protect myself, so I would find the humor. I don't know how many bullies got so pissed off of me because I would find their weakness and just mention it casually. They would smack you, but instead hitting back, you just question their bandwidth.

That's the best way to handle anything. I got a book called The Runner's Bible and it just puts all the good thoughts into different categories all throughout the whole book. I came across one that said, "lose your anger" and I love that. I thought, don't just be careful where you get angry, but lose it entirely. Lose your anger. Because if you lose your anger, then you're left with empathy, you're left with humor, you're left with a lot of positive things.

But the one thing you don't have any more is the danger of losing control, because when you get angry, you actually lose control. And when you lose control, your body gets affected because that's what stress is, a manifestation of that anger or frustration. Hate is another manifestation of anger, and sometimes it could be justified, but for the most part, there's no reason to lose your cool, because that's what happens when you get angry. You just lose it and all of a sudden, you're going off.

Lose your anger and find the humour. It's one of the best things that I've discovered.

Maria-Teresa Zenteno is originally from Chile. Living now in Quebec, she escaped to Canada as a teenager during Pinochet's infamous dictatorship.

MARIA-TERESA
ZENTENO

May is the month my grandmother, mother, oldest son, and many of those I love were born. The 16th of May is the day I arrived in Canada as a teenager, with more anxiety than joy; I had not chosen to leave my country nor my beloved parents, siblings, friends, and university. Being young and progressive was all it took to put one's life at risk under Pinochet's rule. I had witnessed several friends head into exile, prison or simply disappear. My parents understood I was not going to abandon my pursuit of social justice; thus, it was safer to have me studying elsewhere. I miraculously escaped before it was too late.

Challenge became my day-to-day companion, but I met amazing Canadians who were there for me from day one. I dedicate these memories to them. Ten years later, in May once again, struggling to master the English language and raise two children alone, I received an acceptance letter from my chosen university and met a supportive academic advisor. She became my guiding light and, knowing I was an atypical university student, encouraged me to pursue my dreams; she said the magical words: "Yes, you can!"

My imagination wandered, envisioning how wonderful her job was in empowering and persuading others that yes, in fact, they could achieve their dreams. I graduated from university and overcame a challenging audiological disorder in order to learn French. From timidly beginning ESL courses in Alberta, to becoming an advisor of students with disabilities at a Montreal university, the students I served for 25 years confirmed every day that "the impossible just takes a bit longer". This is a legacy I carried on from that professional advisor whom I admired so much, and whose words I frequently repeat in my coaching sessions: "Visualize your dreams and they will be fulfilled."

Now, working from my home office, I know I will never retire. I will always be that person who reminds every single coachee that "the impossible just takes a bit longer", while success can only be defined on their own terms.

Oh! I almost forgot... magnolia trees also blossom in May.

Maria-Teresa Zenteno

Rebecca Bollwitt is the CEO of sixty4media, a digital agency founded in Vancouver in 2008 as well as the publisher of Western Canada's most award-winning blog, Miss604.com. She is a nonprofit board executive, a magazine columnist, and has co-authored and edited five books on the subject of blogging and social media.

REBECCA
BOLLWITT

Photo credit: Bob Lai

I was biking down Fox Mountain in Williams Lake, rounding the final corner when I saw a crowd in the parking lot below. This was the inaugural ride of the new trail and I was invited to experience it while I was in town. I hadn't been on a bike in ten years. I waved to the folks below then my tires skidded on gravel and from their perspective, I disappeared into a cloud of dust.

Poof! I went down and the first thing I thought was: This GoPro footage is going to be hilarious.

I brushed off the gravel, made it the rest of the way, and met up with a local tourism representative, Beth, for dinner. Our post-event conversation was captivating, and we got on the topic of imposter syndrome, thinking we're not worthy, and in particular about when opportunities knock, how we as women should react.

Obviously I like to take on unique opportunities – hence the mountain road rash up and down my thigh from earlier in the day. Beth put down her fork, looked me in the eyes and said: "You always have to ask yourself: Why NOT me?"

Really. Why not?

Doors appear and opportunities knock every day: from big things that could change the course of your career to something small like an experience that will make for great memories.

Why not you? Why do you think you're not good enough? Why might you think you're not the most qualified or deserving? You absolutely are.

I started a website in 1997, was offered a position at a "dotcom" company in 2000, and moved to Boston in 2002. In 2004 I started a blog and in 2009 I was told "blogging is dead" and I should get a real job. As of 2022, I have published multiple books, won thirty awards for online publishing, and I've been invited to throw out the first pitch at a Vancouver Canadians game.

Why not me, eh?

You deserve options. Be on the lookout for these opportunities, and make some of your own happen as I did. Be prepared to dust yourself off and stand up again sometimes, but know that you made those experiences happen. ⸻

Rebecca Bollwitt

Bruce Gallagher from Victoria has a library of images that challenge the viewer's imagination. They exist because of his experiences.

BRUCE CG GALLAGHER

In 2006 I was finishing up an eleven-month period of therapy with an energy healer. It was a necessary chapter for advancing my personal growth; I had lost my partner of twenty-eight years, who died in 2004, and had a rocky relationship with my daughter.

When my therapist created a course on learning the techniques of energetic healing and other skills, I signed on.

On the first Saturday of the course, I found myself with thirty other people who held similar goals to mine. We had just formed a conga line with a guest from California who was leading students and staff around the room while pulling in energy from the Universal Energy Field. She caused all of us to move our bodies forward at a forty-five-degree angle without toppling over, and did the same backward with no ill effect.

Four Saturdays later, I was standing with the same group again, reciting the opening lines to 'The Prayer For the Six Directions'. My nose was about fourteen inches from a basement cinder block wall. As we started to recite in unison, 'Grandmother Spirit of the East, Gran...,' at that precise moment, this large powerful ball of energy came through the wall and hugged me in the chest area, specifically my heart. There are no words to describe the sheer power and presence, but I did know this was God, the Divine... and I was changed indelibly forever.

As we came to the conclusion of the prayer, I shouted out: 'Did you feel that?! Wasn't that incredible?!" Thirty-four people stared at me with question marks in their eyes. They had experienced nothing. From that moment, I knew that religion was illusionary and that God is love. Love unconditionally. Period.

From that point on, I have seen into the dimensions. I experienced telepathy. I have images of orbs, elemental light photons, and some events so mind-boggling that they can't even be captured at this point. This is a passion for me as I persevere with one new revelation after another.

I give a wonder-filled talk called 'The Gift' complete with photographs.

138

Kathi Moore is a lifelong fashionista with a passion for creativity and truth. She is a stroke survivor and an award-winning costume designer who knows the best is yet to come.

KATHI
MOORE

In my 20's, I was one of the young women who had a rare side effect from the early higher strength birth control pills. I was a healthy and active 24-year-old. The world was my oyster. Then I had a stroke. In fact, I even ended up in a wheelchair. But that is not my story. My story is that I am blessed to have a strong support system filled with loving family and friends that got me through my recovery journey. I worked hard to regain my movement and from there went on to a truly amazing life.

My story is that I travelled the world – places like India, Nepal, Egypt, and Vietnam – designing clothing and jewellery along the way. I climbed the second highest mount in Southeast Asia – Mount Kinabalu – AFTER my stroke. There was a hail and lightning storm. Everyone turned back for obvious reasons. I hid in a cave until it passed and then made my way to the summit. I sat looking at the earth and the clouds above me. It was there I truly recognized what a blessing life is and what is important.

On my return, I opened a bohemian-style boutique that ended up wholesaling to over 400 customers. I took courses in stunt driving and circus school. When the boutique closed, my lifelong love of fashion then led me in a new direction.

For the last 20 years I have been privileged to be immersed in the movie industry as a costumer and designer creating wardrobes that help define the characters. This career is not glamorous. There are long hours, early call times, paperwork, and lots of responsibility. But it has also taken me on the most incredible journey, introduced me to the most amazing people and is one I am completely passionate about.

Never let the hard moments in your life define how wide your future can be. I am here as living proof that your dreams are possible.

Kathi Moore

Jodi Brown lives and leads with power, inspiration, and authenticity. During 20 years as a CFRE-certified nonprofit executive, she raised and managed millions of dollars, and more importantly, built solid relationships and established links between critical organizational needs and donor interests. Jodi lives her motto that every interaction is an opportunity to change a life.

JODI BROWN

Broken Fences

At 33, my white-picket-fence life included the beauties and challenges of marriage, raising four children, and degrees and certifications that enhanced a career I loved, as a non-profit leader. I'd checked the boxes of all the goals I'd set for myself in my younger years.

And perhaps, the idea of living my so-called perfect life made reality harder when I was diagnosed with a tumor around my brainstem and suddenly lost control of everything I knew.

Time stopped, yet the clock hands sped in fast-forward motion at the same time. Moments and hours interchanged every day.

Without realizing it, I crossed the threshold between my old life and new life, forever leaving "normal" and "comfortable" behind.

What I learned from three craniotomies, 35 days in neuro intensive care, a spinal fluid leak, 12 years of facial paralysis, and 12 reparative and reconstructive surgeries cannot be defined in one sentence or a single life lesson. But what I can tell you is this: No matter what I did or could have done, alone, it would not have been enough to preserve my life. But when the right combination of people come together, lives are saved, children are cared for, bridges are built, and possibilities are opened. Sometimes miracles take time, but they are still miracles.

My new life entails becoming anti-fragile, growing stronger from the challenges that try to weaken and destroy me. To truly thrive, we must take control of the things we can control, and let go of the rest. I've let go of much, but I've gained more. Now I know that survivors are not mythical heroes, they are simply those who slammed the door when death came knocking. They persevere, day after day, no matter the pain, discomfort, or struggle. They know every day is a good day to be alive.

I'm no hero, but I am a survivor. And I keep going, not just for myself, but for the people who fight with me when I no longer have the strength to fight for myself. My white-picket fence disappeared forever, but I am now living a beautiful, messy life, and appreciating every moment.

Fifa Tran is the founder of FeiModern Creative Studio and is a blossoming introvert with more faith than fear.

FIFA
TRAN

Either you do what most people do: fear failure, keep that drive inside, and apply for that company job that doesn't look too bad. Or you can act on that talent, turn your passion into a business, and let your dream shape reality.

I've always been an artist at heart. I started drawing at the age of five and found myself building websites by the age of 10. I went through the same conventional path as everyone else; graduating and getting a bachelor's degree in a field I'd never get a job in. Faced with a language barrier and a lack of experience, I settled for mundane admin jobs and used them as my venture capital for six years to experiment with a ton of random side hustles. Some of which included calligraphy, influencer marketing, stock trading, reselling sneakers, dropshipping knockoff designer bags... you name it. Some failed miserably and put me thousands of dollars into debt, and others allowed me to earn some chump change for my next venture.

My hope with all of this was to be able to strike it big so I could call it quits.

But in 2019, the universe played its part and I eventually got fired.

Instead of looking for another job, I decided to take a chance on myself. I decided on a whim to pack my bags, rent out my condo and move to Toronto with no concrete plan. Only a thirst for new beginnings and nothing but faith that things would work out no matter what.

That's when I decided to hire my first business coach who helped me finally figure out the ONE thing I was truly good at—design.

This became the start to something much bigger than myself. For once in my life, I finally feel a sense of accomplishment and fulfillment in what I do. The growth I've experienced throughout this entrepreneurial venture is one I'd never trade for anything else in the world.

When you decide to shine your light, you inspire others to shine theirs.

Let this be your permission to take that leap of faith. Life is too short for you to settle for anything less than extraordinary.

Golfo Tsakumis is an internationally recognized artist and philanthropist whose work is featured in private and public collections around the world.

GOLFO
TSAKUMIS

Destiny and self-determination are the themes of this baby boomer artist's life journey.

To say my life today is in total contrast to how it began is an enormous understatement. Being born in a small, picturesque seaside town during the post WW2 and Greek civil wars meant I lived with food scarcity, parents that were constantly preoccupied with how we were going to survive, and dependence on neighbours and family for food and clothing. All these years later, I can still vividly remember waiting at my elementary school for the Red Cross to deliver packages of food to us from the U.S., and experiencing foreign foods like cheddar cheese and powdered milk for the first time.

Similar to many other women's stories, growing up in a lower middle class environment resulted in my getting married young; this would have the biggest impact on me as a human being and on the trajectory of my life. Immediately after our marriage, we arrived as a couple in Canada and the person I am today began to take shape. We were two young immigrants taking a huge leap of faith, beginning a brand new way of living. Nothing came easy. Newly-married and far away from our main support systems, we navigated loneliness, language barriers, homesickness and the typical stresses of daily life. Separately and together, we were determined to make our new marriage and our new lives a success. We chose to focus on our five children above all else. Their well-being and best interests energized us to hold onto our faith, remain loyal and be selfless to endure whatever hardships we would face.

The love and respect of the family we created has given me the most joy in my life and has unquestionably contributed to my self-worth. My husband, children and grandchildren inspire me to create art, to evolve, to keep learning, and to endure. I am proud and appreciative of both the smooth and bumpy roads; all the easy and difficult moments of my life now jump out of me and onto my canvas the moment I pick up my brush, resulting in the myriad of colours and genres that represent this immigrant girl's beautiful life.

Golfo Tsakumis

Bill Tsakumis is passionate about helping his community and is motivated by his faith and love for his family.

BILL
TSAKUMIS

When I think in 2022 how my journey began in 1941, I am filled with humility, gratitude, and pride. Born and raised during WW2 and civil wars that ravaged my home country of Greece, meant that I learned early on that I couldn't take a single day for granted. Pivotal moments in my childhood, like my father being taken by political extremists from our family home in front of my mother and us five young boys, and captured as a hostage for two months, would prepare me for the lifelong realization that nothing in life is guaranteed. Recent catastrophic world events like the refugee crisis in the Middle East and the war in Ukraine bring to the forefront for me such memories of the human consequences of political conflicts on children and families. Imagine living with foreign enemy armies set up right next to your home; we socialized with them, ate foods they gave us, knowing any time we walked by them could also be our last. I lived with worry, terror, mistrust, sadness, and sacrifice every day.

Yet, I managed to choose happiness for what I did still have, and I resolutely believed that there was always hope for something better. That hope brought me to Canada. With only 30 dollars in my pocket, I arrived with youthful idealism, strength, and an unwavering determination to work hard, save, and eventually return to Greece with money to help make our family farms a success. I had two older brothers in Canada already, but it still wasn't easy being a teenager away from the country and people I fiercely loved.

Eventually, I created a successful life here and it would ultimately become where I settled with my wife to raise our own family and create our permanent home. Blessed with a spouse that believed in me, I had the freedom to chase any dream that this immigrant boy wanted. My self-worth has always been tied to my spiritual faith, providing for my family, and service to community. It is who I am. However, the greatest joys in my life can only be attributed to my family; it is, undoubtedly, the reason that I choose happiness even during the hardest days.

Bill Tsakumis

LIZ
BENNETT

People often say, "once you have an eating disorder you always have an eating disorder" and, speaking from personal experience, that doesn't need to be true.

When I was young, I experienced sexual abuse from men who were supposed to be safe, and, when that happened, it made me seek things to control. I didn't consciously choose to start controlling any area of my life in a deliberate way, but it happened. I didn't like that someone else had control over my body, so I decided to micromanage and control everything that my body did and consumed. At 16, after being hospitalized, I had to attend the eating disorder clinic. I talked with a counsellor for years until she said I was fine. But I wasn't. I wasn't willing to look at the parts of my life that hurt or the reasons I felt that need to control.

When I became a personal trainer and helped others get fit and healthy, I realized I wasn't judging any of them by what their body looked like, but I did that to myself. At age 24, living in the discomfort of my unhappiness, I started working on the trauma that caused the disordered eating. The discomfort of living in my body began outweighing that of looking at my pain and trauma.

I started doing vulnerable work- counseling, energy work, exploring feelings, meditation and realizing patterns that I no longer wanted to continue. As that part of my story unraveled, my relationship with my body shifted. I began to appreciate my body for what she could do. I started enjoying flavours and food became a sensory experience, rather than a means of judging myself. I began choosing exercises for joy, and because of how I felt doing it - not for the aesthetic outcome. I'm still not perfect, and have moments where I'm critical of my body, or feel the need to control, but I don't live in that space anymore. It would be a stretch to say that I fully love myself and my body every day, but I'm getting there! I like myself and my body more than I did, and that's a pretty great place to be.

Medical Esthetician, business owner, and Mom to a beautiful daughter and a fur baby!

MARGOT
O'CONNOR

Growing up in a village in Nova Scotia, I was taught the power of faith and the gift of a close family. Both have carried me far in life. I never seem to take the easy route in life. Life lessons have left their marks. My inner voice became stronger, in my early twenties. I knew those dreams inside me had to flourish, so off to British Columbia, I went. I built my new life. I've spent my entire career in the spa industry, which served me well. My passion for the industry is as strong today as 26 years ago. I feel very blessed to connect with people the way that I do. I have been told that I should have been a counselor!

Helping people with their beauty needs is one thing, but listening to their problems or challenges, and empowering them, is rewarding on a different level. I have always been a big believer in pushing myself to continuously grow as a business owner, a friend, a mother, a sister, and a person of faith. I have learned the power of manifestation and putting needs out into the universe for the things I want. As the saying goes, be careful what you wish for! If I could give any advice based on experience, it would be, do not to stop believing or praying. Miracles do happen every day.

Turning the big 50 this year encouraged me to reflect on my life and allowed me to realize that I still have so much living to do. I'm now armed with the confidence and the wisdom I did not have when I was younger. My greatest accomplishment is being a mother and being aware of the example I must set for my daughter. I still have much that I want to create and learn. I continue to dream and make mistakes. I still love with my whole heart. I still forgive, pray and never lose hope. I refuse to settle. Life is far too short for anything less than amazing!

Margot O'Connor

Joanne Turnbull is a passionate advocate and philanthropist who genuinely enjoys being a part of the solution.

JOANNE
TURNBULL

When I was fourteen, my family moved from Toronto to a small town an hour and a half north of London, Ontario. I went from a fast paced metropolis to a rural hobby farm. I didn't stay long and I never looked back.

During the COVID-19 pandemic, I decided to go back to that small town. I was in a very rural area this time. I learned to drive a tractor and I loved being close to the water. Then, winter came, and during a pandemic, it felt even longer. I experienced hardship in a way that forever changed me.

I learned what loneliness really was. I was away from my loved ones and the rural isolation and pandemic taught me that my friends and family are an absolute 'must have' in my life. I was losing so much of me that I didn't even recognize myself. I did everything humanly possible to stay mentally healthy. I lost forty pounds and my health started to rapidly decline. When the province cancelled all elective surgeries, I had surgery. When I recovered I knew I needed to take better care of me. I was so used to caring for others that I completely forgot about me. I couldn't see a thing for what it actually was.

I fondly recall a grocery shopping trip. I wasn't in a good place to say the least. I had three women at the Walmart in Goderich stop me that day and each of them paid me a compliment. I was so touched by their kindness; something I hadn't seen in a very long time. I hadn't talked to anyone outside of the house in so long that I forgot how good it felt.

To this day, I think of the kindness that this little town offered me.

I am not leaving this small town stronger, but I am leaving wiser. I have another pursuit and it's to advocate for the brave women who are isolated in rural areas, and like me, weren't able to have a voice.

To those three women who stopped me in the Walmart that day; I will never forget your kindness.

Amanda is a mother, Founder of Radical Transformation, Creator of Transform Your Life Methodology, Certified Life Coach, EFT Tapping Practitioner and Numerologist.

AMANDA
CONNELL

I can pinpoint two distinct periods of time in my life that I would call a "dark night of the soul." When I was a kid, I decided a whole bunch of things to be true about myself and life; life is hard, you're not good enough, smart enough or worthy. Combine this belief system with unresolved past trauma and you've got a perfect storm. Not surprisingly, after a series of poor decisions, I found myself on the verge of mental breakdown, homelessness, and addiction. As I was flirting with how far rock bottom could really go, something inside of me awoke. I had suffered enough, and I knew there was no one coming to save me. It was time to take responsibility for my life and make some BIG changes. And that's where my transformational journey began…

Fast forward to 2020….I received therapy, I got married, had a baby, had a full-time corporate job, started my own business on the side, and life was perfect. Or was it? Just when I thought I had it all figured out, another 'dark night of the soul' experience would change my life forever. The Universe has a funny way of redirecting you when it's time to call yourself higher. I had two devastating miscarriages, lost my job of 8 years without warning, lost friends and family members, and our family income was slashed to just 25% in a few short months. At that moment, I knew I had a choice - react or respond. I chose to respond.

It was in this new awareness, realizing that I had the power to choose how I respond to life, that something deep within me shifted. I had a belief that I didn't have the power to change my life. I believed that life was happening to me and the answers I was looking for existed outside of me. But the truth is, everything I needed I found within myself and understood that when I transform my belief system my entire blueprint changes.

147

Photo by Darren Ballingall / Blondies Boutique Dress

Jill Maria Robinson is an independent social media relations consultant, magazine publisher, actor, interviewer, and writer.

JILL MARIA
MATEAS
ROBINSON

Sunday mornings are special. That's when I walk through Nose Hill Park, the highest point in Calgary, and gaze eastward, thinking of my family almost 9,000 kilometres away in Romania.

Thirty years ago, when I was three, I made news across Canada. There were many stories about thousands of babies adopted in Romania; I was one of those babies. But the story of my adoption told to my Canadian parents was a lie. It wasn't until I finally worked up the courage to travel to my birthplace that I was able to find the truth about my biological family, heritage, and myself.

Two years ago, I traveled back to meet my Romanian family. At the Bucharest Airport, my brother Fernando and two cousins, whom I had never met, embraced me, rushing me off to my birth mother. Tears streaming down my cheeks, I ran past 200 relatives and hugged Garofita Mateas. Amazingly, my first words were: "Oh, we look so much alike."

I knew for Romanian babies to have been adopted, there had to be 'just cause.' Papers my Canadian parents received from corrupt government officials were filled with lies about my parents being unfit to raise children. So, I was put up for adoption. Officials received kickbacks from unknown sources. My Canadian parents were tricked, told I was living in an orphanage when I was living with my family.

When my mother and I were reunited, I learned my birth father had died over 20 years ago. My mother explained how my Canadian father, Ian Robinson, who recently passed, had come to Romania in 1991 and was introduced to Garofita by 'officials.' He and his wife wanted to adopt a child that they could love and give a 'new life of opportunity.'

My birth mother cried as she told me how she agonized over making such a dreadful decision. She revealed I had medical issues and believed my life would be better in Canada. She said she prayed one day we would be together again.

Now I have two families. Both so different. Both so loving. Both that I am so thankful for. The future and truth does unfold in mysterious and unexpected ways.

Jill Maria Robinson

Christa is driven to continue following her dreams, always being creative and artistic with a desire for constant learning, improving.

CHRISTA
RIVINGTON

Born in North Vancouver BC., I've lived most of my life in Nanaimo and have resided in the Fraser Valley since 2012. As an entrepreneur, a professional photographer, screenplay writer, producer, director of independent films and an actor, I have the strong belief the superpowers of women are numerous and exemplifies my characters when writing screenplays. I've been a professional photographer since 2002 and began writing screenplays in 2019. I thrive on being creative and artistic.

As a child I had a strong bond and love for animals, almost on a different plane. With this great empathy towards animals, I've surrounded myself with dogs, cats, horses, and birds all my life, including rescuing many over the years. I'm fiercely committed to several advocacy groups for the protection and humane treatment of wild mustangs and burros in the U.S. and Canada, among other advocate groups for all animals.

As we navigate through life, I believe things happen for a reason, to teach us what we need at the time. This is something I believe in and remind myself of when experiencing the lessons of life. Life is hard sometimes, and it can be very difficult to find the drive or desire to go on. I know, I've been through some horrendous things most people have no idea about. Is there a reason I needed to go through these bad things in my life? Was it to make me stronger? As bad as it was, I know it could have been a lot worse, and I'm thankful these experiences taught me what I needed. Life's journey is all about learning as we go; if we don't learn the lesson, we go through it again, until we do. I also truly believe people of similar mindsets or life paths are brought together. We need to be aware of these people, they were sent to us for a reason, as guides or true friends. As women we have powers that men do not possess, we're much stronger than we know. We have the ability to conquer our fears, our doubts and can rise above all to be the warrior we're destined to be.

Lili Wexu is a prominent Canadian and American voiceover actress. She's also an author and has written extensively about her field.

LILI
WEXU

Hands down, my favourite metaphor for life is the one about lemons: "When life gives you lemons, make lemonade." It was written on the obituary of an actor with dwarfism who always remained optimistic and became a legitimate stage actor despite other people's views about his disability.

Having grown up under difficult circumstances, I often felt like I got the short end of the stick, and that the deck of cards was stacked against me. While I generally did the best I could with what I had, I wasn't always able to notice what actually worked in my favour. Like how resilient, intuitive, hard-working, determined, and energetic I am, and the important role those attributes would later play in helping me rise above my circumstances, creating my own success.

One of the most painful episodes of my early childhood forced me to become perfectly bilingual at a young age. This is now one of my most valuable assets and it helped me carve a unique path in my industry. Looking back, my entire 25-year career as a voice actress seems at once a crystallization of everything I am, and a revolution against that terrible hand I was given.

So, would I be who I am without those "lemons" I got? Hard to say. But, feeling short-changed made me:
- Determined not to settle;
- Want to define myself on my own terms;
- Seize opportunities and act upon them.

It also made me a very hard-working individual who always gets up after a fall.

In the end, those lemons fueled me. They enabled me to make a living in three different countries, they gave me the privilege of announcing at the Olympics, and allow me to continue lending my voice to exciting gigs, clients, and campaigns, 25 years in.

So, those lemons turned into pretty fine lemonade after all. Today, I can't help but be grateful for those lemons. In fact, the one thing I go to bed with every night, aside from my husband, is gratitude. The rest, I've found, is just good old-fashioned hard work.

Shelly Smee is a realtor, educator, arts patron and dog mom. 25+ years industry experience, 5+ years as managing broker at Oakwyn Realty.

SHELLY
SMEE

Holding on and letting go. When to push, when to pull. The sun, the moon; this is the Yin and Yang of life. In trying to understand what the universe has sent to me over time, I appreciate a fundamental shift has occurred simply because I stopped reacting. I have cultivated a quiet confidence. I stand in my own space feeling like I deserve to exist. This may seem a natural state of being for some, however, for me it is a new sensation that still catches me off guard. When it does, I take a deep breath, smile and let the knowing flow through me.

Covid has been a blessing. Yes, I said it! In the last two years I did all the things: ended an 11-year toxic relationship, bought a home, renovated said home, got a puppy, invited a relative to live with me, formed a real estate team with a long-time friend and colleague, and located a new creative studio space. I closed 2021 by moving my office one door down the hall. I've contemplated every item I own and curated each space. Fresh energy in every facet of life feels revolutionary.

What I learned from this (other than I have too much stuff) is it is possible to reinvent your life in a really short period of time. It started with a single decision, then an action. The next logical steps fell into place as the universe rejoiced in my re-alignment with my purpose. Magik.

The initial decision was to put myself first. It sounds easy when Oprah says it, but it was one of the hardest actions I've ever contemplated. It forced me to examine every relationship and decision.

Saying no to that which does not serve my purpose is easy. I no longer feel burdened by obligation, as I have already vetted my commitments. There is true power in living like this; for that I am truly grateful.

Putting myself first. No Excuses, no complaining; I'm taking responsibility for every facet of my life. It is not selfish, it's what a mature grown ass woman does when she is not willing to settle.

I am enough.

151

Nadine Sands - 2x best-selling author, fitness instructor, vice president of Project Wellness (parent's society that drills wells in Africa)

NADINE
SANDS

I am told she waited patiently in the driveway for me to arrive home for the first time. She invited neighbourhood friends. She was five. Since that day, my big sister Elanna has been by my side.

She welcomed me under her covers at night when I was afraid, praying with me even way back then. She coached me on a two-wheeler, and later, in the driver's seat of her Chevy Chevette when I was barely sixteen—going way too fast for her liking.

When I ran off and eloped at nineteen, she didn't say one critical word to me. She happily threw me a bridal shower. She has always showered me with unconditional love.

When I was a young wife and mom, she assured me that I was doing a good job.

After my husband Mike was diagnosed with ALS, she and her husband and children opened their home to us. We could no longer manage the stairs in our house and struggled with other things. They even did renovations to accommodate a wheelchair and additional equipment needed.

She accompanied us to Mike's neurologist appointments. She brought snacks and provided laughs.

She fed Mike through his feeding tube and massaged his hands and feet and rubbed his head. She sometimes helped me get him to bed, especially towards the end.

She was right beside me when I said my final goodbye to him. She was devastated too—they were wonderful friends.

From proof-reading my manuscripts, to my book signings, speaking engagements, an ALS advocacy award — every step moving forward, including falling in love with another man and getting married again, she has been right there beside me.

Elanna, you are an example of fierce loyalty. You model many exemplary qualities, including steady faith, exceeding compassion, and a love that goes above and beyond. Thank you for being a rock, and a soft spot for me to land. Your encouragement, support, and prayers have been invaluable to me over the years and continue to bless my socks off. I am grateful beyond words for you!

Every woman should have a sister who is a best friend, or a friend who is like a sister.

Isabelle Honing has achieved her Reiki Master qualification since writing her story. She's excited to graduate school and has a very bright future ahead of her. Her movement of #beinclusive on June 1st is the catalyst to having her feel seen, heard and that she's enough. We all need to feel these things and Isabelle's #beinclusive movement is all about that!

ISABELLE
HONING

I tell my mom, "I love my life" every day. I am very grateful for my family, friends and teachers. I have two brothers that love me to the moon and back and the best mom and dad in the world.

Every June 1st is #beinclusive day. My mom started this movement for me because I was bullied. We decided to wear blue because blue represents the throat chakra. The throat chakra is about communication. Please wear blue June 1st and post pictures on social media. Love each other every day, not just on June 1st.

When I'm not in school, I'm singing and drawing while playing Minecraft. I'm also known as the puzzle queen and have a photographic memory. I have been dancing since I was three and I pride myself in picking up choreography.

This past summer, my mom, Reiki master Lynda Honing, taught me Reiki level one and two; I'm very proud of myself as it was very challenging. I know when people need my loving, healing touch. I am also good at massage and so is my brother, Makenzy; he's an RMT like our mom. Makenzy is smart and artistic. My brother Spencer is an author and computer wizard. He can make anything on his 3D printer.

I love to walk in the woods, hug the trees and exchange their energy. I say a prayer and give thanks for them standing tall and cleaning the air for us. I love to skip rocks in the ocean and smell the fresh air. I close my eyes and breath in and out. I learned to sail last summer on Pender Island and can't wait to do it again. I love the outdoors and the stars.

I love to laugh, play Uno, cook, hike, camp, play badminton, hula hoop and swim. I'm looking forward to all the adventures ahead of me. I hope that one day I will sell my art and become famous. I'm graduating this year and can't wait to see what's next.

Most importantly, when I look in the mirror, I say to myself, "I love you, I am beautiful, sweet and caring. I see you Isabelle... I believe in you!"

Isabelle Honing

Lynda Honing, owner, The Urban Oasis. Reiki master teacher ~ massage. Dancer, athlete, gardener, visionary, co-author: Pursuit: 365, creator: #beinclusive movement

LYNDA HONING

Defining moments.

Being hit by a drunk driver at 19, having my face cut badly, among other injuries. Turning this traumatic experience into a lifelong quest to be my own best advocate. I ran my first marathon at 20 as part of my recovery, which led to several more marathons. This life event taught me that I am strong and can do anything with the mindset of determination. It set me on a path of healing and perseverance that I still live by 44 years later. I've been in 9 MVA's since then; those accidents remind me that life is precious and to embrace every moment. I learned that falling down is a reason to get back up. I feel I'm a better healer because I understand pain and suffering.

For the past 15 years I danced in a competitive group, cycled in the ride to Whistler, cycled up the Mt Baker Hill Climb, participated in several triathlons with the most challenging being "The Escape from Alcatraz." Swimming across from Alcatraz prison was the most difficult thing I've ever done. Jumping out of an airplane at 10,000 feet was easier! These races proved to me that I had confidence in myself to overcome anything!

I've enjoyed many careers: ECE teacher, dental assistant, financial advisor, hairdresser, bistro manager, family resort operator, chiropractic office assistant, Reiki master healer teacher, massage specialist, master gardener, home decorator and most importantly... MOM of two beautiful boys and my gifted daughter.

I've lived in Whistler, Mexico and Kelowna, which is where I found my love for mountain biking. I've travelled to many parts of the world, embracing my love of adventure.

So many jewels I've learned along my journey. Grateful...

As I've "grown" through my life, I've allowed myself to adjust my ideas and reinvent myself to match where I am in that moment. There's been many versions of me. Growth is necessary, how we respond is the magical part. Finding a way to make it a great day no matter what has been my motto.

I'm a visionary, adventurous and inspiring. I intend to teach Reiki to many and aim to have my #beinclusive movement for my daughter go global.

Roman Rozumnyj is a practicing West Coast modern artist, interior architect, and set decorator. Artworks are influenced by life!...

ROMAN
ROZUMNYJ

"IF I COULD EXPLAIN IN WORDS WHAT I AM FEELING... I WOULD NOT HAVE TO PAINT IT"....

Is it too cliché to say I draw my inspiration/motivation directly from my family... my wife, Andrea, my daughter, Ulyana, and my son, Yurdan?

I'll just tell you this: absolutely no one has a magic book or magic wand that makes everything perfect and smooth...

We all stumble through parenting, we all stumble to say and do the right things, we all try to lead by example and simply hope and pray that whatever we do and say resonates. In fact, we stumble and fall, a lot! And I'm now convinced that I am now learning more from my children (soon to be adults) than they are learning from myself and Andrea!

"Be in control of your own destiny!" is what I tell them, and what I hope for.

It is never too late to start something new. Be bold! Embrace who you are and always finish what you start. It's okay to be scared, it's okay to be lost, it's okay to be overwhelmed!

How do you eat an elephant? One bite at a time.

Life is a journey... embrace it! And always be true to yourself!

It is difficult to put into words the emotions one feels for loved ones. Sometimes it is better to be an ear and listen than lecture... because THAT is what is sometimes needed!

You don't always have to have the right answer, because a lot of times, you don't.

Raising a family is a journey that has no map, just a winding road which you must eventually stop at and allow them to continue alone, with nothing more than the wisdom you have given them. To see them look over their shoulder as they dissent into the horizon, and catching a glimpse of that reassuring smile beaming from them. That is what I truly hope and live for.

Too many times I stumble, and too many times I didn't quite get it right. All we can do is try, try, try... till we?...

I bundle all this energy up and explode it onto a canvas. This is why I paint. Life is art and art is life...

Roman Rozumnyj

Aurelia Vida is an entrepreneur and business owner, helping people reach their full potential by empowering them to take charge of their own health!

AURELIA
VIDA

Success is measured by how many lives we change!

I have always wanted to help people heal. I believed that my hands were special and had healing powers. At 18, I came to Canada. I had a hard time adjusting to this culture, away from my mother and taking care of my younger sister. I had to mature right away and take life seriously by getting a job and going to university full time. After seven years of studying the nursing program, I became a registered nurse. But I realized that this didn't fulfill me; instead it brought me so much sadness. At 30, I got injured while at work due to a heavy workload. I was treated badly by management and I could barely walk for two months. That is when I realized that no matter how much effort I put into my work, I will never be appreciated or respected. That is the moment when I went casual and opened my own clinic where I could make a difference in people's lives by reducing pain and inflammation using various technologies, intuitive massage techniques and protocols. In the last four years, I have made a difference in the community. I am proud to say that I truly helped people recover from their injuries and reduce their pains by at least 70% without medications or invasive treatments. Money can be borrowed, but health cannot! We need to take care of this body as much as we can, in order to enjoy life to the fullest!

Looking back, I can say that all the suffering I have been through was a blessing; it taught me to be strong, it pushed me to become more creative. It changed me into who I am now. I realized that I have within me the power to change my life, and then, I felt empowered. Now I can empower others.

Now I live in alignment with my purpose; I live a life beyond my dreams! Never give up on your dreams! Never underestimate your power to make a change in this world! Remember why are you here on this Earth! Pursue your purpose and enjoy the journey. Life is magnificent!

Danielle Comeau is the CEO of risk advisory firm, Wesben Global, a creative circus performer and passionate community contributor.

DANIELLE
COMEAU

The pivotal factor. That one event, person or moment that happens, unforeseen, unplanned, and for which you are often completely unprepared. This has redirected my course more than once, but also gifted me with a depth of experience I never otherwise could have imagined.

I am both creative and scholarly – I love music, art, language, community, and performance culture. I'd say that my younger self was also very deliberate with my life plan. Focused on my goal of becoming a humanitarian lawyer, I studied law and politics with a lens concerning international development. I envisioned a corporate career as the necessary means to this end.

Enter the pivotal factor – an opportunity to live and work in Afghanistan to support the Canadian military. This shaped my humanitarian awareness, but for years thereafter, I was underwhelmed by my own achievements. Despite completing two additional degrees and having worked for three of the largest global firms in my field, I always felt that I should be pursuing something more meaningful.

Until now, there was always the next degree, next client, next project, and next plane to catch. But in my 40th year I forcefully shifted, and for the first time maybe ever, I had the luxury of time. I slept a whole night, uninterrupted. I barrelled down a ski hill on NYE, waking up on a Caribbean beach in January, pausing to exhale the stress. I spent quality time with family (not rushing to catch the next plane), sat back and watched quietly as the world slowed down, yet still I thrived through a pandemic.

I played the guitar and keyboard for the first time in years and became lost in my love of music, centering myself through my passion and performance of circus arts. I rebalanced, but to do this, I had to park perception, and most notably, my own, about whose opinion really matters. This led me to become the CEO of an advisory firm, and more connected to those who share my passion for true sustainability and social values.

Mostly, I came to appreciate the irreplaceable value of time, slowing down to realize my greatest happiness is living holistically and enjoying life in the moment.

Danielle Comeau

Michele Young-Crook is an Author, Consultant, innovator, retired CEO, and loving mother.

MICHELE
YOUNG-
CROOK

"If it doesn't bring you joy, don't do it." I gave too much energy to things that didn't make me feel satisfied in the past. I am now making more of a conscious effort to ensure I am spending my time and energy on things that bring me happiness and positively impact others.

I sacrificed so much more than my time when I was climbing the corporate ladder and feeding a ravenous ego. I was always in such a go-go mentality to prove that I could be successful at the top. I stepped back recently and realized how all of that was negatively affecting my family's mental and physical health and my own.

The last year was a real awakening to me and that I was not making my family or my health my number one priority. I now make sure that whatever I am taking on doesn't take away from their emotional needs when it comes to business. My children and husband keep me motivated, and they are why I have grown so much in the past few years. We started a weekly family check-in, which truly put things in perspective. I want to be present in their lives and understand their daily worries and wonderings.

Since 2022, I have pivoted my priorities substantially. Now I choose to work with only those that align with my values through my consulting work. I just finished writing a series of non-fiction children's books that are in the process of being published in May 2022. I have partnered with a few Indigenous and women-run organizations to assist with their growth and how they can hit their target audiences. I recently created a Tik-Tok account as a segway to get back into standup comedy. I did standup for four years and had to quit when I became CEO of a national organization as it was time-consuming.

It has taken me a long time to love myself through my imposter syndrome. I realized that I am a lot stronger and more intelligent than I gave myself credit for, and everything I am going through is shaping me to be someone who will make a difference and help others. The same can be said for us all!

Michele Young-Crook

Kris Hall is travelling the world on his motorcycle living out his dreams.

KRIS
DENNIS
HALL

As a little boy growing up, riding my minibike was a big part of my life. I would come home and tell my family about the people I had met, the animals I had seen and the amazing stories from along the way.

I have spent a lifetime putting on my helmet. I've put on my helmet with family on weekend snowmobile trips, riding around the local trails and backwoods with my friends, and I have put on my helmet racing at the highest level, when you are so nervous you can't even feel your legs.

But now, when I put on my helmet, it all goes quiet and it's just me and my motorcycle. I feel an incredible sense of freedom.

There is a saying things happen for a reason. I honestly believe things happen and you make your own reasons. In 2020, so many things came together in my life to allow me to fulfill a dream that's been burning inside me for as long as I can remember: to ride my motorcycle around the world.

This isn't the life for everyone, but it's the life I have chosen for me.

I've always said, you don't know how strong you are until you need to be strong; these are words I live by.

This next adventure won't always be easy. There will be challenges and adversity. There is a sacrifice to everything in a life worth living. I have left everything I have known my entire life for what I now call my biggest "quest."

From a little boy riding around on his minibike, to the man I am today, riding his motorcycle. The truth is, I'm still that little boy inside, just doing what I love to do. Meeting new people, seeing amazing things and riding around this great big beautiful world.

Kris Dennis Hall

Experience life, cultivate friendship, create memories. Life is good.

BELINDA
HIEBERT

How interesting… this year my guiding word is "discipline" and my personal goal is to quiet my voice and listen better. So, naturally… I'm using it to compose these words. When I agreed to write, my intention was to show support to a woman who has been a quiet, constant voice encouraging me to be brave and take action, but agreeing to write also felt completely incongruent to my goal.

I questioned how to bring this exercise into alignment with my person as it is right now, as well as who I'm trying to grow into. As I contemplated what to write about, the words began to filter in a cohesive direction. This time I didn't try to push it or invent the moment as I had so often in the past. I listened. Carefully. I allowed myself to observe how the words I wrote affected me and if they were a true reflection of what I wanted to accomplish. Three thousand words later, they weren't, so I'm quieting my voice.

Instead of my story, I invite you, in this space and time we are sharing, to tell yours. Even if it's just a whisper only you can hear. Not all words need to be told to others, but neither should they fall on deaf ears… and maybe your story makes you feel uncomfortable, or justified, or hurt, or supported. Whatever feelings are brought up… hold on to them, and when you're ready, ask… are they true? Do they help me move forward to becoming a better self? Look for the words and actions that make you feel truly supported and capable. There's no right or wrong, and certainly no judgment… not from me. I'm simply a page in your life, holding space for you to take time to reflect and be honest with yourself. To work through what ever you're in right now.

I can't give you an unshakable faith in yourself, that faith which gives you the resolve and confidence to follow your voice. I can, however, offer you an opportunity to start listening, to experience each moment fully aware and present, because its these moments, when strung together, that create your best life.

Belinda Hiebert

A creative soul who trusts her purpose and is embracing her gifts

JESSICA
JEWELS

Trusting in the universe and myself has not always been easy. Like others, I have lived a life that included childhood trauma and turbulence. While loving my family, relationships within the clan have been tumultuous and held trials and tribulations. I learned to channel my emotions into drive. This drive and natural inclination toward the physical had me use sports as an outlet. I was blessed to compete in two national-level sports, wrestling and bikini bodybuilding division. The challenges inherent in this level of competition taught me to push harder and enthusiastically offer my best effort. Always putting your best foot forward allows you to live without regret, no matter the outcome. I can accept that. Overcoming my challenges taught me to be persistent, resourceful, and a creative problem-solver.

Post Nationals four and a half years ago, I pulled myself up on my chin-up bar, dislodging the bar, which sprang loose, striking me in the face, driving me to the ground and leaving me unconscious. I roused but passed out a second time. Past concussions due to sports were mild, but this cranial trauma threw me for a loop. Talk about the universe's ultimate redirect. During the second blackout, I had an out of body experience, watching my unconscious self from above. It was life changing. I also lost my speech and then re-developed my communication skills and function again. Constant conversations with myself about what I used to do, what I wanted to do, and what I was currently capable of doing ensued.

I have overcome many frustrations as I've embraced my new gifts. I retain some difficulties with my memory and executive function. The concussion has forced me to slow down, become more aware and re-evaluate my priorities. I dance to my rhythm with optimism and recognize that my beautifully chaotic and colourful past has contributed to the unique spunky person I am today. Trusting in universally shared energy with my intuitive sense, I focus and find love in helping others. We are powerful beings, stronger and more capable than we realize. The power inside us is magical. I am choosing to step into potential, possibilities, and magic!

Jessica Jewels

Franco Cavaleri is the founder of Biologic Pharmamedical Research, a biomedical lab developing nutraceutical and pharmaceutical technologies, bestselling author and IFBB bodybuilding champion.

FRANCO
CAVALERI

Initially driven by a passion to better understand nutraceuticals and nutrition in order to enhance my performance during a quest to win the title of several North American bodybuilding competitions, I was struck with Ulcerative Colitis, a serious autoimmune disease. This disease derailed me twice with hospitalization and with a prognosis of surgical intervention with prohibitive lifestyle consequences but was also the impetus that changed the course of my research forever. My research into anti-inflammatory strategies, originally used to support recovery from training, quickly became focused on better understanding the pharmacology of natural medicinal agents to rehabilitate my condition without surgical intervention. I was able to overcome this disease without surgery and successfully won five bodybuilding titles including the 1992 IFBB Mr. North America Bodybuilding Champion.

Subsequently, I built three successful businesses in the NHP industry from concept to successful merger and acquisition and worked on completing my PhD in Experimental Medicine. My research has led to pharmacological discovery and multiple patents that are used in medicinal products globally. After an expansive review of our research which centers on inflammatory pathways and the pathologies of related diseases, Health Canada approved clinical trials to evaluate one of our patented medicines as a COVID-19 treatment for those at risk of morbidity or mortality upon infection. We are proud and excited to be contributing to human wellness at this level.

Today, I'm the proud dad of two beautiful children. I find great pleasure and pride in mentoring my children and others in the community to help them be the best they can be, from sports to academics. My books focus not only on how our bodies respond to nutrition, but also on empowering people to develop a positive mindset and skills to optimize their mental and emotional well-being.

In order to improve your own skills, intellect, and character, you need to hone your God-given gifts with which you are expected to contribute to the advancement of humanity. It is your moral obligation to persist with discovery within and outside of yourself and to apply these findings to serve your community passionately in the hope of making a positive global impact on mankind and the environment.

Jeanne Beker is a renowned Canadian journalist, media personality, and fashion entrepreneur. Among multiple notable media roles, Jeanne was the host of internationally syndicated Fashion Television, which aired for 27 years and was broadcast in more than 130 countries.

JEANNE
BEKER

Photo credit: Colin Gaudet

I wanted to be an actress. I thought fashion was a little too superficial. I didn't consider it a great art form. I knew there were designers and that there was a certain amount of creativity inherent in the scene, but for me, I wanted to be a great actress and I saw fashion as a tool for that – costumes to really express yourself properly. I fell into fashion in the mid-eighties with Fashion Television, but even then, it wasn't about fashion to me. It was about people and reporting on a scene that was exploding and filled with the most colourful characters. It was about storytelling for me, but of course the more I got into it, the more I learned and the more I fell in love with the applied art and craft of it.

I grew up feeling very loved, and I was always encouraged to dream big and to believe in myself. Although my parents had great expectations for me, I never felt pressured. I was encouraged to be an original. Both my parents had a lot of pride in the fact that I stepped out into the world on my own and that I was gutsy from a young age. I think the older we get, the more we get to know ourselves and the more comfortable we are in our own skin.

I've always really admired and appreciated people who put themselves out there, people with drive and talent, and people who really want to share and give of themselves. I am a strong believer in you get what you give, so it is important to always be putting that energy out there and the good vibes, and whenever you can do good deeds – that too.

I think essentially, that's what fashion should be; make the planet a more beautiful place – a better place – and make life easier for all of us.

Jeanne Beker

Chad Kowalchuk is a strong and compassionate person who, despite being through so much, still pushes forward towards his dreams.

CHAD
KOWALCHUK

The past many years of my life I have been brought down and defeated by the many obstacles life has thrown my way. I was first diagnosed with an incurable disease when I woke up in the ICU after almost dying; that was almost too much to deal with. Eventually, I accepted it. Two years later I was diagnosed with stage 3 avascular necrosis in my left hip. That resulted in having a complete hip replacement at the age of 32. My mental stability after experiencing all that wasn't the greatest. I tried to focus on what I wanted, what was going to make me happy. I was slowly starting to succeed; I was doing better. My personal life then went down the toilet.

This was the point in my life that I completely lost myself. I didn't feel like I was good enough for anything. I was broken. I attempted suicide and failed; I was in a dark place. I finally decided to reach out and get help. That was one of the hardest things I have ever done. Asking for help does not make you weak. It makes you stronger and was a crucial step I had to take.

I realized that I am an extraordinary human being, as we all are. I began focusing on me and what makes me happy. Focus on the positive and how we are making a difference in the world. No one is insignificant, we are all here for a reason. I am now focused and pushing to take my small business to the next level. Sure, it is scary. Stepping outside your comfort zone makes most people feel uneasy. Seeing the positive results from all of my hard work has been so fulfilling and the ones around me have noticed the difference. I am becoming the person I want to be. I am happy, focused, and persistent; I won't let anything stand between me and my goals and dreams.

We are the only ones standing in our way. Believe in yourself and what you think is impossible, becomes possible. Never give up. Keep pushing forward.

Zach Mansbridge-Fafard is passionate about having a positive impact entrepreneurially in sport, wellness, mental health and mentorship.

ZACH MANSBRIDGE-FAFARD

As a young adult I was working a good job and generally enjoying life, however, I had an uneasy feeling that I was unfulfilled. I decided that to find fulfillment, the road would be through service to others. I began to search for opportunities that would get me involved with helping people.

During my search I took a job as a sports coach in schools. On paper, I was grossly under-qualified for the position, and a part of me certainly felt that way too. However, at the end of my first day, I sat in my car and felt the most passion and satisfaction that I had ever felt from a day of work. I decided at that moment that my way of positively impacting the world was through sparking a love of sports and life in the next generations.

From that moment on, I have dived into any learning I could do to grow that mission. I now have a business in which I can interact with a multitude of amazing students who have given to me one of the most valuable things in this life: a purpose. I would like to think that I have given them as much as I can in return. Sports and physical literacy are what Zach's Athletics was built on. Over time, the most exciting part for me has become forming valuable relationships with my students and being able to work with children who may not have had the opportunity or interest in participating in sports, or perhaps they were labelled as difficult and cast off to the side.

As a child, I had comically large goals about changing the world. After spending time in the 'real world,' I began to think those goals were ridiculous and unachievable; my world-view had shrunk exponentially. The most important lesson I have learned from creating a purpose driven business is that those goals are not unachievable. When I am told that a young person has started something they believe in and it had something to do with me, I feel that changing the world is possible, not as a lone fire, but as a spark.

Zach Mansbridge-Fafard

Carolyn Turkington, co-founder of The MomBabes, braving their legacy through storytelling. Coffee in one hand and confidence in the other.

CAROLYN
TURKINGTON

Have you seen the movie Shrek?
Yes!? Great, now stay with me here.
Do you remember the scene when Fiona sings and her voice causes one of the birds to explode?

Fast forward 25 years, and here I am in my classroom of grade six students, and we're silent reading.

One of my kiddos, who is autistic, got up from his chair, walked over to the window and started singing the song from Shrek like Fiona. I was a little confused, but noticed birds outside the window. My gut was to react and respond, "Shhhh, we are reading," and re-direct him, but instead I walked over and started whistling along. We finished the song and he said, "Dang, no birds exploded! Maybe next time," and walked back to his desk, sat down, and continued reading.

I didn't say anything and neither did any of the other children.

Once you have met one child with autism, then, you have met one child with autism.

Even as teachers, we too often generalize, stereotype, label and assume. I know I am guilty of this. Not in terms of having ill intent, or to humiliate, but from general lack of knowledge or a care to understand.

My son was diagnosed with autism in summer 2021, and since then, I have learned to never underestimate one's abilities just because they may see things a little differently.

We all see things differently. Not better, not worse, just different.
I am proud of our differences, and the reality is, it's not different to us. It just is.

Whistling at the window, I realized the power and weight actions can hold. We all want kids to feel included and that doesn't always happen, autistic or not.

My wish as a mother is that my son always feels included and welcomed, so I hope we can all start to do this more. Simple actions of meeting people where they are. Then, asking them to join the table, without judgment.

The classic school cafeteria rule still applies. Choose a table, sit at it, and make room for others.

The MomBabes are braving their legacy through storytelling. Coffee in one hand, confidence in the other.

CHRISTINA
WALSH

Four years ago I sat in my therapist's office feeling lost and suddenly unemployed. Sitting across from me, my therapist asked, "If you could do anything, what would it be?" I blurted out, "I want to be a writer."

In that space, without fear of judgment, it came out of my mouth before I even had a chance to judge myself. But writing or being a "writer" didn't feel sensible or financially stable. A hobby maybe, but not a career. Just pushing the dream to "maybe when I'm retired." Then I could be a writer, that's much more logical.

When does a dream become not a dream, meaning, when do you stop fearing an outcome and just believe and leap into the unknown?

For me, it was standing at my dad's funeral in front of 300 people, delivering his eulogy alongside my sister, when I realized life only gives you so many chances. We shared his stories, his legacy filled the room. What was my legacy? Something had to change.

I felt so pulled towards something, I couldn't explain it. Like Kevin Costner in Field of Dreams, when he does the unthinkable and builds a baseball field in the middle of his corn field.

The whispers became loud. I couldn't wait until I was retired, or my daughters were out of diapers or we're no longer in a pandemic. I started writing and I wanted to keep writing.

I want to write my legacy now. Every day is a celebration of life.

I know my daughters won't ask for the family china sets that still sit in a Tupperware bin or our flat screen TV. They will want pictures of us, to know the stories of our lives. My greatest accomplishment will not be what I do but who I raise and sometimes life is about the risk, the second chances and the leaps of faith. My girls will know they are destined for great things because of the great people who came before them, and it's my job to write the stories and to show them it's never too soon to listen to the whispers in the cornfield.

Christina Walsh

Zoonie is a passionate "enter-training" speaker and entrepreneur who loves delivering interactive talks to hungry, curious audiences with a fearless voice.

ZOONIE
NGUYEN

What did I sign up for, and can I quit now?" I asked myself, sobbing, as I left the public speaking class.

A few minutes earlier, I had been standing awkwardly before an audience of professionals and business owners and felt blood rushing to my face. Their eyes were staring at me, a stay-at-home mom with no self-confidence. "I don't belong here; I'm just a mom," I thought.

Three weeks earlier, my baby daughter had been diagnosed with the Kawasaki virus and was fighting for her life in the ICU. I was 39 and had a wonderful husband and two lovely children, yet I was miserable. I deeply desired to reinvent my work life to fit my home life. When Maggie miraculously recovered, I promised myself I'd have a career that would harmonize with my values – with who I am.

That's when I took the brave step to enrol in the public speaking course at McGill University. I followed all the rules, but it was scripted, felt unnatural and had no heart. I wanted to quit.

That night, looking at my sleeping daughter, I remembered how courageously she fought and how she overcame the disease. What kind of role model did I want to be for my daughter? How could I give up so easily?

So, I decided to stay in the course. I learned to speak from the heart. I learned to deliver stories of hope and courage. Every week, I left each class feeling accomplished and exhilarated. My confidence increased week by week as I found my voice. I began to see myself as an inspirational speaker helping others accelerate towards their pursuit of happiness.

A year later, I created TalentelleTV, an inspirational training firm with a supportive and thriving environment for women to grow, network and collaborate. My purpose is to help them realize their full potential by expressing their talent and passion.

Today, after delivering keynotes and conferences to appreciative audiences worldwide, I am the living proof of a most important message: you are worthy, and you have every right to pursue your life's dreams.

Zoonie Nguyen

Maggie owns Fotografia Boutique, a premier Portrait Studio in Ontario. She is an artist, cultural arts event producer and philanthropist.

MAGGIE
HABIEDA

As a child, I would spend much of my time lost in my daydreams, admiring nature's beauty, and drawing princesses. These drawings were my dolls and my toys. I was born in a small and poor village in communist Poland. My mother raised her eight children alone with almost no support. My father committed suicide. To say I had little is an understatement.

"If you can't speak the words, you can't communicate." This statement paralyzed my life. I was by nature, an extremely shy and self-conscious person. The women in my family had been for generations the subjects of domestic abuse, and I was always taught to keep quiet. It was hard for me to find words to express myself. I believed that authentic communication was verbal.

I knew that I was an artist; it was my life. Art was my path to success and freedom. I applied to an Art School in Poland and was rejected not once, but twice. I was devastated and my world collapsed around me. For a time, I found myself in a depression with a future without hope.

It wasn't until my aunt helped me change my life. At sixteen, I immigrated to Canada. Where one door closed, another, magnificent door opened. I later graduated from the prestigious Ontario College of Art and Design in Toronto.

There is a saying, "One picture says a thousand words." Instead of worrying about something I couldn't do, I concentrated on what I could, which was a thousand times more powerful. Without saying a word, I am now able to capture the essence and soul of a person. I can communicate my emotions, and the emotions of my subjects, through visual art.

To build my self-confidence, I took photos of myself and created a visual representation of how I saw myself. Experiencing and understanding both sides of the camera became therapy. Through this process, I eventually found myself turning into the person I knew I was. I finally broke free from my childhood constraints. Personal growth, self-awareness and self-acceptance are a constant focus for me. Often, we find ourselves trying to be someone else, when in fact, being yourself is the key to success.

Maggie Habieda

Lynda Moffatt is a visual artist with a home studio in Southern Ontario. Celebrating wildlife and their environment!

LYNDA
MOFFATT

Fun Facts!

Yes, I was an avid boater and scuba diver. Documenting to scale, shipwrecks with Bowling Green State University, underwater archaeology for the Wisconsin Shipwreck Museum. These drawings are documented in the U.S. history books 1997.

Juried into International Artist of the year! Winning an online residency from 2020-21.

Juried into Artists for Conservation 2022.

Exhibiting, in many juried galleries exhibits over the years. All while making some great connections, acquiring wonderful collectors, supporters and friends.

How did this all happen?

Truth ~ "I always knew, this is what I was meant to do. Didn't know how, only knew it would!"

What kept me going?

The world could seem to be crashing down, as when I was moving back to Canada over September 11, 2001. What saved me, through all the turmoil? There it was again! Art!

I kept plugging along like it was meant to be. Believing in myself!

Living through these times of Covid-19, art is still my go-to! I guess that's what it's all about. Taking care of yourself, with what you know will nurture your soul. Having a great belief system and a few angels who come when needed really helped!

The art journey prevailed even when other journeys didn't. It's my true journey!

Why wildlife and nature?

Through our adventures, my husband Kevin and I have had some very close wildlife encounters! We know these must have taken place for a reason. Through visual stories of these incredible creatures, we share them to bring interest, knowledge and help support our national treasures through conservation areas and parks which help to sustain them.

I truly believe this worthwhile work needs to be done. If we keep learning, teaching and sharing, I believe we have done what we are meant to do for the betterment of society!

The future will be that much better because we cared!

If there is anything that I leave you with, it is to please listen to your inner voice and keep true to your beliefs. The world needs you!

A mortgage specialist who is committed to well-being!

LEANNE
MYLES

Happiness is an incidental result of physical and mental well-being. Health is a priority over all things. Focusing on your own physical and psychological well-being will improve all facets of your life. What is health? It is a human's ability to function at optimal levels. All our systems are interconnected. If one of our cogs is out of whack, then the rest of our network can also go offline. Focusing on my health was a game-changer.

Reaching the end of my husband's cancer journey and finding him in remission was a gift, but getting there had left me exhausted. Also, my new career path with a young and dynamic team underscored my lack of energy. Tired of feeling tired, I shifted my focus to my health, and that is when I began to see significant change. Changes to my productivity, energy level, and overall outlook on life came about when I focused on my well-being.

I didn't do it on my own; I worked with a coach for over three years. Educating myself was one of the primary steps in living a healthier lifestyle. The coach talked to me about my mindset; you cannot change anything until you change what is in your brain. I learned to silence negative self-talk and replace it with constructive conversation. Accepting that I was perfectly imperfect helped me move past lapses and apply myself to future successes. When you can stop judging yourself harshly, you extend that same courtesy to others. Judgement falls away.

Changes to my diet and fitness level increased my available energy, and since energy drives connection, I experienced improved relationships with family, friends, coworkers, and clients. Building solid habits began to extend into all facets of my life, and I viewed relationships optimistically and with generosity. Goal setting for my health spilt over into other areas, including work. I began to enjoy setting targets and obtaining my objectives while remembering to retain balance.

My happiness and optimism are directly related to the time spent caring for my mind and body. Yours can be too by committing to your health. Make the commitment!

Leanne Myles

JODI
BROWN

My life was turned upside down due to an illness, literally, in 2011. After a few years of medical appointments, the diagnosis was permanent inner ear damage; no surgery could help, I would have to learn to live with it.

In 2014, my long term disability work insurance was wrongly cut off, and in 2015, I ended up on social assistance. I had no clue we gave so little to people. I was given $875 a month to cover everything; that was for all of my bills, including rent, groceries, personal hygiene products and so on.

After a few months of not getting the help I needed, I took to social media. That's where I found my calling! My story was picked up by mainstream media; the newspapers, radio, and TV news channels interviewed me, which got me the help I needed from the government.

With the "fame" of being in the news also came the haters, which fuelled my drive to continue standing up to become a voice for others. We shouldn't have to share our struggles publicly to receive help in obtaining our basic rights. I experienced public humiliation, I know first-hand! That's why my voice has become a voice for the people.

My voice will not be made silent because of others' discomfort.

Megan Lammam, author of Your Heart Compass, is an advocate for social emotional learning and literacy.

MEGAN
LAMMAM

For as long as I can remember, I longed for a home. A safe place of belonging where family and friends gather to share meals, stories and moments of connection. I lost this sense of home when I was ten years old. My father left abruptly to create a new life and my mother subsequently became severely ill from depression. My life upended with my mother's attempted suicide. At seventeen, I was forced to take on the role of her primary caregiver and bearing witness to her devastating struggle was, at times, paralyzing. In the trauma of my childhood experience, I lost my sense of self. It would take me twenty years to recover my purpose and discover the true meaning of home.

As a teenager, through the grace of people in my community, I found a support system that helped me to stay on track with my education and emotional maturity. I quickly learned that, although my suffering was painful, it was not a barrier to love. In fact, my pain was a catalyst for connection. It allowed me to reach out to others and ask for help. More importantly, it gave me the desire for joy.

Ultimately, my painful circumstances brought me together with people in truth and compassion. I learned that being true to myself led to authentic relationships and, in these places of connection, I found my home.

In my forties, I have dedicated myself to researching the concept of home in the context of emotional literacy and connection. I identified four pillars that support a strong foundation of love: joy, kindness, courage and calm. Using these four feelings as core value points, I developed a lifestyle practice that became the essence of my work as an author, a mother, and an advocate for mental and emotional wellness.

Like all good homes, it takes gentle love and hard work to maintain the integrity and stability of connection. I am grateful to share my life with my husband, Hani, my children, Leila and Tarik and my dogs. I am honoured to build a safe and welcoming space for children and adults to connect through stories and activities in books and online.

founded the Organization of American and Canadian Women in Public Relations, and is president of Pink Pearl PR.

TALIA BECKETT DAVIS

My happiness wasn't what I dreamed (it was better).

Many of us grow up dreaming of our future success and happiness. I imagined I would finally be happy if I became a successful executive working in the city, with a corner office and a view. I attributed my career accomplishments with being happy, and I worked hard for years to make this happen.

When I became a new mom, I faced the realities of not being able to work long hours or attend evening events. I would go for walks on my break just to get a sense of calmness, and that's when I knew I had to leave this work environment. The corporate world I had worked so hard to become part of no longer felt welcoming to a new mom.

My family became my priority and my responsibilities had shifted. I didn't want to give up my dream of being a successful businesswoman, but I knew that something bigger was waiting for me, I just hadn't found it yet. It was hard to adjust, but I left that job and started my own business.

I fell in love with my family and passion for my career when I pulled away the layers of who I used to be. When I held my child, the happiness I discovered was more profound than what I achieved when I was climbing the corporate ladder. I found a passion for who I was as a woman in business, and what I was becoming as a new mom.

For the first time in my life, I fell in love with myself, and it was genuine. I let go of the girl who claimed to be enthusiastic about becoming an executive. By simply being myself, I experimented with discovering my unique purpose and giving back to others.

I uncovered the true meaning of authentic joy through acceptance and calmness. Happiness is no longer a destination to which I must fake it until I make it. I always assumed that if I had my life and career figured out, I'd never be scared.

To truly find happiness, love yourself, your life, your family, and your passion on your own terms.

Maddison is a children's book author and theatre professional. Her first publication, *Victoria's Playhouse*, unites her passions for theatre and writing.

MADDISON
BELL

At the age of 10, my doctor suggested I start breathing into a paper bag. For fear of cramping my own carefully curated 'Lisa Frank meets Raven Symone' style, I chose to circulate carbon dioxide with hands cupped over my nose and mouth. It was around this time I retired the sugary watermelon toothpaste and opted for Colgate's clean mint. Looking back, the paper bag princess would have been a cuter look than the neurotic kid with chronic halitosis.

My early onset anxiety was accelerated by perfectionism and climate change. Despite my frequent panic, I was a good leader from a young age. I would convince my posse of fourth graders to skip recess for discussions on taking immediate action to save the polar bears. Admittedly, extinction is a complex concept for little girls who would rather be playing double Dutch. I secured their allegiance with duo-tangs and paper to draw cute polar bears. Not entirely knowing how to convince one of our moms to get us to the Arctic, as the girls doodled, I hyperventilated into my cupped hands. This time, acting as if all the talk of polar caps had made them cold. *Thursday was out for saving the ozone, we had Brownies, and I was falling behind in badge earnings.*

From the ozone layer in middle school to boyfriends in high school, and then eventually myself in university, I realized that there sure is a lot to be fixed in this lifetime. I got better over the years at letting go of the immense pressure I put on myself to be a 'fixer' (I held on to perfectionism). Not to say that I don't try to fix anymore; that just wouldn't be me. But I have learned to be passionate about the effort without feeling the responsibility of the outcome. That adjustment has ushered me from a good leader to a great one.

Trust me; there is still a lot to hyperventilate over. But thanks to everyone catching up to the whole saving-the-world effort, there is also an endless supply of large paper bags.

Please use the rest of this page to draw your cutest polar bear and evaluate your sustainable choices.

Maddison Bell

175

Sharon Marshall is a student, author, artist, facilitator, trainer, and social entrepreneur dedicated to Indigenous women's empowerment. Sharon Marshall offers HOPE by Helping Other People Excel.

SHARON ANN
MARSHALL

My childhood and upbringing lacked any measure of cultural influences or positive role models. For example, I only knew I was Native because I looked Native, and my mother occasionally spoke Cree to her mother (mostly when she didn't want us to hear what she was saying). Oh, and, in junior high, I was taunted and tormented by two boys who called me horrible names like "Wagonburner," "Squaw", and "Dirty Indian."

Shortly after turning 14 years old, after experiencing enough trauma in my life to last a lifetime, I ran away from home. Little did I know this was only the beginning. My story spans decades and is about my life as a survivor. I have survived sexual and physical abuse, suicide attempts, and falling in love with a serial rapist and murderer. I should be a statistic; however, I have survived. After years of denying my ancestry to remove myself from a past fraught with alcoholism, poverty, sexual and physical abuse, and murder, I finally realized there was a part of me that was missing. My mother was raised in a convent —just another word for residential school. By the time I realized this, both parents were deceased. My healing started when I forgave my parents for the trauma my siblings and I experienced, which helped me come to terms with my Indigeneity. And that was when I started to feel like a whole person, feeling more like myself than I can ever remember.

As I fully embrace my gifts, I realize that everything that has happened to me has prepared me to be the strong, resilient person needed to help other women who have experienced similar traumas. I now know and embrace my purpose, and I have dedicated my life to empowering Indigenous women, to help them let go of less than and realize their magnificence.

We are far more powerful than we realize!

Jennifer Dawn has risen from the ashes like a Phoenix, over and over, many times in her life. She is the owner and CEO of Jennifer Dawn Ltd. Currently, she resides in Chilliwack, BC with her partner, her youngest of 3 sons, and her stepson.

JENNIFER **DAWN**

Have you ever felt a challenge absorb you to the point that it engulfs your inner being? Perhaps, to the point where you don't know who you are anymore? It may feel as though the challenge feeds on fear and swallows your being. Challenges in life do occur, but we can overcome them.

I have experienced a tremendous amount in my life. At the age of 17, I died on the operating table. I was revived. I rose from the ashes stronger than I was before.

I was held captive at 17. The capturer was going to use me for sex trafficking. I was rescued. I overcame this challenge. I rose from the ashes stronger than I was before.

I was married and had three sons before I was 25. I ended my marriage because of physical abuse. My sons were 7, 5 and 18 months old at the time. My youngest son would be diagnosed years later with several special needs, including an intellectual disability. I raised all three sons on my own. I worked full time and even worked extra hours in order to provide for my young children. I struggled. I cried a lot. I pushed through it. I rose from the ashes stronger than I was before.

I was diagnosed with very aggressive cervical cancer in 2010. I went through all the pre-stages and was in stage 2 and 3 throughout the cervix. The cancer developed rapidly. I had many surgeries, including a full hysterectomy. It felt like it would never end. I rose from the ashes stronger than I was before.

I had been diagnosed with Endometriosis when I was a teenager. I did not realize that this diagnosis was the beginning of several chapters of struggles and endless pain. Jobs and relationships ended. My quality of life has been impacted greatly due to the disease. This disease brought incredible suffering, mobility challenges and over 13 surgeries. I rose from the ashes stronger than before.

I believe that we are all phoenixes. We rise from the ashes stronger than before. Our challenges don't define us. We choose how we are defined. I choose to be a phoenix! How about you?

Lisa Broome is a financial coach and CPA who believes you can thrive living life based on YOUR unique values.

LISA
BROOME

If you looked at my life five years ago, you would have seen a very successful woman, by society's definition. I was a CPA within a large public company, managing a team of high-performing professionals, living in a beautiful home with an amazing husband and a fur-kid I adored. My life looked like a complete 'success'. Yet, deep down, I knew something needed to change. Work no longer excited me, my health deteriorated with the increase in stress and I never felt like I had enough time for what was most important to me.

I thought I just needed a few more years and then we would be set financially, but I kept moving the goalposts. Then, at the age of 35, life stepped in to give me a nudge, or what felt like a push over a cliff.

Within the span of a few weeks, my life as I knew it was gone. My job ended abruptly. Our dog passed away from unexpected cancer and my health took a turn for the worse. I felt raw and exposed, the identities I'd worn as armour had vanished. I started asking: who was I, really? What truly mattered to me? What was going to bring me joy? What kind of life and impact did I want to have?

In asking these questions, I was able to begin rebuilding my life intentionally, based on what I truly valued – joy, authenticity, wellbeing, growth, financial flexibility. I created my own definition of success: living in authentic alignment with my values. And I discovered my vision and passion for life: supporting amazing professionals and solopreneurs in creating financial prosperity and success on their terms.

Success looks different to each of us, with unique values and visions for our lives, and that's a beautiful thing! You know deep down what truly matters: embrace those values and begin to live them. Start now. Look at where you spend and invest your time, energy and money. Does it align with your values? If not, give yourself permission to shift. You have the power within you.

Decide what success and prosperity looks like to you and watch your life transform!

Alana Brandson works as a sales professional in the CPG industry. She is a mom of two boys and has a love for light and photography. She has embarked on a journey of self healing and transformation in her own life.

ALANA
BRANDSON

As a child of a type one diabetic, I became a caregiver at a very young age. If someone you love has type one diabetes, you will be involved in day-to-day care for the rest of your life. It truly is a family disease. My father struggled to manage the disease and would go into diabetic comas frequently. I worried about him every single day, up until the day he passed away.

In my adult life, I chose a life of caregiving. That is what I knew, what I was comfortable with, even if it created a life of disruption and chaos. I had never associated myself with the word trauma; I grew up in a super loving family with devoted and kind parents. Transgenerational trauma occurs when adverse experiences are transmitted to children environmentally or socially. My childhood trauma dictated my choices in my adult life, which put my children at risk of repeating the cycle. I needed to alter their experience and my own.

When I made changes in my life, I began to understand my mother's choices, and through that, we had a much better relationship. Talking about this has resolved any tension or resentment I felt previously. It is easy to lose pieces of yourself in caregiving. You move from crisis to crisis, giving a bit of yourself away each time. It's exhausting.

Now, living on my own, I am healing and learning about intergenerational trauma, as well as the wisdom of seeking out support for children who have experienced trauma that can have a lasting impact. Examining my story is helping me reframe painful events and change the future. You must want to heal, seek support, practice mindfulness, and incorporate self-care. I am learning to live in the present and enjoy it without being overwhelmed by the past. Taking responsibility and owning the trauma in my life has allowed me to create a life full of peace. I feel I'm in charge of my own story for the first time. Change can be scary, but liberating, too. Embracing transformation allows me to transform my life; my greatest hope is to minimize the trauma my kids will experience in childhood.

Alana Brandson

Katsumi Kimoto is a painter, art curator and gallerist. He grew up on the West Coast, and is an island boy at heart, having spent his days by the ocean surfing, fishing and now creating his abstract art.

KATSUMI
KIMOTO

I've always had an optimistic outlook; my glass has always been more than half full, in fact, it's often running over. I always seek out opportunity and new projects, I tend to view work as recreation. Growing up in the coastal community of Ucluelet, my friends often voiced complaints of boredom and unhappiness, but with an ocean at my doorstep and a surfboard at the ready, I was more than happy to enjoy everything I already had.

I consider myself lucky – I was raised by parents who, despite their separation, were loving and supportive. My father taught me the value of hard work; we would rise before dawn and work on the fishing boat, while my mother nurtured me with her kind and caring heart.

I have always envisioned obstacles as part of the process; they weren't there to merely challenge me, but rather to guide me. However, making art for me is not a harmonious process, it's also about challenging myself. Just like the seascapes I paint, the surfaces of my panels are not often calm.

One of the biggest hurdles I've ever had to face changed this outlook completely. When my father passed just over ten years ago, it was the first time I lost that sense of optimism. His death shook my core, it was a loss unlike anything I had experienced before.

Facing death and mortality has changed me, but it was life on the ocean that shaped me and my art. I didn't fully grasp this until my mid-thirties. I had an epiphany when noticing the water-like quality to my brushstrokes; I had never really thought about it before, this undulation and fluidity of movement. My art was imitating my life this entire time, the ocean is a part of who I am, and it always will be.

Now that we have our own children, a daughter and a son, I only wish we had made the leap towards parenthood sooner. I never realized how much joy I would derive from this chapter of my life; my children are my paradise. They are a constant reminder of why I continue to seek peace and brightness in my life.

Anthony J. Baldwin is a film director, writer, and producer. Anthony J. Baldwin is also a born troublemaker.

ANTHONY J. BALDWIN

Growing up, I was always the troublemaker in my family. I didn't like rules, I didn't like being told what to do, and if I wanted to do something, I just did it. Some would say I was the black sheep, but I never let that stop me. So, it came as no surprise to everyone when the troublemaker dove into the unpredictable world of film.

Film was something I was always passionate about. I have fond memories of the hours spent watching *Teenage Mutant Ninja Turtles, Batman*, and an obscene amount of Disney. No matter what I was going through, I always knew films were my escape from reality. When I was 13, my older brother taught me about screenplays and showed me how amazing storytelling can be. This was the moment I discovered my passion. Writing stories was the perfect outlet I needed to channel all the emotions I had inside me from my childhood.

After graduating from college twice – that's right, the troublemaker went to film school and business school, graduating with flying colours – I decided to turn my escape from reality into a career. I founded my own production company, Steel Hammer Productions, in 2016.

As I said, I was never one to follow the rules – I tend to find ways to do things differently, and that is what I truly love about filmmaking. There is no rule book. Film dares and challenges you to be different.

I felt like an outcast for most of my life, and the film industry greeted me with open arms into an entire community of outcasts. Any lingering doubts or fears I may have at the time, instantly wash away the moment I step onto set.

Being the troublemaker allows me the opportunity to knock people on their ass by surprising them with my accomplishments. The name Steel Hammer reminds me of where I came from and how far I've come. If you want my advice, it's simple. In the words of the great Jack Nicholson, "No one gives it to you. You have to take it!"

Kathleen Lafferty, BA, MCP, RCC, is a Registered Clinical Counsellor and owner of Cadboro Bay Counselling in Victoria, BC.

KATHLEEN
LAFFERTY

Joseph Campbell said, "It is by going down into the abyss that we recover the treasures of life. Where you stumble, there lies your treasure."

I am incredibly grateful to be in the place I am now, after much personal work. It is our inner experience that creates outer reality, and the most profound part of my journey was this realization. It is necessary to go into the depths of suffering because this is the biggest catalyst for growth.

I was very young when I encountered issues with my emotional wellbeing. I fell into a very deep depression when I was eleven. I remember feeling so confused as to what was even happening. It culminated in a suicide attempt, and visiting a psychiatrist for medication to manage depression. It was many years of constant feelings of unworthiness and fear that played out in my life in emotional distress, volatile partnerships, and problematic family dynamics. It never occurred to me that it was even possible to feel good and enjoy life, and that this is actually our birthright.

I was in university when I tried counselling, using a technique where you focus on your inner experience and really let yourself be present with your bodily sensations and emotions. This led to an amazing breakthrough in my healing. The pent-up traumatic energy that had been keeping my system in a frozen state began to unwind itself.

It was like a light had been turned on; I felt like I had been wearing sunglasses for my entire life, then one day they were removed. I saw the world differently, less fearful and much more loving. And while not everything changed overnight, this was my initiation, where I felt deep self-love and joy.

I now enjoy meeting life fully, whatever the experience. That is the purpose of being here, to live fully present in each moment and embrace what the universe offers. Since I arrived at that point on my healing journey, the most important work became about helping others.

I have since began my own private counselling practice; I love doing this work, and I continue to expand my own consciousness through spiritual growth.

Caroline Latona is a beauty photographer who is motivated to show women how beautiful they are, despite societal pressures.

CAROLINE
LATONA

Our society has been gatekeeping how and what a woman must look like. The fashion industry and media have successfully set an expectation for how women should grow. When we deviate from these standards, we feel unworthy, unaccepted, and broken. We're so fixated on these ideals that we can't even assess our immediate environment by looking at the general population of women around us. How can we all be the problem at the same time, when there is only a tiny fraction of people in the limelight?

Skincare products are riddled with "anti-aging", as if aging is something evil that we must avoid. We have even perfected the labels on women, judging women that do not live by the standard of our physical perfection. Yet, when she cares enough about her beauty and her physical appearance, she is deemed vain. Society can't make its mind up, can it?

The self-confidence and self-esteem of everyday women is at stake, those who are constantly trying to navigate these standards. How much should I care about my looks? Am I being modest enough? I want to look good, but not too much. I want to feel beautiful, but I don't want them to think I'm proud. Where does it end? The psychological connection between beauty and self-confidence undoubtedly accentuates why it is important for women to feel and look beautiful. The world cannot make its mind up with its ever-changing standards, so it is up to us to choose our own happiness.

It is the highlight of my day to help women come to a place of appreciation for who they are. Knowing that they have something tangible they get to enjoy every day, that is a deserving reminder of who they are, and what makes them happy. As a beauty photographer, I see the transformation every day and how women go from nervous, withdrawn, and shy to embracing their light when it reflects on them in their photographs. I may not rid the world of its unrealistic beauty standards, but I will, one woman at a time, fill the world with more confidence, beauty, and happiness.

Dear woman, it is up to you to choose your happiness.

Caroline Latona

Betty Anne Chulumovich is an entrepreneur mother, grandmother and outspoken human rights speaker who has a passion to help, encourage and empower people to joy, strength, and healing to move forward.

BETTY ANNE
CHULUMOVICH

A wonderful gift can come into your life in the way of a friend, a calling, or a grandchild. For me tragedy followed by a blessing from God has a way of taking the pain and turning it into a lesson. I do my best to be encouraging to others who are going through similar life challenges. In writing this I reflect on my life, the struggles, and the victories.

As a mother of two, I moved to Vancouver from Prince George B.C when I was 21. I am a free spirit and always had an entrepreneur mind set. I have been working for myself since I was 24 years old. I have always done sale in fashion as well as the health and wellness industry. I am motivated to make money never afraid to take a risk. I think that is due to all the moving we did in my childhood. I was by my mom with the help of my loving Grandmother who had faced many challenges herself. Despite her hardships she was always there for my mom and her other 6 siblings. My Grandparent's place was like my home.

Being a single mother of 2 is not easy. Vancouver is expensive, especially when you are living above your means or trying to keep up with the Jones. But that mind set keeps you working. Sometimes we single parents try to overcompensate so the kids do not feel they are suffering. We make silly mistakes that I now know I would not repeat, but it is all part the journey.

I have various streams of income and work from home. I had to learn to stop and smell the roses and forgive myself for past mistakes. I have a strong connection with my creator and ever since Covid hit I have been very involved with standing up for our freedom to choose what we will allow in our bodies, and the right to speaking up against some of this extreme overreach by the Government. Canada is not looking like the country our fathers fought for, but I believe we will win this battle.

My daughter lost the man she loved, the father of my grandchild, in a brutal murder just one week after he celebrated his 30 the birthday. He was shot outside of his snack store and died within minutes. Two weeks his death my daughter found out she pregnant. The trial date has yet to be set. Life has a way of giving and taking. I now have some sunshine and I feel this little blessing was sent right from heaven to bring joy and love to my family. What the devil wanted to use to destroy the lord turned into a blessing.

Ashika Lessani has a Registered Holistic Nutrition and Holistic Culinary Certification from the Canadian School of Natural Nutrition and is a Certified Life Coach.

ASHIKA
LESSANI

Growing up, I would watch my mother give all her energy and time to her two daughters and husband while leaving no space for her desires, dreams and health (she would share them with us from time to time) made me have deep regret and empathy for her. As I grew up, my desire grew to become a woman who practices the tools to fill her cup and be a role model in creating anything their heart desires without restrictions!

Even though I wanted to create a life of love and joy, my journey was never picture-perfect, although it appeared to be so. Unable to own my singularity or inner truth, I lived for everyone except myself. My childhood conditioning took me to where I lost myself. After a significant life shift in my early thirties, I realized that I had been living my life to other people's expectations and boundaries. After becoming a mother to my beautiful son, the journey I embarked upon was everything but a stroll in the park. Deciding to leave my 13 plus year relationship and marriage was not only a decision that brought me to rock bottom but made me rethink my values, boundaries and standards as a woman, mother and partner.

We are conditioned to believe that something will go wrong when things are going right. We easily shame and criticize ourselves. We adopt the belief that we are not worthy of love, abundance and success. Through mentorship and guidance from my coaches, I was able to reprogram my mind and break my own limiting beliefs. I slowly started to become aware that everything that had taken place in my life was happening for me, not to me. My mental, emotional, physical, and spiritual health, including self-forgiveness, had great power. I wanted to share these tools with women globally!

Becoming a holistic nutritionist, certified coach practitioner, and leadership coach has allowed me to do just that. My innate drive to help women find clarity in creating an authentic and intentional life for themselves has become my purpose. I am truly grateful.

Ashika Lessani

Shawn Bergman and Canuck the crow are from Vancouver, British Columbia on Canada's beautiful west coast.

SHAWN
BERGMAN

If you would have told me 10 years ago that my entire life would become changed forever because of a crow, I wouldn't have believed you. Regardless, that is exactly what happened.

While going through a very dark period in my life in 2015, I was introduced to a crow. Canuck, as he was later named, was a baby crow that was raised and released by my landlady's son. On the day of his release back into nature, I took the time to have what I thought would be a one-time, up close encounter with a wild crow. Was I wrong.

From that day forward our friendship developed and Canuck would eventually become everything to me over the four years I knew him. A brother, a best friend, a son, and the one thing that stopped me from taking my own life. Canuck made me look at the world differently. He opened my eyes to the simple joys in life and what is truly important. Such as watching a crow have fun, doing crow stuff. However, Canuck's influence wasn't just felt by myself.

With being a wild crow in this day and age of social media, Canuck introduced himself to the world through a series of encounters with people in Vancouver. Most famous of course being the knife he attempted to steal from a crime scene in May of 2016. Many of these stories told and filmed encounters shown online went viral.

After starting both "Canuck and I" Facebook and Instagram pages to create awareness of his existence and let people know who he was, I had no idea the effect it would have on people from all around the world.

The story of our friendship, also made into a documentary, became an inspiration to others facing their own dark times. Canuck's daily adventures brought smiles to the faces of people from all around the globe, including one living in a group home who hadn't smiled in over 12 years, and one trying desperately to adjust to a new life in a senior's care home.

Canuck also became an ambassador for crows. He changed many people's hateful views and opinions about crows into an understanding of how beautiful and intelligent crows really are. And that shifting of people's opinions continues to this day.

I am, and will always be, honored that Canuck chose me to tell his story; and I will continue to do so for the rest of my life.

Jim Cassel is living his best life in beautiful
Victoria, BC.

JIM
CASSELS

From humble beginnings, I was always focused on doing better and succeeding. My dad was a policeman, so we were raised with not a lot of extra money. When he decided to leave that career, we moved to the United States so he could have a fresh start, which led the family to the restaurant business. After selling the restaurant we returned to Canada.

Determined to succeed and make something of myself, I took on four jobs as I was finishing school. I was a manager at Koffler stores, moonlighting at Dylex, Woodwards and McDonalds, whatever I could do to secure some extra cash.

My family finally got a chance to run a Danish import furniture store and with a lot of hard work we eventually turned it into a very successful import china shop named Tradewinds Imports.

I was offered an opportunity at George Straith Limited which I quickly accepted. He quickly became my mentor. This turned out to be one of my best career decisions. I was honored to meet Giuseppe Battaglia, the man whose influence created Rodeo Drive in Beverly hills! Having gained so much knowledge I began opening 17 retail shops across Canada. I soon learned that managing 100 plus employees was not what I wanted to do. I wanted a business that would showcase the best of everything in luxury goods, hence "Simply The Best "was born. I love people and the highest of quality goods and I am happy to say that our store has become a meeting place for people of all walks of life in Victoria.

Leoni Tea' Rivers is Gitxsan and a member of the Squamish Nation.

LEONI
TEA' RIVERS

My name is Leoni Rivers, Gitxsan by birth, Wilp Hanamuxw and a member of the Squamish Nation. In my early years, I was brought up by my grandmother on an Indian reserve in Kitwanga, northwestern BC. I attended Indian Day School for a few years then relocated into three foster homes between the ages 7 to 13. I quickly learned to speak only when spoken to. The sixties saw many First Nations children get apprehended and I was no exception.

At 13 years old, I was reunited with my mother and siblings until high school graduation at 18, when I moved to the big city, Vancouver, BC to attend university. At age 15, I worked after school and weekends at two jobs: in a fish cannery and waitressing, while saving for my university tuition. I also gave my single parent mom half of my monthly pay to help her run the household. Despite the abuse I experienced in my early years, I stayed resilient and strong. When not volunteering at the hospital, I was playing basketball.

Faith, hope and love got me through. I knew I did not want to stay on the rez and get pregnant. I wanted a career and graduated at UBC with a Bachelor of Arts, Diploma in Public Sector Management and a Certificate in Administration of Indigenous Governments through UVIC.

My motivation, determination and tenacity inspired me to make something of myself. Today, I have my own Indigenous Consulting business. I have had the honour to work with various First Nations in BC, Alberta and the Yukon, along with some of the largest companies on multi million-dollar projects as the Indigenous lead in negotiations, legacy agreements, LOI's and MoU's.

I had the privilege of being the National Women's Association of Canada representative and advocated for Indigenous Women and Children at the First Ministers Conference at the Kelowna Accord. I was moved (empowered) by making a presentation to the United Nations Interlocutor on the treatment and conditions of Indigenous Women and Girls on Indian Reserves in Canada.

With the current government's acknowledgement of Reconciliation, I have confidence, that Indigenous Youth can achieve anything they put their minds to! *Just do it!*

188

Kelsey is dedicated to the world of philanthropy, giving back to her community through her work as a director for Unique Get Together Society.

KELSEY
McGREGOR

On this journey, this memory will forever remain:

With tuna dripping down my face, I stood there questioning why I had quit my steady nine to five. With all the command I could muster, I charged into the kitchen and looked at the entire kitchen crew.

They stopped, as one would predict, seeing a server with tuna sandwich residue clinging all over.

I grabbed a towel and demanded that the kitchen remake the tuna salad sandwich for the unhappy customer who had waltzed in off the 18-hole green.

We were the pit stop for the high-end country club golfers. We were the afterthought recharge station on the larger loop, and somehow got away with serving tuna fish sandwiches and hotdogs. We rarely sold anything but liquor, which was probably half of the problem at hand.

The chef tried to sputter a rebuttal, but I stopped him with an even keel sternness that surprised even myself.

"I don't care if that tuna salad is premade. Someone in here is going to remake it and deliver it out on the green. Take a golf cart for all I care. Do I make myself clear?"

I calmly picked up a towel, turned on my heel and pretended as if I hadn't just chewed out an entire group of cooks, making my way back out to the tables that were awaiting my attention.

The next day I came in early for my shift and saw that the beverage cart girl had made a pitstop. But she never came by. Curious, I followed her into the kitchen. She appeared to be having a conversation with the head chef.

Beverage cart girl: "Who remade that tuna salad sandwich yesterday?"

Chef: "It was sort of a group effort."

Beverage cart girl: "Well, whoever it was, I want you to thank them directly, because that particular client made a rave review about the service and he has quite the pull in certain circles. Good job everyone, keep it up!"

I backed up and pretended to appear busy as she breezed past.

Two days later, word got out, and I started sitting in on management meetings to inform the senior staff.

Kelsey McGregor

Adam Mckinnon is a Dancer, choreographer, videographer, and creator. Being creative changed his life.

ADAM
McKINNON

I found singing and dancing late in life, at least in industry standards. I pursued my dream of being a professional dancer and singer, having success in both. I was signed to a record label by the time I was 18 years old and that was the biggest moment of I life so far. After I felt that I'd accomplished what I wanted to with singing, I put all my energy into dance and choreography. I spent the next couple of years training and competing as a dancer and choreographer, but I wanted more. I wanted to be in music videos, on TV, in movies, anything to show I had what it took to dance with the best. So, I took the leap and moved to Vancouver. I quickly made a name for myself in the dance industry and worked my way to the top. I got the agent and started booking music videos. I was working with some of Canada's biggest artist like Michael Bublé, Nelly Furtado, and Mariana's Trench. I then booked So You Think You Can Dance! It was a dream come true. I had accomplished so many of my goals, from being in movies, commercials and working professionally as a dancer and choreographer. I then pivoted again in my dance career, finding fulfilment in the competitive dance scene. I wanted to become the top choreographer in my field.

It took me years to finally reach the top of the competitive dance scene, but I did it! I was recognized as one of the best choreographers in my field and was so happy to have accomplished so much in the dance world. I also started a new career with a videography and creative content business. I have taken the skills I have learned from my time in dance and found a new way to create and fulfill that passion behind the camera. I still dance and am very active in the entertainment industry. I believe that struggles are required to survive in life, because in order to stand up, you have to know what falling down is like.

Raugi Yu is a professional Actor, Director, Educator, Mentor and Coach. He advocates staying in the present moment through genuine curiosity and love.

RAUGI
YU

My Dad was away a lot on business in Taiwan. He would come back to Canada once a year.

He had achieved his PhD in aeronautical engineering while studying in France, and then he applied to many companies in the United States and Canada. Only one Montreal company saw past the colour of his skin and the shape of his eyes to the talented human inside. He worked there happily, providing beautifully for the seven of us for years.

He got laid off due to budget cuts, and his mom, still in Taiwan, got sick simultaneously, so he ended up going back and forth. I was 9 when this started.

When he returned, we played catch up each year, filling in the time we had missed. The years went by. I grew older; he grew wiser. I had deeper thoughts and questions about life. When I was sixteen, I said to him, "I'm going to be an Actor. I'm not going to get married or have kids. I won't have time for that." He took a long hall off his cigarette, looked at me, and drew a line on a piece of paper. On one end of the paper, he drew a dot and the letter A; on the other end, he drew a dot and the letter B and then he said.

"You're on a train from point A to point B. Just as you pull out of the station, you find out it's raining in point B, and you don't have your umbrella."

He took another drag off his smoke and then asked me, "What are you going to do? Worry about the rain at point B the whole time, or just have a good f*@#in lunch? Son…it's too far away. You don't have enough information to think about that now."

I didn't know what he meant at the time. Fast forward 33 years later, I'm married to an amazing person who is the mother to our two amazing kids, and I am amazed at what my life is.

Thanks, Dad. For keeping me on track.

Nicole Gardiner is a proud mother of two soulful daughters. She is a naturopath, outdoor enthusiast, artist and writer.

NICOLE GARDINER

I am no stranger to car crashes and their devastating consequences; they have taught me to transform trauma into hope.

He died instantly, and thankfully, did not suffer. My father was only 38 years old when he was taken from earth that beautiful October morning. I suppose now, he could take better care of us from up there, as an angel, perhaps? I always looked for the silver lining and believed this to be true.

I was only 17 when angels came to my rescue one hot, summer night. I was not wearing a seatbelt. My head cracked the windshield and brain trauma ensued. Miraculously, I survived. The years that followed proved to be quite challenging.

I had severe memory loss, speech impediments and difficulty learning. I could no longer take in and process information easily. I struggled to remember anything at all. Life became a series of frustrating blackouts. I found myself asking, "where am I right now? what am I doing? am I safe?" I lived in the present moment all day, every day. You would think that this would be a good thing, but living in the present moment was all I had. Climbing down stairs without falling was not automatic anymore. It was as though my brain could not remember how to do it. I found myself grabbing the stair rail and counting the steps to descend. It took great conscious effort to not fall.

My brain had to create new routes, taking the road less travelled, so to speak. But against all odds and with perseverance that I inherited from my father, I continued with my work and studies.

Soon, my brain repaired itself and I developed a photographic memory. Years passed before the realization of exactly what my brain had done; it built new neural pathways around the damaged area. This is called neuroplasticity and I was fascinated. Just like exercising the muscles of the body, the brain also needs exercise to maintain optimal function. Intense study on this subject led me to my passion: helping others achieve their own optimal brain health, moving from devastation to hope, and encouraging others to never give up!

Nicole Gardiner

Janine Rogan is an award-winning CPA, TEDx Speaker, and passionate financial feminist.

JANINE
ROGAN

I come from a long line of financially ambitious women, who have continued to break down gender norms and smash the glass ceiling.

My grandmother was one of the first women to attend the University of Saskatchewan in the 1950's, and my mother earned her CPA in a male dominated industry.

Following in both of their footsteps I started off in sciences, graduated with a business degree, earned a CPA designation, and started my own business

How long do you think it will take for the women in my family to see wage equality?

My children's generation?

Grandchildren?

Great grandchildren?

Great-great grandchildren?

Great-great-great grandchildren?

Great-great-great-great grandchildren?

My great, great, great, great, great grandchildren will finally see wage equality, and the closing of the gender pay gap. 2571 years to close the gap – the year is 2278... that seems completely unfathomable that it would take that long.

Now in 2022, white women are paid 84 cents on the dollar for the same work as men, and this inequality is compounded by the fact that women live longer than men and are less likely to be involved in financial decisions. The more intersectionality we apply, the larger the wage gap becomes.

If you don't think the gender pay gap exists, I encourage you to look within your organization and ask.

I did.

Turns out I was training a man, in the same role who was earning $13,000 more than I was, meaning he was being paid 23% more than I was.

When I found this out, my first instinct was to feel shame and embarrassment.

But this experience drives the work I do, advocating, educating, and empowering women to lean into their finances and build wealth to ultimately close the wage and wealth gap, and we can do this through embracing financial feminism.

Financial feminism is financial equality for all.

We achieve this through the individual decisions we make as humans but also through the way we decide to build and support the women in our society.

I don't want to it to take 257 years to close the wage gap, I'd like to see it happen in my lifetime – and I think you would too.

HARRY
ALEXANDER
CONAN

Communication is key! It doesn't matter what form we use to communicate; it just matters that we do!

As the youngest of four siblings' communication was essential, and my siblings were quick-witted and verbally astute. Reading and written communication was where three of the four siblings needed support. While reading the Irish Times, my mum came across an article that listed the characteristics of Dyslexia, which described my middle two siblings' challenges perfectly. Dyslexia often has a genetic component, and mum, now a seasoned veteran, soon recognized it in me, her youngest child. Even after extensive testing, it took until age twelve to have a diagnosis of Dyslexia in hand. Armed as I was with a diagnosis and support, difficulties in secondary school abounded. The school system fostered learning for neuro-typical children, not for neuro-divergent children. At fifteen, after mum had a conversation with the head of the school support team, I returned to the doctor's office, only to leave with a new diagnosis – ADD. Some children wear their diagnosis as a badge of honour and find ways to bend the system to suit themselves, but it meant I was "different", so I struggled with my self-esteem. People with ADD/ADHD are not just their diagnoses; they are often verbally gifted, have excellent problem-solving skills, and are outside-the-box thinkers, attributes of the entrepreneurial spirit.

Entrepreneurial spirit or not, I still needed a degree to work in my area of interest, so I set off for college. Continuing in a system created for the neuro-typical was challenging, but I completed my degree in Wildlife biology, allowing me to do what I love. My education could take me where I was most happy – outdoors, assessing the natural world and ecologically making it a better place. Living on four acres in Bray, Ireland, with a botanist as a grand-parent, I grew up exploring the natural world and loved it. Do what you love, and you will never work a day.

I have applied for permanent residency in Canada because, as the second-largest country in the world, it is full of endless possibilities for a Wildlife Biologist and space to communicate my innovative ideas in my way.

Harry Alexander Conan

Deborah Drummond, CEO of Mission Accepted Media, speaker, trainer, direct sales specialist, anti-aging expert.

DEBORAH
DRUMMOND

In 365 words is it possible to "let you in?"

It seems to me the circle of life is the circle back to who we truly are.

My early days weren't the easiest. I've had, like many of you, situations that shaped me for a time, until I was brave enough to shape myself back!

Was it easy? No. Was it worth it? Yes.

If you're a sister or brother survivor… I hear you.

Now, on with life…

My creativity was God given; it took me time to accept that it wasn't a valued asset of the generation I was born into. I always saw things a little differently.

Since I was two, I had things to do and places to go.

My mother would find me hanging out at the top of our apple tree that I had somehow climbed, or hopping my crib over to the window and escaping. It was a pretty regular occurrence for my mom to get calls from the neighbours saying I was running down the street… again

It's probably no surprise I ended being an ultrapreneur and serving others to be the same.

I've been a woman entrepreneur for over 30 years so "I get it," you might have to be the first, so be it! You might need to break down a few doors, "so do it."

You might lose… you'll recover.
You might win… you'll always win.
You might intimidate people…that's a definite.

But that's what bravery and legacy are made of.

I'm not one of those people that say, I wouldn't change anything about my life, as it made me who I am. If there were things I could have a "do over" on, I just might. If I could've avoided some of what life threw at me and throw it back, heck yeah! I would throw it back. I have been seasoned in life enough to say… no matter what has or will happen, we may or may not have control. But it's our job to do what we can to recover, become wiser and weave WITH life in a way that makes you feel whole and is done in service to your heart.

Deborah Drummond

NICKY ARNDT

Staying in the moment is more complicated than it sounds!

We live in a world that continuously has us preparing for the future. High school preps us for college, college for our first job, our first job for our second, etc. We do not even realize that we are not truly living in the moment but preparing for the next.

After my cancer diagnosis in 2019, I was stopped dead in my tracks. Living, something I was clearly taking for granted, was no longer a given. I lived like time was limitless and realized I had squandered it on occasion. The thing you want most when you get that diagnosis is more time. Time is a precious commodity. You realize you want time to see your kids on their way, time to meet your grandchildren and time to see the world.

I was told I was in remission in May of 2020, but life had changed. I had neuropathy and tinnitus from the chemo and had to retire due to my health and covid. Every new minor symptom had me worrying that the cancer was back, and I was hanging on to my daughters too tightly for fear of missing out on time with them. Things had to change.

I had an epiphany while doing art therapy at Wellsprings in London, Ontario. We were asked to paint something from our gardens, so I ran out and grabbed some figs and began to paint. When our instructor asked us to stop and show the class, I wasn't quite finished, which was annoying. She then asked us to cut it up and create something new. I told her I didn't want to because I liked my painting just like it was. She pointed out that I had enjoyed my life before cancer just like it was but was forced to create something new.

My new life is a work in progress. I have a job I can take with me. I am now an editor, not a vice-principal. I am currently writing this from a cross country tour with my daughter. Canada is stunning! I am stopping to savour every moment!

Teresa Syms is a transformational coach, award-winning author, speaker, and podcast host who incorporates real life experiences into her work.

TERESA
SYMS

How does facing death change you?

I've looked death in the eyes, but was left alive for a reason.

I have grown and re-evaluated my life in order to come out the other side of tragedy.

In 2007, I was hit head-on by a truck. Seconds before impact, I braced myself, prayed, screamed (silently of course), and waited. I truly thought I was going to die! I was not ready to leave! I had just gotten remarried, had a new career in human resources and was looking forward to life.

Three days later, my job and HR career ended. I was left alive but with a brain injury, spine damage, multiple soft tissue injuries and ten fractured teeth. For five years, I lived in hell. Not only did I have to repair my body and brain, which meant multiple treatment plans, therapies and hard work, but I was now locked in a battle with the insurance company. I was treated like I was guilty and put through the red-tape ringer. Frustration, anger and the injustice of the entire process did not aid me in my recovery, but it was there... it was always there under the surface.

Once the dust of the legalities settled, I was left with "what now" syndrome. How could I contribute when I cannot sit, stand or walk for more than 20 minutes without pain. Of course, on the outside, I looked like I always had. Well, maybe a bit more tired. Therefore, people didn't understand or believe how badly I was hurt, even my own family didn't understand. I was called a "catastrophic injury" by the doctors.

But the truth is... I am not a victim! There are ways I could still contribute. It began with writing my first book, *A Century of Secrets.* That led to three coaching certifications, NLP, and cognitive behavioural therapy training. I was now armed with experience and education; I knew I could change lives. I've combined coaching with a podcast called *Powering Through Life*, and truth be told, my new, revived life, designed by me, emerged. I became powerful, living with purpose.

Bonnie Mills is a realtor from White Rock, BC who enjoys spending time with her family and friends.

BONNIE
MILLS

As a little girl, I dreamt that I would grow up, get married and raise a family. I gave little thought about who I wanted to be as a woman or what I wanted to contribute to the world. This was all going according to plan until one morning on September 1, 2005, when my husband was killed in a motorcycle accident on his way to work. In the blink of an eye, my whole world was shattered and I found myself a widow, with three young children aged three, five, and six. I felt lost and hopeless. Shortly after that, my eldest daughter was diagnosed with a life altering neurological condition that caused her to lose her vision in her left eye. It was during that time that I was connected with a counsellor who had a profound impact on my life. She would drive us to appointments or just meet me for coffee. There were days that I couldn't bring myself to answer my phone. I just checked out. I remember she gave me a piece of paper that said, "what would a 34-year-old woman do?" I put it on my fridge and would look at it when I felt paralyzed with indecision. It sounds so simple, but when you feel like life has cracked you wide open, even the simplest tasks can feel daunting. Little by little, I built a tool box, so that no matter how overwhelmed I felt I had a plan of action. You can overcome any obstacle if you start with a plan.

My kids are all grown up now with lives of their own, and I have a beautiful grandson. I decided last year that it is time for a change. At 48 years old I went back to school and got my real estate license. It was empowering to take charge of my life and pursue a goal that I have been talking about for so many years. It was also terrifying to put myself out there in such a competitive field. I'm very much a work in progress but it's so exciting to have my future a blank slate. Anything is possible.

Elizabeth Oates finds peace in trusting life's path, taking what it gives her, and embracing the journey along the way.

ELIZABETH **OATES**

Faith, the Art of Silence, and Surrender

Faith is often defined as "belief in something unseen" or "complete trust or confidence in someone or something". But for those who are driven to succeed, this concept may be hard to embrace, and that's been me. I want to control my circumstances, avoid disappointment, have things go my way, know the future, and have it all happened fast. It's hard to meet these expectations. Unfortunately, through my life experiences, I have learned to respond by trusting only myself.

This mindset has been fatiguing. I think we all have an innate desire to trust someone or believe in something outside ourselves.

Then comes the silence.

When transitioning out of my corporate career, I sat in silence for over six months. Surprisingly, this brought me refreshment and peace. I started to trust the silence. Little did I know that a path to successful entrepreneurship was on the other side of the silence. Greatness was forming for me without the need to orchestrate.

Silence is resting in the confidence that greatness will happen. It's just a matter of time.

It's an art to be silent and still. Nothing to control or act on, just silence. This, for me, has been my most significant act of faith: just to believe.

Silence leads to surrender.

Surrender means letting go of the need to grasp things tightly. It's yielding to a power outside of yourself. But how can I surrender when we all know you have to "do" to "get"? Surrender is counter intuitive.

I had to relinquish the fear of being hurt and the perception that surrender is weak. It was the opposite: there was strength in knowing that I didn't control everything. I could embrace risk, disappointment or even failure by knowing that there was more power outside of anything I could say or do. Surrendering daily control brought contentment. And this contentment brought confidence to keep moving forward.

I am learning to embrace faith.
Believe in something unseen.
Trust the silence.
Live with confidence.

Kwantlen member and an entrepreneur who serves on several local, provincial, and national Boards.

BRENDA LYNN KNIGHTS

Where I am today has been the direct result of my journey and the lessons I've learned along the way. In difficult moments, the greatest life lessons are learned.

It's very hard in the moment while going through adversity to see or understand what the purpose or life lesson might be. So how does one stay grounded? By surrounding oneself with friends and loved ones that bring strength, positivity, and love. We also must stay connected with the teachings. In my case, it comes from my Coast Salish teachings that have existed since time immemorial:

1. Trust in the Creator

   I have learned to trust that the Creator only gives as much as one can handle and prepares us for something later in Life.

2. Living by the seven laws of Life

   a. Health – A healthy mind, body and spirit keep stress levels in check.

   b. Happiness – work every day to not speak negatively and then take it further by challenging oneself not to think negative thoughts.

   c. Humbleness – the ego has a way of taking over thoughts in one's mind, and so when stress arrives, it is easy to want to blame someone or something instead of remaining humble.

   d. Generations – Be conscientious about the consequences of decisions and how they affect the next seven generations.

   e. Generosity – be open to finding common ground in conflict, thank and be kind to those who help you, and give kindness generously.

   f. Forgiveness – dwelling or continuing to harbour anger toward others only hurts oneself and not the other party.

   g. Understanding – try and understand why the other party acted the way they did, even in the most challenging situations.

3. Change takes seven generations – Knowing that real and meaningful change can take seven generations is a reminder that things don't always happen on the expected timeline.

Stress can be a difficult thing and by no means do I pretend to have mastered these teachings. I'm not perfect, and the important thing is to try my best each day.

Joël Fafard is an international touring and recording artist who, along with his wife Megan, runs JVGallery.ca

JOËL
FAFARD

Photo credit: Thomas Schleiken

Stage fright! Sometimes I forget that I ever had it, but I did, and it was crippling. Long before my career started, I was terrified that it was already over. I attended music college in the early '90s, and there was a live performance class where we would form student groups and perform and critique each other, the final word coming from our professor. I am sure it was a good idea, but it was too much for me. I immediately developed performance anxiety and stage fright where there had been none before. I was frozen. My hands were stiff and musical ideas were evaporating quickly.

I knew I had to face my fears head-on to get past this new development. The most frightening thing I could think of was to take the #10 bus to Granville street on a Friday night, forcing myself to perform for an hour to disinterested passers-by. Surprisingly, that's what I did. I did this for a few months before it started to feel a little easier, but it always required a few hours of psyching myself up each time. After a while, two friends wondered what I was up to and started to join me with their guitars. Sean, Duane and I worked up some Hank Williams, Steve Earl, and Traveling Wilbury songs, tied strings of bottle caps to our ankles for a bit of rhythm, put out an open case and gave ourselves the name the Twisting Hics. The three of us started to draw crowds that we could count on to support our beer needs for a good night at the pub. I soon forgot about my stage fright and fell in love with performing once again. Truthfully, it took several years of touring for it to fade completely. The first few years of touring, I used to act as if I was not nervous, and I convinced the audience that I was bursting with confidence.

My wife Megan helped me build a pre-show meditation, which has become a ritual for me. Now I feel connected and at my best on a stage, alone with my guitar and voice, ready to share with an audience.

Megan Mansbridge is a painter and mixed media artist based in BC. She had her beginnings in sculpture and has moved into working with oil on canvas. She loves to paint the West Coast rainforest and poultry with attitude.

MEGAN A.
MANSBRIDGE

As a child I could easily spend hours happily entertaining myself amidst nature, making art or singing. I never felt lonely or alone. Instead, I found a deep sense of contentment and peace in my own world and that quiet place within me.

Early in my teen years I began to experience a myriad of health challenges that grew to be chronic and have followed me throughout my life to the present day. After learning that Western medicine had no answers or solutions to offer me, I turned inward, going back to nature almost like a bee going to the flower, or a monarch migrating thousands of miles. I had the valuable example of my own mother turning to natural healing methods and her instincts for her own health during my childhood, so I had a solid foundation from which to spring.

The most powerful a resource in my life for bodily, emotional, mental, creative and spiritual well-being has been my relationship and connection to nature. It has always allowed me to quiet the din of the world around me and return to that place of peaceful and quiet 'being'ness. It provides endless scope for exploration and inspiration for my art. It grounds me in wisdom on my path as a mother. It has sheltered me and accepted my deepest pain and grief when I have had no way to transform that suffering on my own. It has provided plant medicines when I need them in times of illness and trial. It resets my inner rhythms and my very heart beat when the world around beckons me to tune into its madness. It brings me back to myself and reminds me that I have everything I need inside to heal myself and return to balance.

So, when I have gone too far into or stayed too long in the world outside of me, when I feel it luring me into the disharmony, I remind myself to return to the well that feeds my whole being; the forests, the hillsides, the shorelines and rivers. I breathe that energy into the very core of my being, and then I am whole once more.

Tina Pashumati James: A natural born survivor, entrepreneur since her 20s. She is a single mother with two incredible sons, an environmentalist, mentor, game changer.

TINA
PASHUMATI JAMES

We are never defined by our story, no matter what it is; we are our own reality.

I loved writing for Pursuit:365. This is all about me, me, me!

In the beginning…

I have had so many pivotal moments in my life. One thing I have learnt is that we are the masters of our own destiny. There is no quick fix, only hard work and passion, deep compassion and kindness for all beings.

My life has been very traumatic, but I came here to experience life, not to avoid it. The good, the bad and the ugly.

It began when I was diagnosed with dyslexia at nine years old. At the time, it was misunderstood, with no formula on how to work with it. I lost my first boyfriend in a motorcycle accident, I experienced a toxic work situation in Italy at age 17, and had major surgery.

At 19, a drunk driver drove into me whilst riding my horse in a country lane. I suffered a major brain injury, massive trauma to my face, and a spinal injury. I was in the hospital for a month. In 2014 I was diagnosed with cancer and had lymphatic nodes removed. I chose to use alternative medicines; turkey tail mushrooms, which I later started to grow, my yoga program, meditation, and Indigenous ceremonies which are now part of my life.

I moved my family to Canada in 2005, and in 2012, as a single mother, built a yoga studio with Indigenous collaborations. I battled for years to finish our permanent residence, and then citizenship success in 2021.

I would never let all the drama of life become my story, it's so self-limiting. I work with introspection to ignite empowerment in my life. When life has its inevitable pain and we feel broken, you get the potential to reconstruct your life and fill in the cracks with love. It's an art of acknowledging our precious scars and letting go.

When we repair and work with trauma in a positive way, this is the essence of resilience.

All you can do is the best you can, and that's enough.

Happiness is my family and mother nature.

Inhale, "let." Exhale, "go." Let go.

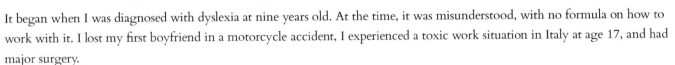

Katherine McEachnie is a wine educator, vineyard owner, best selling author and food & wine event host.

KATHERINE
McEACHNIE

Being told I had three months to live at age 26 made age 60 seem impossible to achieve. It's 2022 and the year I turn 60 years young. Winning the battle against cancer makes me feel incredibly grateful to be alive.

The fire in my belly has always burned brighter than the fire around me. My favourite quote is: "There is no chance, no destiny and no fate, that can circumvent, hinder or control, the FIRM resolve of a determined soul." I know that with persistence and determination, I can achieve anything.

For over 30 years I have had an immense passion for wine. I knew that I had to educate my passion if I was going to share it with the world in a purposeful way. This took enormous effort. I travelled to over 12 countries to meet viticulturists and winemakers. I studied most extensively in France, and as a result, became a French wine scholar. Through my love and passion for champagne, and frequent visits to the Champagne region, I studied to become one of only 75 Masters of Champagne in the world. My WSET diploma gives me a solid understanding of the global business of wine. I always wanted my own vineyard and was leaning in with intention.

In 2017, my dream came true, and I now own a private ten-acre vineyard estate on the Naramata Bench. Moving to the Okanagan made me want to learn more about the local geological history, plant physiology, soil chemistry, etc. I went back to school at age 55 and graduated from the viticulture program at Okanagan College. We tend to seek permission and confirmation that what we want isn't selfish. We need to stop asking for permission and enjoy the fruits of our labour.

Living in the heart of wine country, I am fortunate to make a living writing professional tasting notes, scores and winery profiles for several wineries and the Okanagan Wine Club. At my private vineyard, I create customized wine tastings, wine and food pairings, and vineyard tours by appointment only. My business gives joy to others and puts education at the forefront of the experience. My cup is full when I am sharing my passion.

Live with intention, lean into your passion, and you too will find your gift.

Dr. Divi Chandna is a family physician turned intuitive coach. She helps people live happier, healthier & more joyful lives!

DIVI
CHANDNA

I have been blessed in my life, but that doesn't mean that I haven't had my share of hardships.

After medical school, I got quite sick with anxiety, allergies and crippling pain. I was only able to heal myself through alternative methods. For an in depth description of that journey, check out my TedX talk.

I have spent much of my time after medical school understanding the human mind and human experience.

What I have discovered is this:
We are all capable of greatness.
We are all here to serve each other.
We all have access to infinite joy, infinite health and infinite wealth.

But in order to begin that journey, we have to start to unpack our stories.

Each of us have these stories that are stuck in our subconscious, in our bodies and in our lives. They keep replaying themselves like a bad movie on repeat!

By the time we wake up when we are 40 years old, we can look back at our lives and see the repeated pattern of pain. For example, there may be a pattern of abandonment, loneliness, or rejection. These are just a few examples.

These repeated stories originate in our childhood experiences and are necessary parts of our growth.

It is only when we look at these stories, bear witness to our pain and heal them with love and forgiveness that we can create new stories.

The wildest thing that I have seen in my decades of this type work is that our soul chooses these experiences for the growth of our soul knowing.

When I started to truly understand this, then I began seeing the contrast or hardships as a huge gift. I started to see that it is only through pain that we can evolve as an individual and as a human race.

So what I do now is help people individually and in classes to heal. I use intuition as one of my skill sets to help others grow. Everything we encounter from physical pain to financial difficulty to mental health challenges to relationship havoc is part of our soul growth.

Each of us is being asked to step forward and heal.

Cadi Jordan is a wife, mum, business, and marketing consultant that brings her clients results through Led to Listen© framework.

CADI
JORDAN

One of my favourite quotes is Proverbs 29:18, "Where there is no vision, the people parish." I share this because of the grave lack of vision that can come with business owners and entrepreneurs when they get stuck in one area of either their business or life. Sometimes things become out of alignment and the right orders need to take place to create change in their business.

I started my own business back in 2008 without a clear vision other than to be available and at home with my family. The vision came into play after living through sporadic work times and late nights, something that no one signs up for. I quickly shifted into full serve marketing, social media strategy, and services to help business growth from behind the scenes. After a while, I added teaching workshops and started speaking at conferences.

What I have found over the years is that clients had goals but didn't have a vision to match, similarly to how I started out. It's one thing to tick the boxes and feel accomplished, but if it doesn't align with your vision then you're still not getting very far. It's important to spend that time, not only for your business, but for your family and relationships as well. This is where true growth comes. Our inner game reflects our outer game, so you always have to start with vision.

Starting with a vision in mind is an important part of the work I do, because it is an integral part of the initial framework. This is the time when you get rid of what doesn't serve you and do more of what works to move you forward. Having a solid plan and strategy built on a firm foundation is longer lasting, not only for your business, but for your relationships with others and the overall connection of every aspect of your life.

We see a lot of "finding your purpose" in the self-help space, and I truly believe that you can improve your life "with purpose". Gaining clarity on what matters most to you is how you will make an impact and keep moving forward in life and in business.

Salley-Ann Ross, MA, RCC is a registered clinical counsellor with Alyson Jones and Associates.

SALLEY-ANN
ROSS

I believe that life's struggles are common for all. Each person no matter what age, culture, gender, or abilities, share similar struggles. However, the language that each of us use to work through these struggles may be different from one another.

As a key member of the counselling team at Alyson Jones and Associates, I see the potential in every person. I believe that we are pioneers in our own experiences and working through them starts with exploration, followed by the discovery of growth, learning, accepting, and finding how to let go. As a keynote speaker, accomplished musician, music therapist, clinical counsellor, and guided imagery therapist, I work with individuals of all ages and circumstances.

I am no stranger to the challenges that life may entail and have navigated my own travels through life with both a tenacity and enthusiasm as a lifelong learner. I enjoy contributing to the psychological field through education and continue to build practical solutions and experiences for my clients as I assist them on their own journeys of healing and growth.

As a person of mixed race, I have brought the gifts of my ancestral stories to model this for my three amazing daughters. I continue to bring forth a strong and healthy matriarchal legacy, with pride, endurance, wisdom, strength, and humility. I do so whilst continuing to maintain my relationships with my partners in life who are reflections of these qualities, whether it is my life partner who has co-parented with me or my lifetime partner who is my support and mentor.

Modelling this through life, teaching, sharing and unconditional acceptance of where individuals currently find themselves are the keys to understanding, awareness and authenticity. Now, I continue upon the path of discovery and endeavour to pass on my knowledge not only to my own children but to my many clients.

My biggest accomplishments are my sense of truth, motherhood, humility, and commitment to whatever I put my mind to. I believe that everything in life requires each person to work through areas to their fullest potential. It is not a fifty-fifty process. Truth, success, relationships, learning, and reaching any goal is not attainable without always doing our best.

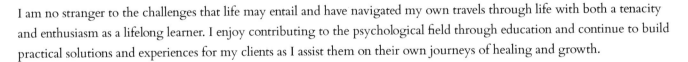

Carolini Arco is a Reiki Master Teacher, ICF ACC Life Coach and Breathwork Facilitator who believes in the power of connection.

CAROLINI
ARCO

The other day, while watching my five-year-old nephew transform a few logs of wood into a giant spaceship during playtime, a question crossed my mind, "When do humans stop believing in magic?"

I remember being a child and believing in fascinating things that the eyes could never see, but I can't remember the moment I stopped believing. Yet, I know that I did stop believing for a while. I became too busy trying to succeed in a big, grown-ups world. While on the outside it looked like I was on the right path, inside, that blank world was slowly killing me.

In my early twenties I was already bitter, already sad. When I felt I didn't have anywhere else to run to from my negative thoughts, I came across an energy healing art called Reiki. I started studying it, and eventually, without me even initiating it, my friends started asking for healing sessions. One of my first healing sessions was through Zoom with a woman in Brazil. As she lay down on her side of the screen, I was taken through a visual journey of her soul. In my mind, I saw her as a five-year-old girl. There was a hand was reaching out to her and giving her a small truck toy. She seemed happy, so I just observed the scene in awe. After the session was over, I shared with her the vision that I had seen. Her eyes began tearing up as she told me she had lost her mother at a very early age, and one of the few memories she had of her was this one moment when her mother gave her a little toy truck. The love she felt from her deceased mother was palpable through the screen. While for her it was a gift to receive, the gift was even larger for me. Somehow, that experience in all its innocence, reminded me to believe in magic once again.

There are many things we might never understand in this world, and perhaps we aren't meant to anyway. However, maybe the point of it is to simply remember, that we can every day, in many ways, believe in magic again.

Alisha (Ali) Moser is an innovative thought leader and activist committed to inspiring a culture of inclusive and equitable change.

ALI
MOSER

Path to Freedom- by Alisha Moser

For much of my life I've admittedly been lost.
Either on a quest for acceptance, love or a greater purpose…

Just.

Lost.

Looking for something external to fill me as if I was looking for permission to exist in a validation of living life correctly.

It wasn't until I hit my thirties that I began to understand the power of standing in my own truth, how freeing that can be when you release the expectations and framed failures of your past that others bestow upon you to instead…be free. To live in acceptance of the history that has shaped you and in turn welcome and celebrate life as textured chapters unwinding the essence of your beauty and being in each moment that leads to this exact presence.

I learned to look inward to develop a relationship with myself, to sit in the heaviness of generational traumas to release and forgive. To both choose a new beginning, abandoning feelings that no longer served me and were never mine to own. Recognizing that the love and acceptance I seek in others may never be feasible because that would be assuming that they are in a place to meet me in true equity. After years of relinquishing my power to others in definition of myself, I've come to the truest acceptance that only I can define me. I am unencumbered by external oppressions, the words and judgements that used to paralyze my self-worth now slide off the back of my free spirit. I was never broken; it was a perpetuation to believe I was. Free from the shackles of expectation, I honour my light. I accept interactions with others for what they are… perfectly imperfect. I am here for a purpose, on purpose; what I do with that is mine and mine alone. In truth, I realized my purpose was never lost, through each trial and tribulation it evolved, it sharpened, it grew into an undeniable force that wasn't years out, but with me daily, in each moment of existence. I was living it, I just needed to be in a position to receive it trusting its guided path to my liberation.

Photo credit: Grace McClure

Teresa Altiman is an Ojibwe Artist.

TERESA ANN
ALTIMAN

Optimism, gratefulness, and acceptance are key!

As an Ojibwe woman, I recognize and accept that life has a natural ebb and flow, a rhythm all its own. Like the waters, life is fluid, and we must move with it. We can plan our futures but not grasp them so tightly that we miss the opportunities presented. Trials and tribulations are also part of life's natural tides, and like joy, sorrow is fleeting. Live in the moment, but do not get stuck there. Mourn with purpose, but when happiness returns, greet it and rejoice. Like the seasons, life changes.

At 73, I look back and marvel at the path my life has taken. My art career is more solid now than it has ever been. I am an artist but have also been a daughter, sister, auntie, friend, caregiver, learner, and educator. I have tried to wear every title with honour. Raised by two residential school survivors, my parents valued having us all at home with them. Love was always present. As a child, I could not have imagined the turns my life would take. A natural curiosity and passion for recording my observations had me drawing on every available scrap of paper or anything else I could find as art supplies were scarce. In elementary school, a teacher recognized my potential, encouraged me, and later helped me apply to art college. While away at the Ontario College of Art, my parents passed away, and I began raising my youngest brother. My art career waxed and waned over the years as earning a living took precedence. Over time, I lost my brothers one by one, and now my sisters and I remain to recall the shared laughter and tears. We respect them by talking about and remembering them. They contributed to our happiness, and we are better for having shared in their lives.

Gratitude is part of my daily life. Through daily prayer, I focus my thoughts, find my centre and embrace the gifts which gizhe-manidoo, the creator, has bestowed. As life unfolds, I flow with it, doing the things I find most meaningful. My happiness is deep-rooted in flexibility, optimism, and gratitude!

Teresa Ann Altiman

210

Chantelle Hansen, business owner, industrious
farmer, and dedicated mother!

CHANTELLE
HANSEN

When you get to do what you love, it doesn't feel like work at all!

Growing up in a small town, coming from a loving and supportive home, I learned to be a hard worker. My work ethic was instilled in me throughout childhood by my parents and has driven the choices that have led me to live the life I have always wanted.

In 2011, a desire to expand my career took my two small children and I to a new town. Leaving the familial support system I had always known, in the community where I had grown up, was scary, but the personal and professional experiences and benefits gained were terrific.

After several years, a second move brought us to another new community. We chose to live on a small, picturesque hobby farm. My husband and I worked on farms growing up but had no idea what was involved in becoming farmers. I have always enjoyed the outdoors, and the farm provides plenty of fresh air. Working in the fields or gardens and watching things grow gives me personal satisfaction and happiness. Buying the hobby farm and figuring out its best use was an exciting time. Involving the children enriched their lives immeasurably.

In 2017, I shifted again, leaving the corporate world and starting my own business. I continued independently to build my professional human resources career, but striking out on my own gave me the flexibility to spend additional time farming. In 2018, we put in our first crop and by 2020, we had our first harvest. It was so exhilarating!

I believe I am most fortunate to have the opportunity to build a farming business and provide professional services in a completely different industry while raising extraordinary children. This takes time, planning, and hard work. It means taking courageous risks, managing fears and expectations, and moving forward to achieve my goals. Living life to its fullest while enjoying and learning from all experiences is something I try to instil in my children. I relish the diversity and flexibility of my work, and I love the life I get to live.

Chantelle Hansen

Rishma credits her cancer for the way she pursues life with faith and gratitude.

RISHMA
DHALLA

Having cancer at the age of forty was a game changer for me. Through leaning into my death, I determined how I wanted to live. Searching my soul through books, prayers, meditations, and deep conversations, and forgiving myself for being imperfect, afforded me the freedom to start over and be who I was meant to be. By keeping my two young boys at the forefront, I was able to glide gracefully (with some trips and falls along the way) through my two-year journey.

The physical pain brought with it resolve I never knew I had. The uncertainty of my future brought with it faith and acceptance unlike anything I had experienced before. Losing my hair led to a depression so scary, it brought me to my knees. And from this place of humility, I began my slow and steady rise. But not alone. My family was there throughout, with homemade meals, daily messages, lots of laughter and hugs. And my therapist supported me through her wise words: "One day at a time; one moment at a time; one breath at a time."

I asked myself: "How do I want to be remembered when I'm gone?" And then I lived that way. I became forgiving, understanding, non-judgmental, deeply spiritual, and more empathetic than ever before. I stopped taking myself (and, in turn, others) so seriously. I sang out loud in the car, I tried new hairstyles, we traveled more, I became friends with my boys. I paid attention to the synchronicities in my life and saw a larger purpose to my cancer.

I met my soul sister in those two years, and I was by her side as she faced her own mortality. I prayed with her, read to her, dreamt and giggled with her. And on July 31, 2014, I said goodbye to her. But not forever. I know without a doubt we will be reunited on the other side.

And so I live each day to the fullest, knowing that this is not all there is. I am not afraid to die, but not yet. I have plans to continue to help and inspire others, watch my sons get married, become a dadimaa, and so much more.

212

Proud Gitsan Warrior Woman, loving mother and grandmother, cultural wisdom and traditional language guide, program facilitator, early childhood educator, guest speaker, mentor, and student of life.

LAUREEN
WEGET

I endured many traumas from a young age when I attended a residential day school in my community. I grew up in survival mode, always watching and needing to protect myself and my siblings from being bullied, beaten, or assaulted. I've always had a voice and known how to use it.

While all of this was going on, I still had unconditional love at home from my Na'ah (grandmother), who was my protector, teacher, champion, my … everything. She taught me never to forget who I am or where I come from and told me to go out and get an education! My parents taught me that if I wanted something, I needed to work for it and encouraged me not to stay on the rez where I had everything.

I found myself in a toxic and abusive relationship, got pregnant at age 17, and had my first child at age 18. As a young Mom, I was overwhelmed and struggled with anger and lack of confidence all the time.

When my Na'ah died, I felt a part of me had died with her, and addiction claimed me for a long 15 years. I numbed my pain with marijuana and alcohol. But still … my spirit was fierce.

Due to the teachings from my Na'ah and parents, I became a go-getter, am often self-taught, and I believe you need to move-move-move to do and get what you want.

My husband (a relationship of 30 years) provides balance, support, and love. I have been alcohol-free for 30 years and drug-free now for the last 25 years. I am a mother of 5 and a grandmother of 4. When my daughters say, "thank you for being our mom, guiding and teaching us, being our role model, and being so loving and supportive," it fills my heart with joy.

Life is about choices.

To honour the creator, I choose to walk with pride, humbleness, respect, and awareness. I choose to be kind.

Jo-Anne Weiler, psychotherapist, life coach, Mother, Step-Mother, tennis player and an advocate of the heart. Jo-Anne facilitates growth retreats.

JO-ANNE
WEILER

Sixty-something, time to "jump into adventure." I want to be BOLD, not OLD. I am an extrovert who likes novelty, people, travel, and freedom; the things that have been shut down across our globe. On the positive side, I've made some changes I am grateful for (changes that I probably wouldn't have made so quickly if it wasn't for COVID-19).

A grown up since childhood, I'm starting to think maybe I'm living my life in chronological reverse. I was a child-adult and now I'm an adult-child. In the last few decades of life, I brought up two children, got my masters, a divorce, and a remarriage. After 17 years, we are still "Jo(e) to the power of two!" Through COVID-19, I also count on my friends, my community, and my family – all of whom haven't always been in our 'bubble.' This love bubble feels a little rosier to me when these special people are playing with me in my world more. I'm not a fan of social distancing, though I am a rule follower and a team player. Put these past two years in the archives.

A strong need for adventure, I recall my most magical moments in my life as being times when I have jumped, dove, or just said "YES, count me IN on that please." I dove into the open ocean in Maui with my daughter Ashley and 100+ dolphins. And I jumped off a zip line 7,000 feet up in Whistler treetops with my son Justin.

Sharing moments with significant people are imprints of my heart.

There is a finish line. There will be a return to grand spirit. But for now, that transformation can wait. I have places to be and adventures to embrace. I've contributed to family and our community a lot through my careers in fitness and psychology, through volunteer work that stretches the globe.

No badges to earn or awards to achieve. No new letters to add to my name. Time to regenerate relationships that matter. If you are reading this, you are likely on my list!!

Enter the unknown places my heart desires. What is my true life calling? It's JOY. I'll meet you there.

Helen is the founder of 'The Jean Collective' and is passionate about encouraging strong female leaders interested in politics.

HELEN
COLE

As a former City of St. Thomas councillor, non-profit manager, community advocate and founder of 'The Jean Collective, a Women in Politics Initiative,' life is always interesting. My love for learning along with a life that includes a husband, five sons and their families ensure that life is never dull.

Childhood was a tumultuous experience resulting in adoption at 12 years of age. At almost nineteen, I married. Later my employment meant a return to school. Over the years, my career has included work in local government and non profits.

Early in my nine years as an elected politician, I met Jean Macdougall who opened up a magnificent world of wonder, curiosity, risk, and acceptance. Her unconditional love & support allowed me to grow in ways I never could have imagined especially given my early childhood.

After remarriage & a move to Sarnia, I accepted a one-year contract with the Canadian Cancer Society Sarnia-Lambton that turned into an almost fourteen years as Manager of the Sarnia Lambton local office. We provided a myriad of patient services and education programs to the public. I led a team that raised more than one million dollars annually for several years, by organizing major fundraising events such as 'RazMaTaz,' 'Pink Cruise,' 'What Women Want,' 'Do it for Dad', 'Grand Desserts', 'Taking Steps Against Breast Cancer' and 5 annual 'Relay for Life' events. These efforts contributed to the Canadian Cancer Society winning the 2010 Outstanding Business Achievement Award in the Not-for-Profit category.

I continued to remain involved in the Sarnia Lambton community through the Chamber of Commerce, Goodwill, and the Family Counselling Centre. In 2019, I personally won a Sarnia Lambton Chamber of Commerce Outstanding Business Achievement Award, just before the entire world shut down!

My interest in politics continues, and so, I have formed 'The Jean Collective, a Women in Politics Initiative.' A supportive Information/education program designed to encourage strong female leaders who wish to support, volunteer or be involved in politics. The Jean Collective is committed to non-discrimination regardless of ethnicity, race, age, or sexual orientation. Jean's legacy also continues through a fund I have created at the Sarnia Community Foundation that will provide bursaries to those who enrolled in degree level political science programs.

Helen Cole

Inspired by personal mental health experiences and the tragic loss of loved ones, Hibby Bartlett is the founder of World LOVEBank Inc.

HIBBY
BARTLETT

I still remember the last words I spoke to my older brother on the telephone years ago. He was struggling emotionally, and was dealing with addiction issues and trying to cope. I repeated to him over and over, "I love you", which he would deny and say, "no, you don't". I said those words 15 times before he finally said "I love you too". Little did I know that three months later, he would die, and I would never hear his voice again. He also left behind his three-year-old son, who would never hear those words from him.

Knowing these words were heard by him, helped my own grieving process. Yet, I always wished I had it recorded for his son to hear as well. Years later, when I was dealing with my own issues with recovery and mental health, I searched through religion and mental science, where I learned to understand that "love" is at the core of human nature and something we all desire. I believe that if those words are heard enough, they would have the power to impress upon our subconscious mind, and improve our daily lives.

Changing the perception of love into something to be valued, shared and saved is my goal in life. Over the last two years during the Covid-19 pandemic, and through the loss of both my parents, I focused on finding a way to make the perception of love as intangible – to tangible. In World Lovebank Inc, expressions of "LOVE" is our currency, which we can all share in and exchange as our most priceless asset.

 Transmuting the love of those I lost, and turning it into a solution for others to benefit is why I launched the WorldLOVEBank health and wellness app. I want people from all cultures, backgrounds, with diverse emotional, social and economic experiences to feel valued and connected by unconditional love when using the app.

Not only to build their personal emotional wealth, but to be a part of another's journey to find love and acceptance. We provide a central private digital storage where users can access anonymous meditations of "I love you" support, which is recorded and created by users all around the world, as well as create, send, and receive audio and video private messages, to bank in one safe place now and for future use. WorldLOVEbank app is a digital, international space of kindness, support and most importantly a place for sharing the power of love.

Hibby Bartlett

Emily Mackey is a recent Graduate of Western University - Master of Media in Journalism & Communication.

EMILY
MACKEY

My earliest memory is of storytelling—I'm sitting with my grandpa on an old leather couch, reading him a mermaid love story I had written in a sparkly, blue spiral notebook. While it wasn't winning a Pulitzer, I remember the nervous excitement I had in showing him something I was so proud of. I was stuck at a plot point, and my grandpa looked at me and said: you'll figure it out. Simple—but he was right.

When I was seventeen, I was diagnosed with endometriosis. I was studying English and spent a lot of my time writing for pleasure. However, with my diagnosis came a surprising inability to put pen to paper. I felt angry, scared, and relieved. I felt like I had lost a piece of myself. Looking at the symptoms and long-term effects, I thought I had lost my femininity. Most of the writing I did was romance and writing about love when I was unsure of how my diagnosis would impact my ability to love and be loved felt impossible and for a while, I lost my passion for writing.

I've always been a storyteller. I love connecting with people through words. For two years, I found myself unable to do that. When I was nineteen, I started working in communications and telling the stories of communities, families, last days, first days, and everything in between. I discovered in the process that love exists in many ways outside of romance and using words to convey that is incredibly healing. More than that, I found that my lack of writing didn't stem from my diagnosis but from the loss of a love I had for myself after I heard the diagnosis. I'd figured it out, just like my grandpa always said I would.

When I picked up a pen to start writing again, it was one word at a time, and before long, I was writing like myself and for myself again. When I tell people I love storytelling, it's not for the plot—it's for how it makes me feel whole and healed and how it allows me to make individuals, families, and communities feel the same.

217

GRACE
McCLURE

Take a step back, take a breath, and carry on. These are the words I repeat to myself as I work through my life—day by day, month by month, year by year.

Finding happiness is not my greatest goal in life, and this doesn't mean I'm actively living a life void of things that bring me joy. It's quite the opposite. When I was 15, I suffered a concussion that changed my life. I was playing basketball, a sport so ingrained in me it felt like I had been born for it, and within seconds everything I had ever known was out of my grasp before I even knew it.

I spent a lot of time figuring out who I was after that, and instead of taking a step back, I took several, trying to separate myself from the overwhelming way my world had shifted on its axis. I went on an exchange to Brazil, and it brought me some of the best and worst times of my life, through which I'm still working. I lost and gained people. After a year in Brazil, coming back home had been a necessary break, and now I was carrying on.

Carrying on for me meant figuring out what was important to me and what my goals were. I had no choice now but to confront the fact that the life I had left the year before was no longer serving me. Several more years and a lot of self-reflection made me realize that what I wanted in life, was to create and foster meaningful relationships. Celebrate the people I love. Working towards my personal and professional goals and finding contentment in the things that make up my daily life is what makes me who I am.

When I say my greatest goal in life is not to find happiness, it's not that my goal is to live a life void of joy—it's that chasing happiness is not an effective way to live. You miss out on small yet essential things that are meaningful. You mustn't live in an unattainable, dream version of happiness. Let the day-to-day things be your goal, and fulfilment will follow.

Leanne Banga is a Prairie girl who loves spending time with her new grandson, her two mini dachshunds, landscaping and salsa dancing.

LEANNE
BANGA

Change your story, change your life!

"Maybe I went through it so I could help others make it through," are words that I've come to embrace.

At the age of 11, I was sexually molested by a trusted family member. This continued for years, hiding the ugly truth, and remaining silent. I thought it was my fault since I was wearing shorts that first time and began covering myself. I hated my body and became an insecure, anxious, and co-dependent woman. I looked to others to love me because I couldn't and ended up pregnant at 18. I was a single mom with no post-secondary education, no money, and no hope. I fell into relationships with men who were alcoholics, and faced abandonment and physical assault. I wanted love and security, so I got married, but got divorced and then became fat and depressed.

My breaking point was Thanksgiving 2016, when my youngest brother was killed in a plane crash. My heart broke, and I turned to alcohol, cigarettes, and prescription pills to numb the pain. My life was a vase that I just kept gluing back together, but this time it all shattered to the floor, and I didn't have enough glue to fix it.

This was the fork in the road. I got up and I got accountable. I looked to the 11-year-old girl inside of me, giving her love that we both needed and found out she loves to dance. I found faith and gratitude and that happiness is not pursued but created. Our minds are very powerful, and from them will come either empowerment or fear. Every time you go through something difficult it makes you a little bit stronger. My scars tell a story. They are reminders of when life tried to break me, but failed. Life hurts us all in different ways, but it's how we respond and who we become that determines whether a trauma becomes a tragedy or a triumph. We have to choose between being a victim or a victor, but you can't be both. We allow the things that happen to us to either empower us or disempower us, but your power is in the response. Once you become empowered, life becomes limitless!

For the record…since getting accountable; I no longer smoke, rarely drink alcohol, no prescription meds or the likes and committed to a healthy lifestyle of food and exercise and shed over 40 lbs.

LYNNET
ANTONIO-GO

Philippines, 1999.

On our way home from Sunday mass, I told my husband Albert to make a quick stop at a local Mercury drugstore. Little did I know that our family's destiny would start to unfold after a chance encounter at the pharmacy with one of Albert's childhood friends who he hadn't seen in 20 years. We were inspired by stories of his family's quality of life in Canada. Before we even left the pharmacy, our young son, Justin, agreed to the idea of migrating to Canada. Despite the immensity of the plan, it was the fastest decision we ever made as a family.

Our life was constant and comfortable in Manila. We never entertained thoughts of living abroad. Until that moment. Carpe vitam.

My faith in my God is my bedrock. Albert's parents, and mine, are my champions. The immigration process was not easy but I never held any doubts.

My mom, Lydia, dreamt of becoming a lawyer like her father, but the cruelty of her stepmother prevented her from pursuing her dream. Her dynamism never to be extinguished, mom found her passion in socio-civic and religious activities supporting marginalized Filipinos.

At the young age of 15, my dad, Fred, lied about his age so he could enlist to be a guerilla resistance fighter against the Japanese invasion of the Philippines in 1941.

There are days when I would talk aloud to Albert's mama Adoracion, hoping she can hear me from heaven. Mama was the epitome of wisdom and serenity. I can still hear her gentle voice reminding me to "always look for the positive in the negative," and to "let go, let God".

Albert's papa Augusto was from a family of Chinese merchants selling goods in Manila. After China closed its borders in 1937, papa never set foot in his homeland again. Mechanically gifted, he would hone his genius towards a career and business in his adoptive Philippines.

Their early lives were dark, dangerous and uncertain, but they were able to transform it into something good and meaningful. And I never let go of that inspiration.

Canada, 2004. I brought that inspiration with me to Vancouver.

Light and love! Pax!

A member of the Skw̲xwú7mesh Úxwumixw (Squamish Nation), a proud grandmother and mother; she is passionate about uplifting future generations through being a relationship holder, bridge, connector, and source of light and energy.

JESSIE
WILLIAMS

I am honoured to be the Director of Business Development and Communications for the New Relationship Trust (NRT), an Indigenous non-profit organization committed to empowering First Nations in British Columbia. One aspect of my role I am inspired by the most is focusing on identifying, building, and leveraging partnerships, connections and relationships in a way that uplifts and creates space for Indigenous presence, voice, knowledge, wisdom, brilliance, and perspectives. I invite us, from all walks of life, from all four directions, to stand next to each other in this vital work. Before we do business, we must focus first on building reciprocal relationships. There is a word in my language that I live by, Nch'u7mut (to be one, to be in unity). I've been taught that we must always give to receive and listen before we speak. We need each other in this work. The impact is more significant when we share in uplifting communities. I call on everyone to see who is not present in your work but needs to be. And create space for them. Because representation matters. I take great pride in this work as it allows me to use my gifts, strengths, knowledge, skills, abilities, and passion for contributing to social impact through collaboration.

My foundation as a human is my teachings. I make a habit of reflecting on what my grandparents, parents, aunts, and uncles have shared with me. One that always comes to mind is from my late grandfather, who told me I was going to be a leader, connector, relationship builder.

From them I also learned to pay attention to that gut feeling we get about a decision or a situation which I like to call our' spirit voice'. This spirit voice is strong, and when we feel it, listen to it, trust it. It has valuable information about whether something is correct or incorrect for us. As people we have the power to choose what makes us feel fulfilled, vibrant, and impactful. Standing together, in unity we can have social impact and uplift our communities.

SABRINA
ROC

Imagine for a moment you lost everything you had to pursue a dream at forty years old.

Imagine being paralyzed physically and emotionally with thoughts of… "I am an epic failure…" swirling in your mind.

In 2016, I left my home in Montreal. I knew I needed more than a change. When my partner had a job opportunity to move to the West Coast, I was all in. Even if I knew our relationship was not working and our business was not moving forward as expected. When it came to love, I knew something was off. I had no real plan. Soon after we moved, my partner announced the end of our marriage.

I carried nothing but my sad survival story for months until, through much soul-searching, I saw my sad story for what it was. A tale. All made up. This is what I learned from failure. It is subjective, just like success, and neither of them are real. I thought to myself, what if I change my narrative?

Imagine at forty, you had nothing to lose and everything to gain. Imagine you were called on a grand adventure called life. Imagine daring. This version, although it made me feel better, was not factual.

What happened is this: I moved and dealt with the challenges of a new place. I did a few financial transactions that did not give me the expected result. I did not honour my vows to my partner, and I decided to stay and make the West Coast my home.

As much as I wanted this imaginative story to be real, it was not. I accepted it in a way that freed my mind and heart to see I don't need to seek success; I no longer avoid failure. This is how I found the light amidst the darkness. I focus on now, this present life, this new relationship with life itself. I learned failure and success are all made up, and I am here now, with or without it. Please remember, this is your life. You are the author. Imagine it. Create it. Be it. It's now.

Community Leader, Executive Director of
Dze L K'ant Friendship Centre, BCAAFC
President, and dedicated mother.

ANNETTE
MORGAN

I am a proud member of the Gitxsan Nation located in
British Columbia. My traditional name is Nox Stikine which
translates as Mother of the Stikine. Leadership, no matter how
challenging, is the path I have chosen to walk.

My understanding of my family trauma due to my mother's
experience at residential school has deeply shaped who I am
and my life's work. Having to bear witness to her stories and
reactions, having to understand what my mother went through and what those dynamics meant, has made me who I am. Once
you know those stories you can never turn your back on them.

My observations during childhood and young adulthood set me on the path toward truth, problem-solving and reunification.
My goal is to enhance the lives of people, including my own children and Urban Indigenous people. I want a good, kind
community for my children and for all future generations. That's something that has always been important to me. It's about
intergenerational healing and correcting our systems that fail people, not just Indigenous but many people.

My goal is to provide strategic direction, cultural knowledge, and leadership in all that I do. I pride myself on surrounding
myself with relationships founded on trust, compassion, and perseverance. I lead in a way that demands respect, because as a
woman, as an Indigenous person, as a human being I deserve this, we all deserve this.

My greatest strength is communication. For me communication isn't about speaking but about observing and listening to the
opinions and challenges of others. Open communication is part of my cultural responsibility, as is being patient and humble.
My traditional teachings ground me in the importance of making space for a diversity of voices. I strongly believe that there is
no benefit to be had in minimizing the experiences of others. My purpose is to encourage others to find the best in themselves
without any fear or judgement. That is the example I want to set for my children and what I hope to message to people.

Evangelia Kondilis is a decorative artist and muralist who uses art as a grounding outlet for her creative passions.

EVANGELIA
KONDILIS

I have risen out of the ashes, so to speak, from toxic relationships and chronic pain. I have become a multi-talented artist inspired by my surroundings. Whether I am restoring old Greek villas on the rustic island of Samos in my off-season or infusing my client personalities into captivating murals, I live for my passions.

I am a Greek Canadian who is living between Athens and Samos, and Vancouver, Canada. I was raised by a single mother who did everything creatively, so art became a way of life. My early years were full of creative projects. My mother taught me to find creativity in everything I did, whether it be cooking, sewing, painting, or living life finding inspiration in the world around me.

My murals and trompe l'oeil pieces can be seen in restaurants, temples, and upscale homes all around the world. Incredibly realistic and always tricking the eye, I create surfaces for my clients using techniques I learned while studying abroad in France, Italy, the United States, and Canada.

Traveling the world and living between two countries has led me to a diverse array of clients who constantly inspire me. Every creative person knows they need time to recharge and reset; however, there is a delicate balance between giving and receiving inspiration. So, I spend time in Samos, Greece for several months of the year, immersing myself in the small island culture. I replenish my energy and creativity by spending time in nature, swimming every day in the salty waters, handpicking produce, processing my own olives into oil, and connecting with the locals.

Whenever life's anxieties feel too much to bear, I escape into the world of creation and focus on the process of the custom task at hand as it comes together. I find that my creative process helps me tackle the answers to my anxieties.

I pursue success every day by pushing the boundaries of my artistic excellence by creating unique and innovative work. Since most of my work is custom, success means working through my creative process to achieve excellence for each client. Maintaining momentum, I am always open to experimenting with different mediums to achieve an innovative effect and creation.

Blair Kaplan Venables is the Founder of The Global Resilience Project, a social media expert and mentor, best-selling author, podcaster and international speaker. When she's not creating you can find her playing in nature, listening to music, or travelling the world.

BLAIR
KAPLAN
VENABLES

Life is full of challenges and over the last few years I have been given my fair share. Brace yourself, it's gets a little heavy: At the end of 2018 I learned that my father was terminally ill, I lost my grandfather, I sustained a brain injury in a car accident on the way home from my grandfather's funeral, my husband had a heart attack and quadruple bypass surgery, I suffered a miscarriage, I lost my father-in-law a few weeks later and then I lost my mother three months later. 360 days after losing my mother to a three-week battle with cancer, I lost my father.

Nothing can prepare you for this amount of loss and heartbreak. However, I did learn that you can strengthen your resilience muscle. This lesson started back in 2018 when I learned that my father was nearing the end of his life. From sharing our story out of my deep sorrow, I learned that our father and daughter story of heart break, addiction, forgiveness, and resilience was a powerful tool to help others. Our story was inspiring healing in others. So, we decided to build The Global Resilience Project and create a safe space for people to consume and share stories of resilience in order to help the healing process. This project would tell stories online, on a podcast, Radical Resilience and in a published book. The book would with my father's story of living with addiction and end with my story of how I forgave him. This Project would be a legacy piece that would live on, after my father passed on.

On February 6, 2022, I rushed from Vancouver Island, British Columbia to Winnipeg, Manitoba to spend my father's last days with him. We laughed, I cried, we shared memories and he made sure to let my sister and I know how much he loved us. It wasn't until February 18th that he took his last breath. I'm not sure where I would be in life without the strength to forgive. Although I've been in grief vortex for a few years, I am grateful, I love life and am able to be there to help my community through their difficult times.

225

Blair Kaplan Venables

SHANNON
BOAKES

Growing up, I always knew that I could be anything I wanted (within reason). I was a normal, healthy kid and I basically knew (or was told) that I was two things: good at school and kinda chubby.

These things became who I was; I did well in school and graduated with honours from university, all the while winning and losing the battle with my weight for decades. This has been my baseline pretty much my whole life, until a couple of years ago when I met my then regional manager who helped me see how limited my thinking was.

I am blessed to be a wife, mom of two awesome sons and a certified financial planner. I take great pride in my roles at home and in helping people reach their financial goals, but I knew deep down something was missing.

My manager opened my eyes to the power of me! Yep, me! I began paying attention to things like, "your thoughts become your reality" and "your energy is currency." This made me realize that I am not confined to predefined roles; I get to be anyone I want to be, I get to choose how I show up and who I am. In fact, a couple of years later, I am now helping my then regional manager and now most amazing friend run a start-up business – we have such big, big plans!

We dream of inspiring women of all shapes and sizes around the world to move with confidence and be comfortable in their bodies. Wow! Me, helping to launch a business with the goal of helping people be comfortable in their own skin; I truly am in awe of how life unfolds if we're open.

I believe that we are each here for a great purpose and it is our job to figure out what that is. I have now uncovered my true passion – I am here to make meaningful connections and impact lives by showing people that anything is possible, and honestly, WE ARE NOT OUR BODIES! We are so, so much more!

226

Rebellious and bohemian, Lisa Penz's art surrounds the mysteries of our sea, bringing you closer to the water.

LISA
PENZ

From the West Coast to the warm waters of Australia, water's beauty has courted me everywhere I go. My art strives to reclaim a magical world and rebel against one afraid of nonconformity through channeling the duelling majesty and ferocity of this splendor. Never far from the beach, I live and paint in Vancouver where the mountains touch the sea.

"Water is more dangerous than fire." That's what my dad would say when I was a little girl.

To understand where this journey begins, let me tell you a story.

Winter frost painted the landscape. Grand fir trees lined my pathway home as I crossed the little wooden bridge. I loved this shortcut; every third grader did.

The frozen pond beneath the bridge sparkled with the ice-skating patterns of kids at play. The ice thinned towards the center of the pond, beyond the fog where the floating island sat. Chestnut chickadees glided down from the willow tree, barren now that its lacy branches had dropped and fused with the ice. I hated when the birds flew away.

Then the reverie shattered. The raucous voices of three fourth-grade boys crept closer. They encircled me and pushed me onto the frozen pond. As I slid onto thin ice, I heard the crack—so soft, like a zipper. The pond broke open. I fell through as it closed over my head. I kicked for a bottom that wasn't there.

December warmed instantly. My senses adapted; my humiliation evaporated. I saw autumn gold where I had expected the endless bite of winter. Shadows swayed like graceful dancers of light in my mind, composed of mermaids, hidden treasure, skulls of legends.

This secret society of the water has profoundly influenced my art. My coastal lifestyle in Vancouver challenges me to explore our uncharted sea by painting, from my mermaid Talisman to my Abstract skulls.

My style has been refined over 10 years of painting, giving my art otherworldly qualities that possess an uncommon temperature in both culture and color. You are never far from the ocean with my paintings. Hauntingly personal, my art is a siren that will transport you to that golden Bohemian kingdom where we all belong.

Kellie Wesley is a designer, artist, writer and eternal optimist. She always uses the good linens and crystal when dining.

KELLIE
WESLEY

I have always been drawn to the beautiful and creative things in life, such as fine linens, good wine and food. From a very early age I was fascinated with colour, flowers and art. While drawing on walls with crayon and picking the heads off all the neighbour's flowers got me in trouble, I soon learned how to channel my creative and artistic pursuits in a much more effective and positive way.

I've been thrown a lot of curveballs in my life which has helped me become resilient and optimistic. Even when going through difficult times, my mantra has always been, "this too shall pass". I have always believed that there are better days ahead. These past two years have been the most challenging and heartbreaking of my life, yet here I am, moving forward and staying positive. Getting back to painting has been very therapeutic for me, and now, I've started to write again and became a published author; this was a lifelong dream for me. As an interior designer in a small boutique studio, we have won GOLD for best interior decorating two years in a row. Another accomplishment in what I had dubbed my most heart wrenching and devastating period of my life so far. See, there is always that silver lining, and this is what I continue to focus on for the future.

As a wife and mother, I have always put everyone else's needs before my own. Now, being a single woman on her own with just my dog, Kate, to care for, I am learning to put myself first. I've truly learned how to step into my power as a woman and set boundaries. I've learned the art of saying NO! I've stopped being the "people pleasing" person that I was for so many years and it's been freeing!

Looking at my future, I am excited and ready for the challenges and opportunities for continued growth and adventure. There's new art, travel plans and more writing to be done. I still make delicious meals, most nights for just one, but I always set the table with the fine linens, crystal, good wine and flowers. I am worth it!

Kellie Wesley

Kristin is a proud member of the Red River Métis Nation and is a Manager in Indigenous Markets at CIBC.

KRISTIN
RICHARD

Growing up, I grappled with my identity as a white-passing Indigenous girl. Living in the lower end of a middle-class neighbourhood in Winnipeg, I was aware of the effect socio-economic status had on a person's decisions and how it impacted their level of opportunity.

Connecting with the prominent side of my identity as an Indigenous individual but benefiting from the advantages of my European ancestry left me caught between opposing values. In 25 years of being placed in the middle, I have developed a deep sense of comfort from my mediative stance. I know the power insight holds. It is not a gift I take lightly, nor a privilege I ignore.

I found power in my life by claiming oppression and privilege, whiteness and BIPOC status.

I know that I am walking in the faded footprints of the seven generations who trudged before me with every step I take. With deep respect and honour, I am trying to forge a new path for the young Indigenous girls walking behind me. We may not have been given opportunities on a silver platter like our colonial brothers and sisters; however, this doesn't mean we need to play prisoner to their antics. While we cannot change the past, we can use it to our advantage. I try to be the voice and action for those who feel silenced and debilitated.

Creating cherished opportunities within a community is at the forefront of every decision I make. I have found power and freedom as a female in finance. While I may work for a Western Institution, I focus on creating opportunities within Indigenous communities.

In a system that's working to oppress me, I bear witness to the privilege that has allowed to me overcome it.

I live as a token of many identifiers: whether by gender, class, or Metis status, I am nothing if not a symbol of those who struggled before me. I hope to inspire other young Indigenous girls with the sense of power I have found.

Kristin Richard

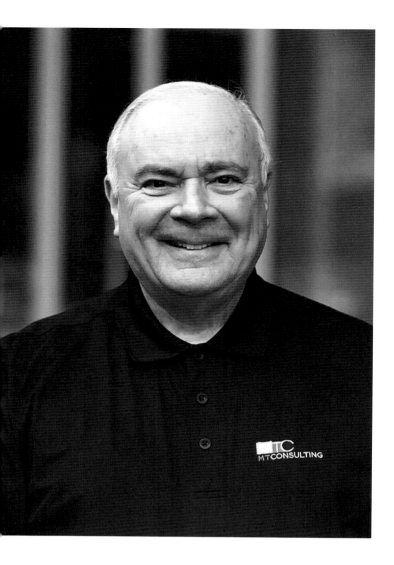

Michael Theodor is the President of MT Consulting Services. His unique background led him to becoming a leader in the Canadian organic and natural product industry.

MICHAEL
THEODOR

It was late in 1972 and I was on the run.

After a few years in Laguna Beach, CA, involved with the Brotherhood (who had Timothy Leary as a New Age role model) I had been in and out of jail at least a half dozen times.

My biggest case was conspiracy to smuggle a gallon of hash oil from Afghanistan, for which I was indicted by the Grand Jury of California, a sure sign that the state could get a conviction.

Out on a reduced bail after around 10 months in jail, I appeared in court for the first hearing of the indicted charge. I was surprised and shocked to see the DA of the State of California (who later ran for governor) appear, along with a battery of state lawyers, to go in front of the judge and advise him that they would be doing everything in the state's power to seek a conviction and the longest sentence possible for Michael Theodor, a leader in the "Hippie Mafia" in Laguna Beach.

I decided then and there I would go on the run instead of facing up to 20 years in a state penitentiary.

Friends I knew in Laguna had moved to Oregon. I went up there and stayed around their wooded property for a week or so, but being wanted in six states was risky and could bring police to their place.

The Oregon folks told me about a meadow with a partially built log cabin on it about 10 miles away, with a two mile walk through heavy woods with no trails (only marked trees). I bought a bunch of supplies to finish the log cabin. No running water, no electricity and not too many skills either. I cut logs, made hand split cedar shakes for a roof, installed windows, made a big door, and built a loft to stash food from bears.

I met a woodsman, Fred, walking through the meadow. He had land in northern BC. He took me to Canada in 1973.

KIM
BAIRD

Kwuntiltunaat (Kim Baird) is a Tsawwassen First Nation woman who is currently the Chancellor for Kwantlen Polytechnic University, the owner of Kim Baird Strategic Consulting, and a director on serval boards.

I descend from the first Tsawwassen Ancestor and a long line of hereditary chiefs.

As an Indigenous woman, I am the product of my culture along with multigenerational trauma based on the colonization of Canada. I am the target of stereotypes and have faced adversity based on my background. Despite all of this, I found my voice, and I am a leader.

I am grateful that I can provide a good life for my three daughters and hope it is a better life than my mother provided me. I am both grateful and resentful for my resilience. I am thankful that I can persevere through trying times yet resentful because my very survival depended on resilience. I am grateful to live in a time of great change, and I remain hopeful for a better future for all.

I support Indigenous reconciliation in Canada and a just way forward for Indigenous peoples based on self-determination. We have all heard Mahatma Gandhi's expression, "be the change you want to see". I am the change I want to see as I do my best to stop dysfunctional cycles and make strive to make things better for my daughters, my community, and this country. Reconciliation within my family is where it all starts.

I try to make peace with the fact that creating change doesn't necessarily make you friends. I know that if I continue to contribute to the best of my ability, that is all I can do. Although I am a work in progress, I am unapologetically myself as I face the world. The quote by Moïra Fowley-Doyle's - "Do no harm but take no shit" are words I live by. I don't know how the next chapter of my story will turn out. But I know that I will continue my journey to make the world a better place for Indigenous peoples and, as a result, for all people.

Tabatha is an Indigenous electrical engineer turned not-for-profit CEO and a proud mom of two boys who is committed to growing the Indigenous economy.

TABATHA
BULL

Journey to Fulfillment

I can easily look back at my 16-year-old self and imagine her sitting in a high school classroom considering what she wanted to do, what she wanted to "be".

As a female Indigenous electrical engineer turned not-for profit CEO, my career has definitely been a unique journey with many twists and turns along the way. I have often found myself as "the only" in the room, the only woman, the only Indigenous person, the only mom. As difficult as that has been at times, as frustrating and demeaning, I have felt strongly that if I am "the only" at the table, I must speak up, I must make sure that not only am I there, but my voice is there as well, and I must bring an extra chair for others to join me.

I am often asked to speak about how I overcame hardship, I suppose because some find that is a better story. The truth is my parents and grandparents overcame hardships for me. They provided me this beautiful gift of not passing their trauma on to me, of ensuring I believed I could be anything I wanted to be. I have been incredibly fortunate to be raised by two extraordinary strong, resilient people who put their children first and who provided us every opportunity, at their own expense. To add to my fortune, I am the youngest of four, and my three siblings, each exceptional in their own path, continuously supported and boosted me in whichever endeavor I undertook.

Since I was a young girl, I have always been an advocate for change joining groups such as World Wildlife Fund or Amnesty International and I knew then that my career should be no different. It is easy to lose your way though, to become too comfortable. At one point in my career, one of my boys asked me why I went to work when other mommies didn't. I was on an easy path. I am fulfilled when the work I am doing is creating positive change, when I'm setting an example and making space for others and when the impact, I have is well beyond my career and into the next seven generations.

Finding a passion in your life and knowing your purpose can justify our happiness and with a great level of discipline dreams come true.

BEATA
JIRAVA

Finding a passion in your life and knowing your purpose can justify our happiness and with a great level of discipline dreams come true.

My athletic background and experience in multiple universities, studying on two continents, guided my level of passion for health and strategic consultancy. Since 2004, I have been involved in senior-level management, ranging in roles from a strategic consultant to being a partner, director, and shareholder of companies, including engineering, property management, medical cannabis, mental health organizations, and most recently, wellness centers set for a global initiative. My focus is now on strategic collaborations with scientists, medical practitioners, alternative medicine, and biophysicists with the goal of enhancing one's vitality at the cellular level.

Over 25 years ago, I came to Canada to improve my English and compete for Canada. To my surprise, it wasn't easy. After one year of working at the local bakery on Robson Street, and cleaning homes to pay for my school and living, I found myself alone one rainy day. The tears were falling from my cheeks and rain started to pour. Sitting at the North Vancouver bus stop, I felt lonely, with no place to go, only $100 in my pocket and two suitcases by my side. One beautiful soul walked towards me and said, "come and stay with me for the time being." And this is how my journey began in Canada, with hope and love.

Studying and earning certifications and degrees in both Europe and Canada has only enriched my intellectual knowledge. My mission is to create a global restorative impact at the cellular level by combining a series of modalities, including pulse electromagnetic frequency, dry salt therapy, nuga bed, infrared, chromo, and respiratory therapy.

I am a former competitive athlete and winner of multiple medals at the national and international levels in both track and field and swimming. This taught me to never give up. In the last decade, I have coached athletes on the provincial and national levels in Canada. With honor, I have become a part of a pilot project with the USA, Canada, and England for halotherapy and post Covid recovery research. I'm part of the World Council of Health and sitting on the council at Global Wellness Institute supporting halotherapy, and also a member of the World Halotherapy Association.

Beata Jirava

ALICIA
RENY

As I sit back and look at my life, I couldn't be more grateful, more blessed. I'm my own hype girl; high-fiving myself in the mirror, affirming, "yo, girl, you on FY'YA!" But trust me when I say this, it certainly wasn't always this way.

Let me rephrase that: I used to really hate myself...

Until the age of 30, my constant state of mind was self-loathing, self-hatred and never feeling I was enough.

I know that we are all authentic, and that each of us is affected differently through our hardships. What initiated my darkness was my parent's divorce when I was four. That created an instant hole in my heart. I didn't understand what that meant. Eighteen years ago, that wasn't talked about.

Living in two separate households that were very different was the beginning of learning my way through this world. In one house, full of light and love, and the other house, what felt like walking on eggshells. You can imagine how this would mould a little love.

I grew into my teen years, where I would experiment with hard drugs, allowing men to treat me in ways that were convenient for them, placing myself into very dangerous situations. For a moment, when I was high or held by a man, I felt a piece of love, I felt 'worthy', I felt 'enough'...

Enough to lead me into addiction.

Enough to lead me into abusive relationship after abusive relationship.

Enough to be forced into sexual activities I didn't want to be a part of.

Enough to become homeless.

Enough to lose everything I had.

All I wanted was to feel was enough.

Until one day, I did feel enough; enough of living in darkness.

I found a force within me I never knew existed. I reclaimed myself, healed, mourned the loss of the illusion of me and found self-love.

I am sharing my story because it's not mine to hold. It's for others to understand that no matter what this world throws at you, you are you, and that's enough! That there is no one in this world that will love you more than you will.

You are a warrior.

ROSALYN C.
RAINDANCER

My culture has a rigid way of defining success. We're supposed to work hard, and success would follow. I was taught that certain people were luckier than us. If I wanted to succeed, I had to work twice as hard and be smarter than everybody.

As a teenager, I struggled to pursue my passions and be true to myself. I wanted to uphold my family reputation, but I also wanted to follow my heart. I felt like a "bad daughter" because my choices didn't align with cultural expectations. It was painful being the black sheep. Do I risk bringing shame to my family? Or do I conform and risk betraying my heart? I longed to be fully embraced.

A decade after college, I chose to live freely. But my success was short-lived. Inevitably, I encountered adversity that would trigger my trauma of being an outcast. Ghosts of the past and self-sabotage often overshadowed any accomplishments. Endless therapy sessions and self-help books never healed this seemingly inaccessible part of my soul.

Eight years ago, I hit rock bottom. My business partners betrayed me, and yet another romantic relationship failed. I had never felt more defeated.

Serendipitously, I met a shamanic medicine healer who introduced me to The Medicine Wheel. This system of healing and wellness is practiced in many Indigenous cultures. After five years of intense healing, I reclaimed my fragmented soul, healed my lineage, and restored my spirit. Due to childhood and ancestral trauma, I was disconnected from the Source of Life. I finally reclaimed my birthright as God's beloved daughter. I realized that everything I was seeking was already within me. This solid spiritual foundation allowed me to live with purpose and joy, and create beauty in abundance.

Society reinforces the idea that success is "out there". In the pursuit of success and happiness, we may attain everything we desire, and yet we still remain unfulfilled and spiritually empty. When we tend to our heart and soul, that's when we have true success. Success isn't about the destination, but rather who we become in the process. May we all have success that feels as good as it looks, knowing that we belong in the beautiful tapestry of life.

LESLEY
DIANA

Photo credit: Mitchell Parsons

Openness to opportunities can change your life's path

I am a genuine example of how life can provide you with opportunities. I could never have anticipated the doors that would open for me over my career and the change of course I would navigate that would take me from the classroom to the red carpet.

I started teaching kindergarten when I was 19, which led me to teaching physical education to high school students after I graduated from university. At a weekend workshop focused on the lack of physical fitness in women I was approached by one of the participants who introduced me to the program director at CTV in Saskatoon. The audition led me to eleven years of on-air hosting a popular fitness show and talk show. From there, I opened a full-service fitness studio with spa amenities and added author to my resume by writing a fitness book.

When I transitioned out of my fitness career, I opened four ladies' wear boutiques across Western Canada. When they closed I had no idea what was next. As we had received so much positive publicity for the boutiques, doors opened for me. I began executing publicity campaigns for shopping malls and fashion boutiques until a filmmaker hired me to do the publicity for his feature film. I can now proudly say that I have been an entertainment publicist for over 25 years working with my team on incredible campaigns for feature films, television series, red carpets and hundreds of actors.

I was born in England and moved a lot once we arrived in Canada, so I was always the new girl in class with an English accent that the kids teased. Those experiences helped to make me more outgoing and willing to join activities and try new things. I was the social director and sports director on our high school council, which has given me the foundation to be a leader in all my endeavors.

My careers as a teacher, fitness instructor, talk show host and publicist have all focused on helping and uplifting others. Supporting others in achieving their dreams and goals is what gives me the most pride and fulfillment.

Having patience has helped me and others get through many difficult challenges in life. By being open to opportunities, motivated by helping people I have built a meaningful and fulfilling career.

Dawn Williams is learning to put herself first and is a great wine drinking partner for her friends.

DAWN
WILLIAMS

Our son was two when we found out I was pregnant. We were thrilled to round out our family of four!

Almost immediately, I confided in our company nurse about an uneasy feeling I wouldn't carry to term. Roll onto the dating ultrasound a few weeks later, and there was no heartbeat. I was devastated; thankfully, my husband was with me. We drove home in shock and silence. I remember calling our nurse to share the news, stunned that my uneasy feeling had materialized.

Eight months later, I was pregnant again! Given my age, I had the recommended genetic screening. While I had sailed through it in my first pregnancy, this time the results flagged a high likelihood of complications. Referred to a genetic clinic, I underwent tests under the guidance of a fantastic counsellor. What a rollercoaster! Some indicated good news, and others, not, culminating in amniocentesis that confirmed our worst fears. At 20 weeks gestation, with our son having just turned three, we made a heartbreaking and very personal decision to terminate our pregnancy. We know this is not the decision every family would make, but it was the right decision for ours. Almost a year to the day after my first DNC, we said goodbye to our second son.

Those were hard days and I was slipping into a dark place. But I had my son, and above all else, he needed his mum. While it was incredibly difficult, I truly believe having him to focus on was the reason I didn't slip further. After a few weeks, I rallied and went back to work and forced myself to return to 'normal'.

Eighteen months later, we were blessed with a healthy little girl. My sister had questions during her pregnancy, apologizing for dredging up memories. I remember smiling and thinking that despite the grief, if it hadn't happened, we wouldn't have our daughter. And despite her sass – she's 10 now – I wouldn't trade her for the world.

Without my son to look after, things could have ended very differently. But with the benefit of hindsight, I can also appreciate the positive – I can't imagine our life without our two kids.

Sharon Mason is an International Award Winning Realtor and best selling author of "For the Love of Real Estate: Tales From the Trenches".

SHARON
MASON

Apparently, I am a perfect Capricorn. Indeed, I have always looked for mountains to climb. This has led me in many different directions and into various fascinating experiences and lessons. Since I see life as a school, it has been my nature to welcome it all - the good, the bad, the ugly and the beautiful. In other words, life, and plenty of it, and the knowledge that everything we are given has a purpose.

Some of the traits I grew up with were being "petite" and "cute". All my life - "cute". Women already have to work harder and smarter to be taken seriously and being "petite" and "cute" has only added another dimension to that challenge. This was especially true back in the 1950's and early 60's, my formative years as a young woman. Thankfully, times continue to evolve for women. We stand on the shoulders of the suffragettes and the ongoing women's movement, which means that we have many more choices in life than our sisters of the past. But there is still much more work to be done!

When I was a small child of 4 years old, I knew I wanted to be a ballerina. I had no idea what it was going to take, but that particular lesson taught me this, "Nothing is ever what you think it is, looking in from the outside." I did fulfill that 4-year old's dream and performed with the Royal Winnipeg Ballet for Queen Elizabeth and Prince Philip, but that was a very long time ago!

Since then, my "mountains" have included things like full time honour roll student, university graduate, professional actor, singer and dancer in theatre, film, and media. I have been a marathon runner, registered counsellor, school teacher, international award-winning realtor, and published author. However, one of the biggest by far was becoming a mother and raising and educating my kids. My biggest lessons came from there, no kidding. My beloved children have been my biggest teachers.

I am filled with gratitude as I enter "Act 3" of my life. I think they call us "Super Agers" and as I enter my ninth decade on the planet. I'm "all in."

Safina Kataria is a professional Makeup Artist & Hairstylist working in the field for more than a decade.

SAFINA
KATARIA

A happy life is just a string of happy moments. Being a Professional Makeup & Hair Artist, my goal is to make sure that we're not only creating memorable looks but memorable moments!

My greatest influence is my mother, Mrs Veena Gujral, who has been perfecting her passion in the beauty industry for 40 years. My dad, Arun Gujral, encouraged me to take some courses during the summers of 2nd & 3rd year of university. Although I have done Masters in Business Administration, in 2004, I graduated from PIVOT POINT Beauty School. Since then I have worked with many Indian, Vancouver & International Brides over the years creating looks that leave people feeling & looking like their best self. I have lots of experience with every skin type. My clients & anyone who sits in my chair, I make sure they feel comfortable, we have fun taking pictures & making Tik Toks & they leave feeling like a new friend.

I am a mother of two beautiful kids, Sameer (12 years) & Jianna (7 years). My son loves to play soccer & my daughter loves making makeup videos (you know why ;)). I am blessed with a wonderful husband Kanav who supports me in everything I do! In between our goals, there's a precious thing called life that we enjoy by watching Netflix together, going for walks in the park or meeting our friends! I truly believe I'm about to get everything I've prayed & worked hard for & I'm truly grateful for all I have!!

Dr. Sam Winter is grateful for his family, his dental career, Vancouver, Canada, and his ability to pay it forward.

DR. SAM
WINTER

I'm here because of the kindness of others, especially under the worst conditions. My father entered Auschwitz's gas chamber. A former neighbour checking tattooed numbers whispered, "walk slowly to that broom and sweep, as your life depends on it. Don't answer to your number." Two weeks later, Auschwitz was liberated. My mother and aunt survived the war in a forced labour camp. They were spared by a superior's love of sweets, having learned candy-making in their father's candy factory.

After the war, my father found my mother. Remembering her from their candy store, he proposed, threatening to kill himself if they did not marry. Already seeing too much death, she agreed. Returning home, to Poland, there was no kindness, only more death threats. Refusing to live in a DP camp, they fled to the German-American Zone, where I was born.

We came to Edmonton when I was 15 months old, sponsored by my great-uncle. He sought a new life; unaware he'd be saving his family. Amongst fourteen siblings, five survived the war; many also lost wives and children. I was stateless until nine.

I was always ahead of myself. Born January 4th, my mother finagled me into kindergarten early. I played with locals to learn English. In University, being younger was problematic. Too young to party with classmates, I was arrested, waiting in a Banff pub vestibule, and fined $25. My low alcohol tolerance and age facilitated cramming eight years of university into six. Living at home, student loans financed three summer trips to Israel.

Another stranger's kindness put my future wife, Randi, on my Sinai Desert tour. It was love at first sight. The catch? She was attending Hebrew University. After finishing UofA dental school, plans changed, facilitating my earlier return to Israel and Randi.

Soon, I was asking another stranger to marry his daughter, taking her from New York to Edmonton. Invited to visit Vancouver, we stayed one block from the house where we raised our children and near my Fairmont Medical Building dental office.

I continue volunteering my time and skills helping those less fortunate, always remembering the random kindness of others that have blessed me with citizenship, family, friendships, and a profession I love.

Dr. Sam Winter

I am an unashamed Christ follower, a pastor's wife, mom, entrepreneur, founder, and community leader, whose passion and purpose help individuals become the best version of themselves by understanding their identity walking in the reality of their true selves.

ADETOLA
TAMUNOKUBIE

I remembered that evening in December 2019; family and friends lavished us with hugs and farewell wishes as we prepared to check in for our flight. Memories flashed through my mind of what life was going to be like away from them.

After I moved to Vancouver in 2019 with my husband and kids, I was afraid of starting again. I had left everything behind–family, friends, a thriving career, business, and the comfort I enjoyed back home.

Everything was different and settling down and fitting in as an immigrant was an uphill battle.

In January 2020, I came to the end of myself, and the only way to make headway was to seek help. I sought help from God. I began to study the Bible more, which ignited a higher connection with the Holy Spirit. I probed deeper into my existence, passion, and purpose and started motivating myself with the Bible's faith-filled words. I began thinking about how I could affect and improve my immediate community and the world at large. Then, viola! I realized God is interested in my well-being and me having all-around success. It occurred while I studied and meditated on God's word daily, my unfailing remedy for finding direction and navigating life's issues.

Daily meditation on God's word changed my approach to situations and reframed my self-image and perception of people. By acknowledging God's love for me, my worth and the value of others, I blossomed and found my community. The quest to reinvent me, build relationships, network, and inspire confidence in others, especially new immigrants, resulted in increased community involvement. I believe that every action can make a difference in a community, and collective action can impact the world.

In 2021, I founded "Canada Christian Moms", a community of purpose-driven Christian moms with a mandate to shine God's light on earth and help others come to the knowledge of Christ.

I see a learning journey of reinvention and growth when I look back.

Adetola Tamunokubie

Aeryon Ashlie is the founder of Aeryon Wellness Supplements, CHN, Speaker and Amazon Best Selling Author. She resides in Vancouver, BC with her daughter and 2 Poodles.

AERYON
ASHLIE

In the spring of 2011, my daughter's father and I separated. As a single mother, I knew that now, more than ever, I had to be a strong and positive role model for my daughter. However, my 25-year private battle with my eating disorder, bulimia plagued me. I kept having episodes.

One day I was in the midst of a purge in the bathroom. Suddenly, I heard a knock at the door and a little voice say, "Mommy, what are you doing?" At that moment I looked up, feeling my panic rise.

As I responded, "Nothing babe, be out in a second," I caught a glimpse of myself in the mirror. My eyes were watering, there was vomit and blood on my face and hand, my veins were bulging on my neck. This was a sight I had experienced many, many times…but in that moment it was suddenly quite different.

My beautiful little 3-year-old was standing outside the door, her innocence, her love of everything. Her body and mind not yet tainted by life. It was my responsibility to protect and love her. But I had none for myself.

I remember my eyes started tearing up and I started sobbing…

I was sick and tired of being sick and tired.

For once in my life, I chose that moment. Not Monday, or the next birthday or holiday but that exact second to get real with who I was, who I wanted to be, the legacy I wanted to leave and what had to happen in that exact second to step into that.

I opened the door and scooped my beautiful little girl in my arms.

As her arms wrapped tightly around my neck, I felt as though I was holding little Aeryon. All these years I wanted the tenderness and love from others but would never allow it to for myself. The all-consuming search for the fill from boys, food, drugs, money, and alcohol clearly would never be enough. That day I chose a path to self-love and started my work on becoming who I am today. My "why" was the little girl in my arms, for what I knew for sure was my story would not become *her* story.

Ami McKay, Interior Designer and owner of Pure Design Inc.

AMI
MCKAY

From a very young age, I have always pushed forward to maintain a sense of purpose no matter what life has dealt me.

My family has a rare genetic disorder called Ehlers Danlos Syndrome, EDS, which weakens the connective tissues in our bodies, caused by a lack of collagen. From a very young age, I had a feeling that I wasn't quite like all the other kids. I was hyper-flexible and had other symptoms which caused me to continually modify my behaviour to accommodate this condition, which I was unaware I had.

My limitations and differences turned into the recipe that created a child who marched to the beat of her own drum, escaping from the world of sports into art, leading me to my career today. I treated my limitations like superpowers, teaching me that I needed to work harder than the average person to overcome the most ordinary circumstances, which is true to this day.

At 23, a volunteer trip to Bihar, India, provided me with a great perspective and was pivotal in changing my entire outlook on life. Seeing people born into a caste system with limited choices about their future helped me realize how truly fortunate I was. As a Canadian citizen, I was afforded freedoms and options, allowing me to be the only person who could choose how to live my life, regardless of my circumstances. It made me realize the only thing that stood in my path was fear itself.

When I returned home, I channelled all my energies into everything that I loved, remembering to use my 'superpowers' for good and always giving back to those less fortunate. My love of art, flowers, fabric and travelling, coupled with a flair for the dramatic and a fair amount of humour, led to my career in interior design. Creating sacred spaces for others through collaboration and conversation and playing with textures, light, and colour truly is my passion and joy. If ever my health issues interrupt my flow, I remember my 23-year-old self and those without choice, and I'm reminded to be thankful.

243

Anna is a Cosmetic Tattoo Artist, Business Owner, Industry Trailblazer, Wife, walker & seeker of better balance in life.

ANNA
RYKIERT

I started my business while finishing University some 20yrs ago. At the time, public perception of Cosmetic Tattooing was not great; It conjured up images of things you probably wouldn't want on your face. Determined to do better by my clients, I decided to carve my own path, find my own style & above all, make the results look natural. And so Lasting Lines was born.

The demand for my services grew quickly & soon became overwhelming. Working 6 days a week, I said "yes" to every client & any opportunity. It's not surprising that 10yrs into my bustling career I experienced extreme burnout, mounting health issues & a complete disconnect from family & friends.

My body forced me to shift. I had to re-prioritize relationships, learn self-care & find space for personal growth. I was also in desperate need of a sabbatical.

On a whim, I bought a pair of hiking boots & decided to fulfill a life-long dream: walking the Camino de Santiago, a 1000km trail spanning across Northern Spain. As I stuffed my backpack & booked my flight, a feeling of panic set in. I had not trained! What if I fail? What if it's just too hard?

I will never forget encouragement from my father: "Anna, remember, it's just walking! One foot in front of the other." That message carried me along the many hills & valleys of my month-long adventure. As I reached Compostela, a new strength grew within me & I learned a great lesson:

You can never fully prepare for the road ahead. You'll have to bend with life's twists & turns. You might get lost & sometimes things just feel too hard. But the best moments are often right around the corner from the worst of moments. Keep placing one foot in front of the other. Somehow, on your own time, you will get there!

I still do a lot of walking today. I like the idea of moving forward. I listen to my body. Yes, I am still tattooing faces! Sometimes we talk about the Camino. I love giving my clients a new kind of freedom, because it's so liberating to not have to "fix" your face in the morning, especially when you are trekking across Spain!

244

Cydney Mariel Galbraithn is the founder of Loves Pure Light Scarves and resides on Vancouver Island.

CYDNEY MARIEL
GALBRAITH

We must never despise the day of small beginnings. The truth is that opposition can be a good thing. It reminds us that we stand for something which leads us to our intended place.

Canadian heirloom scarves began after I hit rock bottom. As a Canadian national team athlete, I believed there was more to life than professional sport. Late one night, I picked up a paintbrush and began painting my clothing with words of affirmation and identity, love and worth. Words flowed from my heart, reminding me of divine purpose. I listened to my inner voice reminding me who I was and my ability to create.

I wore my hand-painted silk clothing underneath my work clothes which reminded me that I was covered with an armour of love even on the toughest days. The word got out about my armour, and I began to do art shows and local artisan festivals. I called my heavenly line of clothing "Love's Pure Light",; a clothing line that took a heart first approach.

After time passed, I set my design ideas aside because doubt weighed heavily.

I began travelling instead, joining global missions' trips and doing outreach work in 25 nations. Each nation inspired a unique prayer mantle to gift to my hosts. I felt blessed that my creativity could have such an impact.

A decade after mission work began, I returned to Canada, picked up a paintbrush, and painted on clothing. My inner voice encouraged me to build Love's Pure Light. Encountering people who had one of my scarves from years ago and wanted others seemed divine.

The celestial spoke directly to my heart and encouraged me to have faith in myself. The moment I put my heart and soul into creating Love's Pure Light, everything moved in the right direction.

Part-time jobs paid for fabric, and after knocking on doors, I had over a dozen retail outlets selling my scarves. Challenges existed along the way, but one can't know success without opposition, a business built from small beginnings.

We all have a calling, a unique destiny based on our strengths. Our greatest calling is to love one another and ourselves, significantly impacting the world.

Cydney Mariel Galbraith

Bonnie Moy supports investment in 'Safe and Healthy' communities. Believing we are blessed to live in a 'Garden of Eden', in this lower mainland from the mountains to the border, to the water.

BONNIE
MOY

Having experienced Real Estate investing as a REALTOR for over 30 years, I appreciate the 'global' value of British Columbia. However, the word 'affordable' in the lower mainland might be considered, an oxymoron.

Supporting the approach of Options Community Services, and the building concept suppling both 'affordable' and transitional housing in Surrey, is not an option; it is an absolute necessity. With this type of housing, we can provide a safe and healthy community

As an Eaton's Department Store Display Production Coordinator in the 1970's thru 1980's, I helped open many new stores in B.C. and Alberta. This was a booming time for department store expansions! Now all gone as things change, and quickly too.

During those years, I was immersed in 'marketing and selling'. Requiring the resourcing of many ideas to 'sell' a product and offer the idea quickly. This left me with the habit of having not one idea but many more up my sleave…just in case needed. If you didn't like the first idea I presented, no worries, I'd have a 100 more! And yes, presenting too many ideas… well, can drive anyone nuts!

One idea that was embraced by the Fraser Valley Real Estate Board, is 'REALTY WATCH'.

In 1994, I asked the Fraser Valley Real Estate board to support the idea of REALTORS using our pager system to find missing persons. My client's daughter, Pamela Cameron, went missing and was later found murdered. The Fraser Valley Real Estate Board, working with the RCMP, vetted the program and Realty Watch was born. Initially using pagers, now using cell phones and social media reaching more than 14,000 Realtors who act as the community's 'eyes and ears.

In 2014 I received the John Armeneu Award, the Fraser Valley Real Estate Board's highest award, for helping launch the Realty Watch program.

My hobby is painting. I will donate 50 paintings to be auctioned, with the theme "Everyone Needs a Home", featuring local scenes in Surrey in support of Option Community Services.

Rita Stoller, Founder of Riwas Designs, graduated from architecture school in Bern, Switzerland before immigrating to Canada in 1979. She and her husband owned and operated a dairy farm for 20 years, and she later fulfilled her dream of designing and building her very own dream home.

RITA
STOLLER

Throughout my life I have always tried to appreciate the small things. It's easy to overlook those little victories when there is so much happening around us, when we are focusing on the next big goal. For me, it's always been important to be present in the moment, to enjoy where you are right now. This is a constant practice of gratitude; I know our time here is limited, so we have to make the most of it.

When I came to Canada, I was 29 years old. I was immersed into a new culture in unfamiliar territory, and it was difficult at times to get used to this new way of life. My husband and I were excited to begin our next chapter; we purchased farm land and began building our new life from the ground up.

Coming from a career in architecture, I had to be diverse. My work ethic learned back in Switzerland certainly helped with both farming and transitioning to life in a new country. We kept a positive mindset through it all, working seven days a week and getting our hands dirty. This lifestyle isn't for everyone; I could have complained about the early mornings milking our cows, but everything we did, we did with a sense of appreciation.

My farming career ended after a knee injury made it impossible to continue with the intense labour that was required. But when one door closes, another opens; our next venture was purchasing an Ontario fishing resort with 20 cabins. This was a whole new world, giving us the opportunity to be social with guests, a huge change from the solitude of farming. Eventually, I was led back to my career in design and architecture. It all has come full circle.

Life is an incredible journey, but when we focus too much on the destination, we can miss the beauty in the everyday. We hold the power to decide our mindset, whether that be positive or negative, so we must choose wisely. Every day I wake up and I choose happiness; I choose to celebrate the small things.

Rita Stoller

Denise Wong, CPA, CA, helps entrepreneurs take control of their business & personal finances because it's never too late to build financially healthy and sustainable lives and businesses.

DENISE
WONG

For anyone who has ever done a home renovation, you know you always get to the end, but the journey will inevitably bring you twists and turns you may never have expected. I think fondly of my favourite home reno shows where a budget is set. The homeowners excitedly put forward all their wants, only to have those dreams crushed when the reno starts. Who knows what gets exposed once the tradespeople get below the wall's surface or home's foundation? Sometimes there are cracks, or worse yet, asbestos. Wiring is often not up to code. If their dreams or expectations do not change, homeowners need extra money to meet current regulations and fix the problems. If additional money is not an option, then sacrificing the powder room or finishing the basement is the only alternative. By the end of the program, the homeowners are usually happy with the concessions they have made and fall in love with their homes all over again despite the stress and turmoil.

Whether personal or business, managing money and finances is like managing home renovations. Money and finances are some of the fundamental building blocks of life. Money and finances are complex topics to master, and sometimes their rules change, like building codes. Like homes, if money and finances are not maintained frequently, there are more unknowns and sometimes major overhauls like renovations.

Below is a very simplistic A, B, C framework to help you start the journey of renovating your money and financial house.

A = Awareness, B = Baseline, C = Clarity

Awareness is giving yourself the knowledge and just enough financial literacy to ask the right questions. Accept offers from financial advisors who offer complimentary sessions. Ask questions about how it applies to you.

Baseline is what you have now? It is important to understand your current financial standing to have a starting point from which to measure progress.

Clarity is the financial goals you set once you set your baseline.

It's never too late to implement the ABCs and get your financial house in order. It will help you avoid significant renovations!

Melissa Rosas owns and operates Violet Dae Communications, a boutique firm specializing in event planning, entertainment production management, digital marketing, and publicity. Melissa believes in celebrating.

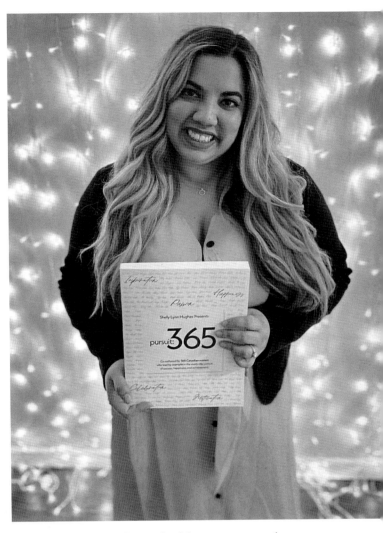

MELISSA
ROSAS

For as long as I can remember, I was always planning something. Honestly, I wouldn't be surprised if I planned my own birthday parties as a toddler somehow. I simply loved the idea of getting people together and celebrating. I seemed to always find a reason to have an event, and while that probably drove my mom crazy when I was young, it all made sense as I became an adult and started my own business as an event planner. The feeling that comes with preparing and executing any type of event is euphoric to me. I love every moment, no matter how tedious or difficult, when everything comes full circle in the end, it's like magic.

As I grew up celebrating the traditional milestones in life, I always felt like that wasn't enough. Why do we only celebrate the big milestones? What about all the other life experiences that make us who we are? What about work, friendship, or adoption anniversaries, mental health recovery, freeing yourself from a toxic relationship, or just surviving a rough week at work? Life is too short to not celebrate whatever victory looks like to you. Glitz and glam aside, events are a way for people to celebrate, and if that's just with two people, or 20, or 200, it matters. If something is important to you and seen as an achievement in your life, that is reason enough to acknowledge it, and no one can tell you otherwise.

Originally, I started my business to make my dream a reality, but soon I realized that my job was so much more than that. Not only am I doing what I love, but I am also granted the opportunity to help others celebrate their dreams through events. That's pretty amazing if you ask me. So, the next time you pass an exam, or finish a stressful project at work, or see a friend you haven't seen in a while, celebrate, because why not?

Melissa Rosas

Dr. John Esdaile is an internationally respected rheumatologist and research scientist who created Arthritis Research Canada.

DR. JOHN
ESDAILE

Boarding school is something most parents jokingly threaten their kids with at least once. "If you don't start listening, I'm sending you to boarding school." In my case, the roles were reversed. I applied to boarding school when I was eight. My mom and dad found out when they received a letter from the headmaster of Trinity College School in Ontario, inviting me to take the scholarship exam.

To my delight, I was offered a scholarship! However, my mother wouldn't let me go until I turned nine. As my family lived in Quebec at the time, I think she needed time to adjust to the idea of my moving out. The following year, still as enthusiastic about the idea, I ventured into the world.

"Developing habits of the heart and mind for a life of purpose and service." That was my boarding school's mission statement. I didn't think much about it at the time. Looking back, it's funny that I ended up doing exactly that. For the past 40 + years, I've worked as a rheumatologist, helping people living with different types of arthritis.

I've trained at some of the best universities – from McGill to the University of Toronto to the Kennedy Institute of Rheumatology in England to Yale. I've also had some amazing mentors like the grandfather of clinical epidemiology, the late Dr. Alvan Feinstein.

All of this experience led me to start Arthritis Research Canada in 1999. I saw people suffering and wanted to find answers for them. Many don't realize that arthritis is a serious and sometimes life-threatening disease or that it's more than 100 diseases affecting people of all ages.

Today, Arthritis Research Canada has grown to be the largest clinical arthritis research organization in North America. We're helping people with arthritis stay employed, start families, reduce pain, stay active and avoid life-threatening complications. I am honoured to be part of a team that's working to change the lives of millions of Canadians.

Carmen Vars is a model and talent agent, freelance writer and creative director with a big heart for both fur and skin people.

CARMEN
VARS

"Excuse me, I am a model and talent agent. Have you ever thought about being a model?"

From there begins the journey for a young person and for me the thrill of becoming a conduit to their evolution from caterpillar to butterfly.

Since childhood I was fiercely precocious at dressing. I insisted on being dolled up for Sunday School long before I was old enough to go. I spent my teenage earnings on magazines, voraciously studying the models, photography, words, advertising and the fashion. I enlisted my mom to sew me things I had seen in Vogue that had not yet hit (our) reality. Thrifting was also key to knocking off runway looks on a student's budget.

My mom and I watched the Oscars and "Miss Universe," voting on the gowns and the talented, eloquent women. Never did my mother act threatened by other women's appeal but rather celebrated it, acknowledging iconic women like "Liz" and "Grace" amongst others. As a figure skater I was more excited for my sister or bestie to win a medal than I was for myself.

In my gawky teens I fell into modeling by default as I grew too tall and lanky to be graceful on the ice. Suddenly geek was chic and I was thrust into a world of beauty and fantasy that I found intoxicating. My mother told me to never expect to get a modeling or acting job, but to be super grateful if I got any; a notion that I continue to pass on to my newbies and their parents. "Your looks may get you in the door, but your brains will keep you in the room," I was told. Expectation management 101.

I never dreamed I would end up where I am now, but looking back, the road less traveled was the right one for me. Like all careers there are highs and lows, but the opportunity to uplift others and to stay creative are my blessings. People and their potential keep me passionate. I am excited for the creative possibilities that lie ahead and vow to manifest my future through the power of gratitude.

Carmen Vars

Michelle is a go-getter with an entrepreneurial attitude, who knew she would own her own business since she was 14.

MICHELLE
BOHONIS

I remember feeling excited about a change I knew was to come. It had felt as if the universe was the soil, and I was just a planted seed ready to bloom. I was living in an apartment in Kerrisdale, Vancouver with my wonderful husband Dustin, who I had met in high school. Our beautiful Kerrisdale home was in the works of being demolished. The city that I was so in love with was becoming a place we could no longer afford.

It wasn't long after my awareness of our current situation, an opportunity to invest in real estate was brought to our attention. Now, I'm a true believer of the saying, "What's meant to be, will always find its way". The developer happened to only want the exact amount of savings we had in our bank accounts for our down payment. Dustin had come home from work that evening and I excitedly blurted out, "We are buying a home in Penticton!". He didn't even hesitate, simply responding with, "Sounds good!".

Moving is change and change can be scary. As humans, we are creatures of habit and need time to adjust and process. I did have some reservations as I knew I would be leaving my job of six years and starting fresh in a new environment. My mom had recommended this book to me called Signs, The Secret Language of the Universe by Laura Lynne Jackson. Essentially, it's all about the signs we receive from the universe. I had told my mom that day that I needed to see a blue hair tie to get clarification that this was the move for us. On my walk to work, hanging on a tree was a blue hair scrunchie. I knew at that moment everything would be okay, I got my sign of affirmation.

Making this move really pushed me to get out of my comfort zone. The realization is that things continuously change, and we learn and grow from those experiences. Making big moves will always be challenging, and the unknown can feel both terrifying and exciting all at the same time. I am open to the possibilities of change and ready to continuously evolve.

Cathy Kuzel is founder of The Connected Woman Association, CEO of the CSuite Learning Center, best-selling author and an award winning business development consultant & speaker.

CATHY
KUZEL

Life has a way of helping you look at things differently and after a death in the family, the sale of my company and time away from business, I was ready to get back into the swing of things. The best way to do that was network. It was 2007 and I had come to a point in my life and career that while existing networking groups had purpose, I wanted something different. I was tired of people pitching and trying to sell me something in sixty seconds or less before I could even say my name.

I envisioned a women's organization that encompassed many industries, levels of experience and diverse backgrounds. It would be focused on exchanging ideas and knowledge; discovering how we could empower other women to move ahead; and engaging women so that we could learn from each other. I couldn't find one locally, so I decided to create one.

Coffee with Cathy™ was where it started. These monthly in-person masterminds were where we would come together to discuss issues that were pertinent to our businesses. I found that women wanted to belong to a community of women who "get it," and who understand that being in business is not a walk in the park. From these conversations, The Connected Woman® Association was created.

Fifteen years and we're still going strong. We've come together for a common purpose: to develop a culture centered on women helping women – serving rather than selling, collaborating rather than competing. We laugh, we cry, we help women through tough times and celebrate the victories both large and small. Coffee with Cathy™ has expanded into our Connection Café™ and now we reach women globally.

I believe that powerful things can happen once you start to make connections, and it all comes back to helping others. If you spent a portion of each day thinking of how you can help those you come in contact with – from the barista who makes your coffee to the top authority in your industry – a world of possibilities and opportunities opens up.

And when you make it to the top? Remember to reach back and give a helping hand to those behind you.

Sam van Born is a health & wellness entrepreneur that helps restore people's health and vitality, specializing in immune system support.

SAM
VAN BORN

What the last 2 years has taught me, if you need to choose anything, choose to be kind. Because you never know what someone is going through. Working as a first responder for the last 22 years and having 2 businesses in the health and wellness realm all I know to do is to help people. Whether it's something that could be life-altering, experience something life changing, or being sick and tired of not feeling well.

So many people must fight a medical system that doesn't seem to get to the root cause. Don't get me wrong, we have an amazing acute care system. However, in my opinion there are other ways to go about getting the help you need. And a lot of those things can be found in nature. That's when I kick it into high gear. I see so many people that need help. It's then a matter of connecting, understanding, and talking about what they need, that could potentially change their lives. By being able to listen to families, educating and connecting them to quality products I feel is my life's purpose. I know what it feels like to hit the wall, I know what it feels like to have no energy and feel like you don't want to get out of bed, I know what it feels like to always feel run down and not feel well, I know what it feels like to be exhausted with the healthcare system and not getting to the root cause, the roller coaster moods. All of it. I see you and I hear you.

Now that I have changed my health and feel better, I educate people about how Aloe Vera can change your health. Imagine something that goes into your cells that heals and has a celebration with you as you start out fresh, with a clean slate. I just want you to know you're not alone, I get it and we will figure it out … you just need to start somewhere. I'm here to help when you're ready.

Founder of Woman Of Worth WOW Worldwide. She adores big bold red wines, has been a #1 bestselling author ten times, believes chocolate is a vegetable (as it comes from a bean), trusts that everything is figureoutable, and has been completely in love with her beloved Manly Man for over 15 years. Visionary, philanthropist, speaker, writer, publisher ... she stands for the empowerment, connection and collaboration of women. Her favourite quote: "Every woman has a story, and your story matters."

CHRISTINE
AWRAM

The WOW Credo

I am a Woman Of Worth

My worthiness is inherent, infinite and persevering — it is my natural state

My value is a reflection of who I AM — and I am magnificent

And… who I am always makes a difference — because I MATTER

I am successful — coming from my true power which lies within

I am empowered — making choices from the clarity of my heart, mind and spirit

I am abundant – manifesting from my core values

I am a Human BEing — as my BEing is of far more significance than my DOing

I cherish my relationships — they are part of what makes me strong

I play, laugh, and bring beauty and light into the world — because I am radiant

At times I despair and I weep – when I feel the pain of a world that has momentarily gone mad

Yet even when I tremble through a dark night of the soul,

I renew my faith and my courage in a single heartbeat — because my spirit is indomitable

I FEEL and I CARE and I am passionately ALIVE — with a heart as open as the universe

I AM A WOMAN OF WORTH, AND I AM GLORIOUS!

255

Daniela is a certified energy and crystal healer, reiki master, founder of Naturally Given, and co-founder of Glarea Elevated Learning.

DANIELA
FISHER

Our wonderful planet is going through a major shift in consciousness. Welcome to the Golden Era, a new type of Earth as humanity re-awakens to its highest frequency of love and truth. Did you know that you came to Earth to remember who you really are? In other words, we came to the Earth dimension to evolve into more powerful beings, what I like to call "Beings of Light".

I believe that we are all vibrational beings in a physical body. We are not only a body and mind, rather we are a soul that has a body and a mind that we are able to use as tools during our lives on the third dimension, also called Earth.

But what exactly is a soul? A soul is the true essence of your being. Your soul has gifts that are unique to you, things that no one else in the world has. In other words, you are irreplaceable and a limited edition, and that's your power. Your soul is also eternal and is one with all that exists in the world. Your soul chose to come to Earth to learn lessons, so it could evolve to its highest frequency of love. In fact, your soul's original form is just that, love.

What exactly is love? Love is the most powerful energy force that exists. Love is a high vibrational frequency that makes you whole again and keeps you alive. Unfortunately, it is what most humanity is lacking. I believe that love is the answer to all your problems. Love is you, and therefore you no longer need to be looking for it outside of yourself. How cool is that?

I am so excited to remind you that you are not only love, but also an extremely powerful and eternal being. With that in mind, continue to do more of what will guide you deeper into love. You may ask yourself these questions: Why are you on Earth? And how can you contribute to and bless this world through your soul's gifts?

On this Earth, I believe that my purpose is to fearlessly elevate humanity to its highest frequency of love.

Love, Light, and Gratitude.

Daniela Fisher

Nicole Oliver is a successful Actor, Producer, Director and Voice Director.

NICOLE
OLIVER

My mother often told me that she only had 3 options for what she could BE when she grew up: a secretary, a nurse, or a wife. Even with her self-expressed limited range of choices, she still picked 2: nurse, which she got paid for, and wife, which she often argues she SHOULD have been paid for. I decided that I was going to be an actress, full stop. Expression was my passion, and I was determined to make a living at it.

I was bullied throughout my school career (and work journey, but that's another story). Bullying and the impact of it wasn't the t-shirt wearing, ad fueled point of compassion that it is today. My mother told me to be thankful for the true friends in my life and that "this too shall pass." My Dad told me to fight back.

Photo credit: Kristine Cofsky

So, I did.

My Dad also taught me that following your heart and dreams are just as important as good grades and an education. He would often say, "The worst thing is to be leading your life and yet to be haunted by the unanswered question of: What would have happened if?"

My father died when I was 25 years old; he was just 52. At my father's funeral, people talked about his character, his sense of humour and his lousy golf swing. Yes, they talked about his work accomplishments, but no one was shedding tears over the reports that would never be written. They were shedding tears remembering all the perfect and imperfect pieces of him. Friend. Father. Husband. Partner.

Even from "the other side," my father was teaching me that my resume wasn't going to fit on a tombstone. Just like he taught me to fight back and stand up to bullies, he was letting me know that I had the power to craft the life I wanted to live. (And that I better get to it, because life rarely follows the path we think we desire.)

Fast forward 27 years, and I am still putting one foot in front of the other as a performer, director, and voice director. My father helped me to embrace those moments where we can change, grow, and not concern ourselves with the challenging answer to "What would have happened if," but only with the infinite possibility of what can be possible.

Arlene Wise is a mother and teacher with a deep passion for yoga and travel; she has found balance in her life.

ARLENE
CATHERINE WISE

I was born in the month of October, a true Libran at heart. I have always looked at both sides of any situation. Finding balance in my life is what I have always strived for. Balance is what keeps me strong, calm and centered.

I've travelled to 27 countries and lived and worked in both Germany and Japan in my 20's. I was doing what I loved: travelling, meeting new people, learning new languages, and experiencing new cultures, which nourished my soul. My life was balanced. A life lesson I gained through my travels was how people with lives so different from mine could cope with existence more easily as they appeared to be more spiritually and communally connected.

We had three children in our 30's. My husband and I experienced the typical challenges of raising a young family while working full time. My life generally felt balanced; yoga and swimming kept me grounded, and time with friends and family kept me socially connected.

As our children grew older and family dynamics changed, I began feeling less centered and in control of my life. One child left for a year to pursue hockey, one developed Anorexia Nervosa and required treatment, while our third child left the country to pursue advanced education. Suddenly, I felt alone.

While I was managing these changes in our family, it became apparent to me that my self-care was lacking; I was the one who needed to be cared for. I was blessed with the support of many women throughout my journey, including medical professionals, family and friends who were intuitively aware of my situation. This all helped me to overcome the most challenging journey of my life so far.

My mental health experience took seven years to overcome. Today, I live a fulfilled and satisfied life with a nourished soul, experiencing life through an entirely different lens. I have learned how to put my needs first in an unselfish way. I have understood through my journey that I am a central pillar of strength; if I am not well, my family is not well.

258   Arlene Catherine Wise

Miranda Diane is a crystal lover, plant hoarder, moonlight and sunrise chaser. She is a coach, nurse, speaker, podcast co-host and mama to four wild little ones.

MIRANDA
DIANE

Many years ago, I met this woman. Over the past two decades, I have gotten to know her in a different way – in the details… and it changed me.

I watched as she ran away from everything that hurt. I also witnessed the moment she chose differently. The moment she whipped around fiercely, declaring "no more," walking right into the middle of the blazing fire and began to unpack it.

I watched her confront trauma and begin the wound work. Abandonment, childhood sexual abuse, loss, marital issues. One after the other, I watched her quietly put it on the table.

I watched her navigate loss and perceived brokenness in her body as she begged for answers around infertility/miscarriages. I watched her become a mother to many, both in Heaven and Earth.

I watched her as she was silenced and misunderstood. I heard the assumptions being made and watched her retreat instead of asserting.

I watched her bury into the tundra. Deconstructing, unlearning and burning it down. I watched her rekindle the fire, nurture and unleash it.

I watched her set boundaries for herself and others. I watched her steadiness when they were criticized by those who didn't understand.

I watched her learn to honour her desires. Yes became yes. No was no.

I watched as she began to let tears fall that she had held in for years, knowing they are not a sign of weakness, but rather that you can feel your strength.

I watched as she learned that love can heal, hurt, blind or protect you.

I watched as she chose kindness and humility in a bed of thorns.

I watched as her word became her word. Her voice, story, grit, intuition, discipline, trauma, wounds, and "baggage" were hers to hold.

I witnessed all of it. Her becoming, her reclamation of her worth. Fully seen and embraced. I embodied her lessons – the good and the challenges. I called in peace. I set simple intentions. I surrendered. I released the expectations and called her home.

I am her. She is me.

Brad King is an award-winning nutritional researcher, product formulator and best-selling author of 11 books. He's appeared as a leading expert on over 1,000 television and radio shows.

BRAD
KING

In order to realize my full passion in life, I knew something had to change. That something turned out to be my belief system. What transpired altered my destiny and allowed me to live a life worth living. Here is what I learned along the way.

Let me start with a quote from an unknown author: "Watch your thoughts, for they become words. Watch your words, for they become actions. Watch your actions, for they become habits. Watch your habits, for they become character. Watch your character, for it becomes your destiny."

In other words, no matter what you do, you will be destined for failure time and time again, unless you truly believe that change is not only possible but merely a matter of time. Trust me when I say, your personality and behaviors will guide you to your ultimate destiny if you allow them to. "Within you right now is the power to do things you never dreamed possible. This power becomes available to you just as you can change your beliefs."

The question is, what is your present reality? For you to adopt and practice the principles necessary to reawaken what lies deep within you, all you have to do is start moving towards that goal (no matter how tiny the steps) and have the willpower to see it through to the end, or in this case, the beginning—of the new you! Change is difficult, as we are often hardwired to take the path of least resistance, or what is most familiar to us.

The key to success with anything worth obtaining is to remember that you are the one in control of your destiny—no one else! So change your old unhealthy habits for new healthy ones. Take baby steps, but always move a little closer to your true destiny every single day. Remember, if you sit back and do nothing, life in turn will do nothing for you!

The great motivational leader Dr. Denis Waitley once said; "If you believe you can, you probably can. If you believe you won't, you most assuredly won't. Belief is the ignition switch that gets you off the launching pad." Awakening your true-life's potential is a lot closer then you may presently believe!

Brad King

HEATHER
LEAVOY

My childhood was full of dancing and singing. I loved it and I excelled in it. It was my life all the way up through high school, when I also started to explore acting. I was rubbing shoulders with industry movers and shakers. And then came my big break… a role in the show Glee! What an amazing moment. But yet, that's all it was. One kiss sent me down a completely different path… motherhood. At the beginning of my adult life, I had to make a choice— after having a clear vision, I chose her. So I surrendered, jumped in and embraced this beautiful blond-haired, blue-eyed baby girl and all that came with her. As I focused on being the best mom I could be, I found a resilience I didn't know I had. My positive outlook on life sustained me through the depths of difficult times… the breakup with her father, the ensuing counselling around abusive relationships, family court/legal proceedings, being strong enough to become a single mother, and the adjustment to my own mother moving out of my childhood home, leaving me to care for my aging father recovering from a stroke.

It felt like my dream of living a creative life was slipping away. I had another choice to make. To just accept my current reality, or to press on. The second option was much more appealing, so I did just that. I kept pursuing work as a voiceover actor, and I went to work for a business consulting company where some of the top thought leaders in the world were sharing their knowledge and teachings. I absorbed everything like a sponge. I found other like-minded women and moms like me trying to make their way to their dreams, all while carrying the weight of the world on their shoulders. I found they leaned on mine and I was able to provide insight and encouragement; it filled me up! Today, I am a life coach and I help people find clarity in their path. I am so grateful for what I thought was my mess, as now, it's my message.

261

Aunalee Boyd-Good is one of the creative forces behind Ay Lelum The Good House of Design. She is a Director, designer and recording artist with her sister Sophia and they work alongside their collaborative family of artists.

AUNALEE
BOYD-GOOD

I feel as though my life has been immersed in the arts. I was raised in an art studio in my younger childhood, which allowed me to be fully creative and yet also taught me self-determination. I had the absolute freedom to play on my own terms, to perform, make art and sell things. This prepared me for my future as a musician, performer, artist, and entrepreneur within my family collaborative.

Photo credit: Helena Lines

My parents were artists raising a family in Nanaimo, B.C. and in my teen years they moved into a house and opened a studio and retail businesses. Mom painted and did pottery; Dad carved wood carvings and gold and silver jewelry. Together they created the first Coast Salish clothing line called Ay Ay Mut. As they traveled their entrepreneurial journey, I worked alongside them, and my younger siblings were the creative children playing in the studio space. As everyone grew up, worked the business together and my parents retired, the dynamics shifted. I spent time as an Optometric Assistant where I engaged my creativity in the fashionable expression of eyewear, performed with a classical choir and pursued my degree in English. I had adulted, but something was missing.

In 2015 I was walking downtown, and a voice came to me that told me to go to the Nanaimo Museum and ask about a textile exhibit for my parents. I immediately spoke with the Manager and booked an exhibition date. Suddenly, we were celebrating my parents' 35 years of artistic collaboration with the Ay Ay Mut Exhibit. Since my parents sold art to support their family, we didn't have many pieces to show. I had the pleasure of borrowing pieces from the homes of life-long friends and collectors who had their art on display and in their closets - decades later. The impact of their artistic contributions made an impression on me, and I saw the importance of art from an entirely different perspective. I was so inspired, and this was the beginning of a new journey for my family. This is the juncture where my sister Sophia and I decided to start the fashion design house, Ay Lelum – The Good House of Design.

Aunalee Boyd-Good

Sophia Seward-Good is a Director, designer and recording artist with her sister Aunalee at Ay Lelum The Good House of Design, working alongside their collaborative family of artists. She is a mother of 5, a grandma and a student at SFU.

SOPHIA
SEWARD
-GOOD

Photo credit: Helena Lines

In a family of professional artists, my sister Aunalee and I forged our path as the creative force behind Ay Lelum, through fashion, music, Coast Salish art and hul'q'umi'num language. When we started our company, neither one of us could sew, this didn't deter us. We had the vision to create a Coast Salish clothing line like our parent's had and the determination to build it for the next generations. As a mother of five children and one grandchild, it is crucial to carry on the family legacy and keep Coast Salish culture alive. I am driven by preservation of our culture through art, music, language and in passing it on.

One day we were in the studio recording music for our second Vancouver Fashion Week showcase and we were short one song. According to my Dad William Good's Coast Salish teachings, we originally had a song and dance for everything, but so much has been lost. I had been studying the hul'q'uimi'num language to incorporate into our showcase, and my sister told me to go into the booth and "write a song." What is ironic is that she is a classically trained singer, but she sent me in to write -- it didn't make any sense. The beauty is when I went in, I started singing in our language and the words transformed into songs and she did the harmonies. These songs became part of the garment design process, and the words wove into the essence and fabric of each collection through visual art, music and language.

My late Grandmother Hazel Good was one of the original group of Elders in our Snuneymuxw community who recorded and documented the hul'q'umi'num language in the 1980's. I am proud to carry on her legacy and learn from her body of work, as I am currently pursuing my Masters at Simon Fraser University's Graduate Certificate in Linguistics of a First Nations Language, in hul'q'umi'num. As I learn more language and work and learn alongside my parents, I will continue to create and educate. We have a living, breathing culture, I am determined to preserve and share it through art, music, language and fashion within my family collaborative.

Sophia Seward-Good

Photo credit: Sean Fenzl

William Good is a Hereditary Chief from the Snuneymuxw First Nation, a Master Carver and Coast Salish Artist, Storyteller, and a Cultural Historian. He is also a feature artist at Ay Lelum The Good House of Design.

ts'usqinuxun' WILLIAM GOOD

When I was a teenager in the 1960's, the late Leslie John told me I was going to be a world-renowned artist, the next foremost artist in Nanaimo doing hul'q'umi'num art. Leslie was a well-known artist who worked with his family in the John's carving studio in the 1950's-60's and sold in Canada and the US. In those days, the hul'q'umi'num, or Coast Salish artform was almost extinct in our area. I didn't think much of it at the time, as I was young, and I didn't have the patience for art. I couldn't even draw a straight line.

"No, William", he would say, "you were brought up right and you listen to your elders", so I had to listen to him. He told me I had the visions, and I had the dreams, and he professed, "You are the next one to carry out the art and stories of the Snuneymuxw people". I started a life-long journey dedicated to the research, documentation, and practice of hul'q'umi'num art where I combined the oral history I had been taught by my Grandfather, William Good, with visual art.

I ended up carving and making art with a lot of different artists throughout the 1970's and 80's, with Tsimshian, Nuu-Chah-Nulth, and mostly Kwakwaka'wakw artists, but my main goal was to revive the hul'q'umi'num artform. As it wasn't well known in those days, I had museums all over the world send me photographs of hul'q'umi'num art. When I started selling hul'q'umi'num art in the 1990's, gallery and store buyers didn't believe it was Coast Salish, and it was hard for me to sell. Now, to see more artists switching over to hul'q'umi'num art and to see the art come back is like a dream come true. It took many years to get to this point. With my family carrying on the art, it is the way it is originally supposed to be in our culture, the way it was passed on to me. It has to be handed down to the next generations and Joel and my two daughters are taking over the artform now and I have grandchildren that are interested, so that makes me really happy.

Joel Good is a traditional Coast Salish Artist and carver from the Snuneymuxw (Nanaimo) First Nation. He is also a feature artist at Ay Lelum The Good House of Design working with his sisters and family.

W. JOEL
GOOD

Photo credit: Sean Fenzl

My parents were both artists and very well known in our community, famous if you will. My dad always loved to bug me. When dropping me off at high school, he would sometimes blast pow wow music as loud as possible. I was super embarrassed, and he thought it was funny. When I got out of the car with my head held down, people asked, "who was that guy"? I told them he was my dad. They were like, "he's cool". My parents being artists, I decided I'd never be one. When everyone knows your parents and appreciates their work, you have conflicted feelings about being an artist's child that I can't explain. You crave the 'normalcy' that your friends have while living this alternative creative lifestyle. All of my siblings and I have experienced this feeling growing up.

Around the age of ten, I started to carve in cedar. I worked alongside my dad for many years. We have since completed many public masterworks together on display in Nanaimo, B.C. Carving seemed to come naturally to me, but really, I was raised learning it all my life. I learned painting and art principles from my mom and have combined them with the Traditional Coast Salish Artform and family cultural teachings from my dad. I have been able to fuse the best of their styles into one and now feel so fortunate for my upbringing.

Later in life, my best friend Josef said, "I always knew you'd be an artist", and when I asked him why he said because whenever we did schoolwork, you were busy drawing. I was a hyper child diagnosed with ADHD, and my mother managed it naturally, refusing to put me on medication. I grew up with a strict diet, many creative outlets, and my family's love. I was able to pursue art, and I am still busy drawing. It is my calling, and I listened. It is my life's work and my passion. I still work alongside my family here on Snuneymuxw First Nation, and I wouldn't change a thing!

Photo credit: Sean Fenzl

Sandra Moorhouse-Good is a multidisciplinary artist, painter and garment designer. After having taught art classes and produced artwork for decades, she is now a lead couture designer and the design mentor for her daughters at Ay Lelum The Good House of Design.

SANDRA
MOORHOUSE
-GOOD

My lifelong journey as a living artist began when I was a young child. As a wartime baby, I grew up with my mother and family in Ontario while my father was away at war. My family said I was an artist, but there was a definitive moment when I knew I was an Artist. I was travelling on a trip with my mother between Vancouver and Toronto by train, where she had bought me a new colouring book and crayons. I was sitting colouring, and the train porter, an older, distinguished black man, stopped me, and told me how beautiful and special my colouring was. I turned and looked at him with conviction and said, "well, I am an Artist, after all". At this moment, I knew who I was, and everything I did after that was to follow that through.

We moved West to Victoria, B.C., where I began formal art training by my grandfather, Herbert Moorhouse, who had Royal London Academy papers. At six, I began studying classical oil painting from the late 1800s. By the age of nine, a series of my paintings travelled in an exhibit across Canada in 1953. I devoted myself to a lifelong journey as an artist, and throughout the 1960-the 70s, I developed my visual language.

In 1977, I opened The Art Studio at 61 Nicol Street in Nanaimo, where I moved my family and raised the children. Living in a free and creative environment, I instilled in my children the importance of learning artistic discipline and classical techniques in all art forms. I have always maintained a deep appreciation for classical and Traditional cultural art forms. This proved essential later in my career working with my husband, William Good. As I continued my work alongside him and supported his devotion to revitalizing the Traditional Coast Salish art form and applying it to other media, we created many collaborative works, including the Ay Ay Mut clothing line.

We are a multi-generational family of artists, and it is simply who we are. This is how the children were raised and how we continue to work together, creating as a family.

Sandra Moorhouse-Good

Christina Weizmann is a Digital Transformation Strategist, Vegan Mompreneur, Animal Activist, and Amazon Best Selling Co-Author for several publications.

CHRISTINA
WEIZMANN

Innovative Sustainability is the New Hustle...

I'm very inspired to be in the company of so many accomplished changemakers – drawing from a wealth of life experiences. It is my hope that we may all fulfill our life purpose and leave a positive legacy in life – this fleeting existence on an ailing planet. Time is not on our side!

We are facing a massively chaotic time with big changes that are deeply unsettling for most of us. However, I'm embracing the disruptions because I see Mother Nature forcing humanity to get back in our lane. As a young rebel who disliked nonsensical rules, the word WHY has been at the epicenter of my curiosity – questioning the status quo – especially when things didn't make sense and I knew there had to be a better way. It may have started when a Homeopath cured my Eczema after conventional doctors told me that my diet had nothing to do with the state of my skin (insert massive eye roll). My Eczema disappeared within a month of treatment and hasn't returned in three decades. This was the start of my penchant for alternative therapies and solutions… always looking for a better way.

While we witness magnificent talents as humans evolve there are still deep corporate roots anchoring us in the old methodologies for the sole purpose of profit, driven by greed at the cost of our future existence. Globally we need to embrace fast, innovative change throughout all industries, with very simple and logical innovations. We need to get back to basics and strip away the lies, mediocrity, apathy and basic fear of change.

Which is why I'm very honoured to introduce a new nutraceutical project –NUNU BIOCEUTICALS, that breaks free from the old monotony and duplicity when it comes to nutritional supplements and health strategies. NUNU technology is designed to reinvigorate, rejuvenate and regenerate the human existence based on novel science-driven standards that reach beyond convention; and boost traditional wholistic strategies used successfully for millennia with 21st century health science discoveries that extract a new level of efficacy. We're excited to introduce a family of innovative products that supports the body's ability to heal itself.

267

Heather McMullin is a Mortgage Broker, Commercial Equipment Manager, and dedicated mother.

HEATHER
McMULLIN

Happiness is a state of mind dependent on our perception. Perception is our reality. That which we perceive to be true is true. My happiness comes from recognizing and using my skills, trusting in myself, and finding life balance.

As a woman in my twenties, I was always interested in problem-solving, finances and investing. I started contributing to Registered Retirement Savings plans when I was 19. My interests and skills led me to my first career in telecommunications and supply chain logistics, a field primarily dominated by men. During meetings, I was often the sole female in a room full of men and was referred to as Sweetie and Honey. I pointed out that my name was Heather, not Honey. People continuously underestimated me because I was a wife and a mother, as though those things might interfere with my productivity. When a man holds the same position, we do not assume because he is a husband or a father that, he cannot be productive. I did exceptionally well in my chosen fields.

In 2002, I moved to Newfoundland and had a career change. My father owned a mortgage brokerage and asked for help with the logistics part of the company. While working on the logistics, I learned about the lending process, client requirements, and government regulations and enjoyed it. Many people lack financial training, so I act as a mortgage consultant and advisor. People dream of purchasing a house but aren't quite ready sometimes, so I help them prepare. Having worked as a broker for both the bank and under an franchise organization, I prefer working for myself. Working from home in a calm environment allows me to structure my day to work with my clients in two different businesses and be present for my family. Work doesn't have to be nine to five. The bottom line is that I am happy, my kids are content, and my clients are getting what they need, advice and a home.

I believe the reasons for happiness vary. Each person needs to figure out what gives them fulfilment and pursue it! Only you can make yourself happy.

Heather McMullin

Holly Decker is an award-winning Makeup
Artist,BeautyEditor, and creative mastermind.

HOLLY
DECKER

As a makeup artist and working in the beauty industry for twenty years, I see beauty in all faces.

I love what I do for so many reasons – the artistry, working with people and the intimate conversations in my chair.

Over the years beauty trends have changed and I have ridden the wave of them. In the last few years, I do believe beauty needs to be redefined.

The pressure to be "perfect" is at an all-time high. With so many filters and apps, our expectation of what real people look like has been distorted.

Real skin has fine lines, pores, texture, and uneven skin tone. We all need to stop comparing ourselves to filtered and photoshopped images and appreciate beautiful real skin.

This is an unachievable comparison game, and we need to be kinder to ourselves and others. What are you saying to yourself? Is the language positive or negative?

I encourage you to speak kindly to yourself. "I am beautiful" – these are powerful words to speak.

As a young girl, I was influenced by beauty in many ways. From real women in my life, to Magazine covers and television. That was my form of social media, and it did have an impact on me and how I defined being beautiful. Fast forward to 2022 and young girls are being influenced by 24/7 non-stop filtered beauty in the palm of their hands. As a leader in the beauty industry, I hope I can influence and educate our youth on what it means to be truly beautiful.

I see the impact this has had on the young girls and women I work with.

Every time a client sits in my chair, they apologize to me. They apologize for their skin or their nose or their lips.

It's heartbreaking to hear as I only see the beauty in them. Makeup does not make you beautiful or define you. Makeup is my art form and a creative expression for me.

I see beauty in everyone and love being able to capture and showcase that beauty.

Let's redefine what it means to beautiful. Beauty is REAL and we need to embrace it.

269

Photo credit: Kristy Powers Photography

Marilyn R. Wilson is a freelance writer, interviewer, published author and speaker who gives wings to the stories of others.

MARILYN R.
WILSON

Growing up, my interest in people's lives and concern for their suffering led me to pursue psychology as a career. I had this idealistic vision that clients would come in broken, I would work my magic, and they would leave happy and healed.

The day I spoke with one of my graduate professors who was working in the field, the truth he shared of a low success rate for this type of therapy and having to deal with the suicide of one of his clients, hit me like a ton of bricks. In just a few minutes my dream was shattered. I walked away, lost; it would be three decades before I found my true calling. It still came from the same passion, but was focused instead on interviewing and writing – giving wings to the stories others shared with me.

As much as I wish I had been able to come to interviewing and writing at a much earlier age, several things had to come together first. I needed to grow up and deal with some of my insecurities. I needed the computer to be invented to keep up with my racing mind, and the internet a reality.

As well, as an older person with no credentials, I found no one was waiting with open arms for me saying, "Finally, you're here!" I had to create my own opportunities and build my own doors before I could walk through them. However, when all the elements came together, I leapt without thinking. I leapt with abandon. The journey that followed was hard, but I don't regret a single moment. And this journey began at the moment it was meant to.

Some of us find what we are meant to do at an early age. Others find what makes our heart sing much later; but if you keep your heart open to the possibilities, it will come to you at the perfect time. And know that no matter how hard the journey, if you just keep putting one foot in front of the other, you will be unstoppable. It's truly never too late.

Marilyn R. Wilson

Jarrett Jackson is someone who enjoys saying yes to experiences that he once would have only dreamed about.

JARRETT
JACKSON

There is never complete recovery from insanity, just moments of relief that can only take place in the present, and I'm perfectly okay with that.

Even when I was a kid I knew the outcome of situations, but the end scenario never really occurred to me; I craved instant gratification. I needed that chocolate bar my dad strictly told me was for after dinner. Years later, in similar fashion, I needed to go spend money on alcohol when only moments earlier I had said to myself that "This money is for rent," but that didn't matter.

I lied to myself saying it would be different, but it was never different.

Imagine your head being your own worst enemy. I know my mind is its own version of Dr. Jekyll and Mr. Hyde and one day I was hit with the realisation that I couldn't let that pair make the decisions anymore. I made the decision, I needed help.

At 24 years of age I quit drinking. I made the decision to change. It was an easy choice, simply because I would have been dead if I hadn't made it. While the road hasn't been the smoothest, I am able to look back at the things I've endured, and despite many of the self inflicted wounds, I can breath and get back to the present. "If you made it through that, you can make it through this."

I've been able to tackle my anxiety, get my health back, and be a trusted friend, partner, brother, son & member of society.

Today I have been given a gift. I used to drink to escape my emotions, but I've learned from my past mistakes and chose to tackle them head on. I choose to live my life today through action, as it is the only way I know how to be a role model. Attraction rather than promotion, I can't help others if I have not helped myself. This may not be the easiest way of life, but I can tell you personally that there is beauty in the struggle. My biggest struggle today is just remembering to stay present, and you know what? I am perfectly okay with that.

Jarrett Jackson

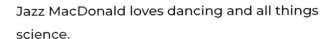
Jazz MacDonald loves dancing and all things science.

JAZZ
MacDONALD

When I was growing up, I knew I wanted to help others and make a difference in the world and have time for various artistic endeavors. I modeled professionally and appeared in films and on tv. I worked for the RCMP and other law enforcement agencies. I went back to college a few times all while being a single mother. I have also had the opportunity to write poetry and lyrics for musicians and work in the Medical Laboratory field, while navigating empty nest syndrome. Then Covid hit the world.

Having survived the stress and grief of two tragic deaths in my immediate family gave me the strength to keep going. My baby brother drowned, and my father was killed by a drunk driver, which forever changed my mother's life, my younger brother's life, and my life.

Life is a gift! Aging is denied to many. I cherish everyone that has come into my life. I love life! I choose to be an example hoping to inspire others to keep going and never give up.

272

Joan Samuels-Dennis is a trauma recovery specialist, mother, wife, community builder, and spiritual teacher.

JOAN
SAMUELS-DENNIS

Most people, when asked about 2016, will recount a rather significant shift in their lives. That year, I left my full-time job to start a not-for-profit. I was going to convert an old barn into a 24-bed shelter for women experiencing domestic violence. I was ready to integrate all my research and clinical counseling experience into an innovative model that would dramatically shift service provision for this population.

But I and the team were not ready for the task ahead. When we're not ready, we fight for power, control, and choice. Conflict becomes our point of focus instead of the vision and the road ahead.

I had started my healing journey in fall of 2015, but the death of this baby took me way back. There I was, a 10-year-old girl watching as a car came towards me and my brother. We drew close to the banking of the road and waited for it to pass. The driver focused on us, not the road ahead. The car hit my brother and he fell. That same week, we were to immigrate to Canada. My brother lived, but ever since, whenever I am to transition into something new, the proverbial car shows up.

Here it was again.

Have you ever kissed someone at the airport, go on with your day and never wonder if they will return? In November 2016, I said goodbye to my husband as he boarded a 14-hour flight to Shanghai, China. On that flight, he had a massive stroke that destroyed his ability to speak and move the right side of his body. My husband came home - 90% recovered - but, my 21-days in China changed me forever.

The last 7 years have been a powerful journey of transformation and healing. As I healed my childhood trauma, I rewired my brain, created new thought patterns, and spiritually transformed. I expanded my private practice and created a model of trauma recovery called Smashing the Mirror. The 24-bed shelter became something much bigger – a corporation focused on transformation called Becoming Inc.

I have witnessed so many miracles in the last 7 years, but the biggest was experiencing a state of complete inner peace. In 2019, I wrote my first book 490: Forgive and Live Fearlessly. My new mission is to eliminate fear from the heart and psyche of every human being.

I am ready now!

Joan Samuels-Dennis

Teresa Teschner, executive producer (film industry), co-owner of Cherry Lane Homes, mother, wife, tea-ma (grandmother of Isla), friend and connector.

TERESA
TESCHNER

Throughout my life I've learned to ride the waves, the ups and downs, highs and lows that come and go. It was 10 years ago at the age of 48 that I found my passion in a sport that is at first challenging, then addicting. Once I mastered letting go of the rope, it was exhilarating, the best way to destress from all life's worries and troubles.

My parents, immigrants from Hong Kong, raised me to be strong, resilient and hard working with a giving heart. They also taught me to be fearless, to be a survivor, to accept changes, to not allow circumstances dictate my path, marching to the beat of my own drum. I was born a middle child, but somehow I knew I was a born leader. Fighting discrimination as a kid felt like a David and Goliath battle. I protected my siblings even as a kid! I did not like feeling and looking different from everyone around me; being raised in a predominantly white community, we were faced with bullying by very cruel children. It wasn't until I published a children's book, Seeds In the Wind, in 2011, about accepting differences, that I finally learned to accept myself completely.

Those early years of education from my parents and institutions shaped me into who I am today. But who I've become is the result of the journey I have taken and the path I have chosen. As challenging as life was, I kept grinding the wake, I kept reinventing myself; when I see an opportunity, I jump in, I take risks, I wing it until I learn it. I found strength in what I have learned, from the large circle of friends I have created, the love of my two children, Alisha and Trevor, my family and husband Peter, a loving man who has re-instilled faith in men for me.

There is no perfect life; it is accepting the imperfections, letting go of the rope, just riding the waves with determination and a smile in my heart while living life to the fullest.

Confucius said, "Our greatest glory is not in never falling, but rising every time we fall."

Teresa Teschner

Josh Montana is currently the Vice President of stewardship and relations of a national wide private consulting firm in oil, gas, potash, and renewable energy.

JOSH
MONTANA

I was raised by a strong woman who has passed down to me strength, courage, and an understanding of who I am as an Indigenous man living in a white world. She taught me to always do the right thing and strive to be the best at whatever I put my hands to.

My generation is the first to break free from the Canadian legacy of Residential Schools. However, the obstacles I've had to overcome are a direct result of that legacy. When I say break free, I mean break free from being forced to physically attend an institution that was created to kill us off. My responsibility is to ensure that the hardships passed down to me, stop at me. I want to guide the next generation and show them that we belong wherever we want to belong.

As a new father, I've had to think about how I want to raise my child. I don't want my daughter and future children to face the things my family and I have had to face. I fear bringing my daughter into a world without equal opportunity or to be discriminated against for being First Nations.

As an Indigenous man in business and sport, I've had to work twice as hard to be successful with half the opportunity. We have much further to go regarding equal opportunities, combating discrimination and racism, and undoing the years of harm imposed upon First Nations peoples. I want to pass down what I have learned to provide greater opportunity for growth, healing, and success. As Indigenous people, we also play a part in the solution.

As a Canadian National Team athlete in Fastball, Vice President of a private consulting firm, and a new father, I have a lot to share with the world and my community.

I live by the motto, "If I am going to be a janitor, I'm going to be the best janitor there is. If I am going to be a CEO, I am going to be the best CEO there is. It does not matter what I am doing, I am always going to strive to be the best and outwork anyone in my realm."

Josh Montana

Joy Peirson currently lives in Victoria, BC and uses the amazing surroundings and vibrant cityscapes as inspiration for her artwork.

JOY
PEIRSON

I was furious. The doctor had said, "Go home and get your affairs in order, I better see you next week." As I left the doctor's office that day, I thought to myself, "Not likely". I wasn't just angry at the abrupt message I had been given, but I was also infuriated by the diagnosis of having Parkinson's. At the time, the easiest thing I could do was try not to believe it.

So, I went home and started painting, which is something that I have always done. When I was younger, my father was adamant against me going into the arts, even stretching as far as telling me to never even consider an art career. This kind of suggestion was damaging to my ego, but I obeyed his demands at the time.

Now, I can look back on all the accomplishments I've made since deciding to take on a career in the arts. I have had many successful art shows, and I have continued to sell my work online. I also have my own art studio where I feel I can escape into my work. I've even made it into the Art section of the newspaper. Thanks to my perseverance and passion, I now have the confidence to don myself with the label, "Artist" in the occupation section of any form I have had to fill out.

Ten years later, I am still alive and have taken some much-needed time to come to terms with having Parkinson's. My hand may shake sometimes, and I find myself having to take a nap most days now, but I still paint all the time. Thank goodness I paint. Painting allows me to step into a different world. Who knows what takes place between looking at a physical thing, the fingers holding brush and paint, and reproducing the image or idea in front of your eyes? When I pick up a paintbrush, time passes, and I don't notice any physical changes. I just feel normal. I do all the physical exercise I need, and I take the required medicine for Parkinson's. Yet, despite these traditional practices of healing, the best remedy for me has always been making art.

Donna Vachon is a construction safety professional who is also a 3 year breast cancer survivor and mentor to other cancer warriors.

DONNA
VACHON

In 365 days, your whole world can change. So much can happen in only a short amount of time. The challenge is how you manage and cope with it all.

I found a lump in my breast. I was only 42 years old. I went for the mammogram, which came back as normal breast tissue. Great, I went on with my busy life. However, something didn't feel right to me. Every night, I felt this lump before I went to sleep and thought to myself, this doesn't feel normal, but what do I know? They are the doctors.

Three hundred sixty-five days later, I was at the doctor's office. I asked him to feel the lump again because it was taking over my chest. They fast-tracked me to the breast health clinic. Soon after, I was diagnosed with stage 3 breast cancer, which had spread to my lymph nodes. The doctors told me I might get five years of life with a treatment plan. I quickly began what would be a three-year journey, which included four months of chemotherapy, 36 days of radiation, a double mastectomy, and a total hysterectomy followed by 14 more reconstruction surgeries. I underwent a total of 16 surgeries with debilitating neuropathy. There are some days I still struggle to walk. There were many days when I was haunted by the pain and the knowledge that I might not survive. Doctors don't really prepare you for the inner mental battle. Luckily, laughter and the love of friends and family somehow got me through the darkest days.

Doctors are trained to diagnose our ailments, but they don't know our bodies as we do. As humans, we trust their knowledge. The truth is, we know our bodies better than anyone. If you feel something strange in your body, you must challenge your doctors and ensure you stand up for yourself. If I had insisted, they follow up on the lump as I felt it grow, maybe it wouldn't have spread to the extent that it did.

I'm fighting Breast Cancer, and I'm WINNING! I'm rebuilding my life and getting stronger every day! Don't ever give up on yourself. You know yourself better than anybody else.

Donna Vachon

KAREN
HOLMES

My parents raised me to be independent, which involves determination, resourcefulness, and optimism. This independent spirit had me complete high school and head for Europe, where I toured different cultures, learning lots. Knowing an education would help me attain the goals I had set for myself, I attended university after returning to Canada.

After graduation, I worked in Graphic design. I loved the diversification of the design business, and so in 1988, along with a co-worker, we purchased the graphic design company for which we were working. I realized that my entrepreneurial spirit was born from my independent nature. It wasn't attached to anything tangible or particular; it was about my mindset. I was proactive about learning new things, and I loved what I did. In 2004, it became apparent that the business was changing and would no longer support two partners, so I decided to make a significant career change.

In 2006, the Hospital hired me to do Fundraising. I loved the Hospital environment and the aspect of helping people. Putting potential donors together with projects in the Hospital that needed funding was gratifying. At the end of 2008, the economy was in financial crisis, and my position was terminated. I was devastated as I loved that job.

In August 2009, I was trying to shake off the devasting blow of being unemployed. Something I had never been. I thought hard about what I wanted to do, and entrepreneurship began to call. I had always loved clothes and enjoyed owning my own business, so I approached an existing clothing store and asked the owner if she was interested in selling. She was. I worked in the store for three months for a free – crash course in retail ownership. In Jan 2010, I bought the business and then moved it to grow it.

Instead of matching donors with projects, I'm helping women feel and look their best. I love being an entrepreneur again; I have control over my destiny. Not all women know what suits them when they enter the store. I love being able to work with women – helping them feel confident.

Nerissa Allen is honored to share her journey of finding authentic purpose in her career in this amazing book!

NERISSA
ALLEN

Refocusing my priorities has led to purpose leadership. My long and varied career path was not always a smooth one, but it has supported my growth and led to strong self-awareness.

As one of few Black employees and, at times, the only, I was acutely aware of the fact that I had to work double duty in job performance to overcome the seemingly innate biases and unconscious stereotypes from my colleagues. Quite honestly, it is just exhausting being aware of the stereotypes and feeling as though you must carry the flag of equality for the entire race – every single day.

I believe the luxury and privilege to just be you and to exist is vastly underappreciated. However, what I did learn was the ability to adapt to situations, people, organizations, teams and opinions. The ability to adapt is an asset that I advocate to everyone that I coach. This ability to adjust with change has been instrumental in my life progression of realizing my purpose.

With every pivotal moment in my life where I was able to adapt, I was also capable of refocusing my priorities, moving a step closer to my "harmonious purpose". For me, this is finding internal fulfillment and purpose, while being my true authentic self.

In 2010, after nearly ten years of working a 9-5 job, I shifted my priorities and started my online business – Heavenly Lox. In 2018, I refocused, partnered with my husband, and opened our own RMT clinic, Chattelhouse Health and Beauty Inc. In 2020, we were forced to pivot due to the pandemic, and another refocusing moment brought me to a crossroads where I asked myself: "what do you really want to do with your life?"

This manifested into my current role of leading a purpose driven organization, the Black Business Association of BC, where I share the knowledge and experience I've gained along the way, all while feeling a sense of harmony with my true self.

As I let go of the shackles and the weight of everyone else's expectations, instead listening to my own voice and what I truly wanted from life, that is when I was able to refocus with impact.

Nerissa Allen

Kristin Sayn is a 39 y/o Momma to 3 boys. Wifey, Nurse, Metis, gestational surrogate, Entrepreneur to 2 home-based businesses, and lover of the earth (being in nature fills her soul).

KRISTIN
SAYN

At a young age, I knew I wanted to be a nurse. I had a yearning to help and be helpful. I also have a mantra "I want to do as much "good" as I can in my lifetime and leave this earth better than when I found it. I want to teach and instil this mantra and way of life in my sons.

I have been a nurse for 15 years. I love my job. It has long hours, and I missed being with my family. My children are only little once. So, I started a business, and then in 2019, I took over another thriving business from a dear friend. My home businesses allow me more time with my family and more flexibility. I also love being my own boss. I love a good challenge, and I always need to be busy, either learning new things or creating new things. It's almost like a passion, not a job. Also, my boys love to help; they think it is pretty funny that mommy works downstairs, and they love helping whenever they can. During the Pandemic, my family and I were able to help another couple become parents. I was a gestational surrogate and gave birth in April 2021 to a healthy baby girl. This couple could not have their own children. My family was overjoyed to be able to provide this gift for them. That moment they held their daughter for the first time was just something I cannot even begin to describe. It was pure awe and bliss.

I luv is very proud to offer our new eco-friendly packaging, which is entirely compostable, degradable and is truly zero waste—printed with vegan, eco-friendly dyes right onto the container. We use only six pure, clean, and natural ingredients, so aligning our packaging with our pure ingredients only made sense. Natural for your body and easy on the earth.

We have an exciting new product launching sometime this year. It has been in the works for over a year, almost two years! We are VERY excited, and we know you'll love it.

Kristin Sayn

KYLA
DUFRESNE

Growing up in a rural, industrial BC town, I struggled hard for most of my youth. My mom worked 12-hour days for most of my childhood and my dad worked in the logging camps; I only saw him every other weekend. Being left largely on my own left me feeling unloved and without guidance, and I grabbed control over my life any way I could. I drank, used hard drugs, self-harmed, dropped out of high school, and even ended up in the hospital three times attempting suicide. Drug and alcohol use ran strongly through my entire family, and it was my main coping mechanism to deal with stress, depression, and everything else.

But I also come from a family of hustlers who will work their butts off. When I was 19 I got my high school diploma online, became a full-time bartender, and used my tips to learn how to do Brazilian waxing. When I opened Foxy Box Wax Bar in my home, I was doing something I loved, and I began to make good money. But even though my business was thriving, I was still going too hard. I used alcohol as a crutch, reaching for a bottle of wine every time stress hit after running myself into the ground.

When my dad got terminally sick three years ago, that all changed. I would go from meetings trying to sell franchises to spending the weekends with him while he was dying. It was such a crazy, different life, and it put everything in a new perspective. Because I had to be so strong for everyone, I had to learn how to take care of myself. I let go of my toxic habits, I picked up boxing, and for the first time I allowed people to help me.

It was an amazing feeling to see friends come out of the woodwork and realize how much they loved me. It allowed me to let go of some of my control, especially learning to delegate and trust in my business; it made me realize what's truly important. You have to let go to grow, and this whole experience really taught me to do that.

Kyla Dufresne

Gina is an award-winning entrepreneur and mentor, she works with business owners to take the next step in their success.

GINA
BEST

Staring down at my leg encased in a brace from my ankle to my hip, all I could think is: are you kidding me? How has this happened, not the accident, but the situation? Yet again, there is another obstacle I have to face. I had a pity party moment and went through the thinking of why me, why is this happening? I am not a bad person; did I do something in a past life, and I am being punished?

Thank goodness it was just for a moment (or a few hours), and then I put my big girl panties on and got on with it. Facing challenges and dealing with shitty things is part of life.

Life doesn't stop when bad things happen. You still have to do what you need to do. Sometimes it is just getting out of bed in the morning and doing the basics, while other days you find the motivation to do more than the bare minimum. The reality is, life goes on. It comes down to a choice; you can let it suck you down, or you can put one foot in front of the other, doing what you need to do to get through it and come out on the other side amazing.

I know far too much about this choice, how easy it is to just pull the covers over my head and stay in bed. During my breast cancer adventure – five surgeries – there were many days I wanted to do just that, yet I had things I had to do. I had two businesses to run and two boys to parent. So, I found balance in taking care of me, honouring my feelings and doing what had to be done. And I got through it.

Life is filled with ups and downs, joy and sadness and everything in between. It is up to us in how we navigate it. I have had to navigate a lot, and with every challenge, I become different. Getting to know this different me has been an amazing journey. Now in my business, I support other women through this process in both business and life. That is my gift.

Stephanie Chenoll is a young professional experiencing life to its fullest in British Columbia, Canada.

STEPHANIE
CHENOLL

Online dating has been an incredible way to bring people together. It has become a cultural revolution, changing the way we communicate and how we find partners. After a while of being single, I decided to give it a try. That decision has led to some incredible discoveries about what I need in a partner, and more importantly, what I need for myself

Chatting with matches has been a fun experience. Sometimes it even felt as though I'd found my soulmate in those text bubbles. Other times, messages like 'nice tits, wanna fuck?' never resulted in love. However, most matches were thoughtful and sweet.

The dates I have been on have ranged from moonlit strolls and adventurous hikes to romantic dinners that turn into breakfast. Others were not quite so idyllic. During one of my dates, I found myself at a Brazilian BBQ. The kind of place that brings the grilled meat to your table on a sword and they carve it right in front of you. The concept is a fun novelty, but my system was not used to eating every kind of animal at once. By the end of the meal I was so full of farts I could barely think. He invited me back to his apartment but all I could focus on was how I was going to sneak a few farts out while remaining as ladylike as possible. He wanted to be romantic, I wanted to release the pressure in my stomach. Eventually, I made my way home, still single.

People have given me some weird and wild dating advice. Everything from useful tips like making a list of my must haves and my absolute deal breakers, to less helpful things like, I should wear more makeup, as if that would change my personality. Ultimately, I have discovered that being myself is really the best way to be. Even though I am still single I have never been more content in myself than I am today. If you are single and reading this, take yourself on a date, celebrate all of the wonderfulness that you are and don't let anyone give you less than you deserve!

283

Lynn Anderson has many talents, from being a clinical hypnotherapist to a graphic designer. She also does intuitive readings and mediumship.

LYNN
ANDERSON

From Marriage to Murder
Lynn Anderson

Being a woman who is a veteran online dater, I've met countless men globally online since the 1990s. I started at 37 and am now 60.

I left an unhappy marriage; I was very naive and desiring to find my soulmate. Dating was alluring!

My first relationship was with a local Kenyan man. He was an educated social worker and we had amazing chemistry. One year later, I discovered he was a sociopath, pathological liar and married with five kids! That destroyed me emotionally, but the lessons were invaluable.

Later, very cautiously, I flew to meet men in New York, San Diego, London, Manchester, Africa and India. After ten adventurous years, I met an exotic, handsome man who lived in Kashmir. My soulmate – finally! In 2008 we married there.

Immigration took three painful years before he arrived here in 2011. Two years later, homesickness and pressure from his family caused him to move back. My heart shattered. My soulmate was an illusion.

Later, feeling hopeful again, I met a local Iranian man. He was a perfect gentleman, classy and fun. After three months, my intuition cautioned me to step back. I met the lady he dated next, and she later broke up with him. He brutally murdered her in her home in Coquitlam, along with her male friend visiting from Israel.

These and other distressing experiences hardened me. However, I am happy to have also met wonderful men I call my brothers from other mothers. Lifelong, loving friendships blossomed. They share stories about their families and some ask me for dating advice. I feel honoured to have them in my life.

I'm very grateful for these profound experiences; I can now confidently advise and help others to be vigilant online daters.

Arleen is on a mission to travel and "play" in her retirement!

ARLEEN
CHENOLL

Who will I play with after a demanding career and the sudden death of my husband? How can I find someone youthful, healthy and with compatible values? Online dating options seemed unnatural and frightening to me, but after learning of three women friends who had success with it, I was convinced to sign up.

There I found brief descriptions, old or even dishonest photos. It was fun to "flip the pages", like catalogue shopping. Soon, a charmer I dubbed as "The Italian Stallion", a great-looking, well-dressed, dark-haired hunk, was interested in ME! He "liked" my smile, a huge ego boost. We never met and I stopped taking his calls when he presented a great story about how he needed money. An array of other characters came and went over the next four months.

I was reluctant to meet Max* at first. I really wanted to find someone younger who could keep up with my energy level and would travel with me. I was coy with personal information. He told me all about himself; he was a widower, married to the same woman for a long time. I thought, "he must be well broken in". I Googled him and found everything he told me was true.

I told him, "you are not in my age bracket". He reminded me that "age is just a number, I am very healthy and active, I work out," etc. Plenty of telephone conversations followed, he made me laugh. So, we finally met one warm afternoon at one of our city's most beautiful places. We spent four hours having brunch, walking, talking and laughing. We had some serious discussions as well, telling each other our stories. We were both in mourning and agreed we needed to take advantage of the years we have left. We kind of bonded right then and there.

After four years with Max, compromise and patience remain my personal challenges. The greatest thing about having a new mate is the opportunity to make new memories and, of course, love and affection come into play. I now encourage women of a certain age to "go for it". Be careful, but be open to the possibilities.

Real name has been withheld.

Lee Hawn is a Creativepreneur who left the corporate world to pursue her dream of owning her own store.

LEE
HAWN

It was September 3, 1980. The first day of school and I was five years old, excited to start kindergarten. That day my mom, who was over nine months pregnant with my brother, got me ready for school, walked me to the school bus, gave me a hug and kiss, told me she loved me and sent me on my way. It would be the last time I would see her. She went into labour with my brother that day and suffered an amniotic embolism. My mother and brother would not come home and my life would be forever changed. I can remember when my dad told me what had happened, and in my childhood innocence I said "it's okay daddy, you and I are going to be okay." Even though I didn't fully understand the situation, this moment truly defines the resilient woman I am today.

Growing up, it was just me and my dad, who I always looked up to. He ran his own business and that is what sparked my own entrepreneurial journey. I always wanted to be like him and have my own business, I just didn't know what I wanted to do.

My life turned upside down again when my dad passed away from a massive heart attack in 2011 at the age of 63. I felt broken; he was my rock and his death brought a flood of emotions to the forefront. My first marriage dissolved and I found myself starting over as a single parent. In 2015, I married my now husband and he has given me the support and encouragement I needed to start my own business. I had always been interested in reclaiming furniture and I made signs from my home. This has grown from an interest to a business, and I was able to open my own store in Uxbridge, Ontario in 2018. We have persevered through major construction outside our store and a global pandemic, but we are surviving through pivoting, and I really enjoy growing the business. Every day I get to show my daughter the rewards of hard work and I also get to have the career that I love.

Monika Baraniuk resides in Lambton Shore's, Ontario, Monika has worked in the fashion industry for years and still loves the art of sales.

MONIKA
BARANIUK

As I age, I now realize I did contribute to others. Perhaps, through verbal reassurances, support whether financial or emotional. In recent years some of these people came to me to tell me how I have shaped their lives due the commitment they felt I had for them. I am humbled because I thought I was just being a friend. I did not understand the impact I had on them.

How did I get this amazing gift I did not realize I had? My Parents. I am the daughter of Polish immigrants. They left Poland just as WWII ended. They were 18 and 21 years old.

At 16 my mother lied to her mother that she would be at a neighborhood library. Instead, she crosses a bridge in Warsaw to another library. This was the exact day of the German Occupation of Warsaw. She was taken to Germany to work in an ammunitions factory. Forced labour, but at least not a concentration camp. She did not see her mother again for 25 years.

She met my father, a Polish paratrooper. He had fought in the battle of Arnhem. They married and soon after moved to England. They found work in factories. They saved whatever monies they had left to send money back to Poland. Eventually, they moved to Canada. They only had 5 dollars in their pockets.

They worked hard, prospered, and continue to send money and packages to family and friends in Poland.

Father died of dementia complications. Mother took care of him to the end. Mother now started failing. Nursing home was her worst fear. I knew I had to take care of her. Unfortunately, my siblings offered little or no help. They loved her but they were busy. I took it in stride. She was my mother. I held her in my arms as she passed away.

She was my greatest example of how people should cherish their close ones. She taught me strength, perseverance, resilience, and humility. I hope her kindness and legacy carries forward through her grandchildren.

Monika Baraniuk

Lila Bruyere is a second-generation survivor of a Residential School and educator. She attended St. Margaret's Residential School from the age of six to 14.

LILA
BRUYERE

I am the youngest girl of a family of 11 siblings, which consists of nine brothers & two older sisters; one brother is the youngest in the family. I have personally witnessed intergenerational trauma and suffer from PTSD. I live with anxiety attacks, depression, and disassociation. I was in therapy most of my teen years, a recovering alcoholic of 33 years.

I started my education at Rainy River Community College in International Falls, Minnesota and didn't quite finish my Associates of Arts degree, but went on to gain my Honours Bachelor in Social Work degree, graduating in 1998 from Carleton University off campus. Working in the field of addictions for fifteen years was something I enjoyed because I could well relate. In 2013, I entered Wilfred Laurier University along with my middle son, Shawn. We both graduated with our Masters in Social Work from the Aboriginal Field of Study Program, which is all Indigenous based.

Presently I'm an educator and public speaker in regard to Residential School issues. My son Shawn and I developed a workshop entitled " Intergenerational Trauma, A Mother & Son Story" and we have travelled across Ontario and the NWT presenting to classrooms and front-line workers, educating them regarding genocide and reconciliation within their people.

One of my greatest accomplishments is being nominated by Shawn to sit on the Elders Circle for the Truth & Reconciliation Commission in Winnipeg from 2019 to November 2021. Due to the pandemic, decisions were made for the TRC regarding the plans to action through the Truth & Reconciliation Commission. I remain active within the TRC by presenting workshops students across Canada.

What motivates me today? My grandchildren. Happiness in recovery is something I'm working on every day. I'm a people person and enjoy being in the presence of others who have a sense of humor; I enjoy a big laugh. My biggest dream is to travel to Hawaii and watch the ceremony of the Samoan people, as long as I am able to travel.

Meegwetch (Thank You}

Lila Bruyere

LISA
CHANG

I unexpectedly landed in Canadian media, naive and knowing absolutely nothing about it or the cutthroat culture. I taught myself early on, that to survive in the heaviness of "imposter syndrome" I'd have to deeply focus my priorities on proving myself through what I was DO-ING, and how I appeared, rather than who I was BE-ING and more importantly BE-COMING. We all tend to attach our self-worth to what we can produce and who we can portray vs showing up as our perfectly (and sometimes messy) authentic selves.

And yet, despite the promise of peace in the surrender to just BE, we flip our channel on to the noise of the outside world. The one that subscribes us to the standards that are set so high, that we're told we could never "win" even if we tried. So, we go the opposite way, and start streaming in the things that bring us instant satisfaction and soothing. We move further away from the truest answers that sit so deep within ourselves.

It was this exact script that I saw so clearly in this new world that I was in. The day that I put down the standards of others and set higher standards for myself was the day that the script was re-written, and I started speaking, living, learning, and leading by my own example.

What I've learned is that sometimes the biggest decisions and changes will often come with questions of doubt in yourself. The answers will never be found externally.

So, I question, what are you tuned in to? Listen fiercely to what your heart says and what feels right. That's intuition and is your greatest guide. That deep wisdom that emerges from the quiet voice within your vs the noise in your head and the world will never lead you astray. Once you hear the direction, take the intentional steps you need to walk on that path each day. You have the answers. You possess the understanding. You just have to trust YOU. The love story you have for yourself will be the greatest script ever written and set you toward the life you most deeply desire.

Sandi is an entrepreneur from Vancouver BC, who is saving the planet one human heart at a time. She makes natural home and body products, and runs a monthly membership guiding midlife women into their Wholeness & Autonomy.

SANDI
JOHNSTON-YU

I don't crave being around others, but I do really enjoy intimately and authentically connecting with people one on one. Building strong bonds through vulnerability and long conversations. Truly hearing and seeing one another for who we are in that moment and showing up as support.

I used to think that loneliness meant needing to be around others. I see it differently now.

What if lonely is the state of feeling disconnected from ourselves?

What if the solution to loneliness was going inwards and fostering a strong bond with ourselves? What if we could have long, authentic, vulnerable conversations with our souls? And, truly see ourselves for who we are in that moment and show up as support?

How do we get there? Presence is the key.

I use nature as my guide. I go hiking a lot. I slow myself down as much as I can to meet the pace of the forest. The trees are patient and easy. There's no resistance, no agenda, no need for anything to be other than it is. The vibration of the forest itself is peace. That's why we're attracted to it. Some people can stop and feel it, others have an idea that it's there but don't have the tools to slow themselves.

I take my socks and shoes off. I walk on the muddy, needled ground. I enjoy feeling the cold, feeling the tree roots, feeling the pulse of the forest.

My feet become the same temperature as the earth. I'm made of the same things; carbon, nitrogen, hydrogen. I am the earth. I contain the same electrons and neutrons, vibrating in synchronicity with the land. Vibrating in synchronicity with all things natural, everywhere.

This is home. This is family. This is the language of my soul, the language of all things. I'm in communion with All Things.

How could I ever be lonely knowing this is available to me anytime?

I can be there in the forest, or I get there when I meditate. I can put myself in this state sitting at the dinner table in just a few minutes.

It's accessible to EVERYONE with just a few tools and a bit of practice.

Lorraine Bear is a business woman, educator, opportunity seizer and loving mother.

LORRAINE
BEAR

I was born and raised in the Peguis First Nation community in Manitoba. Our family of eight, two parents, four girls and two boys, was considered average size on the reserve. I was the second youngest. My siblings and I attended Day School, which juxtaposed the Residential School Experience. These circumstances helped shape who I became.

When they married, my parents were young and still entertained on weekends. Mom and dad supported one another, and they parented well. Life was pretty good at home. Dad was a full-time farmer. Mom was in the process of completing her high school diploma along with working in a garment factory.

When I was nine, everything changed after relocating to a new home. One evening, my dad arrived with two of my sisters in tow to say my mother had been in a terrible car accident. I heard the words but couldn't comprehend their meaning, and after some time, I am not sure how long - my mother died.

Life changed forever. Dad went from weekend drinking to drinking every day because he was depressed. Our home and farm deteriorated inside and outside. The grain farming dwindled, and the cattle were slowly sold off. There was no happiness left at home.

At fifteen, I knew it was up to me to make myself a life, so I chose to dust myself off and go to the city. No matter how lonely I became (and there were plenty of times), I had to keep moving forward. My mother had impressed upon me that education would change my life.

Like all young people trying to socialize, care for themselves and graduate, schooling suffered due to my being too social. University took an extra year, but I came away with a teaching degree and a vehicle to move forward. I did it partially for my mother and partly for myself.

After 19 years of intermittent teaching, running a service business for 12 years, and raising a now 25-year-old child, I can't believe all I have accomplished. Education set me free.

Life is a ride! Create your vehicle, learn how to drive it, and it can take you anywhere.

Lorraine Bear

Photo credit: *Karolina Turek*

Manjit Minhas is a Canadian entrepreneur, television personality and venture capitalist. She is co-owner of Minhas Breweries & Distillery.

MANJIT
MINHAS

I am scheduled to the hour in my life, and that's how I get the most productivity out of it. That really works for me. I am a very disciplined person also; I think that for any entrepreneur to be successful over time you have to be because not every day can you be motivated. It is important, I think, that you take time out to be creative and to enjoy life, but it is also important to be the most productive with so many things going on. I'm not a big believer in multitasking. You have to choose one thing and focus on it and then move on to the next you can't expect to do 3 things at a time and do them all well, that's why my life is like it is hour chunks at a time because I think that for me that is definitely the most efficient way to do things.

I think the most fun thing about being an entrepreneur is that no two days are alike, and you never know the challenge and the monkey wrenches that are going to be thrown in the middle of the day that you had planned. That always happens too, what disaster am I going to have to solve today or what success do I get to celebrate today? I definitely always believe that entrepreneurship is 350 days of hard work and 15 days of pure glory, so hopefully mix those days of glory in with the hard days and it all works

Life is going to throw you some interesting challenges along the way. Be patient. You'll figure it out. But have fun, it'll be a fun journey. Definitely all the plans that you have, some will come true but there'll be a lot of new things thrown your way. And continue to say yes more than no more often. It'll be an exciting journey.

Paul McCart resides in London, Ontario and lives by the words "He ain't Heavy, He's my Brother".

PAUL
McCART

On the eve of my 23rd birthday, my brother Greg, older by a year and the eldest of six, was senselessly murdered while driving a taxicab. He was simply doing his job, trying to earn a living. The wrong passengers put him in the worst place at the worst possible moment. He was my best friend. He was my business partner. He was my older brother.

Not a day goes by when I don't think of him and miss him dearly. Selfishly, my thoughts go to what might have been; we had already accomplished so much together in his short life. We had plans. Even by our early twenties, the two of us had already built several small but successful businesses together. We started selling Christmas trees together in our teens and within a few short years we had already graduated to selling cars. We talked of investing in real estate. We had plans.

Everything I've done in the interim since my brother's murder has been my attempt to answer that question.

My brother wasn't perfect, but he was a good, decent, hard-working young man. He was honest in his dealings with people, and his goal was always to be the hardest-working person in the room. He knew how to build lasting relationships, and he knew his own personal integrity and high standard for his own conduct were the key to making that happen. Our parents taught all their children some very good life lessons. Greg embraced and embodied their wisdom better than any of us.

Looking back, I have done well for myself in this life. With rare exception, nearly all of my good fortune was earned through hard work. Always be the hardest working person in the room. I am proud of what I've accomplished so far. I've carried the example my brother set in his time with us close to my heart for over 40 years now. I've tried to be the man Greg should have been; or at least someone he would have been proud to call his friend and brother.

And still, even after all these many years since we lost him, I wonder to myself, "what might have been?"

Paul McCart

Mary Ann Morin, a successful CPA-CMA, CAFM is of Metis, Cree, Dene, and French Ancestry, originally from Northern Saskatchewan, a mother of 4 and Kukum of 3 wonderful little people.

MARY ANN
MORIN

Living in isolated Northern Saskatchewan was considered a life spent preparing for survival. The Catholic Religion provided schooling in English only, which was how it was. My home was traditional. People spoke Cree and French-Michif and spent summers at the lake, picking berries and preparing for the next season.

After spending twenty years in Accounting/Finance, I put my name in for Treasurer of Metis Nation-Saskatchewan and took on the role for four months before Provincial Metis Council passed a motion that I had resigned as Treasurer. I spent the next 3.5 years in a court battle with Metis Nation-Saskatchewan regaining my position as Treasurer and obtaining the court decision that I was Treasurer from 2017 to 2021. I learned that nothing is as it seems and politics has no rules.

The traditional ways, my education and experience ensure that I continue to be successful in my career and can address the inequalities of women in leadership. I watch for government officials pushing their agendas on a new government leading the way for the Metis people. The Metis are moving quickly and getting involved in politics offering essential ideas to make changes in a world that lists monetary gain above adequate nutrition and climate change.

People have forgotten that Good Leadership is a requirement for surviving bad times like the Covid-19 pandemic. As necessities became scarce and the threat of disease brought back memories of previous generations, our government provided funding to support the communities' needs. If that wasn't enough, our hearts became heavy with sorrow when we discovered children's gravesites at Residential School sites throughout Canada.

These issues helped me prioritize the importance of the things in my life; my children and my community. As a single mother of four children, I am proud they live healthier lifestyles and achieve dreams. I am building strength in our young people and sharing a vision of equality based on the values of our ancestors' matriarchal system.

Although obstacles will come your way, we can accomplish anything. You can change the world depending on how you handle it. Breaking the cycle of colonialism is hard, but it starts with teaching your children their history of strength, courage, resilience, and understanding.

Mary Ann Morin

SELENE
JADE
EMBERS

As a child, I dreamt long and hard about moving away from my small, country hometown. When I as a teenager, a trip abroad opened my eyes to world travel. Adulthood came and I moved away, then back home many times over. I married, had a child, and the cycle continued. When my marriage ended, I was home again. Years passed, second marriage, more kids, I continued moving around the USA. "What are you running from?" was the most asked question amongst my friends. It puzzled me that I could never answer that. Life wasn't bad, I just wasn't happy. The fantasy of world travel I had envisioned still alluded me. I couldn't possibly travel the world with three kids, I was a stay-at-home mother, and my husband didn't like

traveling. I refused to leave them at home as all my favorite childhood memories were of my infrequent travels. As I moved yet again, I discovered world schooling through a friend. The concept of teaching one's children through life experiences. It was practically all I imagined doing, and we were already homeschooling. I was sold.

I did a few trial trips, spending two-month blocks in different countries. We thrived while traveling, learning, and making new friends on the road. Then Covid happened, and we were locked down. My second marriage was ending just as travel restrictions were lifted. I knew it was now or never. I then left the USA to embark on our full-time world schooling journey, and I knew it was the right decision. I'd lived in seven states, never staying in one location longer than 3 years.

Now at age 40, almost two years into our travels, I finally realized the answer to the age-old question. I'm running from nothing; I am running towards this magnificent world to discover all it has to offer. Towards the personal growth I continue to experience. Towards the change of scenery, culture, language, and new adventures on which my nomadic spirit thrives. Most importantly, I'm running towards the happiness that I've found and the connections I've made with those like me. Will I always travel? As long as it lifts my spirit and is my happiness.

Retired physician after 30 years in health care. Living my best life as a newly minted yoga instructor, author, and traveller of the world.

DR. JACQUELINE FOWLER

Waves. It's how we start our lives. Bathed in the warmth of the womb. Taking comfort in the movement within and around us. Feeling safe and serene.

Grief has power like a wave. You don't know when it's going to hit and there's never just one. Some days will churn and churn. Others will be calm and quiet like glass. It's always waves.

You can fight the wave if you want. You spend energy resisting it's pull, as it courses through your mind. You end up tired. Feeling like you're drowning. Pushing the feelings down only to have them rear up with more intensity.

It helps to lean on the people around you for support. However, the effects of Covid have created isolation and loneliness, making relying on our communities more difficult. It's hard to mark a loss alone, isolated and scared about what is to come. Strong people become anxious and feel helpless. The waves of grief churn into what feels like a tsunami, threatening to overwhelm the mind.

Or you can ride the waves. Embrace the motion and the uncertainty. Dig into the feelings of loss. Let them in and honour the emotions that surface. Dive deep, where the water is quieter. Give the mind some time to process the feelings with mindful movement and meditation. Find words to express to others that you're off balance, homesick, lost your center. Share support with someone that is also grieving. Light candles for your loved one. Let the tears come if they need to. Treat yourself with love. Healing is a process for both the brain and the body. Acknowledge when the day is going well, and also when it is challenging. Mental health IS health.

It's important to manage the process of healing, accompanied by the movement of the waves. Those waves of grief etch into the bed of the mind and shape the course of your thoughts as you move on, never to be the same again.

Dr. Jacqueline Fowler

Michaella Shannon, a member of Frog Lake First Nation, is a television host and personality, actress, model and facilitator.

MICHAELLA
SHANNON

It's true, a lot can change in less than a year. In fact, I've always believed that if things are still the same as they were a year ago than you aren't growing. Who I am now is not who I was a year ago and that's a good thing. That's how I know that I am growing and evolving into the person I am meant to be.

A new mother, a new wife, and still a strong Indigenous Woman breaking generational barriers so that my daughter doesn't have to experience what me or her father have.

The meaning of life, my purpose, my vision, my goals, have become so much clearer, stronger, and apparent. With fear of the unknown also comes insight. Insight into who you are and what it is that you were brought here to do.

I've always felt like I was searching for something, sort of wandering around trying to pinpoint exactly what my purpose was. After accepting the journey of motherhood, it all just fell into place and suddenly I no longer felt like I was missing something. To be honest, it wasn't until I became pregnant that I started to feel like a Woman. Becoming a mother has been the start of womanhood for me.

Womanhood and motherhood are sacred. In my culture it is a time of ceremony. During pregnancy, women are connected directly to what we call the spirit world. We are the conduits, the "middleman", the bridge, whatever you might call it, between Earth and the spirit world. It is important for us to protect that connection, protect ourselves from any outside negativity, protect our energy levels, protect our mind, body, and spirit. That is why they say stress is bad for the baby. How you bring your baby into this plane of existence will set the path for his or her life.

As I embark on this next chapter of my life, I reflect on my own upbringing and experiences walking through this world. I know I hold a responsibility to ensure that any intergenerational trauma stops at me.

In our culture we are taught that children are gifts from the Creator, that our babies choose who they want to be their parents. As my husband and I receive our first gift, we know that it is our responsibility to ensure that our children have greater opportunities than we did to succeed at whatever they set their minds and hearts to do.

Michaella Shannon

Michael Soltis is an American/Canadian visual artist currently residing in Delta, BC. Soltis was a film and television actor for several years, however his passion has always been visual art and his work has been shown in several galleries throughout North America.

MICHAEL
SOLTIS

Creating art is the one activity I have pursued where I find total freedom. Much of my early life was spent hiding who I was and carefully curating a person that was acceptable to society and those around me.

As I grew up, my brain learned to be anxious and to constantly be thinking about outcomes and creating expectations of what could or should happen in my life. This turned me into a person who was too busy worrying about how I was going to be perceived by others, instead of actually being true to myself. Living this way for so long has affected both my work and my relationships and has shown to be a very difficult thing to change about myself. However, working in art has helped immensely in distancing myself from my own self-critique and doubt, because it has given me a new way to exist.

When I create art, I never have any expectations around what it could or should be, instead it has always been a place to just let go, explore, and see what happens. I allow myself to have no expectations. When I am creating, I am fully immersed in possibility, and I can let it take me anywhere.

Being able to escape into my work is a fantastic feeling and it's why I work in abstraction because nothing is pre-conceived. People often ask me what I'm trying to say with a piece of art or what the meaning behind my work is. In truth, I'm not trying to say anything or find any specific meaning. Rather, I am just trying to be fully alive. Fully me. Working in this artform is the thing I do that turns off my need to control the things around me or try to find the "right" way. I just simply pick up my tools and work with whatever colour or element that finds its way onto the piece and continue to change and shape it until it feels finished. I never go in with a plan. I never know what the piece is going to look like in the end, but I always find myself through the art that I produce.

Sheila Neufeld is an immensely talented abstract painter, a world-traveller, and brings a sense of adventure to everything she touches.

SHEILA
NEUFELD

One of the greatest skills I have learned is to follow my gut instinct. This has not always been easy for me, and sometimes I overthink my decisions. However, there have also been times where my sixth sense overrode my desire to please others. This intuition has proven to be the wisest voice I could ever listen to.

One of these instinctive situations that has stood out in my life was when I was freshly out of high school and working my first job away from home. I was working in a resort motel as a housekeeper, and I had very friendly relationships with the female and male staff there. A new hire came in and there was something about this man that, even though he was friendly, bothered me and I didn't trust him. My boss asked me to train him about cleaning protocols at night in a certain area of the resort after the guests were done with it. This housekeeping job was always done by myself, and I enjoyed the quiet night walk home alone after. However, I knew right away with every ounce of my being that I did not want to be alone with this man, especially at night. Nor did I want him to know my path home in the dark. I said no instantly, and I didn't care about the reaction I got. It wasn't brought up with me again.

Several days later, this man did not show up for work and we found out he was a violent sexual predator with previous convictions. His criminal record had not been checked when he was hired as this was a transient place where people picked up jobs easily. I cannot tell you how many times I shudder thinking about what may have happened if I had overridden my instinct and just said yes to please my boss.

I encourage people to learn to listen to, trust, and follow their intuition whether it is in business, relationships, or any other area of your life. Sometimes it is a quiet voice that softly guides you, and sometimes it's a loud roar to wake you up. It is always there. Use it.

Sheila Neufeld

Pat Dubreuil, serial entrepreneur & powersports enthusiast on a mission to promote a Northern Ontario town baring his family name, Dubreuilville.

PATRICE (PAT)
S. DUBREUIL

I know there are people who think I work too much. Others, that I am continually adventure riding and having fun on a motorcycle or snowmobile. Some ask what I do for a living and those who know me say, "what doesn't he do?"

Luckily, I am surrounded by resourceful people; friends and family who make up the network of doers that help me get things done. Having a vision and executing it are two very different things that one cannot accomplish alone.

An inspirational friend who passed away from ALS once told me, "you can't control yesterday and you can't control tomorrow, so you should appreciate today." He lived and died by this philosophy. He appreciated everyone in his daily life. He survived beyond his three to five year medical prognosis and went on to live 26 years, 9 months, eventually succumbing to pneumonia. "Let's roll" was his mantra, and Let's Roll "Ideation" Consulting became the entrepreneurial vehicle I used to finance and diversify my various business start-ups, which help sustain the economic tourism activity inside and around the small town of Dubreuilville, both Eddy and I's hometown.

Dubreuilville is a special place where people live and play in the great Northern Ontario outdoors. It was founded by my grandfather and his three brothers in 1961; they were known as the "Dubreuil Brothers". Diversifying and creating a sustainable lasting eco-system is key to its future. Developing the Magpie Relay Motel & Resort, the MooseBack trail system and the CTRL2Market service eco-system make it possible to attract tourists who help ensure long term sustainability and a diversified economic base for Dubreuilville. Money earned is re-invested into tourism assets.

I choose to invest time, money and energy into the vision and mission started before me. As a third generation Dubreuil, it is important that I continue to help create a place where people enjoy to work, live and play. I therefore encourage powersports enthusiasts and outdoor adventure seekers to seek out and visit the little French Canadian oasis we call "Dubreuilville". You might run into "me" somewhere along your adventure. I invite you to "Let's Roll".

Patrice S Dubreuil

Norm Danniels is a retired entrepreneur who is enjoying a full happy life with his family.

NORM
DANNIELS

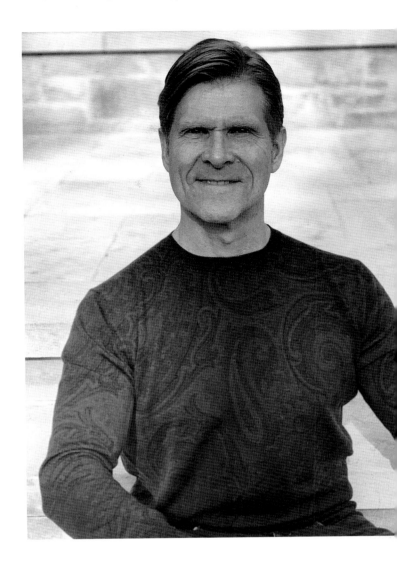

My first full-time job was with a company that manufactured industrial insulation. The general manager was abrupt, condescending and rarely made an appearance on the shop floor. Communication between departments was poor and often unclear. Both morale and productivity were low. Each afternoon, there was a line-up of people waiting for the time clock to strike 4:30pm so they could punch out.

My next job was at my brother's record company. The office had a fun, casual feel and was often filled with laughter. The staff were hard working, dedicated, and adept at every task. Both the energy and productivity were great, and no one watched the clock. The contrast was striking.

They had a team mentality, sharing their victories and overcoming any challenges together. It didn't hurt that my brother was respectful, supportive, had an easy smile and was more than generous. But it was his work ethic and positive leadership style that I admired most. It was an awesome place to work.

I have always had a passion for health and wellness, and within a few years I started a nutritional supplement company. As our staff grew, I tried to replicate that same culture. We kept our goals clear, and the credit and rewards were always shared. It was an exciting time, and our company grew quickly. Where possible, we provided an entrepreneurial experience that linked our team's performance directly with their compensation. We also tried to build in a healthy dose of fun. We had beach volleyball nights, go-karting outings, and an annual Employee Appreciation Day where we would close the office and head to an amusement park for the day.

Clearly, I'm suggesting that the tone of any business comes from the top. I don't pretend to have done everything right, but I certainly gave it my best shot. I think everyone wants to have a rewarding career that feels worthy of their time, and it's up to the employer to create opportunities that live up to that expectation.

If you get it right, or at least mostly right, great things can happen. Careers can be made, missions can be accomplished, and lifelong friendships can be formed. What's not to like?

Supneet Chawla is the Founder and CEO, ACE Community College, ACE Trades and Technical Institute.

SUPNEET
CHAWLA

Being an immigrant herself, Supneet Chawla, now a qualified Canadian Electrical Engineer, an approved Canadian Electrical Code Instructor from Technical Safety BC, and Founder and CEO of ACE trades and Technical Institute and ACE Community College, had a very little support from the local colleges after migrating to Canada 20+ years ago. Along with challenges due to language and being a brown female in a very male dominated career, she had to jump a lot of hoops to prepare for seven challenge examinations to get her P.Eng. designation with Professional Engineers and Geoscientists of BC (PEBC) to practice Engineering in her field.

Supneet did not forget the experience of coming to a new country, starting from scratch in her career and re-training herself to become equivalent to a Canadian Engineering graduate. She decided to then help immigrants like herself to get the training they need in construction trades including challenge exams, TQ as well as prepare for Red Seal Examinations.

Supneet, an immigrant woman of color, an entrepreneur, a wife, and a mother, is still a teacher at heart and continues to teach Electrical programs for ACE. With a team of 50+ employees and contractors working with her at ACE, she still motivates and supports on e-on-one all her students to get their career goals without giving up because of language barriers, racism, and community pressure. Supneet's journey is motivated by her desire to leave a legacy for her daughter. *"Every person has the right to education and choose a life he or she wants, and no one, I mean NO-ONE can dictate what we can or cannot do. Teaching my daughter to always stand up for what she believes in and not back down because of social barriers or circumstances is the life I live by and is very well reflected in all my actions. We ladies are powerhouses, and nothing can stop us in achieving the life we deserve!!"* says Supneet.

302

Hoai Dang-Lachance is a business professional and contemporary abstract artist, with creatives reflecting ebb and flow of colour sought from past and present journeys.

HOAI DANG-LACHANCE

At a young age, I discovered my happy place was simply to create, which paved a path to designing ladies' accessories for retail. Having set aside my creativity for years to immerse myself in the corporate world, it is with much irony my journey has led me back to creatives once again.

I had read about other women experiencing burnout within the corporate world; I never imagined it would happen to me. The thought of having a work-life balance was something that existed in a land of rainbows and unicorns.

Perhaps my hustle train of thought and work ethic comes from being raised by a single mum, whose selfless and unconditional love for her children, strong will and courage, enabled her to live through colliding worlds of fortune to poverty as a result of war.

Having traveled through unthinkable journeys and surpassing truly dire circumstances, I was provided with a new life and a fighting chance. Embracing my roots, I had built my life around actioning sacrifice in order to succeed at any cost. Let's say "sacrifice" won for a moment in time. It's as though I had run into a brick wall, with absolute mind and body exhaustion. The feeling of shame, sense of failure wrapped with anxiety took a toll on my mental and physical well-being.

Looking back, there are certain life lessons that hold close. The action of loving you, putting yourself first without guilt is freeing. Who knew, self-care and the fact you cannot be everything to everyone is indeed acceptable? Surround yourself with humans who will lift you up and inspire you, as you're never alone. Never forget you are capable of change, embrace the possibility of self-improvement. Let go, embrace the feeling of being comfortable with uncomfortable and learn that you can truly create your own life balances.

As my path evolves, so will my desire to create art that will bring joy and enable those who embrace it the opportunity to conjure up inspiration through their own journeys as experienced.

(With a grateful and empathic heart, I dedicate my journey to my mum and all those who have turned their own lives from impossible to possible.)

Hoai Dang-Lachance

Anna Piloyan is happily married to the love of her life and the mother of three beautiful daughters. Anna wears many hats including realtor, beauty clinic owner and the friend everyone can rely on.

ANNA
PILOYAN

Growing up in Armenia when it was part of the USSR, I witnessed the loss of my grandparents' home and my mother's own struggles to find a house for us. These events led to a deep desire to find peace, stability, and one day being able to afford my own home.

As a teenager, I moved to Victoria, Canada, and experienced what it was like to have my own room for the first time. It is here in Victoria that I fell in love with my husband, discovered a vibrant, supportive community of friends, and realized my dream of starting my own business, Deco de Mode. Now, the spa is one of the busiest spots in the city with another location in Toronto, and a third opening in Sidney soon.

Still, I never forgot my first dream of buying a home and how much that journey meant to me. Not only am I an experienced business person, but I also own three investment properties and a commercial space downtown. Armed with this knowledge, a degree from the University of Victoria, and the wisdom that comes from being mother to three beautiful daughters, I have turned my focus to helping others realize their real estate dreams too.

For me, helping buyers find their first or dream homes is about more than just the brick and mortar, it's about listening to their vision and understanding exactly what a home represents to each of my clients.

Tracey Lundell has a passion for helping people. She's an active volunteer, business and career mentor, wealth advisor & cheerleader.

TRACEY
LUNDELL

Could anything sound more boring and drier than Financial Literacy? It doesn't have to be.

I am on a mission to make money a less intimidating and more acceptable topic of conversation. This begins with a foundation of financial literacy. I want everyone to feel more confident and knowledgeable about their finances so they can achieve great things. But where to start that journey? It may sound strange but talking about money can be the first big step towards financial success.

How is your relationship with money? Money has been a taboo point of discussion for decades. Not talking about money keeps people from balancing financial needs with other needs – like relationships, self-worth, employment, physical and emotional health. My goal is to help more people open that internal and external dialogue to reveal your history and develop your future relationship with money. What is your personal money story? It's basically a personal narrative that impacts your financial behaviours through your feelings, experiences, thoughts, and beliefs about money. How many times do we question ourselves when it comes to defining our personal financial worth – negotiating a salary with a new job, determining an hourly rate for a contract, asking for a well-deserved raise? When you understand how money flows in and out of your life and know how to best utilize the money that comes your way, life can get much more exciting.

Money doesn't bring happiness but having a deeper sense of the value of money can be a force of good in your life and others. When you are the custodian of money, you can do great things in the world! So, have the hard conversations, have the FUN conversations, dream big and be confident in your ability to generate money and spend it well.

Sometimes you need a coach, a sounding board, a cheerleader – I aim to be all those things. More than anything, I just want people to lead extraordinary lives. Money isn't the answer to everything, but it sure helps!

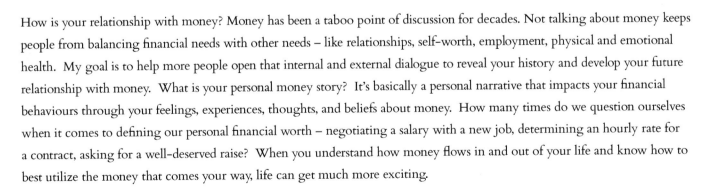

Tracey Lundell

SUE
RANDHAWA

Sue Randhawa is a recognized style maven in Vancouver – voted as one of the best dressed people in Canada. She is a wife, a mother, and the owner of The Optical Boutique in Vancouver, where she serves an ardent clientele who appreciate her carefully curated collections of eyewear. Sue realized early on the power of a first impression and made a commitment to herself that she wanted hers to be a memorable one.

There was no shortage of hardship growing up. My father was a man that most people feared – a look from him meant trouble. A beating or some sort of torture treatment would follow. Amidst this there was sexual abuse and constant emotional degradation. I never felt safe or protected. Most days were a living hell but the one thing that I always had was hope. I believed with all of my heart that God had a plan for me. My life changed when I met my husband. After our first meeting and conversation we both decided that we were perfect for one another. I was 18 and he was 20. This was the start of the fairy tale that I had spun in my head.

Nothing had prepared me for what was about to unfold. Both of my children were perfect in every way – one went on to become a lawyer and the other a doctor. I had made a promise to my younger self that I would make sure that my children were protected from abuse. In 2016, I came to know that my child had suffered sexual abuse at the hands of a very close family member. My world turned upside down. I had to dig deep to find strength that I thought I had already depleted in my own childhood. I turned to the same God and asked for help. Not only did I still have the strength, but my children had it running through their veins too. I was ready to fight this fight again. The scars of sexual abuse are deep and never go away but in time the pain lessens. I am a testament to that. My children are too.

Sue Randhawa

Peter Twist is the former strength and conditioning coach for the Vancouver Canucks and is currently president of Twist Conditioning Incorporated. Peter is also a stage 4 cancer Thriver.

PETER
TWIST

Let the good vibes flow.

You attract + feel the energy you give. Share good energy.

And make sure your tribe exudes good vibes + get into environments known to elevate mood & mind.

Wake up saying thank you for this day. Live grateful, think positive, be kind.

Set goals to laugh more & choose friends who can help.

Happiness is indeed an inside job. We each own the process.

Travel lighter. I take what I do seriously but do not take myself seriously. Take things less personally. Let stuff bounce off as you hold your positive state with strength & grace.

Definitely do not sweat small stuff. Go with the flow and don't stress – just do your very best, forget about all the rest.

Today like every day is a perfect day to create a great day!

If that's what you desire, choose to think, speak, & do what makes it so.

Whatever is good for your soul, say yes.

Bring uplifting energy to everyone on your path, and you will be uplifted.

Sending you peace, strength, good energy, and high passion for this very day.

Let's go – let those good vibes flow!

If you can catch that wave, let this get your perspective positive & mood in motion then keep feeding your mind body spirit what it needs to live elevated.

Inspire It Forward – tag who needs a lift or who shares their good energy with you.

Each day has unlimited potential for co-creation of beautiful moments. Show up leading the way!

Man's most popular cry has always been, "what's for supper."

JEFF ANGERS

Coming from a home with a diverse ethnic background, the desire to pick up a utensil and "get 'er done" has always been a passion. The smells of French, Italian or Ukrainian fare slowly simmering tempted my pallet and the many friends that found their way to our dinner table. To this day, my sister and I still get requests for Mom's pasta and homemade sauce. Thankfully, we can produce a very close copy of that recipe. As we get older, the passion for repeating these classic homemade dishes grows stronger. As you hover over a pot, the urge for creativity overwhelms. A pinch more or less of this? Mom's was thicker or spicier.

The comfort of having the creative wheel so to speak, to the final outcome of the planned fare is intoxicating. Your total focus evolves around quality and not quantity. The clatter of empty plates and minimal leftovers is the grandest compliment the chef can be paid even with a bought pumpkin pie! As our next generations and families grow up, we welcome their involvement in the preparation of these foods. It gives me great pride to say, "your Grandmother used to make it this way"- (chicken hearts and livers included). Ensure you make the time when the need comes for assistance with a meal. As a suggestion, start out small with comfort food and leave the "Art of French Cooking" for a later date.

The goodness of family tradition can be found in a variety of places. The internet is the most readily available for relatives and family to share. I was impressed to see my mother's tattered cookbook, bulging at the seams, full of her most treasured recipes. Rummage through her mother's utensils and find out what is most used (besides her famed wooden spoon for bad behaviour). Keep it simple and keep in practice are the keys. My retirement has not been a rush to extravagant dining or cooking. It has allowed me to focus on key cultures and a few dishes that hopefully will be passed along to everyone.

Estrellita is a fearless and conscious entrepreneur, politician, parent and in her newest endeavour, creating and hosting retreats that celebrate the divine feminine.

ESTRELLITA
GONZALEZ

When I was a little girl I often dreamt of adventures to exotic locales, such as Egypt to unearth lost treasures, or scuba diving the blue seas. A recurring dream was having a small hotel on a white, sandy beach where I enjoyed fun and sun-filled days with interesting people. Dreaming and imagining were a constant in my life.

As an adult, dreaming was replaced with goal setting and responsibilities. After many years I felt disconnected from myself. I didn't take time to dream or to use my imagination as I did when I was younger. A few years ago, I embarked on a path of re-discovery and introspection; doing inner work to tap into my deeper, feminine self. I needed to get clear on what I wanted, where I was going and how I wanted to feel in my life.

In doing this work, I learned of several tools which I continue to use. One was creating a three word feeling mantra: loved, abundant and free ("LAF"). These are the feelings I connect with to help guide me in creating my ideal and daily life.

Like most people, my life has been a journey of many ups and downs, much of it influenced by other people. I needed to get intentional about what I wanted. I also had abundance and prosperity blocks. Clearing these allowed for a huge shift in the quality and direction of my life. And I recalled my hotel dream, realizing that the future I was creating was connected to this childhood memory.

With my son now in university, my business turning ten and my political term ending, 2022 will be a year of great change. I am excited at the prospect of combining my love of travel with my spa and hotel management experience to develop my next venture: hosting women's retreats with a focus on the divine feminine. Now more than ever the world needs the feminine in its caretaking, direction and leadership.

We are never too old to dream or to tap into our imaginations, and recalling our childhoods can help us create our dream lives in order to live our best lives.

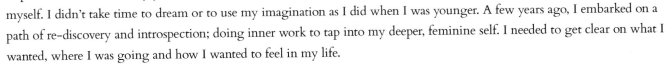

Rebekkah Stainton is the Founder of WestCoast Vitality, a counselling clinic that walks alongside people coping with a variety of struggles. Her two main areas of specialization are working with stress management and anxiety in high performers as well as working with trauma, with a focus on sexual abuse and assault.

REBEKKAH
STAINTON

What makes a hero? As someone who has struggled with anxiety and feelings of inferiority at different points in my life, this is a question I've given a lot of thought. Christopher Reeves once said, "A hero is an ordinary individual who finds the strength to persevere and endure in spite of overwhelming obstacles." It's not that the hero doesn't experience fear, rather that they acknowledge the fear and choose to move forward anyways.

When I was 29 years old, I was diagnosed with cervical cancer. It didn't immediately register. This wasn't supposed to happen. Cancer wasn't part of the plan. At first, I didn't tell anyone. It felt like if I said it out loud, that would make it real. I didn't know if I had the courage to face it. When I did let people in, I discovered just how amazing support could be.

A year or so later, the surgeries I went through to get the cancer out of my body had left me experiencing daily debilitating pain that the doctors were unable to explain or ease. After months of watching me go through day after day of agony, my (now ex) husband said to me "Why haven't you killed yourself?" I understand that this question seems cruel, but I knew it was coming from a place of confusion and fear, and not from a desire to wound. He simply could not understand what allowed me to keep going without knowing if there would ever be an end to my pain. My drive to keep going, to keep seeking answers, and to survive had absolutely nothing to do with not being afraid. Of course, I worried that this was what my life was going to be like forever, but to me, my life was worth facing the fear for.

Today, I'm healthy and honoured to walk alongside people facing their own fears in my counselling practice. Courage comes in many forms, and each of us has our own fear to face. It isn't up to someone else to determine what brings out the hero within, the only person who can do that is the person in the mirror staring back at you.

Rebekkah Stainton

Founder and CEO of MisMacK Clean Cosmetics, a beauty product company that aims to redefine the cosmetics industry by combining the high-quality application with ethical and ecological manufacturing. Missy MacKintosh built MisMacK from the ground up in her basement in small-town Canoe, BC, Canada.

MISSY
MacKINTOSH

Empowering through makeup is my passion. My personal tagline is, "Makeup Does Not Define You, it's Merely a Tool of Empowerment." I believe that makeup is designed to bring out your most beautiful natural features, it isn't to cover them up or change them. When I was young, my mom didn't use makeup, so I was the kid found snooping through others' makeup bags, testing products on my hand. I was obsessed. I love makeup can also be a form of 3D art where you can create magic.

When I was fourteen, my mom became a Mary Kay makeup consultant, and I thought I'd died and gone to heaven. When I discovered there were careers in makeup application, I enrolled at Blanche McDonald and moved to the big city, where I established a flourishing career.

Things pivoted after my husband, and I suffered a silent miscarriage. We decided to return to our roots in the small town of Salmon Arm to start our family. I believed moving back to my hometown meant giving up my dream in makeup, so I managed a travel agency for a while, but makeup followed me. After side hustling for six years, I returned to the world of makeup in 2014. In 2016 I was introduced to Clean Beauty; I fell in love with the integrity behind it. It was then I realized, I didn't just want to apply makeup, I wanted to create makeup – but who does that? I'm in small town Salmon Arm, BC. After much research, I discovered there was not a Professional Performing Clean Makeup line on the market. I took matters into my own hands and created MisMacK Clean Cosmetics Inc., the first Professional Performing Clean Makeup line, which launch in 2019. I single-Handley build every aspect of MisMacK from the ground up in my basement of Canoe, BC. I'm so proud to say that I grew out of my basement and into 2 Brand Concept Stores in 2021 – Downtown Salmon Arm and Downtown Victoria BC.

There have been failures along the way, but I have learned that failure is where growth happens. I firmly believe that if you're not failing, you're not growing.

Shannon Rey is a Certified Life & Solution Focused Coach, Nutrition Educator, Reiki Practitioner and Desire Map Facilitator who has a BA in Human Development.

SHANNON
REY GIBBS

There's a lot of love in my family, however it wasn't always okay to have a voice growing up. Conflict was avoided and questions were left unanswered. I was confused about who I was and felt like I didn't have a voice.

I was terrified to speak any truth that rocked the boat. Thus, I quietly learned to do and say what I thought would please others. By the time I reached my mid-20's I felt so lost. Who was I? What did I value? So, I began a soul-searching journey that opened a whole new world. A world with so much beauty. For the first time, I felt free and liberated. I realized that I could choose what life looked like for me and began to embrace my very own uniqueness and sense of purpose.

The path was bumpy, as I awkwardly navigated by trial and error what it felt like to speak my truth. It felt so foreign. There were consequences to face — I lost jobs, relationships, and opportunities. At times, I wanted to retreat as I continued to build courage one small step at a time.

I soon discovered that it felt better to use my voice and face any fallout because on the other side of that boldness was so much joy, love, and adventure. I signed up for singing lessons and became a public speaker. I pushed myself to use my voice.

My newfound boldness began to inspire other women, which motivated me to keep going. I realize now how women are often socialized to not speak their truth. I'm excited to be on this side of bold — where true freedom lies. Where there's more love, more joy, more aliveness, and more alignment with who I truly am.

I discovered I was so much stronger than I thought, or anyone thought. I'm still learning. I have seen that when I speak, people listen. I have something to say. My words heal and empower. As my journey continues to unfold, I see how my stories deeply affect others and help them to be a little bit braver. You too can step into your bold joy, one brave step at a time.

Sunni Hurley is a new hair salon owner in Woodstock, Ontario. Doubling as an Artistic Educator for PRAVANA, she spends most of her time strategically dissecting hair colour. On her off time, she a mother to her now 8 year old daughter and a bonus mom to 3 stepdaughters, all ranging in age from 6-11.

SUNNI
HURLEY

When I was little, I used to dream about being taken away and sent to a different family, one that I truly wanted. This isn't to say my family was horrible; they weren't most of the time. I grew up in a divorced family with parents that were addicted to their own vices: one house was sober, the other loved to party.

Over the years, I turned to my demons and embraced my addictions, following exactly in my parents' footsteps. I was smart, I was witty, I was popular, but I was also an addict. If it could help me escape, I would take it. This happened from 11 all the way to 21. I don't recall much of those years. During that time, I suffered from suicidal tendencies, battling my own mind every day, yet the darkness always held me closest. This of course led to many abusive partners, including my child's father.

I became a mother in 2014. People always ask if you'd die for your child; I chose to live. Every single day, I choose to be better for her. Feather is my biggest inspiration, and I've pushed myself harder than ever before to ensure she never has the life I lived. I got sober, put an end to the abuse and we moved to where we could be safe and thriving. Before my husband, abuse was all I knew. I've forgiven those that hurt me, but I'll never forget them. I never want my child to experience what I experienced, and after what she went through as a baby, I'll never stop being her protector. From homeless to business owner, I now own a successful high-end, edgy salon in Woodstock, and I couldn't be happier. I have a husband that loves me and my daughter like she's his own, and somehow, he's found room for her in his heart along with his three daughters. We have a fantastic life where we love fiercely, and we do our best to not cause harm. Instead of being taken away, we're going to keep making our dream life happen! This is the life I've always wanted, and we're not even done creating it. SLEY!

TALIA
FADEL

Have you ever heard yourself say, "Well, I won't do that again"? It turns out that past experiences are a road map for the future. They inform our choices and help us learn to trust our own judgement.

At 23, I didn't think I would have anything to say that could help anyone else, but my family assured me that this could not be further from the truth.

I started life in a war zone. Dad had difficulties with self-medication, and mom was fed up. When I was four-ish, we moved houses and cities as soon as she finished teachers' college. Starting over in a new place and finding new friends is tough, but I managed. My Oma and Opa were a stabilizing force. At six, I lost Oma to dementia, and Opa became my person. At eight, mom remarried, and we adjusted again. My stepdad was a good man and cared for us as his own. At fifteen, I lost my Opa to strokes, my confidant, and my friend. I righted myself and carried on, but signs of wear and tear showed – a little eating disorder here, some minor depression, anxiety, and ADHD there. I scraped through the first year of college, but the second year wasn't shaping up well when I received the phone call that my stepfather had died suddenly.

I returned home to stay because I was worried about Mom. Rightfully so, because as my sister and I restarted college, excited to move forward, mom received her cancer diagnosis. She wanted us to focus on school. Crazy!!! But we did, both graduating as she received news of her remission. Life is full of wins and losses, and through it all, I have learned that the heart is amazingly resilient. Your first heartbreak hurts so much more than you think it will. The next one doesn't hurt less but is different, and you build resilience. You are creating your future road map.

I have learned that my feelings are my own, and I am on a journey of self discovery. The journey has had it ups and downs, but it isn't over. I'm just not there yet but I will be.

Peter Eastwood is a photographer with one foot in Canada, the other in Sri Lanka; his heart is in both.

PETER
EASTWOOD

Photo credit: Linda Mackie Creative

I have always been a keen traveller, but it wasn't until 11 years ago, after a personal trip to Sri Lanka, that I found my true raison d'être. Taken with the people, culture, food and beauty of the island, I made a conscious effort to engross myself in projects that would lead me back time and again.

My first was to photograph and film survivors of the December 26th, 2004 Indian Ocean Tsunami, where 30,000 people perished along the shores of Sri Lanka. Over two years, I travelled the entire circumference of the island in a tuk tuk driven by Wageesha Kumara, who introduced me to people and translated their stories of that fateful day. (This would later become an exhibition, book and short film.) I found their stories filled with emotion, hope and in many cases, healing. It was life changing for me; to see people that have suffered so terribly only confirmed how lucky I was on so many levels. It changed my entire outlook on life and from these experiences, I swore to myself that from that point on I would focus on helping as many people in Sri Lanka in any way possible way that I could.

Since my exhibition, I've been travelling back on a regular basis and have since helped finance and build an eco-lodge and home for Wageesha, his wife Dinaseka and wonderful children: Hansa, Dilaksha and Sasande. Through this family I have been given a joyous new lease on life; their love, laughter and uncomplicated approach to all things have given me such fulfilment.

I am also fortunate to have had many experiences in my life that have given me so much; my 44 year relationship with my husband, Philip, my own family back in England, my friends from my time living in Hong Kong and now my extended family in Canada.

My advice to anyone who is reading this, is to try to look beyond what is happening in your daily routine and imagine how hard it is for people less fortunate, to reach out in any way, be it large or small. Small gifts of love can give you so much in return.

Peter Eastwood

Patricia Clarke is an artist, author of the best-selling book 'Unknown Sister' and a speaker who draws much of her inspiration from her real-life experiences and the splendour of nature.

TRISH
CLARKE

I opened the top dresser drawer where I found the brown folder. I opened it there were canceled checks and receipts and a set of folded documents on the heavy paper.

I opened them up carefully and read the word ADOPTION.

My eyes quickly scanned;
Childs name: Patricia
Mothers name: Pearl
Fathers name: —————————
Adopting father: Norman

I was NOT Norma's daughter ???????

The man I loved and treasured was not my father!!

I was not his daughter? This morning I had a father, now I didn't! Half of my identity has been stripped away. The thing I suspected, and felt intuitively was accurate.

I felt my soul had been raped. Half of me was gone.

I stood and looked in the mirror of my "parents" bedroom.

I was surprised a whole 16-year-old girl was reflected back to me. I was an unrecognizable soul with a missing parent.

I slowly put the papers back in folder as perfect as when I had found them.

I wasn't going to tell anyone what I had done. I wanted to be a good girl. I wanted a mother and a "father."

I loved Norman and I wanted him to be "my" dad who made me laugh and taught me to dance. But he wasn't.

Life appeared to go on as before. But it wasn't.

I felt "I" was unwanted and unsuccessful as a daughter. I was not the sister I thought I was to Doug, Richard and Bernice.

I grieved alone.

Mom and dad had their families to supported them and their "untruth."

I was isolated with no one to support my "truth."

If Norman had died in the physical I may have had some support.

No one knew "my dad" had died. Was I some other fathers discard? What was my truth? Wasn't I good enough to have my own dad? My heart was broken as my tears drowned me from the inside but never left my eyes.

I kept up the façade of being Norman's daughter to survive.

Genicca Whitney is a wealth activator for those who are ready to manifest financial liberation and lifestyle creation, through entrepreneurship and investments.

GENICCA
WHITNEY

FORGIVE THE PREDATOR, SET YOURSELF FREE

30% of all women aged 15 and older – have been sexually assaulted outside of an intimate relationship at least once.

A shocking statistic that I never bothered to learn about because when it happened, I became completely numb.

I spent a good chunk of my life unconsciously living in shame, guilt, fear, anger, disgust, rage and totally disconnected from my body....

Because of a monster who got away.

It was through my personal and spiritual growth journey that the one thing I refused to ever acknowledge or look at... came to the surface and rocked my soul. My intuition told me that if I ever wanted to do BIG WORK in this world... If I ever wanted to FEEL SAFE in my own skin, that THIS needed to be addressed, healed and energetically released.

What I learned is that... The things I experienced in those moments were in fact, TYPICAL. The things I felt in those terrifying moments, were in fact, similar to those who have ever been victims. I had no idea that I wasn't alone. I had no idea that THIS was common.

For years, I was unconscious to the ways in which the trauma impacted me; the relationship I had with myself and my relationship with others. It was my decision to finally bring to the surface what I spent a good chunk of my life pretending wasn't there, that I experienced real liberation..

The shame, guilt, fear, anger, disgust, rage and total disconnection from my body.... Did not have to paralyze or define me.

Through the healing, I developed a relationship with myself that I forgot existed... I was able to forgive myself... and forgive the predator.

I came Home to my body, my power, my sense of safety and security in who I am. Through the healing, I found me.

I live to share this experience with you because YOU DESERVE TO BE FREE.

You need to know that it was never your fault!

You were never the one who caused it, encouraged it or allowed it! You were never in the wrong for being where you were, for what you were wearing, for what you said or for trusting your safety with this human!

SEXUAL ASSAULT is not ok.

And you are not alone.

Face it. Feel it. Heal it.

I promise... You will discover an unshakeable power through it.

317

Genicca Whitney

Shashi Maharaj is a wife and mother who also helps others in a Global Patented Health and Beauty Business.

SHASHI
BHUSHAN MARARAJ

I had a creative entrepreneurial spirit in my early childhood years and planned many lemonade stands, candy stores, garage sales and a haunted house that would draw lineups out the driveway.

When I think back, school, family expectations and childhood trauma stifled my creativity. I chose a more traditional path of academics, a "good job", and marriage. After graduating with a business degree, raising three beautiful children, and spending 28 years in the corporate world, I felt unfilled and lost. I knew deep inside that I wanted to have a business but couldn't decide what type. I was also fearful about the risk of failure.

Once I started connecting with my inner self and being honest about wanting more, using my potential to impact the world and help others, it was like the universe started to bring the right people and situations to me.

I connected with an amazing business mentor who was a self-made multi-millionaire. She changed thousands of lives through a global business specializing in advanced in-home beauty devices and anti-ageing supplements. In my fifties, I linked arms with my mentor and have been able to help hundreds of others start and grow their businesses and create generational wealth for their families. I have also embraced my skills in real estate investing and have a solid network that has helped me grow my portfolio in the Vancouver real estate market.

Thankfully, my loving husband of 29 years fully supported my transition from employee to entrepreneur. As did my children, two of whom were entrepreneurs themselves!

My goal is to empower one thousand women to start and grow their own anti-ageing businesses and create generational wealth for their families.

There is nothing that we as women cannot accomplish when we forgive and heal our past, visualize our dream life, and take aligned, focused action every day. Surround yourself with people who have what you want, and do not take advice from people who aren't living the life you want to lead. When you create the life you want you empower others to do the same.

Shashi Bhushan Maharaj

TULIN
FADEL

When I was approached to share my story in this book, my first thought was, "absolutely not. I have nothing to offer." This was quickly followed by an unsolicited lecture on how I am not enough given by the leading expert in this area, my own brain. I have no business including my (short) story among all these people. Others have experienced far worse and are doing far more. Once again, the idea that I have absolutely nothing to offer ran through my mind and coloured all that followed. After voicing this to a friend, she vehemently disagreed and explained why I was so incredibly wrong. Even knowing she truly believed her kind words, after 19 years of friendship, I have learned she sadly does not believe in false flattery. I was struggling to feel her words for myself.

She couldn't believe that I didn't believe her words and I couldn't believe that she did believe them. How could I make her understand my lack of understanding? Then I asked a simple question.

Do you feel your story has something to offer?

The look on her face was enough of an answer. We sat together in silence. Both of us were in awe of the other and so very uncomfortable with ourselves. No one's life is perfect, not mine, not yours and not anyone else's life either. This book is filled with inspiring stories from humans around the world, all with much to offer. Not one of them, myself included, has the secret formula for the kind of life we all strive for, the perfect one. Sometimes we can feel like we do not know what we are doing. We watch others to see how to be and what to do. The funny thing is that those people are often doing the same thing. No matter how privileged a start you may have been afforded, life will continuously oscillate from the painful lows to the beautiful highs and absolutely everything in between. Some days, you are satisfied with your appearance, performance, or choices, and sometimes you are not, which is okay. Not a single human will ever have it all figured out. Knowing our stories are still unwritten, knowing there will be up days and down days, reminding ourselves that there will be periods of time it all feels more manageable than others, try to ride it all out. Grab hold of the shiny moments, be kind, and forgive others and yourself when *(I want to say when we mess up because just as life is not perfect, neither are any of us).*

Tulin Fadel

Photo credit: Audrey-Mazzega-Ingram

Tracy Kaye Holly owns TKH DanceClub, is a professional dancer and is co-director of the Cory Holly Institute.

TRACY
KAYE
HOLLY

I have always found that I had more energy than most of my family, friends, and colleagues. How come? Well, it starts with a positive mental attitude and the willingness to do the work that most aren't prepared to do. It takes a lot of energy. This doesn't mean that I don't get tired at times, but it doesn't last for long. I analyse the issue, then I pick myself up and carry on.

At 63 years old, I still have a rigorous training regime. I also have a successful dance club and I continue to perform. Being on a super clean diet with extra supplementation daily does work, however, consistency is key. It's not about what you do occasionally, it's what you continue to do every day.

We all age, it's just a fact of life. Don't fight the wave, roll with it. Grey hair and lifelines are beautiful and should be embraced. Peace, joy, and harmony are my go-to words, I even have a small tattoo on my arm to remind me of them when I need it. Finding purpose and having goals sustains me, so I like challenge myself to see if I can do what I put my mind and body to.

I always push myself to be the best that I can be. If it doesn't serve me, then l let it go. I do my utmost not to burn bridges, unless it needs to be, and I very well know it. I'm not afraid of confrontation, if it needs to be said then I say it, however, always with a kind heart. Harmony rules!

I surround myself with good friends, they nourish my soul, and they laugh at my corny jokes - yes, a sense of humour is an asset. Laughter is one of the best medicines. My family brings me immense happiness and grandchildren truly are a blessing. I find great joy in watching them grow into the world.

Keep going, never stop moving forward. Honour your life, because it's exciting to see what it will bring if you manage it and take good care of yourself. Be bold, stand your ground and by all means, have fun!

Tracy Kaye Holly

Zandra Ross is an Indigenous woman from the Williams Lake First Nation who specializes in coaching and facilitation.

ZANDRA
ROSS

I am an Indigenous consultant who travels throughout BC supporting First Nation communities and organizations for the past 30 years. I have been on my personal and professional development journey for the past 12 years. It began when I work up blind in one eye about 12 years ago on Christmas day. My kids were very young, and I was a busy consultant who had a ton of strategic plans to finish for my clients. The kids were having such a good day but all I could think was "When are they going to be done opening their presents so I can get back to work?"

Suddenly, I realized my sight was completely gone in my right eye. I don't know if I was blind when I went to bed or if it just happened in that moment. I was living a very high stress life so was not in tune with my mind, body, or soul at all. My family was worried, but I shrugged it off and didn't go to a doctor for 3 days. When I did, an ophthalmological specialist was called to tell me I had Optic Neuritis, which can be a precursor to Multiple Sclerosis.

I was completely shocked and had no idea what to do. The doctor told me I would either get my vision back in 6 weeks or it would be gone permanently. She asked me about my life, and I mentioned the stress, mental health, life history and my crippling feelings of imposter syndrome and low self-esteem. She said it was time to start doing the work to create the life and more importantly the mindset I needed to be healthy and happy.

So began a journey that has seen me love myself for the first time in my life, grow my consulting business to heights I could never have imagined, achieve goals I never believed I could, help people to dream again, and help my children realize they can be, do, or have anything they want in life if they set their mind to it.

The rest of my life will be spent seeking joy and helping others to do the same. Life is beautiful.

Zandra Ross

Mita Naidu is a community educator & named one of "12 Remarkable Women in the Arts in Vancouver" by the City of Vancouver & the Vancouver Parks Board.

MITA
NAIDU

This year was my 50th spin around the sun. To commemorate this, I created a list of the top 3 things I have UNlearned on this journey:

1. I have UNlearned that vulnerability is necessary in life.

It takes courage to share your truths, but I've discovered that our privilege can be speaking when we pressure women to be vulnerable. When my mother divorced, she had little support from her family and the justice system. She understood her power would NOT come from being vulnerable – but from being stoic, strong and standing firm. She had no choice. When we tell women to let their walls down, we make assumptions about what is POSSIBLE in their lives. We assume that vulnerability is a safe choice. And it often isn't. I continue to check my privilege.

2. I have UNlearned that compassion is a "soft skill".

I grew up believing that success was defined by determination and hard work and that empathy was not part of that equation. I once asked a former employer if I could say a few words to staff about a cultural event I was celebrating. Her words were never forgotten: "We are always in crisis mode. We don't have time for that stuff". I suddenly felt ashamed and diminished. I knew this was not a workplace I could bring my whole self. More importantly, I knew this leader didn't care. I left soon after. I now lead with love.

3. I have UNlearned that all friendships are valuable.

I have finally understood that a lengthy investment in a friendship doesn't mean it is safe or loving. I came to realize that they must ALSO be evolving, supportive and honest. I have finite time and energy as a single mom, and I simply cannot invest in anything less. Yet we are never taught how to process endings. I recently let go of a long-term friendship that was exhausting me but rekindled another one that has filled me up. We need to acknowledge the ebb and flow of friendships without guilt. I am learning grace.

UNlearnings have been a beautiful and critical part of my journey. What are some of yours?

Mita Naidu

Patrick Baylis is the owner and lead artist of Karmma Tattoo Shop, He has 10+ years of tattoo experience and specializes in Traditional & Cover Up Tattoos. Patric resides in Burnaby, BC, Canada.

PATRICK
BAYLIS

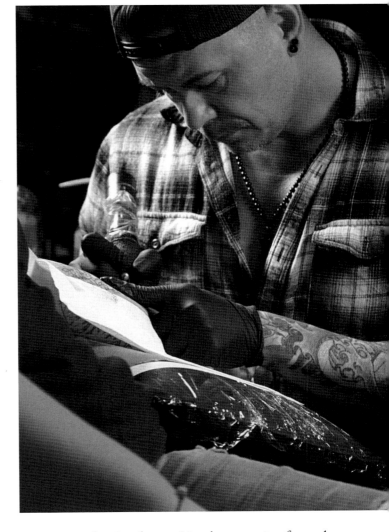

I've lived my life being told I wasn't good enough, that I couldn't accomplish the things I wanted to do. Years of chasing down my goals has built my mindset. I view things as choices that will define myself moving forward. Each day, I make the choice to get up and move towards my goals, no matter how hard it feels. I continue to put one foot in front of the other, trusting I know the steps I need to take. Or I figure them out as I go. No matter what, I make sure I just keep stepping forward, keep moving ahead with strong foundations built to last.

I was tossed between my divorced parents as a kid, troubled and neglected in that. I felt isolated and alone; I was shy and awkward. This led me into trouble during high school, acting out and running with the wrong crowds. Years down that path, I didn't recognize who I was, rolling with gangs and involved in that world. It wasn't a life I wanted and I had to figure out how to change that.

I pulled myself out of it, I cut off anyone involved with it. I started to build a new foundation for myself. I started working as a chemist for my then girlfriend's father's company, slowly climbing within the company. This helped me gain footing and the strength to pivot and move towards my own career goals.

Tired of building someone else's dreams, I finally turned the focus to my own. I studied piercing and tattooing, I started a shop. I've now been running Karmma Tattoo for 13 years. I'm a mentor to artists who I employ and I strive to create an environment where everyone aims to see the best in themselves. I'm proud of the impact I've had on the industry; I strive to create a space I believe promotes hard work and respect. I want my contributions to the industry and the world to pave the way for my kid, so she doesn't have to go through what I did. I try to stay present and take things as they come, take a deep breath and keep moving forward.

Patrick Baylis

Roxanne Baird is an explorer at heart who embraces both the external and internal adventures of life!

ROXANNE
BAIRD

You are magnificent!

I'd spent years teaching this in classes. I wholeheartedly believe it. So, imagine my shock when I discovered that I also held the strong unconscious belief that I am not!

This discovery didn't come in meditation or through my journals, though I see now it was evident in both. This discovery came the way most simple, yet profound discoveries seem to. It came while ugly crying under the covers, spiralling because I felt lost. Those profound discoveries really know how to kick you when you're down!

Six months before the world went crazy, my husband and I moved from Alberta to BC. We had the urge to experience life in a different way. Stepping into lockdowns, losing jobs, with no close community or friends, we certainly got it!

That chaotic, yet quiet period of time, caused me to dig into my beliefs about myself and the world. I found I had lost sight of who I was. I came to discover that not only had I placed my self-worth on external validation, but I also took for granted and talked to the most important person in my life (aka: me) like shit!

I wish I could say I jumped out of bed to "fix" things immediately. I wish I could tell you what finally had me crawling out. But the truth is, I stayed under those covers for quite some time. Then one day, I simply made a choice and found a mentor who challenged me to mirror work.

"Self-love is the foundation for EVERYTHING," he said.
I just thought it sounded cheesy.
But I was desperate, so three times a day I locked eyes with myself in a mirror and said "I love you" ten times.

The first few times, I cried.
The next few times, I couldn't maintain my own eye contact.
The times after that, I really didn't believe it.
But eventually with persistence, very slowly, it began to seep in.

There are so many layers to self-love, but I now know this - what you say and think (particularly of and to yourself) really does matter.

I still believe you are magnificent, but I now *KNOW* that I am too!

Roxanne Baird

Jana Jorgenson is the CEO at JanaJorgenson.com and resides in Parksville, BC, Canada.

JANA
JORGENSON

I'm often asked, "Why are you always laughing and happy?" Simple. It was a conscious decision I made at the age of four. My entire family were incredible mentors and coaches that inspired positivity and happiness within all of us.

I believe everyone deserves to live their God-given right to be happy, loved and always protected. As a child, I believed all children lived blissfully, but as I grew up, I learned this isn't true for everyone.

My purpose is to positively affect the lives of children by influencing adults to embrace their full potential of happiness and fulfillment. In other words, create a trickle-down effect of goodness. It starts with us.

I am a lion, with lots of room for growth. At the age of 12, I told my Mom I was going to lead a revolution. She was horrified, but I assured her it was for good, more like an evolution.

My life has been a fabulous learning experience with many ups and downs, tragic and happy moments. Many failures and successes, but I always focus on the good times, and more importantly what I can create today to make myself and others smile. I am relentless about being the best version of ourselves, especially in spirit.

It's inspiring to me how life moves and changes constantly. Being personally humbled, honoured and privileged to be chosen as Miss Teen Canada 1970 prepared me to become a life-long ambassador creating a positive legacy with love, intention and gratitude.

I am an entrepreneur and an influential networker. I am a Cidesco International Aesthetician. I love God, my life, my husband, my children and grandchildren, friends, and acquaintances all over the globe. I love nature, music, dance, and my desire to help humanity live better lives. People enrich my life. You make me better. It's not cliche, it's a choice that helps me become a better version of myself.

I have a passion for learning and I'm constantly on alert for cutting-edge breakthroughs to enhance our health, happiness, and abundance. I was recently gifted with one that is truly life changing.

You are powerful beyond measure. Smile, and be someone who makes everybody feel like somebody!

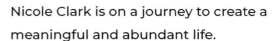

Nicole Clark is on a journey to create a meaningful and abundant life.

NICOLE
CLARK

In the midst of my divorce, I longed for a simpler life. I packed up everything that I owned and moved home to BC. Packing the last of 144 boxes, I realized how much excess I had acquired over the years. I made a quick off the cuff comment about hoping it would never arrive at my new house. I believe I used the word blow up along the way. My wish became reality. My moving truck caught fire and I lost everything except the clothes I was wearing. Because of the politics of insurance, I was not allowed to have anything back. There was definitely overwhelming trauma and grieving in the experience.

Yet in the end, losing everything I owned was a gift. It freed me from the burden of materialistic items that were holding me back and weighing me down. I now make decisions of who I want to be and where I want to live without the ease of falling back into a life that is familiar and comfortable. I had spent a lifetime collecting clothes and things that no longer serve me. I have no desire to wear Jimmy Choo's and get the latest Chanel bag. Don't get me wrong, nice things are great, yet for me, none of those things brought me happiness. Seeking them out was an adventure, a distraction and kept me looking outward instead of inward. I have learned when you live your life authentically to who you really are, things have no value.

I have chosen to live a life where I don't have to hide behind my emotions to protect myself from hurt and disappointment. Choosing this, I have learned so much about who I am and why I have made past choices in my life. I am living proof happiness cannot be found in a manufactured life. I learned this the hard way yet I'm so thankful for the opportunity to pivot and embrace life. Our lives are a compilation of our thoughts and beliefs. I got everything I asked for and wanted in life. I have learned the happiest people don't have the best of everything, they make the best of everything. Always remember your words have power!

Megan Ashley is one of Vancouver's top wedding and intimate portrait photographers who loves connecting with people, dancing around her house to all kinds of music, and making people genuinely belly laugh.

MEGAN
ASHLEY

It was the Summer of 2018. I had my one-year-old business and realized that I was more powerful and beautiful than I thought. My business became an outlet for me; it helped me learn how to love myself and I saw how much I could accomplish. However, I realized how unhappy I was in my personal life at this time. I was unhappy in my marriage and knew something needed to change. I made the most difficult decision of my life and asked for a divorce. Breaking up my family was difficult, but I knew for me to be happy and for my children to flourish, this was something I had to do.

My divorce taught me how to take a step back and see things from a different perspective. I hid away and put my business to the side through that process, which was terrifying because I loved it.

Unexpected things come up during challenging, pivotal moments in our lives. I was left utterly broken, with no clue how I was going to pick up the pieces. I was met with shame and hate and lost a lot of relationships during this time. I had to constantly remind myself that I had made the best choice for myself and my children. It took me a while to surround myself with people who genuinely loved and supported me. My family and a few close friends continued to help me, and through that process I met my incredibly supportive and amazing partner, who showed me what a healthy relationship truly is. I slowly learned how to pick up those little pieces and put myself back together. Once I got to that point, I started to put myself out there again and celebrate myself. I had support like I never had before. I picked up my business again, which is now flourishing and brings me joy every day.

Once I got through that and the pandemic, the biggest thing I learned was to put myself first. Even when it's hard, listen to your gut and trust yourself wholeheartedly. I can genuinely and sincerely say that I love who I am and who I will continue to become.

Megan Ashley

Joey Roo is an Indigenous Makeup Artist working with MISMACK Cosmetics in Victoria BC. Joey loves everything and making big dreams come true.

JOEY
ROO

I am a Two-Spirit, Indigenous Model and Makeup Artist, originally from Simpcw First Nations band, living in Victoria, British Columbia.

I grew up in Kamloops, B.C., without knowing my indigenous roots/culture. It wasn't until late 2018, when I returned to Kamloops from Victoria after battling mental illness and addiction issues and was trying to get my life together, that I began reconnecting with my culture. Having a strong sense of community was instrumental in my recovery journey. After a while, I started to feel more confident and began playing around with makeup more and more. My makeup artistry improved quickly. I enjoyed my results. Eventually, my neighbour asked me to do her engagement party makeup. Word spread, and other people started asking me to do their makeup too!

Meanwhile, I worked full time as a drywall labourer and did makeup and modelling in my spare time. In due course, my modelling photos caught the eye of the Salmon Arm Arts Centre, and they displayed 3 of my portraits. The exhibition's curator introduced me to Missy MacKintosh, creator, and founder of MisMacK Clean Cosmetics because she knew we were both makeup artists. After meeting with her and doing the first-ever guest spot at the MisMacK Salmon Arm store, I was asked to join the team. I would travel between Salmon Arm and Kamloops in my spare time a few times a month, and over the holidays during 2021, I was offered a full-time position as a Makeup Artist at the Victoria location. After being back in Kamloops, working on myself in therapy, and connecting to my culture, I felt like I was ready to take this next step. I followed my dreams and had the support of my family, friends, and community to get me where I am.

Just remember

"Good Things Happen!"

Joey Roo

BRYAN
SMITH

"The child is father to the man" and all that! Explain to me how the pouring of boiling coffee from a percolator up the sleeve of a four-year-old's snowsuit or staring into the watery basement of that same house where frogs hopped in rivulets in the mud contributed to the serial volunteer for social causes that I am today.

Lenses on life are supposed to help you understand it. I gazed through knotholes in the living room sub-floor onto frogs. What was learned? Love of Nature?

Soon after arriving in Oxford, I embraced the work of the Ontario Coalition for Social Justice, a group which no longer exists provincially but which endures in Oxford, working to preserve and restore the environment. "We are all in", I announced when Oxford People Against the Landfill was formed in 2012 to fight (and win) against a proposed dump.

Invited to set out furniture and then clear it for hungry children at lunch, I soon joined the volunteers at a "Supper Club" offering a free meal to those who face food insecurity in a land of plenty. Never missing a chance to combine causes, I recognized that wasted excess food contributed to the garbage and, worse, hunger. I helped found Food Forward Oxford, linking food producers to food access providers.

Waste not, want not, does not just apply to food. Picking up on a great concept of a giant free swap meet, moving one person's rejected but reusable goods to someone else's treasure chest, we called ReuseapaloozAHA.

Sometimes, an activist has to take friends to the seat of power to be heard! Loading a friendly mayor and two more-than-usually-docile cows into a large van, I drove the point home that Queen's Park cannot ignore rural communities' wishes. The scheme attracted the attention of MPPs, tourists and Legislature staff.

As a teacher, I lived what I taught. Staff, students, and community members saw a genuinely concerned citizen and activist. Misquoting Mick Jagger, a guru of survival if there ever was one, I noted that "when you have 30 000 people giving you energy, you have lots to give back".

What's next? Possibly, a retirement to follow the retirement into full-time activism.

Calli Jensen is tenacious, pursues her dreams, and when she has her heart set on something, she finds a way to make it happen. Calli, a master networker and promoter, values her worth and never gives up. Her warrior spirit inspires others.

CALLI
JENSEN

In 2014 I felt my world crashing around me. I lost my clothing store and condo just before leaving Vancouver to save my life (pictured here). I was taken advantage of, victimized, had my vehicle stolen, and robbed of nineteen thousand dollars. My condo, which I bought at twenty-four, was foreclosed on due to my financial loss. I had to liquidate store merchandise to pay for gas to get to Toronto.

I drove across the country three times in less than two months. Imagine driving from Vancouver to Toronto with your dog and a u-haul trailer. I cried the entire time.

My ego didn't want to let go of the life I had become accustomed to, and I was too proud to ask for help. Dead and numb from the pain, I felt unlovable and untouchable.

After being victimized like me, the vibrant, full-of-life woman known to others was lost but has been found again. People seeing me now say you haven't changed, Calli.

Moving to Toronto with Anil saved my life!!! I went through Landmark, a mentorship program, twice, and many other programs to change my victim mindset. Since then, he and I have accomplished much. Although we are no longer together, he remains one of my best friends and always will be because of what we went through. He is there no matter what!!

Together we accomplished great things! We became one of the top teams in our company, earning luxury vacations and cars, doing 3.9 million in sales in fifty-three countries. Yet, the whole time this happened, I felt powerless and unfulfilled; something was still missing.

I'm not saying this to brag. I'm pointing out that when you get out of your own way, what seemed to be impossible becomes possible! It took tons of therapy and working on myself to get back to me, but now I thrive!

Caroline Wedderspoon, MC RCC is a registered clinical counsellor with Alyson Jones and Associates.

CAROLINE
WEDDERSPOON

Seven years ago, having moved from the UK with my then husband, I was a married suburban mother, focused on raising my four kids. Increasing struggles with my relationship, parenting, and with my sense of self led me to a point at which I could no longer continue. So, at the age of 43, I chose to leave my marriage and to come out as lesbian. However, I was afraid of what this might mean for me and afraid for what it might mean for my kids. Divorce itself is hard on kids, and it was also hard for them to adjust to my new identity. They had to navigate homophobia, some intentional and some unwitting, but neither less hurtful. However, I realised that if I wanted my children to be exactly who they are meant to be, I had to be that too, despite the vulnerabilities.

I was in the middle of my counselling studies at the time and struggling to figure out my own identity at that stage of life was scary and confusing. But it was also a gift. I spent a lot of time exploring queerness, what it meant for my life, and what it means for others. This led me to learn more about privilege and to examine my own. Within the context of my work as a registered clinical counsellor, it became increasingly important for me to identify as a queer therapist and to centre queerness in my counselling practice.

It is my belief that queerness is a gift for everyone. Queerness offers unfettered curiosity and the opportunity to see people for who they truly are. Queerness also offers us the chance to name and challenge social norms and constructs that often bind, harm, and shame us. In the counselling space, it offers an opportunity for clients to make new meaning of their own experiences. I feel truly fortunate to have worked with a diverse client population both in community mental health and with Alyson Jones and Associates. I love my work and hope that I can continue to find ways to enable all my clients to find belonging and connection; to themselves, and to the world around them.

Caroline Wedderspoon

My name is Tony Ganton and I'm just a simple man, trying to make my way in the universe.

TONY
GANTON

As I was driving to my university graduation, a song came on the radio:'I Still Haven't Found What I'm Looking For' by U2. Now, like most people, I don't care for U2, especially when they 'surprised' everyone by shoving that damn 'Songs of Innocence' album down our throats and into our iTunes libraries. But in that very moment, it hit all the feels; it spoke to a longing within me, a longing for something I cannot yet name.

Equipped with a psychology degree and six years of varsity football, I was ready to write the next chapter of my life. Up until the moment of my graduation, my life as I knew it had been structured for me — where I was heading was predetermined and how I would get there was clear. This new chapter had no structure or path; where I was heading was entirely up to me. I had no team, no coach, no student perks to rely on, no classes to attend and learn from. For the first time in over 10 years I was no longer a football player or a student. Who am I? Is this what adults feel like, or am I someone who has lost their identity? I considered running away to Europe, deferring my anxiety with a different type of unease. That may be my specialty, actually. Running away seemed to help all my anxieties, but recently, it has felt different, like I was being challenged to stay the course. Four years later, the challenge of what's next still weighs on me. I have had seasons of constantly trying new things and pushing my boundaries, but in turn, I have also stepped back entirely for seasons of nothingness, seasons in which nothing is all I can do. Even writing this has taken longer than anticipated. At one point I might have called this procrastination, but a good friend of mine once told me that procrastination is not doing something because you are lazy, but waiting until you are fully ready to complete that thing.

I still haven't found what I'm looking for, but I do know I am going in the right direction.

CAUVERY
CARIAPPA

My grandmother is my biggest personal influence. In saying that, my Dad is as well.

This is a tribute to one of the strongest women I have ever known. My grandmother lost her hearing in middle school. Yet, she learnt to overcome her challenges by looking for a solution in reading lips. Hence, I can say that "resilience" runs in my veins. She was convent educated and had a thirst for knowledge in the 1930's. She was a genius mathematician. Everything I do today has been inspired by this amazing woman. She sold insurance and knitted sweaters for her loved ones. My grandmother represented our Kodava warrior tribe community in Southern India.

Miracles happen when you step into the light, even when no one sees that but you.

I define "happiness" as a state of mind. I learned that external validation is not necessary for me to be "happy". You cannot expect someone outside of yourself to make you happy, rather its within you, hence you will not hear me blame other people. I am conscious of projecting my feelings onto others and the other way around. My sense of worth comes from "believing in myself", that there is no substitute to hard work.

If I could teach one positive impact for humanity it is to allow yourself to feel pain and stay present. Staying in the now, not to worry about your past mistakes or failures. That does not define you. The future is still unknown, and you can write it the way you desire. Step by step, in the now. I thank my past experiences and failures for who I have become today. I forgive all the people involved. We are all living life the best we know how. I am a peace-loving warrior living an ordinary life.

My greatest influence would have to be Mahatma Gandhi's Ahmisa. Ahmisa is derived from our Hindu Vedic manuscripts and the Yajur veda which states that, "May all beings look at me with a friendly eye, may I do likewise, and may we look at each other with the eyes of a friend."

Passionate about diversity and inclusion. I thrive in being a creative problem solver.

Deborah is strong, positive, focused, and finds happiness in the smallest things. She does more than exist - she lives!

DEBORAH J.
LOHRENZ

In the first Pursuit:365 book, I talked about the physical, emotional, and sexual abuse I suffered at the hands of my father. I was young, naïve, and unable to tell anyone. He said it would kill my mom if I told her! So, how did I get through each hour, each day? I developed numerous skills coping strategies.

To survive, I became very intuitive – from reading body language and tone of voice to sensing energy – these saved me many times from his attempts. There were times I knew instinctively what was going to happen and could escape – but, unfortunately, there were times I could not! Because of these times, I knew I needed to be strong, to be a fighter. At a very early age, I started lifting weights and I learned to box! I vehemently refused to let him do what he threatened. I'm proud to say I was able to keep him from raping me - this word is difficult for me to say, as it was a 24/7/365 threat for years!

Even though this happened to me, life did go on! I want to talk about memories. Unfortunately, bad memories have the strongest emotions attached to them - we remember them in detail! These don't go away and those deep within our subconscious can surface at unexpected times – it happens to me to this day! My way of dealing with my memories is to recognize I can't change them, but I can do my best by not giving them power. Instead of my memories controlling me, I do my best to control my memories and my reactions to them.

There are still challenging days; however, having control over how I react is a choice I made for me, my wellbeing. I also choose happiness over sadness and pain. As I get older, I fully embrace what life has to offer. I do my best to use my life experiences to help others. I strive to be my best, be understanding, and to be nonjudgmental. No one really knows others' struggles and challenges. No one knew mine! I still struggle, and I am truly proud of my successes!

Cherie White is a strong award-winning social justice developer. She focuses on providing housing for women and children in Canada's poorest postal code, Vancouver's Downtown Eastside.

CHERIE
WHITE

As a little girl I was born into a loving Salvation Army home. I remember my grandfather singing gospel songs over me before I went to bed. He taught me about social justice, and I heard stories from a very young age of him finding housing for immigrants that would arrive in bus loads in front of his church door.

Because of these roots that were planted in me, I have devoted my entire life to redistributing wealth, finding homes for single moms and women, and creating social enterprises and ultimately revitalizing Canada's poorest postal code.

My husband and I with our four small children decided that we wanted to move to this neighbourhood to bring light and hope and be a part of a community. Over time, many people would leave drugs and alcohol and join our community, but the hardest part was finding housing. Vancouver is in the middle of a huge housing crisis; if you're wealthy, housing is not a problem. So, I became a social justice land developer, living and working in this neighbourhood.

My company is called Steadfast Developments, an all-female development team that focuses on social justice, affordable housing, and intentional community development. We also provide sustainable economic development and social enterprise.

We are about to purchase property and build an entirely new neighbourhood with an infrastructure of community centers, art centers, cafés, libraries, schools, grocery stores and banks.

However, it's taken me a lot of hard work, determination, and tenacity to get to the point I am today. There were many challenges and setbacks over the years.

Three years later, I have built a successful all-female development company that is ready to revitalize an entire neighborhood. I still wake up between 5:00 and 5:30 Monday to Friday, exercise and meditate on scripture. This is the foundation to my day.

I'm so thankful for challenges that taught me so much, made me stronger and created the woman that I am today. I'm also thankful for the opportunity to be a part of an alliance of social impact entrepreneurs that have a passion to make a difference in this world.

If there's one piece of advice that I would want to pass on to my children or those that are considering chasing their dreams, it's that there is no plan B, only an alternating plan A. Ultimately, we just can't give up. The hope and the support is always out there if we just keep looking.

Cherie White

Nicolass Glim is a member of the International Bridge, Structural, Ornamental and Reinforcing Iron Workers.

NICOLAAS
GLIM

I am a very private person with not that much to share. As an introvert, I open up to only a small circle of people that I trust. Expressing real emotions is difficult, but I would love to change that; this is my opportunity. Hello everybody, my name is Nick.

I am a member of the International Bridge, Structural, Ornamental and Reinforcing Iron Workers. I have been a member of Iron Workers Local 736 in Hamilton, Ontario for about 27 years. Being a member of this union has given me the chance to work in the steel plants of Hamilton, nuclear plants throughout Ontario, Niagara Gorge Hydro, 401 bridges and high-rise downtown Toronto condos. I'm grateful that this job has given me an opportunity to experience differing locations that most don't see without watching a documentary on engineering. Being a tradesman has been rewarding, provided a decent wage, benefits and a good pension.

I live in Port Weller, North St Catharines, where the Welland Canal starts at Lake Ontario. A quiet, peaceful little part of town. My wife Miranda (of twenty-five years) and I, along with our three children, moved here in the fall of 2015. We had big plans with our recently purchased house; it was the home my wife grew up in. She appreciated her childhood home and we were going to live out our lives here.

But in 2016, my wife was diagnosed with non-Hodgkin's lymphoma. How could the strongest woman I know have cancer? That was my response. Miranda was the healthiest person I knew. She ate healthy and exercised. Meanwhile, I didn't care what I consumed. How could this happen? I then realized life is not fair. Cancer shows no prejudice. It doesn't care if you are the most empathetic, good person on this rock that we call our world, or if you are the nastiest thing that ever existed. Cancer can strike at any time – it has no boundaries.

On January 22, 2019 at 3:10 in the morning, as I had my forehead against my wife's, she took her last breath. There are no words to describe the emotions. I was numb. It was just me and her, and then, it was just me.

Like in welding, I put my shield down, focusing on the light to mend things together.

336

Nicolaas Glim

CHRISTINE
BLANCHETTE

How Running Led To Creating Two TV Shows

Growing up on a hobby farm in the Eastern Townships in
Quebec, I always knew that I'd be leaving one day to go to
college and university. I remember filling out the application at
the kitchen table and telling my parents that I wanted to go to
college. I had a desire to expand my wings, even though I was
scared to leave. My zest for adventure and desire to be the best
was the motivating factor and powerful lure I couldn't ignore.

What I appreciated most growing up was there was lots of
open spaces to play sports and running was my favourite.
Though my passion for running started in my youth, it was not until moving to Vancouver in 1989, I joined a running club
and became competitive locally. I exceeded my own expectations by qualifying to run the iconic Boston Marathon. While I've
tried to give back to the sport of running through teaching in clinics and helping others, running has given me so much more.
In 2005 I started writing a weekly newspaper column, which led to writing magazine articles on fitness entertainment, and
eventually inspired me to create, produce and host my own television show, Run With It, which is a monthly entertainment
and educational show about running, fitness and health.

My first media job was working at CBC TV news in Vancouver where I met a colleague who suggested that I get TV
interviewing experience by joining Rogers TV, a community channel. I interviewed sports figures and entertainers on the show
called, Westside Profile. I also co-produced a magazine show which led to winning a producing award.

My passion for running and media created a perfect combination; from running shoes to high heels on the red carpet, I gained
the opportunity to interview celebrities, musicians, athletes, and those who follow a healthy lifestyle. My platform has given
many opportunities to share intriguing stories and make it about the guest. The success of Run With It led to the launch
of my second show, The Closing Act, which is a monthly show about musicians, producers, and the movers and shakers
in the entertainment industry. I enjoy being a promoter of health and wellness and playing a role to the health, sports, and
entertainment community.

Following your passion can lead to a career you never thought possible.

337

Christine Blanchett

Entertainer, actor, gender illusionist and foodie are words used to describe local celebrity Christopher Hunte - aka Symone Says.

CHRISTOPHER
HUNTE

From a young age I was blessed with a light that attracted people. As an adult, that light often shone too bright. It singed some of my closest friendships and left me at times out in the cold. After years of excess and self-destructive behaviour, it was time to take stock of my life, ask the universe what it had planned for me and actually listen. It was the next two life events that changed my trajectory completely. The COVID pandemic arrived, followed by the unexpected passing of my youngest brother. This left an immense hole in my elderly mother's heart. Not being in close proximity to her was the missing piece of my life's puzzle.

Departing Vancouver for Ontario to look after my mother and leave my acting and drag life behind was not an easy decision. It was, however, the right one. It took us 6 months to acclimate. My mother had been living alone for 26 years after divorcing my father and was quite set in her ways. Here I was, now, an adult with a very big life in need of downsizing. In my mind she was still 50, vibrant, quick as a whip and a fashion plate. We both needed a reset. The reality, she was 80, and in need of support albeit still fashionable, fairly independent and it bears repeating, set in her ways.

The child had become the parent. An adjustment to the psyche, a shift in responsibilities, repetitive anecdotes, and the like. It is exhausting, but the pros far outweigh the cons. I take pleasure in creating wonderful multi-course meals for the woman who was responsible for my childhood nourishment.

In yet another turn of events, I have returned to writing. Close to completion are my recipe book, a comedy piece and a series chronicling the life and times of my mother. A talent agent has also sought me out for representation, and I have a handful of drag projects in the works.

When the universe does speak, it is up to you to listen.

My light is back on, this time with recharged batteries and a dimmer switch.

Stay blessed,

Christopher Hunte – aka Symone Says

Cory is an educator and health professional that desires to stay well and live free. Optimum functional health is everything.

CORY
HOLLY

I believe that life is a sport. I mean this not only figuratively, but also literally. It is my contention that life itself is an actual sport, revealed by nature and governed by the laws of physics, biology, and chemistry.

We are the players in the game and like all sports, there is a beginning and there is an end. If one fails to comply with the laws established by nature, this leads to hardship and severe consequences, but if you play the game of life according to the rules, you will be well rewarded. The origin of sport as an invention of man is as old and ancient as man himself. How old is humankind? That is the true age of sport. The ancient Greeks said that sport represents all that is good in man as an ideal and all that is reprehensible. We love sport because it reveals our true character as humans. Sport doesn't build character, it reveals it. Should we follow the herd, or should we rely on reason and critical thinking to construct an objective paradigm of life that creates optimum health and wellness as an outcome?

I live by a simple motto: If you live hard, you die soft. This means that if you exert yourself physically and surpass your own limits, you can live longer and feel better. It requires effort, and you must take some risks, but the dividends are enormous beyond belief. Imagine just for a moment, living a long life free of chronic disease and disability. Living hard means you do the work that needs to be done before you pick up your paycheck. It means you measure progress in the currency of sweat and that you're not afraid to challenge yourself or rock your own boat.

Now what does it mean to die soft? This means that you hit the wall at the end of a functional, full life quickly and without effort. It also means you don't die a slow, miserable death that causes pain and hardship not only for you, but for everyone else around you. So, do you want to live hard and die soft, or live soft and die hard?

DEBRA
ABRAHAM

I'm inspired by this work the people are truly the heroes of the day.

Happiness comes from seeing the joy on the faces of those I serve. I have discovered we all do the best we can and deserve to be treated with respect and dignity. We must honour one another as human beings and meet one another in the space we inhabit at the time.

What seems like ages ago, I was a single mother of six, using social services for addiction issues and support. I waited in lines losing myself bit by bit. I didn't want to be a statistic, another black woman waiting in line for help. I put in the effort to get clean and have stayed that way for 28 years. I set attainable goals while working three to four jobs at a time. At forty, I returned to university to complete a degree and then work for the Ministry.

Once a user of the social system and then an employee of the system, I believed there was a better way to work with people with various challenges such as addiction, mental health, trauma, homeless, etc. The system I was working for had deep-seated inequities inherent in the programs offered, the delivery system and assumptions made by others.

Eight years ago, I took a leap of faith, left my job, and with my son, began the Unique Get Together Society, a registered charity. It is a privately funded not-for-profit organization that helps marginalized and underserviced individuals and families get the support they need. We individualize support using a humanistic approach, asking clients, "what do you need". Trauma creates an urgency, so we respond to applicants within twenty-four hours, so they are aware support is on the way. Services are put in place within the week, and paperwork follows rather than coming first.

We now have a staff of fifty and three different office locations. It's a one-of-a-kind non-government funded agency. I am blessed to work with the most dedicated and loving team.

Joy is found through human connection, being seen, and being heard. My advice: love one another, honour where everyone is on their journey.

Debra Abraham

MARYANN
OKORO

From a very young age, I knew I wanted more out of life. Everything that I've ever accomplished, I first envisaged. September 2017, I gave birth to my precious baby boy in an ambulance after going through a "fast and furious" labor. Arriving at the hospital, he had some hiccups concerning poor breathing and low oxygen, but eventually was discharged with no issues after spending a couple of days in the neonatal intensive care unit. Little did I know that three years later, I would discover my little boy has autism.

Having that assessment on that snowy winter morning left me with so many emotions. "Woe is me," I thought. I had so many questions, but no direct answers, and there I cried. I cried because we are living in a world that is not accepting of all people; the comprehension that certain things may be difficult for him broke my heart. It felt like I would be letting go of all the dreams that I had for my son, my own dreams, and my career. I felt it was all over for us.

After months of solitude, I realized having the result of this assessment gave me the clarity to be able to assess programs to support him. Slowly, I began to create a vision of my dreams again. I left my corporate job and began to chauffeur my son from one therapy program to another. During that time, I also launched my skincare brand, KAMBIIO. One that I have envisioned so many times in the past, but couldn't pull the trigger on.

Different life experiences can break barriers within you. Discovering autism totally gave me a different perspective, and becoming an entrepreneur has since led me to a self-discovery like never before. The fear of change, the fear of disappointment and the fear of failure wanted to have the best part of me. I recognize these fears and I'm not letting them become roadblocks to following my dreams and my happiness. When you are on the path to your dreams, you may experience setbacks and challenges. You will feel like it is all over for you. But remember, there is always another path you can take.

Diane Johnson culminated her successful career in marketing and broadcasting to leave a lasting legacy by founding her company Descriptive Video Works. She has received many awards including, EY Entrepreneur of the Year, A Silver Stevie Award, RBC Finalist for Woman of the Year, The Audio Description Achievement Award and ProfitW Top 100 Female Entrepreneurs.

DIANE
JOHNSON

When I started in radio as a receptionist, I was a single mom with little confidence in myself. I was fortunate to have mentors along the way who taught me that when you care about others and lead from your heart – everybody wins. I have always worked with that in mind, investing in people, caring, and helping others to reach their potential.

As my career evolved through television, marketing management for Disney and into the larger world of broadcasting, I enjoyed my work, but knew that my real passion was yet to be fully activated, and I wanted to make a difference. My chance for that arrived in 2003, when I first heard about a new process called Audio Description.

Hearing about it took me back to a pivotal memory from when I was 7 years old. I had a young neighbour, Darlene who was a gifted pianist. She was also blind. I remember thinking how unfair it was that Darlene couldn't share in watching the TV shows that the rest of us enjoyed.

That memory combined with information about this new process inspired me to take a chance. I started my company, Descriptive Video Works (DVW) to provide television programming to people who were blind or visually impaired. DVW went on to become the leading description provider in North America and Internationally – working with all major broadcasters, Netflix, Disney, and numerous others. We also provided description of live events, and even do video games. Our services were ground-breaking when we started 20 years ago, but now Audio Description is mandated throughout the world.

Starting a company from scratch takes commitment, faith, and passion. I thank my team for the commitment, my mentors for the faith, and Darlene for the inspiration that awakened my passion.

There is a quote by Helen Keller on the wall of our Descriptive Video Works studio in Vancouver that says:

"The best and most beautiful things cannot be seen or even touched they must be felt with the heart."

In following my passion and leading with my heart I made my difference by making the world of broadcasting more accessible and inclusive – and in that, everybody got to win.

Diane Rolston specializes in coaching female business leaders to have more confidence and success, while living a balanced life. When she's not hanging out with her husband and two kids, she's leading events for the Dynamic Women® Global Club, speaking on international stages or hosting the Award-Winning Dynamic Women Podcast.

DIANE
ROLSTON

Are you someone who likes to achieve, improve, and reach your goals? Then we're very alike.

At a young age, I realized that when I achieved, I was praised by teachers, coaches, and family. This fed into being an A-type, goal-oriented, high achiever.

These qualities served me very well growing up: helping me to be captain of sports teams, an honour roll student, and student council president. But they also taught me that our worth comes from our outward achievements, that we can always become a better version of ourselves, and we should be able to do it all without asking for help.

As I've grown up and started running my own business while also becoming a mother simultaneously, I've had to learn a few things so I wasn't burnt out, overwhelmed, and stressed. I'll share with you the three shifts that had the most impact and were crucial for my success today.

Shift 1: Stop measuring your life according to your success instead of your satisfaction. Society uses success to define who we are and our worth. However, when I started to look at what made me happy (using a coaching tool) and what I truly wanted in each area of life (there are 10), it helped me focus on what mattered and design my ideal life.

Shift 2: If you want to reach your goals, you don't need to change yourself; you need to change your actions. Feeling not good enough and always looking to improve yourself kills your confidence and holds you back from DOING what you need to do. Instead, by learning from experts the right actions to take, I sped up my achievements and kept my confidence high.

Shift 3: Don't try to do it all yourself; it's wiser to work with others. Like the synergy of a flock of flying geese, doing life and business with others makes it easier to reach your goals and more fun! I collaborate, hire coaches, and have two fantastic team members to help me reach my goals.

I'm grateful for these shifts and they are part of how I coach women in their pursuit of being dynamic leaders living a balanced life!

Diane Rolston

Margaret Hughes is a mother to four children and resides in Sarnia, Ontario. Margaret's journey has not always been easy but her strength is incredible.

MARGARET
HUGHES

Happiness is a practice. Resilience and optimism take work. We are not born knowing how to overcome difficulty; we practice and learn.

Emigrating to Canada from Northern Ireland, my father started again at fifty to provide a more stable life for us. Adjusting was difficult, but I built relationships, finished school, and looked forward to the future.

At 26, living with my fiancée in Toronto, I was excited; life was unfolding the way I imagined. Then one morning, I awoke without sight in my right eye and headed to the emergency room. After testing, they found that I didn't have an eye problem but a neurological one, Multiple Sclerosis. I was devastated and terrified about what was waiting for me around the next corner. I decided that Multiple Sclerosis wouldn't overshadow my future and running became my refuge and a way to prove to myself that MS wouldn't win.

I married my childhood sweetheart a year later and began planning our family, soon discovering we had fertility issues and needed help. IVF worked, and Sarah was born. Tom and I were elated. Things were looking up!

While on maternity from teaching, I slipped out with Sarah to pick Tom up from work and upon our return, the house was ablaze. We could not believe our eyes. We needed family support and relocated to Sarnia. Life has a way of keeping things in perspective, and that's when I found out I was unexpectedly pregnant with our son, Jack. Pure joy!

In 2003, Tom was diagnosed with testicular cancer, which returned after a year of remission. After the second round of treatment, we enjoyed three more cancer-free years. At forty, I lost Tom to a brain injury. The course we had charted together was now going to be piloted by a single mother.

At 55, I am happily remarried, retired, and the mother of four adult children. I have discovered that happiness occurs during those quiet moments between life's chaos, where we appreciate the journey and those we love. No matter how often you get knocked down, you must get back up because happiness is just around the corner.

Margaret Hughes

Don Wolf is best known for fronting Canada's recording artists "White Wolf". Don is an in demand and well respected Vocal/Performance Coach and is currently based in the beautiful South Surrey, British Columbia, Canada.

DON
WOLF

Respect & Family

Respect and family are two words that can mean many things.

In regards to myself, I've carried these words with me throughout my music career and life.

Coming from a small family whose parents survived the horrors of WWII, coming to a new country to start a new life and raise a family, I quickly learned how family means so much!

Having no relatives such as uncles, aunts, grandparents, cousins etc., because of the war, I learned through both of my parents to love and respect your family, no matter how big or small, fighting or at peace, Love and Respect each other always!

In return, you try and treat others that become close to you like your family.

Music was integral to our family growing up. I remember being woken up late on a Saturday night upon my parents' return home from a wedding or dance, and my dad having invited what seemed like all the guests to stop by for food and drink. They wanted to continue the good time they were all having.

Yes, some seemed to have too good a time beforehand, if you know what I mean. Still, they would all sit around the kitchen table and, along with the many stories and jokes, start singing in beautiful harmonies, songs from their homeland while my mother and all the ladies would help prepare food for the guests, who may have had a bit too much party and could have used the food!

They sang the songs from their hearts, some sad, some funny but all had the theme of family and being together, no matter what.

Music and Family!

As I grew older and my passion for music took over, I remember taking what my parents taught me about respecting others and instilling that in every friendship I made and with everyone in the business I ended up dealing with.

It may not have always happened, but those words were always in the back of my mind.

I raised both my children, now grown, to be the same and do as I was taught in their everyday life.

My Motto to this day:

"Music Is Life; Family Is Everything"

Edina Beeby is groups manager and head of social media marketing for Fly & Sea Dive Adventures, a boutique-style travel agency specializing in scuba diving.

EDINA
BEEBY

It's always hard when relationships break. It hurts. It hurts even more when it breaks at the hands of dishonesty. You can become filled with emotions that don't belong inside you.

I'd like to be able to write that I was blindsided by the betrayal. That I didn't sit in the knowledge and the devastation in an uncertain haze for weeks. That I was as strong and as courageous as I had always believed myself to be.

But I wasn't. And I lied to myself longer than any person should.

As women, we struggle to figure out who it is that we want to be. We are brought up to believe that we have to be so many things to be worthy of love, to feel like we matter.

I knew that I didn't want to be the person whose heart wasn't seen. I didn't want to be the rejected one, the insignificant one, the disposable one.

I fought against that reality. I wouldn't accept it. And in the process- lost everything I had promised myself I would be.

Weeks of dysfunction, days of bare minimum, hours of angry tears- but when my 9yr old daughter put her arms around me and told me, "you don't have to do this anymore"-I finally accepted that simple truth. If I had control of nothing else- I did control who I was going to be.

I started my journey back. First by forgiving myself.

I forgave myself for not being as resilient or as strong as I imagined myself to be. For knowing and ignoring. For letting the lies outweigh the truth.

Next I started practicing radical acceptance.

I accepted that resiliency is not IF you break but what you do after that counts. Not matter how long it kept you down.

I started accepting the reality as it was. To have the courage and strength to live inside it.

The truth is, is that as women, we are capable of breaking our own heart's in ways that no other human being can. BUT we are also capable of mending those same hearts- IF we are only willing to accept the lesson.

GRAYSON
FOSTER

The Beauty of Reinventing Yourself

I'm the youngest of four and grew up poor on a farm in Alberta, Canada. My father was an alcoholic, and my mother suffered from mental illness, so parenting was non-existent. I started working at 14 and left home at 17. I knew I had a choice - either spiral down into that toxic mess that surrounded me or escape the legacy of trauma and abuse. Somehow, I had this never give up attitude, and I dreamed of a better life. My goal is always for progress, not perfection.

My biggest fear, besides spiders, is failure. Despite my career as a former news anchor, reporter, and producer, acting in movies, and commercials, hosting a real estate show, interviewing celebrities, hosting over 400 infomercials, and creating and producing a female-driven reality series, I still have moments of self-doubt. Don't we all? But it's been my dream to have a talk show, so thank goodness for YouTube. I interview wonderful guests who share advice on self-care, health and wellness, beauty, money management, and relationships. I have a "Women and Wealth" series coming soon, so stay tuned!

I've overcome abuse, toxic relationships, eating disorders, and cervical cancer. I have started over many times by reinventing myself. Reassessing and changing my life when needed has become the key to my success. My mother was beautiful, and I believe her savior was makeup and fashion, even though she probably didn't know it. She always got up, put her face on, a pretty dress, heels, and gloves, and held her head up high despite the chaos at home. Similarly, beauty and fashion have become transformative for me throughout my life. I want to share knowledge with other women seeking self-improvement and new directions.

My goal is to inspire women to focus on what's next and not what's behind them. I am living proof that you can face painful circumstances and rise above to have the life you desire. To avoid change, people get stuck in their trauma and fill themselves with food, alcohol, drugs, or toxic relationships. I've been there, but if my life can serve as an inspiration to even one person to make a change, then I'm genuinely successful. I refuse to give up, and neither should you, and that's the beauty of reinventing yourself.

Grayson Foster

Born and raised in Richmond, BC, Gurjit Tiwana obtained her law degree from the University of British Columbia and completed her articles with the criminal firm of Cobb St. Pierre Lewis in Gastown, where she became an associate afterward. In 2019, Gurjit collaborated with Paramjit Malhi and opened Invictus Law.

GURJIT K.
TIWANA

In my life I've been to hell and back more than once, yet I wouldn't change anything about it. I lost my husband, father, and best friend all in a short period of time, spiralling me into depression. It hurt to breathe. I was crying to a friend one day, and she told me that I have one life to live and it's up to me to decide how I want to live it. That is when I decided that I could still grieve for my losses, but it would be an injustice to keep holding on to the sadness. I owed it to myself and the ones I lost, to keep pushing forward. I still had life to live. I then realized the true meaning behind William Ernest Henley's poem Invictus, "I am the master of my fate, I am the captain of my soul". The same things that make us; break us, yet the very same things that break us, make us!

As women, we must remember that we hold the reins and steer the vessel. We are in control of ourselves, and our mindset can determine our outlook, our path and how successful we become. Success can be defined in many different ways and what I see as my personal success is likely different than what success looks like to others. Success came when I realized that I controlled my happiness. Don't let anyone tell you what happiness looks like – only you know what your soul desires.

My father used to tell me that I had the opportunity to help others, and not everyone is blessed with that ability. My mission in life is helping people move their own lives forward. In the practice of law, I generally see people during their worst moments. My job is to help them protect their rights, but I also believe it is my duty to help them discover how they can progress their lives. To provide real service, you must add sincerity and integrity. Smiling and showing love are the best gifts you can give another person. You may never know what someone else is going through, and your kindness can affect their day completely. Smiles and hugs are a universal language – everyone understands them, and you can never receive too many.

Heather Lake BA, MACP, RCC is an individual, child and family counsellor with Alyson Jones and Associates.

HEATHER
LAKE

I believe that even the most challenging, unexpected life changes offer us an opportunity for self-reinvention. Mine came in the form of a career change at the age of 50, following the unforeseen dissolution of a 20-year marriage. Having spent almost three decades in Canadian and U.S. boarding and day schools, I chose instead to pursue a degree and career in the mental health field. I never imagined leaving education after so many successful years, but it was time for fulsome change. I have come to fully embrace the notion that we show true courage by acting, despite our fears.

This transition led me on a path of self-understanding and self-awareness that required both agility and certitude. I began by reassessing and further cementing my core values, and I use these every day as a platform for my work with clients at Alyson Jones and Associates. I believe that human relationships are one of the most important elements in our lives and that we need healthy, supportive connections to thrive. I maintain that clients need to feel genuine warmth and a sense of compassion in building a meaningful therapeutic rapport. I always try to see the best in people and thrive on helping others in overcoming challenges, recognizing their unique strengths, and finding hope in even the most difficult situations.

My experience in education, coupled with my own life experience, positioned me well for a career as a therapist. In my work with teenagers and their families, I have drawn upon my time in boarding schools, for those were the moments when I learned the most about the inner workings of families and the incredible impact of positive role modeling. In counseling couples, I draw inspiration from my parents who have shown me what true partnership, unwavering loyalty, and enduring love looks like.

I am the proud mother of two thriving, resilient young men. For them, I hope that I have modeled the tremendous power of optimism, positivity, and showing resiliency through moments of transition and change. I strive to assist my sons and my clients in tapping into their inner strength, finding joy where it was lost, and overcoming the challenges they are facing.

Heather Lake

Jacqueline Gauthier is a mother, an aspiring creative and now like so many others, a pandemic baker. She lives with her husband, two teens and 3 birdies in a modest rural home near Peoria, IL. Someday she would love to put her toes in the sand in the Maldives.

JACQUELINE
GAUTHIER

I am a woman, a mother, and a poet. My soul is tethered to precious people and the herculean task of their care. I find the sacred in the ordinary. I must, or walking this winding, sometimes spiraling path to an unknown destination loses meaning. Like a leaf tossed in the air, caught up in a damp cyclone of autumn frenzy Or a lost sock spun on an eternal rinse and repeat cycle Like a bird feather whirling in a white water river Rushing around a stone searching for the sweet spot in the eddy The familiar groan of the school bus stopping and starting, loading happy chaos up and down the groggy morning street The house empties, two bodies out the door then one more Sent out to face whatever may come with reassurances of love and reminders of courage The maelstrom dissipates Silence falls like a heavy comfortable blanket The leaf softly swings from side to side as it floats to the ground The click and whine of the washer slowly lowers in tone and stops The feather finds calm in the pool just behind the rock Peace returns Until the familiar groan of the school bus is heard once again But until then, coffee. One of the most magical things on this earth is how starlings move en mass -- it's like God herself is creating living breathing kinetic sculptures in real-time. Lofted free In thrum of wind Slicing through the blue Orchestrated dips and sways Daring plummets Banking left and right Exhilarating calculations In concert Unity with variety Vers libre Equally magnificent is bioluminescent life, emitting light that says, "I am here" or more likely, "Don't eat me." I want to spend more minutes within the hours of my busy day appreciating these kinds of things. I want to shed the tired, worn and worried -- trade it in for awed, inspired and imaginative. Don't misunderstand me, I don't want to be up in the clouds. I just want to sink my toes into warm loamy soil or step into an ice-cold alpine stream. I want to be grounded and alert to the very moment. I want to take it all in.

Jacqueline Gauthier

Melanie Doane is a Juno Award winning artist and the founder of USchool, providing music education to Canadian Youth.

MELANIE
DOANE

I was always going to be a music teacher.

That's what we do in our family. My dad had created an intimidating yet inspiring example for us, working with educators across Canada, building music programs in public schools as he had done so masterfully in Halifax. I assumed from a young age that my two siblings and I would do the same job.

After two years in music school, I took a detour, auditioned, and found myself working in professional theatre. It was a secret dream, and I went for it. I loved it, found some of my best friends there, had a stint on Broadway, met and married my husband and got the courage to start writing and recording my own music.

This led to being signed to Columbia Records, experiencing another secret dream of recording, touring, top 40 radio love and the joy of creating my own music for a living. I went for it.

We eventually had two beautiful children, but the now 20-year marriage was suddenly touched by a crisis and unsurpassable obstacles that our little family could not survive. Faced with a lot of change and heavy responsibilities, I immediately stopped going on the road and started teaching music so my life and schedule could more easily revolve around my kids.

It was a convoluted route back to my initial dream of teaching music, but once I got in that classroom, it was a magical ride. I was delivering my dad's innovative program, using the ukulele to introduce kids to the joys of music. The U School program became a registered charity in 2015, making it possible for me to work with thousands of school children.

My Dad, Mom and siblings are my mentors and I'm so lucky to have them.

My talented sibling Creighton Doane and I have recently collaborated with Bob Ezrin, writing and recording music for a new children's show called Ukulele U on CBC Kids.

It is a full circle kind of moment where I get to be a songwriter, a teacher, use my theatre chops and my musicianship on every episode.

I think I'll go for it.

Jennifer Crawford is proud to celebrate 20 years as an entrepreneur.

JENNIFER
CRAWFORD

When I was 26 and working in a managerial position with a well-established global beauty company, I was presented with the opportunity to purchase a Caryl Baker Visage franchise. I decided to take the leap and while excited to take this journey, I was also nervous to leave a secure and comfortable job.

I had to live in Toronto for three months to complete training to finalize the purchase. Shortly before I was to take ownership, I was in a serious car accident and due to my injuries, I had to delay the takeover for three months. When I walked through the door on opening day November 29, 2002, I was still on crutches, but I was determined to start my adventure.

After three years in the small and established location, I was offered a larger space. While interested and excited for the opportunities it could offer, I was afraid to say yes because of the unknown and the learning curve for the expanded offering of services. But with the support of my family, I decided to take the opportunity.

I was asked by the local college to teach part time evening esthetics classes. Teaching was new to me, and I was on another exciting adventure. When I was asked to join the full-time program, I was also mom to two awesome boys. Looking back, I am not sure where I found the time! I jumped at the opportunity, and I was also able to build a great team for my business by hiring many of my students.

Covid hit and like many others in the beauty and cosmetics business, I was essentially shuttered during the pandemic. As it is my livelihood, I had to be creative and devise alternate ways to market my product. With the support of family and friends, I found the strength and rose to the challenge and my business is more successful as a result.

I truly don't know what is next. I am excited about the future. I am where I am due to hard work, taking risks, learning from failures and the unwavering support of my friends and family. I cannot wait to see what the future holds.

"Nobody gets away unscathed."

JENNY
KRAHN

...that's what my therapist tells me.

Every family has stuff. I struggled for years to understand my stuff. I was the first born to immigrant parents and I ultimately found myself a single Mom later in life. I felt my role in life was to be a solution person. After all, if I did not help people, who would? Codependency at its finest. As a single Mom, I have felt the gravity of ensuring my children learn every single lesson possible from me.

Living my life consumed with helping those I love most with a real lack of boundaries.

Now, currently living in a world where deceit is prevalent with a complete lack of ownership, we are globally gripped with fear. Shifting fear-based behaviour to consciously living in love has certainly been a challenge for a codependent mother like myself, who likes to maximize every teaching moment. This mother's heart is learning to let go one day at a time.

The most beautiful lesson of surrender. This is an art to be sure. Allowing for the journey to unfold. Practicing gratitude. Being still. Self-care. Giving myself permission to live in the present and remember my passions. Singing. Learning. My relentless pursuit of truth. Travel. Adventure. Cooking for others. Family time.

My name is Jenny Krahn and I give great thanks in gratitude for the wonder of life. For the countless blessings. I believe that the act of surrender allows room for miracles. I live in the most beautiful city of Kelowna, BC Canada. In a most beautiful home. With fantastic teenaged kids and a supportive family. I count my life a miracle. I would like to share with you the blessing of my childhood best friend's father each time he ended a message which has become of great value in my life. Cheers my dear friends, here's to love and miracles!

"The Lord bless you and keep you. The Lord make His face shine upon you, and be gracious to you; The Lord lift up His countenance upon you, and give you peace." Numbers 6: 24-26 NKJV

Jenny Krahn

Jonathan is a born humanist at heart, a cautiously optimistic dreamer that believes in the power of the individual.

JONATHON
ADAMS

At the ripe age of 14 a writing teacher in high school made us write an essay on what we thought would make our lives better as we got older. To this day I still remember the intro line of that essay "becoming a better version of myself". Although it took me 13 years to realize and conceptualize what that even meant, at a very young age I knew that deep down that was something I would forever be building upon.

I grew up a single child in a very suburban neighbourhood in a very stable home with two loving parents. One, an emotional compassionate that showed me the true range of human emotion in full colour. The other, an intellectual wizard that could masterfully execute any plan or idea with precise articulation and confidence and bring it to life. As I've grown older, I have realized that I am a perfect model of both these completely opposite people, a human dichotomy that is commonly misunderstood.

I often wondered why I was gifted with such a "normal" childhood, a life free of tragic suffering, however as I have gotten older, I have found myself craving hardship, and longing for the suffering of life to show me something I need to learn or figure out. I think people are shown that in all facets and in all different ways throughout life. What I now understand is it didn't come from the outside world, for me it came from the world within. The battle for a better version of myself has always been within, a harmonious balance between intellect and emotion, a push and pull of two opposite ways of being, coming together to help understand and show myself and others the most authentic version of themselves.

At the still very young age of 32, I have found myself with the everyday trials and tribulations of life but understanding them in a very different way. I see people as myself, both past and future versions, and how powerful that perspective is in relating to others but also to yourself. Being the most authentic version of yourself doesn't vary by degree, but by kind.

354

Jorge Gonzalez, MA, RCC is a registered clinical counsellor with Alyson Jones & Associates.

JORGE
GONZALEZ

Everyone's life is an exhilarating journey that rarely goes according to plan. I have experienced my own life changes and allowed my curiosity to lead me into unchartered waters and eventually towards increased confidence.

I grew up in Columbia and made a big change when I moved myself and my family to Canada to pursue new avenues and adventures. In my early years, I worked as a strategic planner in advertising agencies in South and North America. This background provided a unique perspective when it comes to thinking creatively. My varied background and commitment to curiosity has helped me problem solve, move thorough conflict, and discover opportunities for growth.

I stretched past the advertising world and was pulled towards a career in counselling where I felt I could assist others on their journey. We all encounter unexpected twists and turns, life's own challenges that will test our resolve and ability to adapt. Big and sometimes overwhelming feelings of frustration, anxiety and even depression can suddenly creep in and take us down a dark path where we doubt our ability to overcome and push through. It is during these challenging times that I call upon my own journey to provide some guidance and support to myself and others. With sharpened empathy and a true understanding of how life can take unexpected twists, I believe we can find strength by being curious and open ourselves to new opportunities and possibilities by reclaiming the confidence that's often been undermined.

With over 20 years of practice, I have acquired a vast experience treating anxiety, depression, relationship issues, complex trauma, attachment disruptions and self-esteem. I specialize in child and family therapy and belong to the innovative divorce and separation team at Alyson Jones & Associates. I feel honoured and humbled by the privilege of witnessing human resilience and the ability to adapt to new circumstances. Moreover, through years of working with children, I have seen how properly supported children can heal and move on to live healthy and successful lives.

I firmly believe that a key role of a therapist is to challenge clients to see their contributions to the way things are and encourage them to create better change.

Karen is an executive and force in Canada's tech marketing sector, an author, film maker, order of British Columbia nominee, and mother of two boys.

KAREN
DOSANJH

Growing up, I watched my elegant mother wear the most vivid colours, dressed to the nines in her exquisite sarees and Salwar suits. On special occasions, she would wear matching lipstick and had her hair perfectly done in a polished seventies styled updo. As she aged, I watched her brilliant colour palette start to fade, her glowing makeup went away, and she slowly let her raven hair naturally turn grey.

After our precious father passed away suddenly in the mid-nineties, my mother's spirit further dimmed, and the only colours she would wear became whites, beiges, and greys. One day, I asked her why she didn't wear her boldly coloured suits anymore? To which she replied, "My daughter what can I tell you? Those bright colours are reserved for young women, and these muted tones are more appropriate for women of my age. Besides, what's the point of wearing rich colours of celebration when your dad is not here with us?" Although I understood and shared my mom's profound sadness and loss, I knew Dad would want her to wear her joyous colours again.

A few years later, I bought my mom the most effervescent pink and gold silk suit to match my bridal lehenga on my wedding day. Mom smiled, and knowing this was my wish, she reluctantly agreed to wear it. On that day, I have never seen her look more radiant. Since then, she hasn't stopped proudly wearing her dazzling and splendid colours.

This year Mom celebrates a milestone birthday as she turns ninety, and I had the privilege of turning fifty myself. This milestone caused me to question why older women feel the pressure to dim their light and become invisible for the comfort of others? I believe that all women have the right to shine unapologetically at every stage of our lives. I, too, decided to embrace aging in all its glory and not allow anyone to dictate what is and isn't appropriate for me. Just like my beloved mother, I am no longer allowing cultural barriers or society's rules determine what a woman in their fifties should think, act, or look like. What an honour it is to age vibrantly just like my loving mother.

Keri grew up in Northern BC and comes from humble beginnings. Strong roots and close family gave Keri an appreciation for the little things in life, while always having passion for nature, music and all things beautiful. She now resides in Victoria.

KERI LYNNE
HENDRY

The most meaningful realization I have had in my life so far is that I will spend the rest of my life with me. There is power in being comfortable alone. Whether you want to believe it or not people will come and go, it is inevitable. Accepting this has brought me inner peace, strength, and courage.

Sometimes, the hardest walk you have to take is on your own. Being alone does not have to be lonely. The power lies inside. It is normal to feel afraid to be alone and sometimes that is a choice we make, and sometimes it is out of our control. The key is to find clarity and happiness in those uncomfortable times by looking inward and accepting yourself. Self-soothing has been wonderful for me. I find calmness in a cup of tea, soft jammies, deep rest, a hot bubble bath, music, walking in nature or being on the beach.

Some of the best advice I have received is, "If you could only see what lies ahead, those uncomfortable times would not be as unbearable." I find comfort in knowing that we have to experience the lows to appreciate the highs, and those times will come but they will also go. The lows will not last forever.

We can learn something from every single person that comes and stays or comes and goes. There is something beautiful in that because if you have a deep connection with yourself, you know you will not fall apart when or if they leave. Instead, you can learn from each relationship, but you will always have yourself to turn to.

Taking the time to get to know yourself can be uncomfortable but beautiful and necessary. When I started to connect to my inner self and listened to my intuition, is when I realized being alone does not have to be a weakness, instead it can be a gift.

357

We make plans... and God laughs. Entrepreneur Jenny Gough has had to learn how to roll with the punches.

JENNY
GOUGH

I stood at the midpoint of where the waves began their run up the beach and where they turned back to rejoin the ocean. My feet were buried ankle-deep in the wet sand, and I knew that if a big wave came and surprised me, I'd wind up on my backside. I was prepared for that, just in case.

Living close to this beach was always part of my plans – a life goal come true… but it was a goal that was accomplished only for an instant – and then it was swept away.

As I stood there, gazing at the mirror-like reflections off the water, I wondered why I hadn't been better prepared to be blindsided by a series of hard life lessons.

I'd always valued my persistence – like an ant, I'd never give up once I had something in my sights.

So, while I wasn't prepared when things started going awry, I faced it all headlong, like I was wont to do… but "battling on" wasn't the lesson that life wanted me to learn this time.

Eventually I watched, disbelieving, as a pandemic swept the legs out from under my business and my life, and my well-laid plans crumbled in ruins.

As the old Yiddish saying goes, people make plans, and God laughs.

The lesson that life wanted me to learn was that sometimes I need to give in to the waves – to yield to the current, and let the riptide drag me to where I need to be, instead of exhausting myself with frantically trying to maintain a status quo that no longer exists.

What was left as those waves of lessons swept away is all that truly matters. I'm here, I'm alive, and I have the voice and the ability to share my knowledge with those who need to hear it, so that they can do better for themselves, and for the Earth.

Gratitude underlies my every thought, and every move that I make. I am so grateful for every breath I take and for this beautiful life, and I am especially grateful for those who stood by me when things didn't always go 'according to plan'.

Lenore Rattray is writer, entrepreneur, storyteller, trauma survivor and mother who is passionate about community building and making a difference.

LENORE
RATTRAY

At the age of seven, while catching the school bus on a highway near Calgary, I was hit by a car that was driving 90km/hr.

My injuries included broken bones and a massive head wound that put me in a coma for five days. I have no memory of the accident, and very little memory of my life in the years just before and after, but, I can vividly recall the feelings connected with this time. When I think of myself as a child then, I feel sadness, loss and deep shame for being "different."

As I relearned how to walk, talk and eat, I also quickly learned that being different wasn't okay, and that the more "normal" I looked, the more I was praised. I was determined to be normal again.

Fast forward to 1992, the year I turned 21. As a recent journalism school graduate, I moved to Vancouver from Calgary, determined to begin a new and better life. Three months after I arrived however, I was robbed and kidnapped at gunpoint before disappearing into the woods for nine days.

I survived, but my "different" label returned. Again, the feelings of sadness, loss and deep shame darkened my mind. I fought hard to not let these feelings win, and mostly, they didn't. I presented to the outside world that I was okay… that I was normal.

Until, I became a mom, many years later. And then, the crumbling really began. Both the broken seven-year-old and the violated 21-year-old manifested and, mentally and physically, my strength to fight almost disappeared… and I almost didn't win.

Almost.

This is the impact of trauma. This is the sneakiness of PTSD.

This is my normal.

It has now been eight years and my journey towards post-traumatic growth is ongoing. The feelings of darkness still loom. I've learned to see them in myself and take it day by day.

Today, I see that my normal is that I am different.

Today, I see that I am just like everyone else.

STEPHANIE
TAYLOR

I always thought I would be married to the same person forever. That part of my life was unceremoniously turned upside down when my spouse of 27 years shared she was transgender. In one dinner, my vision of my future unraveled. Confusion was followed by shock, resistance, and grief. I also lost my mother and then my father shortly after. Losing my parents, my husband, and my identity in such a brief period of time jolted me immensely. What did this mean for our family?

Forced with uncertainty and feeling very alone, I asked myself, "what do I want?" In the beginning, I sat in a place of sadness. Over time, though, I found myself slowly moving into the world of being single, while continuing to grow my real estate investing company and taking care of my teenagers. Every day I started by writing down the question, "What do I want?" One answer was simple, a life that would work for all of us.

Healing took me on a path outside the norm – alternative retreats, on-line courses, fasting, even a one-way ticket to Mexico. Finding a way to become comfortable with being uncomfortable was required. Making heartfelt choices was key, as was filling every part of my being with love. When I stepped away from what I felt I "should do" and "could do," and instead asked myself, "what do I really want," my world immediately expanded. I became reacquainted with myself and started spending more time doing things that brought me joy.

In the end, my world became filled with authenticity, vulnerability, and deep connections that could only have been found through the journey my family experienced. Our household is now filled with open, honest, loving communication for which I have an enormous sense of gratitude! I discovered the father of my children choosing to embrace her true self was a gift that allowed me to recreate my life, to experience being fully present. This is the beginning of a new chapter where I create my life in a conscious way, while being grateful for the person I get to be and become.

You're always one decision away from a totally different life. – Unknown

Stephanie Taylor

Linda Bui is a stage 4 cancer survivor, self love and meditation teacher from Vancouver, BC.

LINDA
BUI

I had just turned 33 on May 18th 2019 and suddenly fell ill with fevers everyday and lumps appearing on my body. It was the big C word.

I was diagnosed with stage 4 lymphoma and it was incredibly aggressive. Within 2 months, I had developed over 50 tumors. I was rushed to get chemotherapy, as I had no time. However, I had an adverse reaction. My body shook uncontrollably, and I lost consciousness. The next morning, I found myself in the ICU in critical condition and was told I only have hours to live.

But something inside of me told me not to panic. I just knew what to do, that I get to decide my destiny and choose to live or die. That I had manifested the cancer, because I was so unhappy and miserable with the life I was living and needed a way out. I was so trapped and living out of alignment with my true self. I knew deep down I am here at this time on earth going through these experiences to grow and evolve my soul and accomplish my souls mission. To bring awareness to the power of the mind and body. To share my story and help others wake up to their true self. To help others heal and raise their consciousness. So I decided to stay.

In that moment, I practiced acceptance, letting go and completely surrendered. I immediately felt peace. And I knew I will be ok. Within five days my body healed, and I was released home to continue my recovery.

I had survived stage four cancer and escaped death, but I still had the very difficult task of leaving my abusive relationship.

I was ten months in remission by October 2020, and the right moment came for me to leave my husband. All I had to do was have the courage and strength to push open this door in front of me and walk to the other side. Where limitless possibilities of any life I wanted could be manifested into reality. I just had to let go of all my fears and trust that everything I need will be provided.

From October 2020 to October 2021, I flipped the script and went from a struggling single mom with no home, no job, and a mountain of debt to truly loving myself and thriving in life. I had manifested everything that I wanted and turned my life around in just 365 days.

Liz is an account executive at a start-up called Circle So. She's a lover of all adventures and advocate for marijuana.

LIZ
AVRUTOV

I learned early on that life isn't easy. Growing up, I felt very alone and different from everyone else. The word I'd use to describe my childhood is – strange. I vividly remember lying on the floor, holding a knife, crying, while my parents weren't home. Thinking of how much I wanted to take my life. This was elementary school, maybe grade six or seven. I wondered whether people would finally care when I'm gone. I felt like there must be something wrong with me. I didn't have friends, I didn't feel close to my parents, I was struggling with mental health, and I felt very alone.

In high school, I met Ms. Atkinson – the vice principal for that year. I truly believe she was the light that helped start my progress, which got me to the place I am today. It all started with me being sent to detention in grade nine and her telling me she could tell I'm not this person. That I have such a bright smile and am so kind to others, that she knows this isn't me. I immediately felt loved and accepted by her, I felt like I had someone on my side. I remember coming to her saying I feel like I didn't want to live, I was very suicidal. She was the only one in the world I could share that with. What was it I learned from Ms. Atkinson? Be kind and show care. You never know if you're simply making someone's day or saving their life.

I'm happy to share that I'm thriving as an adult and have positive and loving relationships with my parents. While childhood traumas have created insecurity and doubt in myself, I have also shaped into a kind, empathetic and hard-working person and am so grateful to be alive. Ms. Atkinson (Janet), if you're reading this, you have no idea the kind of impact you've had on my life, in a critical time that would determine the trajectory of my life. I am forever grateful to you and I make sure to carry myself with the same kind of kindness, care and respect for others. The road can look dark. But as per my mom's favourite quote, friends: "This too, shall pass".

Maninder Grewal is a mother, grandmother and banker. She immigrated to Canada in 1981 with the dream of raising a family in a beautiful and safe country, and is very proud of her three wonderful children.

MANINDER
GREWAL

I am a mother, grandmother, and banker. I immigrated to Canada in 1981 with the dream of raising a family in a beautiful and safe country. I am very proud of my three wonderful children and two grandchildren.

Once my children were in school, I decided to pursue a career in finance. I joined a local credit union in 1990 as a teller and currently hold the position of community branch manager. I have more than 30 years of experience in the finance industry. The work I do encompasses many facets, including helping newcomers set up their finances and helping business leaders in the community grow their portfolios.

I enjoy mentoring new employees and working with leaders in finance such as Tochi Sandhu, who was my first manager. I support community investment at Khalsa Credit Union where they donate 10% of their annual profits. As a credit union-based co-operative with principles and Sikh faith, I am actively involved in giving back to communities in many ways throughout the year.

I am an active volunteer in the community as a board member of PICS and a member at large with Mannkind charity and The Saheli Foundation.

I use my platform to support organizations such as Khalsa Aid, Guru Nanak Free Kitchen, Guru Nanak Food Bank and providing scholarships for youth. Feeling privileged to be able to assist in any way I can, I love seeing women help women as some of my greatest support has come from my mother, daughters, and friends. I strongly believe in this quote: "I've learned that people will forget what you said, people will forget what you did, but people will never forget how you made them feel." Maya Angelou. I am inspired by women like Oprah Winfrey and Malala Yousafzai who demonstrated great resilience and overcame adversity.

I also live by the mantra: Don't ever forget your worth, spend time with those who love and value you.

Maninder Grewal

Maria is trained as a health, wellness, and beauty specialist. She is a Physiotherapist, Kinesiologist, Personal Trainer, Health Coach, bikini bodybuilder and business owner of The Body Lab.

MARIA
BEWCYK

What if the life I dreamed of became my reality? Imagine growing up in a family that worked hard, taught me strong values, provided love and encouragement to push through hard difficult times to be successful. I started figure skating at 3 years old. At 16 years old, I started working at 7th Figure Skating Boutique, as well as teaching ice skating. Throughout high school, I competed at a National Level. I had the opportunity to audition to figure skate Professionally with Disney On Ice, then my life took me on an Academic path.

I completed my Bachelors Degree in Human Kinetics in 2006, started working as a Registered Kinesiologist and opened my own Multidisciplinary Healthcare Centre. In 2010 I decided to further my studies, in Sydney Australia, where I completed my Masters of Physiotherapy. I became highly educated working as a Physiotherapist for 4 years, which included working at the Hospital and Rehab Centre for Disabled Children in Nepal. I also had the privilege to work with professional athletes with Wiggle Honda Professional Cycling, Professional dancers, and the National Rugby League. I specialized in treating injuries with light (low level laser therapy) at different wavelengths, to heal tissues at a cellular level. I attended the World Association of Laser Therapy conference in the Gold Coast with high profile practitioners and scientists learning new treatment techniques from the World's Best. I was invited to teach my theory on how to treat tendinopathies at the 4th Multidisciplinary Ultrasound Symposium on Pain Management with the Division of Pain Medicine Department of Anaesthesiology at Hong Kong Sanatorium and Hospital. Working with hundreds of clients, healing with the power of red and infrared light, manual therapy, Pilates, and specific exercises I realized how I could heal the body at a cellular level.

I now combine my clinical expertise, the science of DNA testing, ionized electrolysed reduced water therapy, nutritional guidance, body work myofascial release therapy, chromotherapy and exercise, to create personalized medicine regenerating cells. I recently started working with skincare Medical Devices to promote skin rejuvenation. The sky is the limit with the power of mindset.

My challenge was to find a way to differentiate myself. I now fulfill my passion with the ability to heal hundreds of clients, inspiring millions to fight for their dreams and never give up.

Maria Bewcyk

Jen resides in Sarnia, Ontario with her fur babies, Tucker, Ginger, and Bruin. She enjoys nothing more then meeting new people and connecting them with like-minded individuals.

JEN ANGERS
DAERENDINGER

In September of 2020 I answered a phone call from Shelly. We had met 8 years earlier and instantly connected. Shelly excitedly started telling her about a project she was working on.

It was a book called pursuit:365 that featured 365 co-authors and the co-authors would be featured in Fresh Magazine and would be able to market their business. I immediately said "Yes!". That's how I became part of this last two-year journey of working with pursuit:365.

I spent from September 2020 to January 2021 speaking to women from across Canada, from my artists at ROAM to people I have met over the last 50 years. I was not surprised that the majority were very excited and wanted to be part of this wonderful project. The magic was that they always asked, "Do you need more people?"

By January 1st, I was on a mission to fill the last few spots. I met a woman named April May Bellia, who is also very excited about the book and connected me with the last of our co-authors.

When the book went to press it was expected that my job would be over, but that was not the case. I have spent another year meeting people from across Canada and the United States and filling Volume 2. It has been a pleasure spending my time engaging with interesting people from across the continent during COVID.

Most people I know wonder why I have spent so much time and energy on this project. The answer is simple. I believe in Shelly, and I believe in this project. I feel so blessed to have met so many people that have shared incredible stories of strength and perseverance.

To wrap it up, I am so grateful that Shelly called me and that pursuit:365 has gone into print twice. If I haven't connected with you yet, expect to hear from me regarding our 2023 book.

Carpe Diem

Jen Angers Daerendinger

Adam McKinnon . . . . Pg. 190

Adetola Tamunokubie . . . . Pg. 241
@adetolatams

Aeryon Ashlie . . . . Pg. 242
@aeryonbelaashlie

Alan Wade . . . . Pg. 113
@themagic.within

Alana Brandson . . . . Pg. 179
@alanabrandson

Alex Delvecchio . . . . Pg. 18
@thehockeyhalloffame

Alex Kazantsev . . . . Pg. 66

Alexis Gail Ellis . . . . Pg. 76
@alexis777cdn

Ali Moser . . . . Pg. 209
@alimoser_ftw (Twitter)

Alicia Reny . . . . Pg. 234
@ali.jane.renygade

Allison Lee Patton . . . . Pg. 33
@ardourwellnessinc

Alyson Jones . . . . Pg. 34
@alysonjonesassociates

Amada Jones . . . . Pg. 9
@laura.amada.9 (Facebook)

Amanda Connell . . . . Pg. 147
@coachamandaconnell

Amanda Da Silva . . . . Pg. 29
@amanda.da_silva

Ami McKay . . . . Pg. 243
@puredesigninc

Amy McVeity . . . . Pg. 98
@funmomboss

Amy Sussex . . . . Pg. 53
reviveaswellness.com

Andrea Lee Szopa . . . . Pg. 60
@Szopaphotography

Andrea Menard . . . . Pg. 96
@andreamenardmusic

Andrea S. Barone . . . . Pg. 7
@crystalhillsorganics

Angela Abbate . . . . Pg. 87
@pupsonthepier

Angela K Markusic . . . . Pg. 99
@angelamarkusic

Anna Piloyan . . . . Pg. 304
@piloyan_anna

Anna Rykiert . . . . Pg. 244

Annette Morgan . . . . Pg. 223
@dzelkant (Facebook)

Anthony Baldwin . . . . Pg. 181
@steelhammerproductions

Arleen Chenoll . . . . Pg. 285
@ArleenJean (Twitter)

Arlene Catherine Wise . . . . Pg. 258
@arlene_wise

Ashika Lessani . . . . Pg. 185
@ashikalessaniwellness

Aunalee Boyd-Good . . . . Pg. 262
@aylelum

Aurelia Vida . . . . Pg. 156
@eachoptimalhealth

Barb Pearson . . . . Pg. 102
@barb_pearson

Beata Jirava . . . . Pg. 233
@jiravab_

Belinda Hiebert . . . . Pg. 160

Betty Anne Chulumovich . . . . Pg. 184

Bill Tsakumis . . . . Pg. 143
edc.com

Blair Kaplan Venebles . . . . Pg. 225
@blairfromblairland

Bonnie Mills . . . . Pg. 198
@bonniemillss

Bonnie Moy . . . . Pg. 246
@bonniemoy

Brad King . . . . Pg. 260
@metabolicwarrior

Brenda Lynn Knights . . . . Pg. 200
@brendaknights1 (Twitter)

Brian Mellersh . . . . .Pg. 50
@brianmellersh

Brittany Hardy . . . . .Pg. 24
@emptydesksolutions

Bruce CG Gallagher. . . . . Pg. 138
@brucecggallagher (Facebook)

Bryan Smith. . . . . Pg. 329
@BryanSm27147539 (twitter)

Cadi Jordan . . . . .Pg. 206
@cadijordan

Calli Jensen . . . . Pg. 330

Carmen Vars . . . . Pg. 251
@carmenvarss

Carol Sachowski . . . . Pg. 14
storycoaching.com

Caroline Blanchard . . . . Pg. 51
@simplymecaroline

Caroline Latona . . . . Pg. 183
@franctalstudio

Caroline Wedderspoon . . . . Pg. 331
@alysonjonesassociates

Carolini Arco . . . . .Pg. 208
@carolini.arco

Carolyn Turkington . . . . Pg. 166
@themombabes

Carrie McEachran . . . . Pg. 107
@thefemalerevolution

Cathy Kuzel . . . . Pg. 253
@cathykuzeltcw

Cauvery Cariappa . . . . Pg. 333
@freespritedcauv

Chad Kowalchuk. Pg. 164
@chadkowalchuk

Chantelle Hansen . . . . Pg. 211
mavin-hub.ca

Cherie White . . . . Pg. 335
cherie-white-679b49114 (Linkedin)

Christa Leigh Rivington . . . . Pg. 149
@christaleighlife

Christina Walsh . . . . Pg. 167
@themombabes

Christina Weizmann . . . . Pg. 265
@christinaweizmann

Christina Wyatt . . . . Pg. 117
@cwfinancialguide

Christine Awram. Pg. 255
@wowwofw

Christine Blanchett . . . . Pg. 337
christineblanchette_tv

Christopher-Lee Hunte . . . . Pg. 338
@becausesymonesays

Cindy Stibbard . . . . Pg. 121
@divorceredefined

Cindy Van Arnam .Pg. 77
@cindyvanarnam

Clarissa Gibson. .Pg. 56
@clar-gibson

Cory Holly . . . . Pg. 339
coryholly.com

Crystal Flaman . . . . .Pg. 20
@crystal_flaman

Cydney Mariel Galbraith . . . . Pg. 245
@loves_pure_light_scarves

Dale Villajuan. . . . . .Pg. 38
@dalevill1

Daniela Fisher . . . . Pg. 256
@naturallygiven

Danielle Anderson . . . . Pg. 122
editingbydanielle.com

Danielle Comeau . . . . Pg. 157
wesbenglobal.com

Dannii Freeman . . . . .Pg. 49
@miss_danniifree

David Burrows . . . . Pg. 123
@davburrows

Dawn Williams. . . . . Pg. 237
dawn-williams-03989737 (linkedin)

Deborah Drummond. . . . . Pg. 195
@debdrummond_official

Deborah Gillam .Pg. 75
@fastforwardcoaching

Deborah J. Lohrenz . . . . .Pg. 334
@2motiv8u.by.deb

Debra Abraham . . . . .Pg. 340

Denise Wong .Pg. 248
@being_denise

Dennis Wager .Pg. 36
@denniswager

Derek Miura . . . . Pg. 3

Diane Johnson . . . . .Pg. 342
descriptivevideoworks.com

Diane Rolston . . . . .Pg. 343
@coachdianerolston

Don Wolf . . . . .Pg. 345
@donwolfmusic

Donna Vachon . . . . .Pg. 277
@safety_donna

Dori Howard . . . . Pg. 101
@dori_howard

Dr Divi Chanda . . . . .Pg. 205
@drdivi

Dr Jacqueline Fowler . . . . .Pg. 296
@guerajacquelina

Dr Joan Samuels-Dennis . . . . .Pg. 273
drjoan.ca

Dr Sam Winter . . . . .Pg. 240
drsamwinter.com

Dr. John Esdaile . . . . .Pg. 250
arthritisresearch.ca

Dr. Mark Robson . . . . .Pg. 26
theholeidea.com

Dr. Meg Haggitt . . . . .Pg. 25
@meghaggitt

Edina Beeby . . . . .Pg. 346
@suburbansurfette

Elisha Bonnis .Pg. 73
@nakedsilverdesigns

Elizabeth Louise Douglas . . . . .Pg. 104
@liz_l_douglas

Elizabeth Oates . . . . .Pg. 199
globalleadergroup.com

Emily Mackey . . . . .Pg. 217
EmilyMackey (Linkedin)

Erin Vogt . . . . Pg. 84
@erincoaches

Estrellita Gonzalez . . . . .Pg. 309
estrellitagonzalez (Linkedin)

Evangelia Kondilis . . . . .Pg. 224
@evangelia_kondilis

Fifa Tran . . . . Pg. 141
@feimodern

Frances Michaelson . . . . Pg. 10
@livethewow

Franco Cavaleri . . . . .Pg. 162
@cavalerifranco

Fynn Mansbridge-Fafard . . . . .Pg. 91
Fynn Mansbridge-Fafard (Linkedin)

Genicca Whitney . . . . Pg. 317
@geniccawhitney2.0

Gillian Mott . . . . .Pg. 59
@fiddle.me.ginger

Gina Best . . . . .Pg. 282
@ginaknowsbest

Ginni Mehta . . . . .Pg. 39
@okokocosmetiques

Gloria Cuccione . . . . Pg. 15
@1111wishfacecosmetics

Golfo Tsakumis . . . . .Pg. 142
@golfoart_

Gordon Tareta . . . . .Pg. 65
taretagroupintl.com

Grace McClure . . . . .Pg. 218
gracemclure (Linkedin)

Grayson Foster . . . . .Pg. 347

Gurjit K. Tiwana . . . . .Pg. 348
invictuslawyers.com

Harry Alexander Conan . . . . Pg. 194

Heather Lake . . . . Pg. 349
alysonjones.ca

Heather Leavoy . . . . Pg. 261
heatherleavoy.com

Heather Mason . . . . .Pg. 111
@Mason134211f (twitter)

Heather McMullin . . . . Pg. 268
(709) 685-7712 / heather@ecmb.ca

Heather Nightingale . . . . .Pg. 72
@hnightingale1

Helen Cole . . . . Pg. 215
@thejeancollective

Hibby Bartlett . . . . Pg. 216
@worldlovebank

Hoai Dang-Lachance . . . . Pg. 303
@hoainotart

Holly Calderwood . . . . .Pg. 69
@vancouverluxuryhomesrealtor

Holly Decker . . . . Pg. 269
@hollydeckermakeupartist

Huriye Sefayi .Pg. 97
huriyesefayi.com

Isabelle Honing . . . . Pg. 153
@beinclusive

Isah Nsubuga . . . . Pg. 127
rainbowrefugee.com

Jaala Leis Wanless . . . . .Pg. 82
@jaalawanless

Jacqueline Gauthier . . . . Pg. 350
@jaxident

James Eddington . . . . Pg. 133
@chefjameseddington

Jana Jorgenson . . . . Pg. 325
@janajorgenson._

Janet Walmsley . . . . .Pg. 47
@janet.walmsley

Janine Jones . . . . Pg. 126
@jjonesart

Janine Rogan . . . . Pg. 193
@janinerogan

Jarrett Jackson . . . . Pg. 271
@jarrettvsfitness

Jazz Macdonald . . . . Pg. 272
@jazzfromvictoria

Jeanne Beker . . . . Pg. 163
@thejeannebeker

Jeff Angers . . . . Pg. 308

Jeff Hardy . . . . .Pg. 68

Jeffrey St Germain . . . . Pg. 17
@jeffreystg

Jen Angers Daerendinger . . . . Pg. 365
@roamgallery

Jen Warrington . . . . .Pg. 45
jenwarrington.com

Jennifer Anne Utley . . . . .Pg. 35
kirkgroupmedia.com

Jennifer Crawford . . . . Pg. 352

Jennifer Dawn . . . . Pg. 177
jenniferdawn.net

Jennifer Mercer . . . . Pg. 109

Jenny Gough . . . . Pg. 358
jennygough.com

Jenny Krahn . . . . Pg. 353
@jennykrahn7

Jenny Story . . . . .Pg. 46
@jennystories101

Jessica Jewels . . . . Pg. 161
jessicajewels.com

Jessie Williams . . . . Pg. 221
jessie-williams (Linkedin)

Jill Maria Mateas Robinson . . . . Pg. 148
@jillmariamateasrobinson

Jillian Morris . . . . .Pg. 37
@jk_morris_less

Jim Cassels . . . . Pg. 187
stbpens.ca

Jo-Anne Weiler. . . . . Pg. 214
@jojoe2020

Joanne Turnbull . . . . Pg. 146
@joanneatdesignmojo

Jodi Brown . . . . Pg. 140
@jodiorgillbrown

Jodi Brown . . . . Pg. 172
@jodibrownphotography

Joël Fafard. . . . . Pg. 201
@joel_fafard

Joel Good . . . . Pg. 265
@aylelum

Joey Roo. . . . . Pg. 328
@joeyrooofficial

Jolene Laskey. . . . . Pg. 21
wabanakimaple.com

Jonathon Adams . . . . Pg. 354
@deep_roots_athletics

Jorge Gonzalez. . . . . Pg. 355
alysonjones.ca

Josh Montana . . . . Pg. 275
@joshmontana98

Joy Peirson . . . . Pg. 276
@joypeirsonart

Justin DaSilva. . . . . .Pg. 28
@justinthehappymechanic

Justin Madder . . . . Pg. 119
@justin.madder

Justin Saint . . . . .Pg. 23
@thejustinsaint

Karen Dosanjih. . . . . Pg. 356
@karendosanjh

Karen Holmes . . . . Pg. 278
@garbosfashionssarnia

Katayoon Webb . . . . Pg. 80
@katayoonwebb

Katherine McEachnie. . . . . .Pg. 204
@katthegrape

Kathi Moore. . . . . Pg. 139
@kathi.moore

Kathleen Lafferty . . . . Pg. 182
@kathleen.lafferty.rcc

Katsumi Kimoto . . . . Pg. 180
@mr.katsumoto

Kellie Wesley . . . . Pg. 228
@kelliewesley

Kelly Baker-Pabla . . . . .Pg. 58
@kelly_elizabeth_bp

Kelsey McGregor. . . . . Pg. 189
@etsyketsy

Kendra Vyse. . . . . .Pg. 94
cleardirectionadvisors.com

Keri Lynne Hendry . . . . Pg. 357
@klynne_love

Kerri Anne Kedziora. . . . . Pg. 31
kapcleaners.ca

Kimberley Baird . . . . Pg. 231

Kris Hall . . . . Pg. 159
@kdh__adventures

Kristin Richard . . . . Pg. 229
kristin-richard-988359113 (Linkedin)

Kristin Sayn . . . . .Pg. 280

Kyla Dufresne . . . . Pg. 281

Laura Fox . . . . Pg. 131
@laurafoxflails

Laura Lynn Ross . . . . Pg. 115

Laura Mennell . . . . Pg. 108
@laura_mennell

Laura Traplin . . . . .Pg. 42
@lauratraplin

Laureen Weget . . . . Pg. 213

Lauren Morris. Pg. 103
@laurenmorris77

Leanne Banga . . . . Pg. 219

Leanne Myles. . . . . Pg. 171
@leanne.myles

Lee Hawn . . . . Pg. 286
@lemonade_standca

LeiLani Kopp . . . . .Pg. 89
@sweetleilanicosmetics

Lenore Rattray . . . . Pg. 359
@planitgirlcanada

Leoni Tea Rivers . . . . Pg. 188

Lesley Corte. . . . . Pg. 41
@lesleycorte

Lesley Diana . . . . Pg. 236
thepromotionpeople.ca

Lesly Quiambao . . . . Pg. 6
@lesly.cue

Liam Chernen . . . . Pg. 16
@puckeringpeach

Lila Bruyere . . . . Pg. 288
@dancingeagle

Lili Wexu. . . . . Pg. 150
@liliwexu

Liliane Marie Laurence Ulysse . . . . Pg. 4
lilianemarielaurence.ulysse (Facebook)

Lily Ahonen . . . . .Pg. 57
@blondvagabond

Linda Bui. . . . . Pg. 361
@lindabui.living

Lisa Broome . . . . Pg. 178
inspiringprosperity.ca

Lisa Chang . . . . .Pg. 289
@livewithlisachang

Lisa Penz. . . . . Pg. 227
@lisapenz

Lise Parton . . . . Pg. 125
@ liseparton

Liz Avrutov . . . . Pg. 362
@lizavrutov

Liz Bennett . . . . Pg. 144
@lizbennettlifestyle

Lori Bagneres. . . . . .Pg. 43
@loribagneres

Lorraine Bear . . . . Pg. 291

Lynda Honing . . . . Pg. 154
@lyndahoning

Lynda Moffatt. . . . . Pg. 170
@artist.lynda.moffatt

Lynn Anderson. . . . . .Pg. 284
celestialembrace.ca

Lynnet Go . . . . Pg. 220

Maddison Bell . . . . Pg. 175
@victoriasplayhousebook

Maggie Habieda. Pg. 169
@fotografiaboutique

Maja Aro . . . . Pg. 44
seatoskystunts.com

Maninder Grewal . . . . Pg. 363
khalsacredit.com

Manjit Minhas . . . . Pg. 292
@manjit.minhas

Margaret Hughes . . . . .Pg. 344

Margo O'Connor. Pg. 145
@margooc

Maria Bewcyk. . . . . .Pg. 364
bodylabpro.com

Maria-Teresa Zenteno . . . . Pg. 136

Marilyn Anderson . . . . Pg. 19
marilynandersons (Linkedin)

Marilyn R. Wilson . . . . .Pg. 270
@marilynrwilson_official

Mark Acheson . . . . .Pg. 86
@actormarkacheson

Marlyna Los . . . . Pg. 12
@MarlynaLos

Martin Prchal . . . . .Pg. 70
@martinprchal

Mary Ann Morin . . . . Pg. 294
@mamorin1

Maryann Okoro . . . . Pg. 341
@kambiio_skincare

Megan Ashley . . . . Pg. 327
@meganashleycreative

Megan Lammam . . . . Pg. 173
meganlammam.com

Megan Mansbridge . . . . Pg. 202
megan.mansbridge (Facebook)

Melanie Doane . . . . Pg. 351

Melissa Mancini Burbridge . . . . Pg. 54
@melissamburbridge

Melissa Rosas . . . . Pg. 249
@violetdaecommunications

Michael Hefferon . . . . Pg. 74
@mainframestudios

Michael Lensen . . . . Pg. 2
@michaellensen

Michael Soltis . . . . Pg. 298
soltisart.com

Michael Theodor . . . . Pg. 230
mtconsulting.ca

Michaella Shannon . . . . Pg. 297
@michaella.shannon

Michele Thomson . . . . Pg. 61
@curis_consulting

Michele Young-Crook . . . . Pg. 158
@m_young_crook (twitter and instagram)

Michelle Bohonis . . . . Pg. 252
@saffron.hawk

Mike Reno . . . . Pg. 8
loverboyband.com

Mike Soloman . . . . Pg. 22
@solomanartist

Mindy Zara Small . . . . Pg. 132
summersidemortgages.com

Miranda Diane . . . . Pg. 259
@mirandadianeco

Missy MacKintosh . . . . Pg. 311
@missymackintosh

Mita Naidu . . . . Pg. 322
mitanaidu (Linkedin)

Monika Baraniuk . . . . Pg. 287

Monika Schnarre . . . . Pg. 62
@monikaschnarre

Nadine Sands . . . . Pg. 152
nadinesands.com

Natasha Bruce . . . . Pg. 27
@natashanicole47

Nerissa Allen . . . . Pg. 279
@nerissalallen

Nicky Arndt . . . . Pg. 196
@madcapmaven

Nicolaas Glim . . . . Pg. 336

Nicole Clark . . . . Pg. 326
@itsnicoleclark

Nicole Gardiner . . . . Pg. 192
@balancelifecentre

Nicole Langman . . . . Pg. 129
nicolelangman.com

Nicole Lee McCurdy . . . . Pg. 78
@Horse_guided_healing

Nicole Oliver . . . . Pg. 257
@noliver77

Nila Cook . . . . Pg. 128
@neonaturelle

Nira Arora . . . . Pg. 116
@niraarora

Norm Danniels . . . . Pg. 301

Patrice (aka Pat) S Dubreuil . . . . Pg. 300
@magpierelay

Patrick Baylis . . . . Pg. 323
@karmmatattoo

Paul Becker . . . . Pg. 71
@artrapture

Paul Henczel . . . . Pg. 1
@paulhenczel

Paul McCart . . . . Pg. 293

Paula DeWit . . . . Pg. 85
pauladewit.com

Peter Eastwood . . . . Pg. 315
@bcphotographer

Peter Twist . . . . Pg. 307
@coachpetertwist

Petra Hermes. Pg. 120
@flyandseadive

Priya Mehrotra . . . . Pg. 48
stressfreecareerwoman.com

Rachel Frustaci. . . . . .Pg. 93
@jewel_and_rose

Raugi Yu . . . . Pg. 191
@raugiyu (twitter)

Rebecca Bollwit . . . . Pg. 147
miss604.com

Rebekkah Stainton . . . . Pg. 310
westcoastvitality.com

Rishma Dhalla . . . . Pg. 212
@rishmaot4life

Rita Stoller. Pg. 247
@ritastollerdesign

Robert Amado . . . . .Pg. 32
@amado.salon

Roman Rozumnyj . . . . Pg. 155
@romanrozumnyj

Rosalyn C. RainDancer . . . . Pg. 235
@raindancer.home

Roxanne Baird . . . . Pg. 324

Sabrina Queiroga . . . . Pg. 114
@clickyhealthcoach

Sabrina Roc . . . . Pg. 222
@wojackproductions

Safina Kataria. . . . . Pg. 239
@safinakataria

Saireen Neilsen. . . . . .Pg. 92
menopausitivity.ca

Salley-Ann Ross . . . . Pg. 207
alysonjones.ca

Sally Omeme . . . . .Pg. 95
@sally_omeme

Sam van Born . . . . Pg. 254
@samvanborn

Sandi Johnston-Yu . . . . .Pg. 290
@choosenatureinstead

Sandra Moorhouse-Good . . . . Pg. 266
@sandramoorhousegood

Sandy Rutherford . . . . .Pg. 79
@rfsuccessacademy

Selene Jade Embers . . . . Pg. 295
@wandering_goddess_selene

Shannon Boakes. . . . . Pg. 226
@shannboakes

Shannon Gibbs. . . . . Pg. 312
shannon-rey.com

Sharad Khare . . . . Pg. 11
sharadslunchbox

Sharley Neill. . . . . Pg. 40
sharleycowan.norwex.biz

Sharon Marshall . . . . Pg. 176
@sam_digitaldeva

Sharon Mason . . . . Pg. 238
sharonmasonrealestate.com

Shashi Bhushan Maharaj . . . . Pg. 318

Shaun Peet .Pg. 30
@swpeet

Shauna Magrath. . . . . .Pg. 88
@beautyink

Shauna Zingg . . . . .Pg. 63
@shazingg

Shawn Bergman. . . . . Pg. 186
@shawn.bergman

Shayda Ashley John. . . . . Pg. 13
@shayda.ashley.j

Sheila Neufeld . . . . .Pg. 299
@sheilaneufeld

Shelly Smee. . . . . Pg. 151
shellysmee.com

Sherrylyn Vivero . . . . Pg. 5
@sherrylyn_vivero

Sonja Picard. . . . . .Pg. 67
@sonjapicardfineart

Sonya Janisse. . . . . .Pg. 55
linktr.ee/Sonyajanisse

Sophia Seward-Good. . . . . Pg. 263
@sophia.s.good123

Steph Purdy. . . . . .Pg. 52
@redandko

Stephanie Chenoll. . . . . Pg. 283

Stephanie Taylor. . . . . Pg. 360
evevoproperties.com

Stephanie Wicks. . . . . Pg. 81
@aikinstephanie

Sue Noble . . . . Pg. 100
@suenoble441

Sue Randhawa. . . . . Pg. 306
@theopticalboutique

Sunni Hurley . . . . Pg. 313
sleyco.ca

Supneet Chawla. . . . . Pg. 302
acecollegecanada.com

Suraya Sophia . . . . Pg. 112
infinity-healing.com

Susi Vasseur. . . . . Pg. 130
@susivasseur

Suzanne Durnan. . . . . .Pg. 90

————————

T.J. Corman . . . . .Pg. 83
@t.j.corman_author

Tabatha Bull . . . . Pg. 232
ccab.com

Taisha Teal Wayrynen . . . . Pg. 110
@arttherapytaisha

Talia Beckett Davis . . . . Pg. 174
@taliadavispr

Talia Fadel . . . . Pg. 314

Tatiana Gregoryanz. . . . . Pg. 106
@moose_and_walnut

Teresa Ann Altiman. . . . . Pg. 210
roamgallery.com

Teresa May Teschner . . . . Pg. 274
@teresateschner

Teresa Syms. . . . . Pg. 197
@TeresaSyms

Terrance Richmond. . . . . Pg. 134
@terrancerichmond

Tina Pashumati James. . . . . Pg. 203
@tina_pashumati

Tinuke Adebowale . . . . .Pg. 64
@tempting.delights.canada

Tommy Chong . . . . Pg. 135
@heytommychong

Tony Ganton . . . . Pg. 332
@t.ganto

Tracey Lundell . . . . .Pg. 305
seaglasswealth.com

Tracy Holly. . . . . .Pg. 320
coryholly.com

Trevor Amon Phillips . . . . Pg. 118
@trevor.amon.phillips

Trish Clarke . . . . Pg. 316
@patriciaclarkecreations

Tulin Fadel. . . . . Pg. 319

Tyler Hatch . . . . Pg. 124
@tylerhatch1976

————————

Veronica Plewman . . . . Pg. 105

————————

William Good. . . . . .Pg. 264
@aylelum

————————

Zach Mansbridge-Fafard . . . . Pg. 165
@zachsathletics

Zandra Ross. . . . . Pg. 321
zandrarosscoaching

Zoonie Nguyen. . . . . Pg. 168
@nguyenzoonie

pursuit:365
TEAM

SHELLY LYNN HUGHES

Founder & Creator
"The Visionary Vixen"
@shellylynn.hughes
www.pursuit365.com

ANDREIA MCLEAN

Experiential Logistics & Creative Processes
"The Communications Connoisseur"
@andreiavanessaa
www.getinviting.com

JENNIFER ANGERS DAERENDINGER

National, Sales & Business Development
"The Sales Sovereign"
@roamgallery

CHRISTINA MOORE

Graphic Designer
cmooredesigns.ca

JIALI KIMOTO

Photo Editing.

NICKY ARNDT

Copy Editing
"The Eminent Editor"

EDINA BEEBY

Social Media
"The Social Slayer"

MELISSA SCHILZ

Copy Editing
"Editor Extraordinaire"

"None of us got to where we are alone. Whether the assistance we received was obvious or subtle, acknowledging someone's help is a big part of understanding the importance of saying thank you."

-HARVEY MACKAY

Special **THANK YOU** to the following individuals,

I appreciate you and your support.

Warmly, Shelly Lynn

Jennifer Angers Daerendinger

Andreia McLean

Christina Moore

Jiali Kimoto

Nicky Arndt

Colleen Kirk

Liz Douglas

Melissa Schilz

Marilyn Wilson

Leanne Myles

Oyeta Kokoroko

Jane Stoller

Elizabeth Oates

Missy MacKintosh

Judy Doyle-Sahay

Ruth Geurts

Cori DiPietro

Mandi Sohi Sellers

Ray Macklem

Janice Michelle Rose